Bilingual Games

New Directions in Latino American Cultures

A series edited by Licia Fiol-Matta and José Quiroga

Published in 2003:

Velvet Barrios: Popular Culture & Chicana/o Sexualities,
edited by Alicia Gaspar de Alba,
with a foreword by Tomás Ybarra Frausto

The Famous 41: Sexuality and Social Control in Mexico, c. 1901,
edited by Robert McKee Irwin, Edward J. McCaughan,
and Michelle Rocío Nasser

New York Ricans from the Hip Hop Zone,
by Raquel Rivera

Bilingual Games: Some Literary Investigations,
edited by Doris Sommer

Tongue Ties: Logo-Eroticism in Anglo-Hispanic Literature
by Gustavo Perez-Firmat

Forthcoming:

New Tendencies in Mexican Art
by Rubén Gallo

Bilingual Games

Some Literary Investigations

Edited by

Doris Sommer

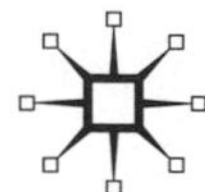

BILINGUAL GAMES

First published 2003 by
PALGRAVE MACMILLAN™
175 Fifth Avenue, New York, N.Y. 10010 and
Houndmills, Basingstoke, Hampshire, England RG21 6XS.
Companies and representatives throughout the world.

PALGRAVE MACMILLAN is the global academic imprint of the Palgrave Macmillan division of St. Martin's Press, LLC and of Palgrave Macmillan Ltd. Macmillan® is a registered trademark in the United States, United Kingdom and other countries. Palgrave is a registered trademark in the European Union and other countries.

ISBN 1–40396–011–9 hardback
ISBN 1–40396–012–7 paperback

Library of Congress Cataloging-in-Publication Data
Bilingual games : some literary investigations / Doris Sommer, editor.
p. cm.
Includes bibliographical references and index.
ISBN 1–40396–011–9—ISBN 1–40396–012–7 (pbk.)
1. Bilingualism and literature. I. Sommer, Doris, 1947-

P115.25 .B55 2003
306.44'6—dc21

2002074848

A catalogue record for this book is available from the British Library.

Design by Letra Libre, Inc.

First edition: November 2003
10 9 8 7 6 5 4 3 2 1

Printed in the United States of America

Contents

Part III: Genders

Part IV: Double-Barreled Canon

Part V: Living Investigations

Acknowledgments

The barrio of Brooklyn where I learned the fun and the frustrations of bilingual games gets my heartfelt acknowledgment here. Hail to the hood for being the space of encounters and disencounters, far from any communitarian paradise and close to the messy ground of democratic coexistence. Growing up between streets named after a Dutch Amboy and a Zionist Herzl now seems like an objective correlative for the bifocal vision we developed there. The double focus and double talk made everything outside any one of our small apartments look elliptical, pulled between two gravitational points of home and host languages. The ellipses were linked up by a series of *puntos suspendidos* that kept meanings afloat, somehow there but never settled. It was a time when Larry Harlow, lovingly called in Puerto Rican Spanish *El niño judío de Brooklyn,* was just starting to feel his piano fingers tingle with Caribbean counterpoints, and when grown-ups in the neighborhood who spoke English without a Spanish or Yiddish or Southern Black or Greek or Chinese accent sounded childlike and too shallow to take very seriously. How could someone be grown up already and still to have only one culture or language? It seemed to us like a case of arrested development. Needless to say, dealing with monolingual teachers wasn't easy. They commanded respect (ambiguities intended), parents assured their children; and we gave them respect, mostly out of deference to our old-world parents. For some time now, I have appreciated the privilege of spending my formative years in a place where we all fit in, more or less uneasily and with the mutual respect that comes from never presuming to be at the center.

Those multilingual lessons about the precariousness of communication and the miracle of contact slowly took the center of my attention, especially after *Proceed with Caution, When Engaged by Minority Writing in the Americas* (1999). A chapter on "The Traps of Translation" put me on the track of a whole set of language games that play on the differences between insider and outsider. Since then, bilingual games have been the subject of courses I teach, of my own research for *Bilingual Aesthetics* (forthcoming, Duke University

Press), and conferences. In all these projects, I have depended on the creative collaboration of an exceptional core of graduate student colleagues. Our first course was literally designed by the group, which included José Luis Falconí, Bill Johnson Gonzalez, Carmen Oquendo, Carolina Recio, Miguel Segovia, Joaquín Terrones, and Esther Whitfield. My gratitude is immeasurable to each one for particular contributions and to the group for their collective lessons in collaboration. Special thanks are due, nonetheless, to José Luis Falconí, who has managed to coordinate this volume and many related projects with the already legendary tact and efficiency that makes his intelligence a gift to everyone in his expanding circle of contacts. To Joaquín Terrones, I owe an irredeemable debt for the brilliance of his interpretations, the mental agility and generosity he lavishes as teaching fellow for undergraduate students, and for his elegant translations here. And to Miguel Segovia, the bibliographer and voracious reader, go the thanks of a follower to her leader.

The contributors to this volume merit, obviously, my profound thanks for their brilliant essays. Many of them presented their work during conferences at Harvard University, where we all benefited from the participation of more colleagues than could—unfortunately—be included in one volume. The work, however, of participants, including Evangelina Vigil Piñón, Tino Villanueva, Ilan Stavans, Ramón Saldívar, Robbie Schwartzwald, Giannina Braschi, Arnaldo Cruz-Malavé, Francisco Goldman, Tato Laviera, Juani Guerra, is present to all of us and forms part of the basic bibliography at the end of this book. Thanks are also due to John Coatsworth, and Steve Reifenberg, Director and Executive Director, respectively, of the David Rockefeller Center for Latin American Studies for the institutional support of the center for some translations of the essays, to Tomás Ybarra Frausto for his advice and bendición, and to Gayatri Patnaik for bringing our games to what we hope readers will judge to be some winning results. Even more, though, we hope that readers will join the games.

Introduction

Doris Sommer

Bilingual games play on the broad field that Ludwig Wittgenstein cleared through his *Philosophical Investigations.* Language had become a problem for philosophy because the field was cluttered by prejudices about what language can or should do. Why worry, he asked, when it evidently does many things effectively? The only way to solve philosophy's problems is therefore to take a fresh look and to see the almost endless variety of existing "language games" instead of perpetuating tired assumptions about ideal functions that came to grief all over the world. Wittgenstein's cure for this self-inflicted anxiety was simply to induce relaxation, because beating a live horse to death, as it were, or asking for *peras al olmo* was causing a whole syndrome of ailments for scholars. Natural language doesn't demand perfect fit as long as it is useful; and it doesn't need philosophy's blessing even if the discipline presumes greater clarity than everyday speech. On the contrary, Wittgenstein insisted, philosophy could advance a bit if it developed some respect for the subtle mechanisms of everydayness that produce intended effects through so precarious a medium as language.

Our essays take the descriptive cure to heart and extend the treatment for anxious times. These new investigations will need to stretch beyond a single language and also past everyday activities, as mass migrations and strained, often double, be-longings push identities and language games to boundaries between codes. And at those frontiers, unconventional speech and writing border on art. *Bilingual Games* develops in both urgent directions: First, it broadens the work of description toward the busy borders between languages, where linguists have been mapping varieties of conversational code-switching in normal communication. And then it deepens admiration for the art of code-switching by underlining its particular and unconventional aesthetic effects. Learning to enjoy those effects may train an attitude of respect for the displaced and culturally overloaded artists who produce them, often on purpose, even when one language feels more precarious than another. So we invite you to play bilingual games, even if you don't have much of a second language yet. Among the rules for playing, after all, are the different positions we take on the field, some at home base and others off in left field. It is a difference to reckon with.

The days of the one ideal reader have been numbered and spent in our segmented societies. A "target audience" today can mean the target of exclusion or confusion. And feeling the unpleasant effect is one valid way of getting the point, or the kick, of a language game. More basic even than these hide-and-seek games is the very fact that overloaded systems unsettle meaning. When more than one word points to a familiar thing, the excess shows that no one word can "own" or "be" that thing. Several contending words point, each imperfectly. Even a proper noun like "Hamlet" is game for competition.[1] Of course he worried enough about precarious arrangements (without code-switching) to be an inviting target. "Whenever you were reduced to look up something in the English version [of *Hamlet*]," Nabokov's Pnin complains, "you never found this or that beautiful, noble, sonorous line that you remembered all your life . . . Sad!"[2] Words are not proper and don't stay put; they wander into adjacent language fields, get lost in translation, pick up tics from foreign interference, and so can't quite mean what they say. Teaching bilinguals about deconstruction is almost redundant. ["Big dill!" Pnin might say.[3]]

Reckoning with positions and their asymmetrical aesthetic effects will be one antidote to multicultural anxiety. "We are all multiculturalists now," admit fellow citizens, often with a tone of resignation if not resentment. A cure for cringing will need to turn the dread of difference into desire for it. Maybe recognizing the charm of a lateral move from one language to another, to poach a word or turn a phrase, will call admiring attention to everyday artists as well as to literary exemplars. Recognition of this knack for innovation and creative survival will make it unnecessary to require that migrants choose and lose in the game of cultural belonging. Perhaps their staying powering two or more cultures can be a model of tolerant sanity for single-minded nativists, just as normal unsystematic speakers were Wittgenstein's guides for getting on with philosophy.

Push and Pull

The stretch in breadth will make good on Wittgenstein's advice to look and listen to the ways that language normally works. But the pull toward literariness takes some liberties with his preference for common speech. Wittgenstein's provocation was to value everyday flexibility over the cramped habits of "philosophese." Ours will be to honor the creativity of a common condition that continues to be pathologized and disdained. Today philosophers are not the only ones who worry about language. Reflecting on what it can mean is complicated by questions about which language(s) to use legitimately for commerce, politics, intimacy, and education. Mass movements of economic and human capital unhinge people from their native languages and unmoor even anchor words such as *nation* and *state, gender* and *mother tongue*. Pieces of personal and collective identities go off on multiple and risky courses. The dis-ease needs remedies because it can be volatile and escalate into violence. One diagnosis assumes that cultural coherence is the normal and healthy state, so it leads to purgative cures. The other observes that we have outgrown simple assumptions about cultural identity and recommends that we get used to the messiness of late modernity. The first remedy would clean up the confusions (restrict immigration; enforce English-only communication; fuel militant patriotism; restore ROTC to campuses; answer jihad with crusade and conversion). The second values the loose ends of identity as lifelines for negotiating democracy (through legitimate dual citizenship, bilingual arts, and a cautious coexistence between particular codes and a *lingua franca)*.

The cleansing option is familiar and intolerant. Born-again Americans, often monolinguals, can bristle at people who speak strange languages. Spanish-speakers are asked to leave bars; Chinese conversations grate on English only ears; the polyphony of a place like Manhattan sounds like the Mad Hatter's raving to people like Ron Unz (*sic*),[4] whose name plays the kind of bilingual game that brings translation close to philology and makes English play "sounds-like" games with German; it evokes the kind of intolerant populism that pits Us against Them. It's not the foreigners themselves who bother Unz, he insists to xeno-baiters, but rather their stubborn cultural ties that tangle the country in "The Bilingual Bind."[5] "They are talking about me," is one self-centered response. (Are you Amerdican citizen?) Self-centering seems self-evident in a powerful United States where it's enough to speak one language, because less powerful foreigners must learn to speak English. Here monolingualism sounds normal. I am normal; you should be too.

The bi- and multilingual options are unfamiliar and fresh: They admit that a large number of people in the world live in more than one language, and they develop a tolerance (even a *taste)* for the risky business of democratic life in which codes coexist and come into conflict. Anticipating the irritation between languages and identities (in oneself as well as in society) will make dis-ease feel normal rather than a case to be cured through drastic and violent measures. And feeling normally irritated will amount to a change of heart about how to pursue the good life. Hearts and minds are the organs of political life; without them, the best designs fail. But our tired rhythms of desire and our cramped approach to language and identity can't keep step with democratic demands. A new sentimental education is on the agenda for this period of global movements of people and capital through multicultural states.[6] It is a tall order for teachers, but an urgent one, because some of our inherited tastes for coherence and predispositions to seamless assimilation have become obstacles for democratic life. That retraining taste is feasible goes without saying, given the astounding success of the relatively recent education in feelings that made us modern national subjects. That program started only about two hundred years ago and had its effect within one generation. It depended on a neat calculus of one language per people, and obviously one per person. National feeling was the *Sprachegeist*, a single and unified spirit of a people. This was J. G. Herder's shorthand prescription for defending rootedness and local self-esteem against what he considered the ravages of eighteenth-century (French) cosmopolitanism. Herder warned that living in more than one culture corrupted the soul and that bilingualism literally caused decay, a physical decomposition signaled by flatulence.[7] (I mentioned this in Mexico, where bilinguals from the Yucatán turned the signal into laughing gas, since the Spanish word for "fart," *pedo,* means kiss in Maya.) The very assumption that monolingualism is normal and the apparent "naturalness" of an imagined community across class and sometimes color lines prove that sentimental education works. Had that early republican effort failed, we would still feel that monarchy was the divine order of politics. The education that novelists, legislators, leaders, and mostly classroom teachers provided for the earlier republican national period practically overhauled the hearts and minds of entire populations. *L'education sentimental* means more than the title of a particular nineteenth-century novel by Gustave Flaubert. It is the program of an entire foundational genre and a generation of republican fathers and mothers.

Now mono is a malady, an adolescent condition for times that have outgrown the one-to-one identity between language and people. Growing pains can't be avoided in the process of maturing toward tolerance for a complicated world. How can we avoid them while people and languages rub against and irritate each other? Is there nevertheless a way to mitigate those pains instead of aggravating them into unbearable tensions? The choice between annoyance with evidence that doesn't fit into inherited systems and the alternative of letting go of systems recalls the change in Wittgenstein's approach to philosophy. He had started with an ambition to map clear relationships between words and the world. But his mature work gave up the goal of tidiness and developed a taste for vagaries. Meanings, he concluded, depend on usage in changing circumstances, not on dictionary entries, or analyzable parts, or any other language elements that had seemed stable. Language plays an almost endless variety of games and defies systematic analysis. The games include storytelling, betting, making lists, mocking, conspiring, praising, kvetching, apologizing, hinting, denying, mourning, commiserating, promising, and repeating. These and many other games are played by flexible rules that adjust to particular situations and can morph into related activities. So Wittgenstein's game of "therapeutic" philosophy amounted to describing its own moves among others. It was, as I said, his remedy for the longstanding "problems" that had engaged philosophers (including himself) about what language could or should do. Worriers were only making problems for themselves when they noticed that words didn't exactly coincide with the world or with ideas. Either you can deduce that words don't quite work, since they disappoint expectations, or you can turn the observation around and notice that the systematic expectations frustrate an appreciation of the ways that words do normally work. Any reasonable person would turn around, Wittgenstein said, once it was clear that philosophy was giving itself headaches by beating its head against an inherited wall. "Do away with all *explanation*, and description alone must take its place."[8]

That work of notation needs to include bilanguage games. They would have figured for Wittgenstein, too, if he had finally freed himself from the prescriptions he claimed to dismiss. Instead, he became cramped and stayed inside one language at a time. This Austrian in England took care not to cross over language lines. In his books, the German original and the English translation face each other on opposite pages, without apparent interference. At one point, Wittgenstein admits that an English word may come to him before the German equivalent, but the foreign word gets lost in a list of other stimuli for language, including feelings and gestures, as if English were also preverbal. Had Wittgenstein in fact described what happens in normal language use, the bilingual moment would have detained him. He might have noticed that it is a fairly common feature of speaking and writing, and that these moments can free up communication that seems blocked, or play jokes that turn bad humors into laughing gas. For some reason Wittgenstein stopped short of these observations. Maybe mixing codes seemed undignified for philosophy. Or maybe the requirement of universal validity needs a single universally visible code, while slips into particularism take language onto risky sidetracks. In any case, language cramps turn out to be a widespread affliction among even our most daring iconoclasts. They include Wittgenstein and Sigmund Freud (whose book of jokes translates away the Yiddish, though the humor depends on code-switching) and also Jacques Derrida (whose monolingualism misses the moves that most minority subjects make in and out of alternate identities). Universalism goes on edge in the field of bilingual games because they don't play evenhandedly. Instead, the players take advantages of the uneven playing field where a powerful language expects to win every match, but where other languages jostle and rub power to win some points. Using more than one language causes problems for universal, across-the-board games of politics, philosophy and aesthetics.

Roughing It

"How does it feel to be a problem?" white people are always asking under their breath, says W.E.B. Du Bois. Monolinguals ask it of newcomers, too, sometimes less discreetly but in a strange language. By the time immigrants or conquered people can answer, some deny being a problem anymore, having managed to forget the home language. Others will admit that living in two or more languages can make them difficult, which isn't a pleasant feeling. But it leaves room for maneuvering. Doubling is a lesser evil than either full assimilation—which can risk humorless self-hatred—or refusing assimilation—which will cost them opportunities. I want to suggest that feeling bad can feel good, both for migrants and for their hosts. The aesthetic advantages of uneasiness and estrangement have been self-evident since the Russian formalists lesson on art as roughness or difficulty and through the Marquis de Barthes's taste for the "hurts so good" pleasure of texts that can taunt.[9] It is the political charms of linguistic overloads and underdeterminations that will need attention and alliances between trainers of taste and theorists of statecraft. Otherwise our polyrhythmic societies will continue to sound cacophonic instead of engagingly contrapuntal.

Du Bois had admitted to being a problem for a country that required assimilation but didn't allow it. "One ever feels this twoness—

two souls, two thoughts, two unreconciled strivings."[10] Double consciousness was a double bind for Du Bois and demanded a structural solution: He proposed amalgamating black and white through a racial alchemy familiar to Latin Americans as *mestizaje*. He proposed it, singing the black blues to call attention to the color line that doubled minority souls and divided them from the majority. Du Bois sang so movingly that Americans could sometimes interrupt their colorblind and monorhythmic dance of equal and reversible partners to hear improvisations on contrasts and mutual attractions. But today, double consciousness and the bilingual binds that add sound to the black and white drama no longer seem soluble nor require solutions. The split soul could look, if we focused, like an intense experience of the general split structure of language and living as human beings. This unhappy consciousness could be a vanguard for our best cultural defense of humane practices because doubleness won't allow the meanness of one thought, one striving, one alchemical gold standard of value.

The color line has barely budged. Today it is a very busy and noisy place, like a border between the rich who need workers and the poor who need work. Sometimes the counterpoint sounds like counterpurposes, especially when the interruptions of one language by another make color a clue to difference. Foreign sounds are metonymies of dark color. Otherwise, what could "Hispanic" or "Latino" mean in response to the question of race? And why would a white face provoke a "You don't look Spanish" skepticism from Anglos? Latinos don't jump to the congenital conclusion about language; they lose one too easily and know the effort of gaining another.

Not fitting easily or well, being both too much and not enough, makes many migrants aware of grammar trouble with themselves and with their neighbors. How is one to identify, when one is more than one, *either/and*? Two languages (often more) and loyalties to a home country and to hosts can seem intolerable to patriots on either side of the border, and on both sides of a divided self. "Say 'perejil,'" Trujillo's troops commanded the border people at the banks of a river already called Massacre in 1937. Speak English without an accent, parents advise children, just to be safe.

But saying "shibbolet" with the accents of both Israel and Ephraim raises suspicions on both sides. To switch codes is to enter or leave one nation for another by merely releasing a foreign sound, a word, a grammar tic, slipping into an always borrowed and precarious language. Migrants aren't at home even at home. The word means somewhere else, a loss for the parents and a lack for the children who would be gringos there and may be spics here. In the Americas and throughout the modern world, linguistic be-longing *is* identity in the still-standard equation inherited from Herder. Today again, the logic of language rights uses the one for one equation. Consider Charles Taylor's "Politics of Recognition" as a contemporary milestone here; and think, too, of the program to distinguish Serbian from Croatian speech so the war could go on.[11] Nation builders have generally tried to reduce linguistically complex societies to simple ones, usually by the force of elimination. Even Du Bois and the ideologues of *mestizaje* perfected one imperial tongue.[12]

Bilingual Prosthesis

Talking with two is a double bind. Bilinguals are not, Ana Celia Zentella says, pairs of monolinguals stuck at the neck, but overloaded, imperfectly doubled systems in which the supplements as well as the missing pieces destabilize both languages. Swiss cheese is the image, with more holes than matter. Verena Conley, for one, has unforgettable things to say about being literally Swiss, weaned in one language and educated in an unwelcoming rival. Even official and elite multilingualism can breed unhappy consciousness. Sylvia Molloy's Anglo-Argentine schooling comes to mind, as does Elena Poniatowska, who learned Spanish from the maids and envied their authentic Mexicanness. How could that consciousness be happy, given the modern language economy of one per people, one per person? Something is always *in* the way or *in* demand. "Bilingual prosthesis" was the inspired mistake that Dale Shuger made when she meant to name "bilingual aesthetics" as the subject of our course one semester. When a concept is lacking, prosthetic borrowings fill in, like Molloy's *cucharite* that stirred up French and Spanish, or like *kosher* and *he's good people* which patch up a few holes in English, while *imeliar* or *beipasear* keep Spanish from crippling. But sometimes bilinguals worry about still missing pieces, because as a translation "miscegenation" vilifies *mestizaje;* "uncle" for a Chinese speaker ignores whether he's on the mother's side or the father's; and "we" should be two words for speakers of Quechua or Guaraní, one to include, the other to exclude interlocutors. The worry is a symptom of care, not of ignorance. Yet monolinguals may mistake this exquisite but commonplace attentiveness as a deficiency in the speaker.

I could go on singing the bilingual blues along with the contributors here, and we probably will, which is to recognize the bittersweet pleasures of bilingual games. These are mature pleasures wrested from reflecting on pain, as therapists and art theorists will know, however slow they are to associate everyday bilingualism with sophistication. A tragic bilingual sense of life tolerates loss because our deformed prosthetic selves survive losses. Bittersweet maturity is close to the experience of the sublime, a commonplace experience for bilinguals who live with the daily shock of disconnecting and the satisfaction of knowing it.

They know that language is arbitrary, material, and fallible; this is the metalinguistic sophistication that linguists notice but don't always defend. Bilinguals anticipate failure in ways that make contact a small miracle, through the strange and delayed meanings that the formalists valued as aesthetic artifice. And running the risk of misrepresentation and misrecognition is a kind of breathtaking vulnerability, a social death wish that brings bilanguage games to a brink. Do I risk addressing a stranger in Spanish? Will it be an invitation to intimacy, an aggressive unmasking, or a ridiculously wrong channel? The question may sound irrelevant to people who don't make these decisions daily and may not worry about the risk. Perhaps they'll counsel us to get over the complication and simply speak English, as if worrying about which language to use were not an exercise in the interpersonal delicacy and caution that amount to civic behavior. Am I making any sense in English, if readers are *assessing* what I say without asking how to *asesorarme?*

Letting a bilingual pun slip in, I ask for less judgment and more help, because the prospect of failure and the promise of a miracle produces a *Schadenfreude* of communication that splits me between jokester and butt of the joke, an alienating thrill that bilinguals learn to survive. It is a Freudian *Freude* of one word betraying another's intention, except that the master was reluctant to follow slippery words past language barriers. Veering from one signifier to a "sounds-like" neighbor is a technique of disguise or escape that marks multilinguals even when we're not trying to be funny. I remember the punctilious old ladies in my neighborhood who had *very close* veins, because varicose made no sense in English. These were the same funny ladies who figured that Giselle MacKenzie of "The Hit Parade" must be famous, because *mir kennen sie,* unlike the already forgotten Sean Fergessen.

Political Predispositions

Political theory has been slow to pursue the advantages of bilingual effects. It is often stuck in the anxiety aroused by migrant workers who strain or interrupt national arrangements. Sometimes, theory responds with compensatory designs to make room for difference, often spelling out rights and responsibilities for citizens who no longer speak the same native language. It hardly ever suggests that the differences could be good for politics, though Bonnie Honig's *Democracy and the Foreigner* (2001) invites rethinking. One political advantage of bilingualism is precisely its nervousness about communication; it demands caution and respectful distance. Another advantage of fitting badly is that *Unheimlichkeit* is unhappy, restless, and available for change. Being at a loss and anticipating unpredictable differences create a margin of disidentification from existing structures and possibly the energy to adjust them.

In top-down systems, bilingualism is a dangerous supplement that signals lateral codes and cagey moves in and out of them. More than one language per person means more than one way to eat, dress, pray, cure, dance, think. Plurals sidestep the "monism at the root of every extremism," Isaiah Berlin's wrote.[13] In a world where lingering colonial arrangements and mass migrations make bi- or multilingualism normal, it remains almost inaudible for theoretical interventions, because disciplines press on in one language at a time. To pose the bilingual question to aesthetics, politics, and philosophy is to ask how the disciplines change when we hear more than one language constitute their games. The gains will go beyond refreshing some tired subjects with the challenge of minoritarian (Latino, indigenist, migrant) practices. Reciprocally, the changing disciplines can dislodge those irritating practices from weary identitarian postures in order to promote engagements with what we call "high theory."

Until now, a politics of language has polarized regional autonomists and centralists. In either case it assumes that people choose between languages rather than live with both. Most have never lived with only one. And it's a good thing. The borders between regional and national, home and host languages map onto people as well as territories. This is bad only for taking sides in a conflict, which is why patriots prefer monolingual loyalties. What can a country expect from double-talking dual nationals? It can expect, I want to suggest, a level of ambivalence so unbearable it might help to deter conflict. Double consciousness is surely a dis-ease of bad fits, but the cure of reducing two minds to one of them can be catastrophically narrow, as Du Bois knew.

Those who don't feel strained by the split may object that bilingualism doesn't necessarily lead to double-consciousness. Or they may call us to order claiming that monolingualism is better for communication. The objections sound prescriptive and rather deaf to differences of class, color, and location. One reason the English and the Irish don't get along even in the same language, Terry Eagleton taunts, is that one assumes that language is for communication, and the other knows it's for performance (the Irish Question).[14] Living in two or more competing languages troubles the assumption that communication should be easy and upsets the desired coherence of romantic nationalism and ethnic essentialism. This can be a good thing, I repeat, since confusion and even anxiety about conflicting identities and belongings are vigilant and insomniac; they interrupt the dangerous dreams of single-minded loyalty. But the condition is volatile and will demand outlets: Either it can seek purgative cures for difference, or it can develop a new, almost perverse, taste for anxiety and irritation as stimuli for partial relief.

A totalitarian danger of one response to bilingual belongings and the liberating promise of another urges an intervention by political theorists. Of course we can assume that all are created equal, but in the real world some feel more equal than others, and those others feel more split. That heightened tragicomic feeling of being too much and too little can be a beacon for a new ironic but active political sensibility. It will be an antidote for the single-minded utopian desire for fullness, just as description was Wittgenstein's antidote for philosophical headaches. Utopia wishes away struggle, and with it politics and desire, along with the creativity that discomfort demands. Appreciating discomfort as the goad for creativity will need a new sentimental education to develop a taste for unfinished pieces.

While teachers of literature already value negativity as room for interpretation and surprise (ambiguity), we seldom make it matter for politics or deign to notice the exhibitionist ambiguity of bilingual arts. In fact, bilingual education is almost always a scaffold meant to get students from one language to another and then to fall away. Today, politics in literary studies seems inimical to the aesthetics of ambiguity; it is more likely to defend a particular identity inside the hegemonic language than to develop maneuverability between codes. This makes criticism and pedagogy lag dangerously behind creative literature, which is alarming for politics, even if social scientists remain skeptical about what humanists do. What we *do* is teach taste, judgment, sensibility—that is, a predisposition for one kind of politics or another. This is an opportunity for a new alliance between politics and literature. Defenders of democracy need pedagogues who can teach a taste for irritation, and literary studies needs something more flexible than identity politics if it hopes to recover the moral dimension of aesthetics.

The alliance can count on some already existing links onto language and literary theory. I'll claim them as precursors (as I claim

Borges as the model for this metaleptic move) in order to project a future tradition and thereby shore up some cautious optimism about reforming democratic feelings. For example, Wittgenstein woke up from the egolotrous fantasy of precise, controllable language to appreciate its precariousness. Language was not a totality but an infinity of unpredictable games that needed room to play, even though Wittgenstein didn't cross from one language field to another. For another example, Ernesto Laclau's advice to engage in irritating negotiations for rights and resources makes feeling "bad" politically good.[15] And Bonnie Honig recommends that democracy stop expecting national romances and face its gothic tensions between dread and desire. The advice sounds familiar from reading Roland Barthes, for whom the point of reading was to get "neurotic kicks," the "hurts so good" effect that he shamelessly called bliss. And though Barthes's lust is a personal incentive, his lesson in literary erotics and the joys of irritation should not be lost for a politics of reciprocal rights and responsibilities. Barthes knew that reciprocity is asymmetrical, that the great artist refuses to deliver easy satisfactions. The effect of bliss is to leave the reader at a loss, panting for more contact. His admission of joy in these frustrating engagements makes intermittence and externality necessary conditions for intimacy (see Winnicott too). But bilinguals improve on Barthes's provocation against complacent "ideal" readers; they multiply the positions and add levels of ignorance and bliss. All are less than ideal because a single ideal would gather up externalities as if the differences hardly mattered. This is no cause for concern. It's a relief in hopelessly heterogeneous societies. We've lost faith in the single ideal national language, and thank God(s) for the loss, because it lets us be imperfectly human and console or cajole ourselves with endlessly creative bilingual games (gains, in a Spanish accent).

The Players

Sylvia Molloy will have a final word in the "Bilingual Scenes" of a life that inspires future investigations. But her essay helps to frame the present collection too. She combines both the literary effects featured in *Bilingual Games* and the critical attention that our collection hopes to promote. Molloy's reflections and her novels make fuel from the burden of both languages; they press unhomeliness into movement and wonder between what can and cannot be said. This restlessness also makes Molloy an outstanding interpreter of literature. Elected president of the Modern Language Association in

2001, she promoted reflections on "Translation" among a membership that tends to stay in the cautious sub-fields of English or any one of the "foreign languages." Anglo-Argentines don't have to choose and lose traditions, and an exceptional model like Molloy can inspire an entire profession toward risky and creative moves. Can teachers and critics afford to miss those moves between languages and traditions while the world is busily crossing borders?

Michael Holquist trumps this question with another. (Why respond to questions with questions? Why not?) In an essay that will center the following *Investigations* for anyone who thinks that bilingualism is marginal, he asks, "What Is the Ontological Status of Bilingualism?" The answer will surprise unwary readers who imagine that the condition is particular to some people and irrelevant to others. No one will remain unaffected, whatever language(s) one uses. Although our collection gives disproportional space to Spanish-English games, the imbalance shows my limited reach, rather than the practically endless range of possibilities. Thanks to Holquist's meditation on the fissured and choice-driven nature of language, our volume begins with a more elegant defense of that range than any possible apologies for exclusions could muster. But his point may be easier to understand than to assimilate for readers raised on the ideal of romance between a people and their language. So this first section called "Choices"? continues with a follow-up rhetorical question by Enrique Bernárdez: "Is Monolingualism Possible?" Asking it is practically seditious from his home in Madrid, the nostalgic center of a lost empire that had forced everyone (Jews, Moors, Amerindians, Africans) to speak the same devotional language, or "Talk Christian!" Ana Celia Zentella is a leader of linguistic sedition against the racist legacies of empire. "José Can You See?" shows the colors of linguistic intolerance by outing racism and monolingualism as accomplices. From the conquered extremes of both Puerto Rico and Aztlán, she upsets authority by outmaneuvering it. These two linguists from both ends of the Spanish-speaking world exercise a tragicomic sense of the vagaries that bring everyday language games to the borders of literary effect. One effect is to bristle at purists and patriots; another is to chuckle over linguistic prudes.

Particular settings will provoke a range of performances and effects. "Some Places," the title of the next section, beg bi- or multilingual questions about who belongs and how to claim pride of place. Five essays explore some effects of polyphonic spaces that pull creativity in competing directions and twist it into lifelines where choosing means losing. A space like New York is Juan Flores's "New York,

Diaspora City," where Latinos fit in as well as almost anyone, but with remainders that tug elsewhere. New York seems to belong to everyone and to no one in particular. The best thing about "the City," a familiar joke goes, is that it's so close to the United States! Friends tell me the same joke is repeated in Miami and Los Angeles and probably elsewhere. Maybe Montreal knows a variation. Sherry Simon's "Crossing Town: Montreal in Translation" is a meeting point for migrants. The unsettled poignancy of too many languages and not enough of one makes Montreal an *unheimlich* home. The mix sounds different, though, when people stay put and empires move in. In "Bilingualisms, Quechua Poetry, and Postmodern Subjectivity," José Antonio Mazzotti listens to contemporary Peru, where Quechua poetry plays survival games in parries with Spanish. Neither language escapes the fragmentation and migration that describe people, too. The movement and resistance can damn whole populations into becoming "men with guns," while dreamers escape to a haven "cerca del cielo." The astounding multilingual movie by John Sayles inspires Joshua Miller to traces the filmmaker's "Transamerican Trail" from Texas to a Central American mountain top, where Maya and birdsong may survive. Survival of indigenous sounds does not, however, seem to be at issue in the Maghreb, according to Réda Bensmaïa. Rather, the challenge is the uneasy coexistence of more language options than any one place might manage. The dry land seems to preserve all the languages that claim it, each imperfectly. The two poles that pull at most Peruvians or Canadians multiply in the "Tetraglossia" of Maghrebi writers. Historical layers of conquest and nomadic nations that refuse to submit add up to (impossible) choices of language that go beyond either/or decisions.

Genders frame the third section to pull the effects of place toward positioning in the ubiquitous game that we might call the "war of positions," to borrow Gramsci's term, between male and female moves. As an incentive to tease language in one direction or another, gender might seem to divide performances along either/or lines between male and female, gay and straight. But bilingual games don't play at choice and loss of positions; they "queer" language, as Henry Abelove quipped after some jokes, by slipping in and out of identifiable roles and rules. Winning those queer games that don't stay in one language or another amounts to upsetting any stable expectation with more creativity than any script can allow. Each surprise is an aesthetic effect that exposes the dimension of artifice in language and gender, the dimension of wiggle room for maneuver in and out of tight spots. Margo Glantz plays along with "Doña Marina and Captain Malinche," as Cortés's consort squeezes past constraints in the double games of political and erotic inversion. Moving among languages and between genders, Mexico's "mother" was always a step ahead of the men who needed her, and wily enough to keep them panting. Breathless too, from reading *El caso Casey,* Gustavo Pérez-Firmat follows the Cuban writer past the male and female wards of the prison house of Spanish to tenuous attachments in Italian. There, where love is possible but precarious, Casey caresses a foreign tongue in "Bilingual Blues, Bilingual Bliss." That a Cuban regime of gender continues to push language to its limits is clear from the "Lexicon" that Esther Whitfield culls in *El hombre el hambre y la hembra* by Diana Chaviano. The adjustment of mere vowels in the title measures the short but significant distances between men and women held together and apart by hunger. Short on money, the island is a mint for subtle sounds and new words that keep foreigners wondering about who's who and how to spend dollars or make contact. From a neighboring island, Benigno Trigo defends existing language. In Puerto Rico, he says, "The Mother Tongue" speaks two languages. Afloat between the strong political alternative of U.S. statehood and the tenuous dreams of independence, Puerto Rico has managed to stay clear of defining decisions (that would cause either a loss of resources or a loss of face). It remains a creatively queer, oxymoronic, "free associated state." Debates about official language(s) are just as lively and inconclusive. They concern politics and pedagogy more than the arts, because island writers almost always perform, gloriously, in Spanish as a charm against the powerful spell of Americanization. Rosario Ferré worked that charm for years in books that became canonical, while her heart and mind strained toward independence. But her writing pulls elsewhere now, in an English that can offend patriotic ears.

Canons may seem to preserve the particular charms of a linguistic tradition, but a double take exposes some central texts in the section titled Double Barreled Canon. This canon enlists foreignness to refresh the waning forces of familiarity. Foreign words help to roughen a home language into producing aesthetic effects, said a grateful Viktor Shklovsky. Polyglossia is the necessary condition for real wisdom and humor, Mikhail Bakhtin insisted at the end of his long book on Rabelais. In the five demonstrations that follow, bilingual games take center stage in a variety of literary performances, not by chance. Borderline moves that strain legitimate languages actually produce the exciting effects that give the language staying power against familiarity-fatigue. Yunte Huang describes Ezra Pound's "Process of

Pidginizing Chinese" for English effect. It was Pound, after all, who canonized his own roster of poets to foreground refreshing techniques rather than pleasant results. Thanks to Huang's multilingual reading, Pound's own poetry is caught poaching and pulling found art out of shape. As self-appointed mentor to other poets, Pound had an extraordinary effect on William Carlos Williams, who began writing with the echoes of Spanish (his mother's, Quevedo's, Lope's) in his English verse. In "Found in Translation: Reflections of a Bilingual American," Julio Marzán tells how the Spanish sounds subsided, but not the affective echoes, or the uneasiness of double-barreled resentments between Mr. Pound and Mrs. Williams. But how might either Mr. Hispanophobe or Mrs. Hispanophile have accounted for the lasting quality of freshly minted Peruvian Spanish? Some of the first home-bred chroniclers knew the language well enough to pass as intellectuals in the motherland; others knew enough to use it with a studied clumsiness that called readers to attention in the war of unequal positions. All of them, Julio Ortega shows, scarred the language with indigenous intrusions and sutured it into renewed life. The technique could describe Ernest Hemingway's English, or Fanon's to mention just two famous double-barreled canonical writers. But perhaps the most notorious case of lending a language new life by borrowing accents from another is the operation of "Kafka's Languages." David Suchoff hears the accents, from Yiddish and from Hebrew, and marvels at the appreciation of effects while their sources seem irrelevant to readers. The very success of foreign effects has the paradoxical result of feeling so normal that German can remain self-sufficient instead of consciously dependent on neighbors, including disdained minorities. Kafka got away with cutting and pasting Jewish material into German texts; maybe he enjoyed a small satisfaction of subtle revenge on the beautiful language would never be quite his. But for Igor Guberman, revenge on anti-Semitic narrowness was explosive and hilarious. Greta Slobin describes his campaign inside and against the normative Russian language, forcing the mother tongue into unorthodox service. His punchy poems often deliver their jabs in Yiddish, but against the backdrop of the classical poetic tradition, thus involving most Russians in his work. Shooting off in too many directions for any canon to contain him, Guberman challenges the limits of legitimate bilingual games.

Testing and tuning our ears to a range of naïve and naughty games, these "Investigations" invite readers to pursue the possibilities of bilingual lives. Sylvia Molloy's exemplary reflections can suggest how playing these games, sometimes by being drafted into them, hones the kind of wisdom and humor that become available only at the borders between languages and between pieces of our complicated personae.

Notes

1. "Grammatically proper name," Bertrand Russell would call it, because unlike "logically proper names," these do not denote particulars but complex descriptions and have no meaning in isolation. "The Philosophy of Logical Atomism"; reprinted in *Logic and Knowledge: Essays 1901–1950,* ed. Robert C. Marsh (London: George Allen & Unwin, 1956) pp. 178–201.
2. Vladimir Nabokov, *Pnin* (New York: Vintage, 1989), p. 79.
3. Greta Slobin, author of *Remizov's Fictions,* does say it, quoting after her daughter Maya's teasing.
4. John Tierney, "The Big City: Polyglot City Raises a Cry for English," *New York Times,* August 16, 1999. "After leading the revolt against bilingual education in California, Ron Unz would like to see one in New York City." The most recent battleground is Boston, a center for higher education: "Bilingual Education Law Gets a New Foe" by Scott Greengerber, *Boston Globe,* July 31, 2001. "The Silicon Valley millionaire whose money helped demolish bilingual education in California and Arizona is bringing his crusade to Massachusetts. Ron Unz will be on the Massachusetts State House steps this morning to join the push for a ballot initiative that would virtually eliminate bilingual education in the Commonwealth, which enacted the nation's first bilingual education law in 1971. Unz bankrolled overwhelming ballot victories in California in 1998 and Arizona in 2000, and he recently initiated an effort in Colorado."
5. Ron Unz, *Wall Street Journal,* May 24, 2001, editorial.
6. See David Harvey, "Cosmopolitanism and the Banality of Geographical Evils," *Public Culture* v12, no. 2 (Spring 2000), pp. 529–564, 531–53, for a summary of many contemporary calls to pedagogical action based on [Kantian] appeals to knowledge and understanding, to which Harvey counterpoises an equally misleading [Foucauldian] taste for heterotopia and misunderstanding.
7. Johann Gottfried Herder, *Against Pure Reason: Writings on Religion, Language, and History,* translated and edited by Marcia Bunge (Minneapolis: Fortress Press, 1992), p. 43: "The age that wanders toward the desires and hopes of foreign lands is already an age of disease, flatulence, unhealthy opulence, approaching death!"
8. Wittgenstein, Ludwig. *Philosophical Investigations.* London: Blackwell, 1995. Translation by G. E. Anscombe, p. 47.
9. See also Julio Marzán, thanks to whom William Carlos Williams can now be read with a depth that monolingual readings have missed.

Our gratitude will surely extend into the future beyond this magnificent book, which inspires us to discover that other canonical writers may also have refreshed American English by being haunted, and nourished, by other languages.

10. W. E. B. Du Bois, *The Souls of Black Folk* (1903) in *Three Negro Classics* (New York: Avon Books, 1965), pp. 213–390, esp. p. 215.
11. See the special issue of *International Journal of the Sociology of Language* (no 151, 2001) dedicated to Serbian sociolinguistics, which deals with contact and separation, especially the article "Language, Nationalism and War in Yugoslavia" by Ranko Bugarski (pp. 69–87) on the sociopolitical processes by which Bosnian, Croatian, and Serbian are moving to become separate languages.
12. Miscegenation has been pronounced with mistrust or revulsion, while Latin American racial mixing, called *mestizaje,* has often been an official slogan in Spanish and Portuguese. Mestizaje endorses the particularity of New World peoples through a rhetoric of national brotherhood that is meant to ease racial tensions, not necessarily to address material equity. Latin Americans would immediately recognize Du Bois's manifesto for merging as a conventional banner of cultural pride. It was, for example, the standard of the Independence movement throughout the continent, when Simón Bolívar proclaimed that Spanish Americans have many fathers, but only one mother; that they are neither Spanish, nor Indian, nor Black, but all of these. A century later, to mention just one more of many examples, *mestizaje* reaffirmed Mexico as a modern country with a mission to the world. For a hundred years, the republic had been torn between indigenist liberals like President Benito Juárez, and Europeanizing monarchists who replaced him with Maximillian. Both sides would contribute, said the minister of education during the Mexican Revolution, to making the new man. Whites and Indians would be joined by Blacks and Asians in the unprecedented culmination of one "cosmic race." This would happen in Mexico, José Vasconcelos wrote in 1925, because no other country was as free from the racial prejudice that obstructs human progress. Anglo-Saxons (like Emerson and Whitman) seemed to prosper by divine will, but, Vasconcelos underlined, "*they committed the sin of destroying those races, while we assimilated them, and this gives us new rights and hopes for admission without precedent in History.*" José Vasconcelos, *The Cosmic Race.* (Baltimore: John Hopkins University Press, 1997).
13. See chapter 1, "My Intellectual Path" in Isaiah Berlin's *The Power of Ideas* (Princeton: Princeton University Press, 2002).
14. See Terry Eagleton, "Postcolonialism: The Case of Ireland" in David Bennet, *Multicultural States: Rethinking Difference and Identity* (New York: Routledge, 1999), 128–134.
15. Ernesto Laclau, *Emancipations* (London: Verso, 1996).

PART I

CHOICES

1

What Is the Ontological Status of Bilingualism?

Michael Holquist

Bilingualism is a topic constantly found in the news media. It is discussed (usually in heated tones) on the subway, in bars, and other social gatherings, as well as in the halls of Congress. At a time when many, even those with the Modern Language Association, question the relevance to society of the humanities in general and the role of language and literature departments in particular, it was shrewd of Doris Sommer to choose so urgent an issue as bilingualism for one of the presidential panels (generally devoted to the topic of translation) at the MLA national meeting in New Orleans in December 2001.

Those panels brought home with new force the gravity and immediacy of bilingualism. The topic emerged as a phenomenon larger than some of us previously had thought. The papers made clear that it is a topic more capacious than its cultural, political, educational, or even economic dimensions, although these are, of course, enormous. Together, they manifested a growing awareness of a new *theoretical* latency in bilingualism. Each paper provided a specific illustration of a general truth about bilingualism, a truth that gave them all their unusual coherence. The larger point that each of them made through their particular examples was this: *The condition of being in at least two languages appears increasingly to be the natural condition of having any language at all.*

More precisely, the concept that a human being might be confined to only one language appears increasingly to be a fiction. At best, we might charitably assume the monolingual thesis (as I shall call it) has held sway in most societies for so long because of a certain theoretical naiveté in the societies where it has been taken to be a fact of nature. It is a cliché of anthropology that certain traditional societies recently encountered in the New Guinea highlands or the headwaters of the Amazon, much as had ancient cultures in the Old World and aboriginal groups in the New, took as their collective name a term that could be translated as "the people," or "humans." Assuming they were the only people in the world, it is not surprising they should also have assumed that the language they spoke was the only one in the world. But of course their assumption of uniqueness was based only on their isolation, not on the teeming diversity of a world outside the experience or dreams of such groups. It may have been only a delusion, but the sense they were speaking the *only* language in existence nevertheless had, for such societies, an effect on how they conceived language itself: In the great majority of previously "undiscovered" tribes, most speakers assume an intimacy between words and things that is denied to citizens of cultures in which other languages are known to exist. It seems to follow that in the wake of such polylingualism, people become more self-conscious about their words, aware of a growing gap between them and the world. Writing, when it appears, only complicates matters. Postphilological societies emerge in which the invention of formal grammars and the presence of literacy mark a gap between sign and referent.

In such postphilological communities, characterized by their more intense experience of cultural and linguistic variety, the monolingual thesis becomes difficult to maintain. Indeed, it becomes impossible to hold without elaborate rationalization for claims of uniqueness. In later, sentimental stages of culture, self-conscious effort is required to create the effect of naiveté. Instead of being able to *assume* a special status for any particular language as a *natural* language, such claims to privilege must be *posited*. Ernst Cassirer has provided a striking example of how claims to a unitary language can be manufactured in the face of manifest diversity.

In his account of totalitarianism in *The Myth of the State*, he argues that the events enabling Nazi accession to power began long before 1933. He goes back to the origins of the political mythology that preceded Germany's rearmament, particularly those that involved changes in German culture: "The first step that had to be taken was a change in the function of language" (282).

His argument is that German, like any other language, can be made to serve many different functions. Two that are crucial he calls "semantic" and "magical" word usage, a distinction found in all cultures. "Even among the so-called primitive languages the semantic function of the word is never missing; without it there could be no human speech. But in primitive societies the magic word has a predominant and overwhelming influence. It does not describe things or relations of things; it tries to produce effects and to change the course of nature. . . . Curiously enough [he writes with heavy irony] all this recurs in our modern world" (282–283).

As an instance of magic language in the present, he cites his own experience in trying to grasp German as it was spoken in the Third Reich: "If nowadays I happen to read a German book, published in these last ten years [1934–1944], not a political but a theoretical book, a work dealing with philosophical, historical, or economic problems—I find to my amazement that I no longer understand the German language . . . words which formerly were used in a descriptive, logical, or semantic sense are now used as magic words that are destined to produce certain effects and to stir up certain emotions. Our ordinary words are charged with meanings; but these new-fangled words are charged with feelings and violent passions" (283). He gives the example of a little book that seeks to translate some of the new German words used by the Nazis into English, an attempt that in his eyes fails utterly: "For unfortunately, or perhaps fortunately, it was impossible to render these words adequately in English. What characterizes them is not so much their content and their objective meaning as the emotional atmosphere that surrounds and envelops them" (283). To illustrate his point, he adduces the two terms *Siegfriede* and *Siegerfriede:* "Even for a German ear it will not be easy to grasp this difference. The two words sound exactly alike, and seem to denote the same thing. *Sieg* means victory, *Friede* means peace; how can the combination of the two words produce entirely different meanings? Nevertheless, we are told that, in modern German usage, there is all the difference in the world between the two terms. For a *Siegfriede* is a peace through German victory; whereas a *Siegerfriede* means the very opposite; it is used to denote a peace which would be dictated by the allied conquerors" (283–284).

What the Nazis sought to do was to erect one version of German into a language that was symbiotic with their party's ideological essence. Others, such as Cassirer, might still speak a language that bore a surface resemblance to the Nazi performance of German. Insofar as they did, their use of the language could be compared with the use made by any other people of their language: That is, Cassirer spoke German in the same sense that Frenchmen spoke French, or even the way that Russians spoke Russian. But the German language of the Nazi party was not like that. For all such apparent similarities to the use made by people of their native languages, the Nazi version of German was perceived to have one thing that made it unique, and thus different from all other tongues. It was a *magic* language precisely because it did not participate in the first condition of all other natural languages—that is, its signs were not arbitrary, but had a primordial immediacy to the truth as the Nazis conceived it.

This is not the place to go into the complex (but relatively well-known) story of how the German language assumed a magic status in post-Romantic European nationalism. Something like the same story could also describe the tortured course of the French language since at least the seventeenth century, and especially after the French Revolution, as attempts to centralize and homogenize the State were prosecuted through attempts to create a centralized version of French. The confusions resulting from the collapse of the Soviet Union have produced even more grotesque experiments to weld language to identity in such places as Moldova and (with bloody seriousness) the Balkans.

I mention these lugubrious, but all-too-well known examples of monolingualism to reinforce my initial argument, that the concept of a single language taken as norm appears increasingly to be at best a primitive misconception of the world, and at worst to be an ideologically driven state policy. The politics of enforcing a single language, no matter what form such a politics might assume, results in oppression of a kind I presume need not be spelled out for most readers of this book. Perhaps too much effort in debates about bilingualism has been expended on denouncing evils the errancy of which is matched only by their obviousness. In this short intervention, I will assume that it might be more interesting, if only for a change, to speculate not on the ethics of bilingualism, but rather on the ontology of bilingualism. Now, I am fully aware of how pompous such a move must seem, so I hasten to add that by invoking the overdetermined term *ontology*, I wish merely to locate what seems to me to be the biggest difference between arguments for the privilege of a single language versus arguments for the virtues of two (or more) languages. And I seek to do so in a form that will cast light on all such debates (later we shall consider differences between bi- and polylingualism).

In all the discussions (including those at the MLA Presidential Forum) about bilingualism of which I am aware, there is ample evidence that whatever else it might be, "monolingualism" has a *fictive* quality about it insofar as it lacks a firm basis in what we have learned about language itself. Monolingualism lacks a theoretical basis that can stand up to the knowledge we have gained about language in the millennia through which it has been studied all over the globe. Monolingualism has at its heart a passion for wholeness, a desire for unity, a lust for order in a world in which variety and contingency seem to rule. Insofar as it does, it presumes a concept of the autonomous self and of the uniquely homogenous state that, outside the emotional universe within which such claims are advanced, is theoretically indefensible.

We have been talking about *language* as if it were a self-evident concept, which of course it is not. So let me specify more clearly what I mean when I invoke the word. It is a view of language that seems best suited to accounting for the reality of bilingualism as it stands over against the phantom dream of a single language. In its major outlines it derives from a variety of East European thinkers, but several of its primary assumptions are found in many other traditions as well.

The founding assumption of this view is that language is best conceived as having its most deepest ground in *relation* rather than in *things*. It will generally be conceded by most that any individual language is best thought of in terms of relations that exist among the elements that constitute it. More significant for the argument of this paper is that the larger *language* of which each particular tongue is a variant should also be conceived relationally. More particularly, this larger language might best be conceived as a contest between two opposing tendencies. Any specific utterance will be erected out of a negotiation between the two larger forces: An utterance is always a compromise between the two. At the highest level of abstraction, these shaping drives might most economically be characterized as those *centrifugal* forces that focus and bind meaning together with maximum lucidity on the one side, and on the other, *centripetal* forces that expand the possibility of meaning by prying apart existing nodes of significance to reveal previously unsuspected aspects in them. These two powers have been called by many different names. I choose *centripetal* and *centrifugal* as they have come to me in my work on Bakhtin, but Bakhtin is, of course, drawing on the great Humboldtian insight that language is energy, an event (*energija*) rather than something finished, a made thing (*ergon*).

This agonistic way of seeing things is a *philosophy* of language (or, as Bakhtin will say, it is a metalinguistics) more than a linguistics because the view it assumes of our words is grounded in a larger vision of existence, the person, and the way the world works. A distinction between actions and words is resisted in the assumption that words are actions, and as such among the building blocks of existence itself. The Russian term Bakhtin uses for "being" is always "the event of being" (*sobytie yitija*), not only because his conception of existence is dynamic, but because the Russian word for *event* stresses the interdependent nature of it: *Sobytie* is a compound in Russian, made up of the prefix *so-* (meaning 'with') and the root *bytie* (meaning 'being'). In other words, existence is always shared and therefore nothing, no one, is in itself.

I have no doubt gone on too long (and at a horrendous level of abstraction) about the metaphysical assumptions of a particular way of conceiving language. I have done so in order to move discussion of bilingualism beyond arguments about Spanish versus English in New York City schools, for instance, or the relation of English to French in Quebec. These are significant issues that need airing, but in the long run if we wish to contribute to such debates as more than simply concerned citizens, we must, as academics, find a more primordial set of categories to meditate the transient arguments that are always with us. In what follows, I will appeal not only to philosophy of language, but to a number of concepts in linguistics that may help us understand the ineluctability of bilingualism, even among those who presume they are speaking a single language.

One category that always casts its shadow over such debates is same/different. For instance, in itself "English only" is a banal thesis. So impoverished a concept can work at all only because of the same/difference distinction that powers it. It rallies those who valorize sameness over difference. But opposition to monolingualism is theoretically insufficient if it simply does a flip-flop and invokes the principle of difference alone, as its battle cry. As those who speculate on language know, as Serge Karcevskij writes, "opposition pure and simple necessarily leads to chaos and cannot serve as the basis of a *system*. True differentiation presupposes a simultaneous resemblance and difference" (51).

In other words, as students of language, we have available to us debating resources that inhere in the nature of our subject itself, for "[i]n a complete sign (a word as opposed to morpheme) there are two centers of semiotic functions, one for the formal values, the other for semantic values. The formal values of a word (gender, number, case, aspect, tense) represent aspects of signification known to every speaking subject, which are more or less safe from any subjective interpretation on the part of interlocutors; they are assumed to remain identical to themselves in all situations. The semantic part of a word, in contrast, is a residue resistant to any attempt to decompose it into elements as 'objective' as formal values" (Karcevskij 52). Monolingulism seeks—either from ignorance or from design—to collapse these two poles of language in order to claim privilege for a particular language. A correlate of assuming that every element in language is the site for an active struggle between centripetal and centrifugal (formal and semantic) forces is that *there are no single words.*

Each word exists as an entity in its own right, of course. But it is also simultaneously a particular instantiation of how the generalizing tendency in language might relate to the no less omnipresent individualizing impulse. Or, as Karcevskij puts it, "every linguistic sign is potentially a homonym and a synonym at the same time" (51).

The English word *watch,* for instance, can be a verb or a noun; after specifying in any particular utterance that I invoke it as a noun, and that I mean a timepiece and not a guarding action, but rather the watch I wear on my wrist even as I speak, I am still unable to claim an utter uniqueness for the word. Not only is the thing on my wrist not identical with the word *watch,* it is also the case that by insisting that I mean not any watch in the world, but this particular watch in this precise moment, I have still not exhausted a certain minimally necessary synonymic aspect of the word, the general watch-ness of the word *watch.* For to understand that this and only this watch is meant in this particular utterance, my interlocutor must know what *watch* in general means in English. In order to achieve a sense of *my* watch he must go to the pole of homonymy. But to do so, he must simultaneously maintain awareness of the pole synonymy, his knowledge of *other* watches.

What this suggests is that every word in all languages is a doublet. The Bible says that in the beginning was the Word; Goethe says that in the beginning was the deed. Perhaps Samuel Beckett was closer to the truth of language when he joked that in the beginning was the pun. But if it is the case, as it seems, that the primordial nature of language is relational and doubled, the question has to arise: Why have so many for so long been deluded by (or have sought to delude others into believing) the chimera of a single language? The reason, as I have tried to suggest, is to be found in confusion about what is meant when the fraught word *language* is invoked. In pondering the meaning of the term, the somewhat fuzzy philosophy I sketched above that sees language as primordially doubled (at least) finds unexpected support in an emerging consensus among linguists, especially those linguists who pride themselves on being hardheaded pragmatists suspicious of all "philosophical" claims. I have in mind here work being done by a whole group of researchers, influenced by Noam Chomsky, among whom the best known is probably Mark Baker. They are adherents of a body of ideas that has several names but is collectively called parametric theory. The group is characterized by a general (but not uncritical) acceptance of Noam Chomsky's argument that all actually spoken languages are embedded in a set of deep structures that constitute a Universal Grammar (UG). Despite the philosopher John Searle's recent claim that the Chomskian revolution has failed, most professional linguists believe it is more accurate to say that Chomsky's ideas have gone through a complex evolution over the last forty years.

A particularly important step in that evolution was taken in 1981 when Chomsky introduced the concept of "parameter" as a means for understanding the relation between universal grammar (UG) and particular languages. The most recent account of how parametric theory might change our view of language has been provided by Mark Baker, and in the brief summary that follows I will draw heavily on his latest book, *The Atoms of Language*.

Two sets of doublets used by linguists will be of help here. The first dyad is a distinction Chomsky introduced almost thirty years ago. As had Saussure before him, he sought to answer the question, What is the subject that linguists study? And he came up with an answer that had two parts. There is first of all what he called I-language, in which I was meant to convey "intentional" and "internal." It was a deep level of structure that supplied the armature for his postulate of a Universal Grammar underlying all languages. I-language is never found in actual use—it is a set of potentials. But the potentials are not laid up in a hypothetical heaven of neo-Platonic otherness. On the contrary, their presence can be deduced and demonstrated through several features that exist in words actually used by any speaker of any language—what Chomsky called the E-level of language, where E stands for expressive, insofar as the level where language is actually produced in human speech. It is this I/E distinction that marks as well the levels between *competence* in knowing all the rules of a particular language (many of which are never articulated in expression) on the one hand, and on the other, *performance*, in which the rules produce actually articulated utterances in everyday life.

Chomsky's assumption of a Universal Grammar met with (and continues to encounter) strong resistance across a broad spectrum of professionals, from neuroscientists and philosophers to other linguists. In further elucidating his position, Chomsky developed another set of terms to define language as a hard-wired set of possibilities present in all healthy human brains. Among the more productive of these terms are those that constitute the second dyad I wish to use in my further remarks, the distinction posited by Chomsky in the late seventies and early eighties (following on the important "government-binding" talks delivered at Cambridge) as P/P, or principle/parameter.

With the introduction of the category of parameter, Chomsky accomplished several goals at once. He first of all gave an answer to those who had accused him of excessive abstraction, of being a theorist whose model had a huge black hole at its center, the void between the I and the E levels of language. Much as Plato had been charged with a too-radical cutoff between his realm of pure ideas and the realm of everyday life, Chomsky was frequently attacked for insufficient thickness of description in his account of how I-level rules gradually transformed themselves into E-level phenomena. The answer Chomsky and his followers proposed after 1981 was an intermediary category between the rules of I-level and the actually articulated words of the E-level. Parameters are the key to this new way of thinking, insofar as they are the links of the chain connecting the highest level of generality with the greatest degree of specificity in language.

Mark Baker, a Chomsky student who has done a great deal of work to clarify parametric theory, finds normative models in the history of physics and chemistry. In asking what linguistics should be able to produce if it is really a science, he puts forward the example of the Periodic Table of Elements. That is, a description of language should be *complete,* much as the Periodic Table of Elements contains every possible element in the universe, even those that had not been discovered when Mendeleev first proposed it and was able "to predict the existence of germanium, scandium, and gallium because he found that his periodic table worked best if he left blank boxes near silicon, boron, and aluminum" (Baker 160). Secondly, a description should be *systematic* in the way that the periodic table manifests system. That is, "not only are all elements included, but they are placed in a natural order. The atomic number of each element is exactly one more than the element to its left, and the chemical valence of each element is the same as the one just above it. Thus the arrangement of elements in the table communicates essential properties to the informed observer at a glance" (Baker 159–160).

Linguists have yet to produce anything so splendidly reliable as the Table of Periodic elements, and probably they never will, but they are at least approaching something like the completeness and systematicity of description that characterize Mendeleev's achievement. Certainly they have introduced a greater degree of rigor to the study of language. At the heart of their proposal is that just as *words* are the atoms of *E-language, parameters* are the atoms of *I-language* (Baker 57).

Perhaps the simplest way to explain a parameter is to think of it as "a choice point in the general recipe for a human language. A parameter is an ingredient that can be added in order to make one kind of language left out in order to make another kind. A parameter could also be a combining procedure that can be done in two or three different ways to give two or three different kinds of languages. If you take the generic ingredients of language, add spice B, and shake, you get English. If you take the same basic ingredients of language, but instead of spice B you add flavorings D and E and stir, you get Navajo. I-languages are recipes, and parameters are the few basic steps in those recipes where differences among languages can be created" (Baker 57). Crackers and bread seem quite different things, but their apparent dissimilarity comes about through the inclusion or exclusion of a single ingredient, yeast.

A quick example of what a linguistic parameter might look like is the so-called null subject parameter. I use it because it involves familiar languages and also because it was an important part of the discovery procedure that led to the formulation of parametric theory in exchanges between Chomsky and his student Richard Kayne, who was teaching in Italy at the time. From the point of view of superficial syntax, a French sentence looks very much like an Italian sentence, insofar as they usually contain a subject noun phrase followed by a verb that is marked for tense. "Jean arrivera."/"Gianni verra." Italian differs from French and English, however, in that the subject can also come after the verb, as in "Verra gianni." But it is incompetent to say in French, "Arrivera Jean."

A second difference between Italian and French (and English) is the way they refer to someone who is already known from context. If Jean has already been discussed, we might say "Il arrivera." But in Italian you may simply pronounce, "Verra," which in Italian qualifies as a complete and well-formed sentence. There are other differences that flow from those I have just mentioned (for instance, you must say "It is raining" in English or "Il pleut" in French, whereas you can say in Italian simply, "Piove."

What is important for my argument here is that all these differences between Italian and French (and English) can be read as the consequences of a single fundamental difference: In some languages (such as French or English and, we might add, Nigerian, Edo [an African language]), every tensed clause must have an overt subject. Conversely, in some other languages (Italian, Spanish, Romanian, Japanese, Navajo) tensed clauses need not have an overt subject. A myriad of differences will flow from the single axis of the null subject parameter, depending on how it is instrumented in a particular language system. If so much is accepted, parametrics, when combined with the Bakhtinian emphasis on the paramount role of simultaneity in language, and with Karcevskij's stress on the asymmetric dualism of the sign, may be enlisted in the argument that says that *there is no such thing as a single language.*

To see how this might work, consider once again the basic claim we are trying to make. The thesis is that language at its heart is a set of dualistic relationships that can never be reduced to the kind of uniqueness that monolingual ideologues wish to assert when they talk about "language." If we consider any responsible account of any given language—English or Mohawk, for example—we will find that such a description must contain three elements. It must first of all account for the syntactical features of English or Mohawk. Second, it must describe the phonological system comprising what will be accepted in English or Mohawk as meaningful sounds (phonemes) as opposed to other sounds it will dismiss as nonsense. And third, such an account will have to be able to say something about how sounds get translated into meanings—that is, the semantics of English or Mohawk. At each of these levels, linguistics tells us there is a duality that governs expression.

In seeing how deep bilingualism sleeps even in the heart of what appears to be a single language, we will be helped by perceiving syntax, phonology, and semantics as a hierarchical set of possibilities. Jakobson has suggested what seems to be the natural order of language priorities in the following scheme: In the combination of linguistic units, there is an ascending scale of freedom. In the combination of distinctive features into phonemes, the freedom of the individual speaker is zero: The code has already established all the possibilities that may be utilized in the given language. Freedom to combine phonemes into words is circumscribed; it is limited to the marginal situation of word coinage. In forming sentences with words, the speaker is less constrained. And finally, in the combination of sentences into utterances, the action of compulsory syntactical rules ceases, and the freedom of any individual speaker to create novel contexts increases substantially, although again the numerous stereotyped utterances are not to be overlooked.

The differing degrees of freedom Jakobson describes here are constrained or permitted according to how closely any of the three aspects of language I listed above are involved in any given utterance. I will note only in passing that in the Jakobsonian tradition, sound is at the root of language; in Chomsky's system, it is syntax. But in both cases, what is at issue is a primordial ground of language that is defined by its ineluctability. At the deepest levels of language, if we for the moment choose the Jakobsonian model, we are not free to introduce new sounds as conveyers of meaning. If I speak English, I am compelled to use the very limited range of sounds that English has selected, out of all the noises humans can produce with their vocal cords, to be meaningful; all other sounds, the great majority of noises humans can make, will be dismissed as nonmeaningful in forming English words and thus nonsense in the technical sense of that word. The Russian phoneme that the IPA [International Phonetic Alphabet] renders as "y" (*û*) sounds very strange (and at first, somewhat off-putting) to native speakers of English, much as English short "I" (as in "hit") sounds quite foreign to Russians, because it is not one of the sounds Russian has selected to convey meanings. Out of all the grunts, groans, squeals, hisses, and other sounds we can produce, we are limited to a very few in any language we speak if we are to speak that language. In describing the null subject parameter above, we effectively described as well the unfreedom that *syntax* can bring home to the individual speaker: As we saw, in Italian you can say merely "piove," but in English you must say "it is raining."

The reason there is no choice at these levels is because they are at the borderline between the I-level language and the E-level language, a border very close to the deepest layer, the mysterious realm of Universal Grammar, the body of rules that says if we are to use human language at all (and all healthy humans do), then we are forced to use things that deploy as nouns, others that work as verbs. Furthermore, arbitrary limits will have to be set on the range of sounds that any particular language will recognize as capable of bearing meaning within it. In dealing with these limits, phonologists use the innocent-sounding terms *phoneme/allophone:* The phoneme for the English sound "a" (as in "hat") is a kind of Platonic idea of the short "a" English speakers recognize as able to bear meaning (as in other words that use it, such as "cat"). But in spoken speech, no one ever pronounces the perfect essence of the short "a" sound. We always voice an approximation of the phoneme, or an allophone. My pronunciation of "hat" is not exactly like any other pronunciation by any other speaker of English of the same sounds. And yet, other English speakers will be able to recognize my sounds as being close enough to the phoneme "a" that they will understand me. The space between a phoneme and an allophone is the difference between I-level and E-level, daily evidence that there is a gap between the parametric and performed levels of language. So at the sound level of even a "single" language, such as English, there is a split marked by the difference between relatively idiosyncratic noises I utter in my unique voice and the Platonic sounds of the phonemes setting English off from other languages.

If we look at any apparently discrete single language ("English" or "Mohawk") from the perspective of what we now know (or at least suspect with greater certainty) about the nature of language, we can draw several conclusions that have a vital bearing on the topic of this book. In conclusion, I'd like to list some of the more significant of these. A first insight will be that we must turn around some of our basic assumptions about bilingualism. It has widely been assumed that bilingualism is a term that describes a relation between two national languages (Spanish/English, let us say). There is, of course, a difference between a child (or adult) who knows both languages, and another who does not. It is on this crude basis that most schemes for curricular reform in schools, psychological theories of child development, or restrictions in the workplace get started. These attempts to "deal with" or to "use" bilingualism have not borne notable fruit. And they have not because more often than not, their essential premise is based on a fallacy: the mistaken belief that there is such a thing as a unified language that can then be specified as endowed with special qualities (national or magical in some other way).

Looking at bilingualism from the perspective of theoretical linguistics makes evident that what appears to monolingualists as a special case (people with two national languages) is, in fact, the norm. Everybody, even the farmer in Kansas who has never left his land and thinks he knows only English, is always already bilingual insofar as he is between the level of phonemes and allophones, the parametric level of syntax in Universal Grammar and the syntax individual speakers actually use. Universal Grammar provides the glue that holds all languages together (there is no language that cannot be translated into any other language). As such, it is a hopeful sign of our commonality. The ultimate irony is that at the same time, Universal Grammar is the certain guarantor of ineluctable variety. Difference is what we have in common. In meditating bilingualism we are very close to the condition in Language that Tolstoy perceived in the center of human existence. As he wrote in the second epilogue to *War and Peace*, "The problem is that regarding man as a subject of observation from whatever point of view—theological, historical, ethical, or philosophic—we find a general law of necessity to which he (like all that exists) is subject. But regarding him from within ourselves as what we are conscious of, we feel ourselves to be free"(Tolstoy, 1921).

Works Cited

Baker, Mark. *The Atoms of Language: The Mind's Hidden Rules of Grammar.* New York: Basic Books, 2001.

Cassirer, Ernst. *The Myth of the state.* New Haven, CT: Yale University press, 1946.

Karcevskij, Serge. "The Asymmetric Dualism of the Linguistic Sign." In Peter Steiner, ed. *The Prague School: Selected Writings, 1929–1946.* Austin: University of Texas Press, 1982. Trans. Wendy Steiner.

Tolstoy, Leo. *War and Peace.* Ed. Henry Gifford; trans. Louise and Aylmer Maude. New York: Oxford University Press, 1921. Reprint, 1991.

2

Is Monolingualism Possible?

Enrique Bernárdez

The Problem

In present-day Spain, bilingualism is a problem in many respects, including literary: Writers can be (and are) sometimes the object of attack due to their linguistic choice. In recent years the public discussion on this issue seems to be slowing down, a welcome development, but the rejection of the non-Castilian Spanish languages in certain areas of the country continues, a rejection that is sometimes genuine and popular but that frequently is the artificial creation of the media and some nonnationalist, right-wing political groups or the opposing hard-core nationalistic groups, whether right or left wing. The first group, of course, rejects bilingualism and defends the exclusive use of Spanish, whereas for the second group Spanish has to be rejected and it is the exclusive use of the vernacular that is the object of their political and cultural struggle, so much so that some people even propounded abandoning the teaching of Spanish at school in favor of English, so that children would be taught Catalan or Basque and English as the second language, whereas Spanish would continue to be acquired naturally (through contact with Spanish speakers, the media, etc.), but no formal instruction in it would be provided. This proposal—which didn't go beyond the stage of wishful thinking among some nationalist groups, mainly in Catalonia—makes full sense in any independent nation; the degree of independence or self-government is therefore an issue that has not been solved yet.

But even if bilingualism has always been there and a serious problem was historically made of it in a recurrent fashion, the situation was made much worse during Franco's regime. As is well enough known, the exclusive use of Spanish in all public affairs, including education, was made mandatory. As the rightist groups in Spain are trying to forget as much as possible of the country's recent history (including the nineteenth century) and a rewriting of earlier historical figures and events is currently underway (although fortunately not on too systematic a basis), much in the spirit of present-day revisionist history-writing, something similar is happening with this issue, so that the linguistic politics of Franco's regime seems to be in the process of revision, too, so that a speech by King Juan Carlos, obviously written by the government, included a reference to the Spanish language having been voluntarily accepted by many peoples of the world and never imposed on anyone. These words, in addition to offending many people[1] and opening a major debate that lasted for several months, were simply false, and unfortunately not only for the period of the Generalissimo's dictatorship.

But let's leave these more general problems aside for the moment. It is frequently forgotten, however, that Franco's regime not only opposed the use of the non-Castilian Spanish vernaculars;[2] what mattered was that Spanish should be the only language around: Foreign movie pictures had to be dubbed into Spanish, a tradition now so firmly entrenched in the Spanish public that it has lead to the opposing swing of the bilingual pendulum, dubbing in other languages of Spain now being favored instead of, or in addition to, Spanish, although fortunately the times have not made it possible to declare such dubbing legally compulsory and exclusive. Teaching and using foreign languages was also rejected, or at least suspected: In an article published in 1952 in a literary journal published by the Consejo Superior the Investigaciones Científicas,[3] José de Entrambasaguas, one of the leading Spanish literary scholars, explained in rich detail how and why learning foreign languages is something that only Jews and other *apatrids* would do, while it is wholly unnecessary in imperial nations as Spain and England:[4] "Casi todos los tontos tienen una veneración supersticiosa por el conocimiento de otros idiomas ajenos al suyo. . . . [L]os judíos, apátridas, incrustados circunstancialmente en tantos países, valoran el poliglotismo tanto como el dinero, su lengua universal."[5] The fact is that until the late 1950s no degrees in foreign languages existed at any Spanish university and the teachers of French, which by then was practically exclusive at the Spanish secondary schools, and later those of other languages (English, German, Italian), had salaries much lower than those earned by teachers of more serious subjects, including Latin and Greek (Lorenzo 10). Some languages entered our universities extremely late, mainly for political reasons, as in the case of Russian; others are simply not there yet.

All this, even if anecdotal, is important if we want to understand the point of view of many Spaniards (I'd rather avoid saying "most") in respect to all languages but their own (whether Spanish or any other); to continue with a real but incredible anecdote, my American brother-in-law was walking with his bilingual son in Madrid and talking in English, as they always do. An elderly lady overheard them and exclaimed: *¡Hablen español!* ("Speak Spanish!"). This linguistic ideology, one of the many deep and enduring effects of Franco's fascism, but one that has much deeper and general roots,[6] could be described thus: Spain is coextensive with the Spanish language; Spain is pure, Spanish has to be pure; every language other than Spanish is a danger to the essence of Spain. In bilingual areas this ideology is not so dramatic, mainly probably because people there have learned to oppose it in order to protect their own language. But as the old idea "a nation is its language" has historically been extremely pervasive, it is to be expected that some people will simply translate the old ideology into new terms: Nation X *is* X's language, et cetera, so that in the worst scenario you can get as far as defending killing to impose the exclusivity of X's language or, in the far more usual case, trying to avoid the use of any other language, including Spanish, at least in certain areas.

So bilingualism in Spain, as elsewhere, is a tricky issue, and while some people abhor it as a menace of language X on language Y, others would rather reject the use of Y in order to give X exclusive rights. For most people in their daily lives, however, bilingualism is either a familiar and constant phenomenon or simply does not exist, so that it is not worthwhile even to talk about it.

The Officially Multilingual Spain of the Twenty-first Century

Nevertheless, the bilingualism issue underwent a dramatic qualitative change with the creation and development of the *Estado de las Autonomías,* that peculiarly Spanish system of political organization of the territory, neither federalist nor confederalist or whatever, which has given some of the autonomies, notably the Basque country and a bit less Catalonia, a degree of self-government unequaled in any other modern state. This autonomy includes the official use of the vernacular alongside Spanish but with an official position of privilege. Of course, between the official and the real situation there can exist a real chasm, but that is basically a reflection of the real situation of the vernacular in its historical area, in such a way that while Galician is nowadays understood and spoken by most Galicians and Catalan is the majority language in its political community, the Valencian variety of Catalan is in a rather difficult situation and Basque is still, in spite of tremendous improvement since the creation of the Basque Autonomous Community, a minority language.[7] In this situation, the non-Castilian vernaculars should have been readily accepted by everyone as yet more of the many idiosyncracies of the different parts of Spain. This has been so for most people, although by no means all. In the same way that some people from Castile or Andalusia resent the high degree of autonomy enjoyed by Catalonia, some Spanish speakers indeed feel insulted when they hear Catalan or any other of those languages "outside their own community" (and even inside it), just like the old lady hearing a conversation in English.

The old ideology is still there, then, and is clearly visible in the constant struggle between the central and the autonomic governments, in which linguistic policies are always an issue. To give a single example of a very well known and constantly repeated anecdote, the night of Jose María Aznár's victory as the leader of the Popular Party in the general elections, hundreds of his supporters yelled a slogan that I prefer to "edit," as it was grossly abusive of one of the most valuable political personalities in contemporary Spain—"*¡Pujol, habla castellano!*"[8]—and thus metonymically ordered the Catalans to speak only Castilian (again). And even outside the strictly political realm, those who defend bilingualism and the right to use one's own language in preference to any other are frequently subject to abuse.

The "Eternal Spain" Had Only One Language

Bilingualism affects not so much the daily life as those more or less formal situations in which a choice has to be made. Today, as ever, Catalans will normally automatically choose Catalan or Castilian according to a number of well-known factors, which I will not analyze in these pages. In linguistic matters, as in many others, the problem arises whenever the possibility of choosing is restricted, limited, or simply totally blocked and the individuals have to follow a course of action—a course of speaking or writing—in whose selection they had no saying at all.

The "eternal Spain" (horrible phrase!) has been strictly unitary and centralistic: a single religion, a single army, a single and unitary political organization (even a single party), a single language. The religion was Catholicism, and all others were prohibited for centuries and until very recently. The political organization was a rather absolute monarchy and a rather suspect parliamentarianism, both of which were substituted by Franco's own organizations for too many years; and the language was Castilian Spanish. This means that the "eternal Spain" is Catholic, centralistic, monarchic, and Spanish-speaking.

Obviously, all this is radically false; never in Spanish history was it true, no matter how you look at it. Spain has always been diverse and multilingual, probably even since Atapuerca's *homo antecessor* of eight hundred thousand years ago. When Spain was officially established as a politically unitary state in the late fifteenth century, no language disappeared,[9] and it was only with Felipe V's French-style radical centralism that measures were taken against the non-Castilian vernaculars (religion had come first, hand in hand with the new political centralism of Ferdinand and Isabella in the late fifteenth century).

This ideological trinity—one god, one king, one language—was a mere wish of the ruling political and social groups, who most frequently had at their disposal, however and unfortunately, the coercive force necessary to transform their desires into realities, falsity into truth, or at least to try to do so, whatever the cost. Thus language has gone together with the civil wars, military coups, dictatorships, and other forms of repression that decorate the recent history of Spain.

Choosing a Writer's (Literary) Language

In spite of that recurrent wishful thinking of linguistic unit, Spain has always been a linguistically diverse country. Many writers had to choose a language to use in their writing, and writing itself—literature—has been affected by that choice and by the languages involved. In modern Spain, gone were the days of the selection of one language among those known by the writer, according to the genre. It is well known that Alphons X wrote his *Cantigas de Santa María* in Galician, not in Spanish, because Galician was one of the only two languages in southern Europe that were deemed appropriate for that kind of poetry: Following the example of Martin Codax's *Cantigas de amigo,* the wise king changed the subject from profane to religious but kept the language. At more or less the same time, the Catalan troubadours used their own version of the other poetic language of the time: Provençal, even leading to the creation of a peculiar literary language that is neither Catalan (or Valencian) nor Provençal, and that rather artificial language became the means of expression for none other than Ausiàs March. Other writers used Latin or found other forms of expression according to their knowledge, their interests, and the conditions of their own lives. The choice of language had consequences, of course, but these were mainly literary: No one incurred any kind of penalty for using a particular language. Of course in the Middle Ages the equation "language = nation" had not been invented yet (or reinvented, because it had existed in Roman times).

In modern Spain, the choice was automatic if the writer belonged to the cultural establishment of his time and felt himself (much more infrequently, herself) to be a member of it: The only real choice was Castilian Spanish, not because it was a better language than any other, although many people said and still say that it really is, but because it was the neutral choice. The other languages were merely regional, and using them for literature would have meant labelling oneself as a "regional writer" and being condemned to the low consideration that accompanied such a label in their own life and even later.

Designation as a "regional writer" could be a nice thing, however, even involving tender feelings, but it would be difficult for such an irresponsible individual to be included in whatever Canon that could be created by the literary intelligentsia: Such a writer could never be a writer, a real writer without further epithet. Nowadays many writers feel proud of being defined as "a *Catalan* writer" or "an *Andalusian* writer" or "a *Murcian* writer" (with the stress on the regional or national epithet), but this is a very recent development linked to the autonomic state. For this regionalistic consideration it should not matter whether they write in Spanish or in a vernacular, but this is not quite so: In those areas where a vernacular exists, for example, Catalonia, only those writers who use Catalan are principally considered *Catalan* writers. What this means is that personalities like Enrique Vila Matas, Eduardo Mendoza, and so many others do not deserve that name. For the Basque country, Jon Kortazar (2000: second part, third paragraph) refers to the Basque literature written in Spanish as an example of those literatures "sin sistema, o . . . subsidiarias." Of course such things do not (or at least not always) amount to a rejection of those writers, of this literature, as somewhat "foreign"; but they are not "really" Catalan or Basque. This indeterminacy should not meet with much amazement, because if the equation "nation = language" is extremely frequent, the other one-"-literature X = language X"—is even more basic. In the United States, a country so dramatically interested in multiculturalism, the "other" literatures are nowadays accepted on equal terms with the "traditional" U.S. literature; even here, African American, Asian

American, Japanese American, Native American, and Latino American Literature have to be written in English, or in a mixed language such as Spanglish. Could Spanglish become a rich literary language as Ausiàs March's Catalan-Provençal? Time will tell.

There Were Other Writers

There have been some interesting exceptions to the pejorative consideration of the regional writers. First and foremost, writers could depict their own region's peculiarities and yet achieve great public and literary consideration: Pío Baroja is a Basque novelist and José María de Pereda is *the* writer of Santander, while the playwright Arniches, in spite of having been born in Alicante, is considered the "regional writer of Madrid," and Pardo Bazán is undoubtedly a writer from and about León. They all have one thing in common, though: They all write in Spanish, and they use of some vernacular words, expressions, or forms of speech serves just to enhance the regional character of their works. But these authors' great literature is written in Spanish, not in any of the vernaculars.

There were a few exceptions, though, mainly in the poetry; as a matter of fact, the vernacular is usually adequate for poetry, but not for more serious, prosaic endeavors ("Está muy extendida hoy la opinión de que el gallego es rigurosamente adecuado para la poesía pero no para la prosa ideológica o crítica" [Alonso Montero 35]; "Es rarísimo el catalán que escribe poesía en español: a la distancia de intimidad de la lírica, el catalán es la única lengua realmente posible" [Marías 366].)[10] Authors were included in the official literary canon and studied, but not always read, and then only in Spanish, in secondary schools. Rosalía de Castro was a bilingual writer and was read as such: Some poems in Spanish and some in Galician are not even simply labelled as "regional" in the current histories of Spanish literature: They rank among the best in Spanish nineteenth-century poetry. Another example, far from Rosalía's poetic heights, is Gabriel y Galán's *Poemas extremeños*, whose regional character is more significant than their literary value. And there is, of course, the Catalan *Renaixença*, especially Mossén Jacinto Verdaguer. He was traditionally called Jacinto, in Spanish, and he was moreover Mossén—that is, a priest. A similar change of name took place with Domingo Arregui, nowadays Txomin Arregi, a Basque poet but also a priest and a conservative personality in politics and social affairs.

These examples—they are not the only ones—suggest that a certain linguistic choice in favor of some vernacular language did not seem to endanger the national unity: at least in certain conditions, so it seems, any of the languages of Spain could be equally used in literature. Of course, in none of these cases did the use of a vernacular affect religious and political unity: a woman not involved in politics and religiously orthodox, and two priests, and a conservative ideology common to all of them. But the unity of the nation was also maintained because they all were strictly regional poets who limited themselves to regional subjects. Arregi "creó personajes irreales y mitificados, personajes que poseen o deberían poseer todas aquella virtudes inherentes al pueblo vasco: sinceros, trabajadores, inteligentes, amantes del hogar."[11]

As for Rosalía de Castro, it is the most *enxebre* elements of Galicia that are visible in her poems and in her own way of dealing with them, not only the language:

> Miña terra, miña terra,
> terra donde m'eu criei,
> hortiña que quero tanto,
> figueiriñas que prantei.[12]

Of course, in the case of Verdaguer, although his views are broader (as befits Catalonia itself), he doesn't abandon his own country even in his magnificent epic poem, *L'Atlantida:*

> Com viatger al cim d'una pujada
> d'on obira sa terra somniada,
> aquí el bon vell sospira de dolçor:
> i veent-la verdejar hermosa i bella,
> passeja els ulls, enamorat, per ella,
> rejovenit sent volar-hi el cor.[13]

I will not dwell on Gabriel y Galán (*El Cristu benditu*), whose *Extremeñas* are his only dialectic work and one of extremely few attempts to write in this or any other dialect of Castilian Spanish.

All this amounts to saying that Spain's great, eternal (and false) unity is not endangered by these or other writers who confirm the rebirth of Spanish literature in the non-Castilian languages. Certainly there were other writers who did endanger it, who saw themselves as opposed to the prevalent religious, political, and linguistic regime. They of course were not included in the canon, although they could become some kind of symbol for the desired new, democratic, progressive Spain; this was the case of the Catalan poet Salvador Espriu, for instance. Fortunately, things have changed a little nowadays. But then, during Franco's regime and until even later for some people, even if some writers who did not use the Spanish tongue were accepted (and integrated), the fatherland could remain one, Catholic, and traditional, and, thanks to its own strength, the eternal Spain in its magnanimity could allow some of its children to sing their own local plot of land using their tender mother language.

The Ideal of Diglossia

This could be, I think, the definition of the bilingualism desired by those friends of the great patriotic unity: Spanish as the language of public life, a noble, universal language, while the vernaculars would rather befit the private, intimate, homely spheres of life. In other words, the desired situation corresponds to what sociolinguists for many years now have been calling diglossia, a situation in which only one language exists that is worth the name, and there are as many regional, secondary forms of speech, dialects or whatever, as you may wish.

This diglossia has had violent defenders, even quite recently, among the most famous Spanish intellectuals. It can usually be said that all those people always have one thing in common: They are not bilingual themselves, so that for them the problem of linguistic choice simply does not exist, as they have to use Spanish or keep silent forever. A case in point is Julián Marías's metaphor of the two-story house in which most Catalans live: One floor is Spanish, the other one, Catalan. Only the "rústicos" (the "uneducated," the "peasants") live on a single floor, Catalan; really, the two languages, the house's first and second floors, are to be used in different conditions and for different purposes. Marías's metaphor is from the 1960's, but similar ideas have been expressed much later, even by such a well-informed linguist as Gregorio Salvador. For him, languages are essentially unequal: "El igualitarismo es doctrina aplicable a los hombres, pero no en absoluto a los idiomas. Los idiomas son objetos esencialmente desiguales, son instrumentos de utilidad mensurable y a sus colisiones no se les deben aplicar jamás los mismos criterios que sirven para resolver los conflictos entre personas (G. Salvador 97, quoted in Moreno 18).[14] Needless to say, Salvador offers a number of "scientific" reasons to "prove" that Spanish is a much better language than any other. Those reasons are equally valuable for the foreign languages and for the Spanish vernaculars: Spanish is necessarily the better language because it is spoken by far more people than any vernacular, it is also better because Spanish—as opposed to Catalan and Galician—has the "most perfect" vowel system with the five basic vowels, a, e, i, o, u, and no such intermediate things (neither fish nor flesh, ni chicha ni limoná, I dare to add) as open vs. closed /e/ or /u/, not to speak of the Catalan neutral vowel, etc.

In such conditions, when even the most respected intellectuals and linguists have been writing on the inherent perfection of Spanish as opposed to the other languages and on the need to keep the unequal system of diglossia, should we wonder why the common people, but also journalists and many others, will think of the Spanish language as the perfect, natural language for any literature that wants to go beyond mere regional interest and value?

The Empire

And one must not forget that Spanish was also the "Compañera del Imperio," that it went anyplace where the Spanish galleons could sail or the invincible Tercios could walk or ride. The position of the Spanish colonial administration with respect to the native languages, in America or the Philippines, was far from clear, in spite of the propaganda that for many years tried to offer an ideal image of full respect for the languages of the indigenous peoples. The situation lasted until the very end of Spanish imperialism: Neither in Equatorial Guinea nor in the Spanish Sahara was anything done to promote and develop any language other than Spanish. And to this day, all of the very few and scarcely known Equatoguinean writers use only Spanish. Remember José Rizal, too, the Philippino writer who only used Spanish to fight against the Spanish colonialists. Of course, his choice of the imperial language was not accompanied by the necessary acceptance of the two other legs of the myth of the eternal Spain, religion and king, so that he never entered the Spanish canon and, what is much worse, was killed by a Spanish firing squad in Manila.

Who Will Read Me?

So for most writers, irrespective of their origin and mother tongue, Spanish was the natural choice as their literary medium. And there are many writers from Catalonia, Galicia, and the Basque country (but also some from Asturias and Aragon), who chose Spanish even though they could have used their own vernacular. But there were other problems, too, of a very different nature. First of all, for many years very few people could read any of the Spanish languages. To give an example of how things were, I can say that in the early seventies, while serving in the military, I made the acquaintance of a number of Catalan boys from rural Girona who had difficulty speaking Spanish but who could not read any Catalan at all. I gave them a couple of my own Catalan books, and when they discovered that they could read them easily once they got used to the new spelling conventions, they were so delighted that I never saw my books again.

At that time, writing and publishing in Catalan and the other languages of the state was completely legal and there existed a sizable production of books in Catalan, but even under these conditions, writers' freedom of choice was limited. If they wrote in their own language, very few people would be able to read them and of course they could never make a living by writing. In the case of Catalan, the existence of an uninterrupted tradition enabled a comparatively large reading public, but it amounted to practically nothing in comparison with the possibilities offered by Spanish. Now think of Galician—by then, a despised although widely used rural language—or Basque—the language of not much more than 150,000 people, usually considered politically suspect by the regime.

Choosing the vernacular was then a difficult, somehow apolitical decision: In spite of the negative conditions, a significant number of writers chose Catalan, Basque, or Galician during the last years of Franco's regime, and the number grew in those languages but also in some others that had seldom been used for literary purposes earlier: Bable in Asturias, Fabla in Aragón, and even some local dialects. Nowadays the situation is well known and has been sufficiently discussed by people who know much more about those things than I do. As a summary, it can be said that even if the normalization of the languages in their autonomous communities significantly favors their literary use, there are still many problems pending, especially in the reception of those literatures in the common canon and the number of possible readers, a problem especially acute for Basque (see Iturrald, Kortazar).

The Old New Problem: Choosing a Variety

But also in the selection of the particular form of language that is being used, alas, the old problem, Spanish versus the vernaculars, seems nowadays to be repeated. Which language variety has to be chosen? For Catalan, even if the language is not fully standardized (is there any that is?), there is a universally accepted form in Catalonia, and with only minor differences it is also used in the Balearic Islands.

But in Valencia things are a bit trickier, as one has to choose to write in standard Catalan or in the regional variety, Valencian, and then with the standard spelling or with the anti-Catalan, more Spanish-looking spelling propounded by some (rightist) groups. The writer has still to make an explicit decision, which in Valencia can bring about some undesirable consequences.

Something similar happens in Galicia, and although practically all the writers used the standard, "normative" spelling (including some specific choices in the vocabulary and, to a lesser extent, the grammar), others prefer the so-called *Lusist* spelling, which tries to enhance the linguistic and cultural relation between Galician and Portuguese. In other languages, such as Fabla, and to some extent, Bable, the writer's choice has to go as far as a selection among the various forms of standardization, and in many cases (particularly in Aragon), learning the vernacular is a necessary first step.

But where things get really bad is in Basque. The official standard, Euskara Batua, "unified Basque" is a somewhat artificial form of language spoken nowhere as a native language,[15] which coexists with a number of very diversified varieties, or "dialects." The traditional "essence" of Basqueness was to be found in the countryside, in the *baserri,* the rural house, where the ancestral traditions continued. The Batua, on the other hand, is more associated with the city and the modern way of life. The creation and initial development of the Batua met with strong resistance among traditional nationalists, and the Basque writers played an important role in its acceptance (Bornaetxea). Even today, some writers prefer to use their dialect, or a form of Batua with some approximation to their dialect, a trend that unfortunately has been blamed for the excessive localism visible in a part of contemporary Basque literature. Of course, all really important writers (and Bernardo Atxaga is the best known example) use Batua. But this situation can remind us of the choices by those Spanish-speaking writers of the nineteenth century we considered at the beginning. It seems that this is an eternal braid: Once the decision has been taken to use a language in preference over any other, one has still to choose the standard or the dialect, the local variety, and once we choose the variety to be used, things repeat themselves again.

Conclusion

In February 2001, Álvaro Galmés, a well-known and universally respected scholar in the field of Romance studies, delivered a lecture on

Las Lenguas de España (the Languages of Spain), at the Academy of History in Madrid. He analyzed the linguistic feelings of the Catalans during the sixteenth, seventeenth, and eighteenth centuries, when they defended Castilian Spanish, which they simply termed "the Spanish tongue." Álvaro Galmés, in the conservative Spanish newspaper *ABC,* humorously explained that these were the opinions expressed by "los propios catalanes," the Catalans themselves, so that if any nationalistically minded person took exception to that opinion, he or she should "complain to those Catalans, not to me." (*ABC,* February 27, 2001).

It is true: Many people in Catalonia, Galicia, the Basque country, Peru, Bolivia, and Mexico[16] historically have thought of Spanish as *the* language for literary purposes, much as Joseph Conrad chose English instead of his native Polish, or Gunnar Gunnarson wrote his novels in Danish instead of Icelandic. But Álvaro Galmés is showing only part of the picture: the Catalan writers who chose Spanish. Of course there are not many examples of Castilian writers who chose Catalan or Basque, although Blanco White did write in English and we already know about Alphons X's Galician poems, and many other examples exist.

Bilingualism has always been present in the literature of Spain, ever since the Aragonese poet Marcial wrote his poems in Latin. He was said to speak the language of the empire with a strong accent, so that he probably had his own vernacular. At the time it would have been nonsense to try to write in anything but Latin, and the same situation appeared at different times in the history of the literatures of Spain. Writers chose their language according to their interests, their political, social, or religious affiliation, and the type or genre they wanted to use. Some writers, however, had less of a choice, as they only had one language at their disposal. But in fact this is never so: There are regional varieties or dialects, social registers that writers can use in their writing. They can even choose to develop a special standard, or a special variety within the available standards. As the differences are not so salient as with different languages, most writers—and critics and historians—did not notice that a linguistic choice had been done. They didn't notice that Cervantes's language was as Castilian as Cortázar's or that Borges's could be Argentinian or García Márquez's, Colombian. This produced the mirage of literary monolingualism, something that in fact has never existed. As the literatures written in the Spanish vernaculars are now rich and varied, it remains only for the rest of the Spaniards—those who don't have the opportunity of choosing—to accept them gladly.

Notes

1. Who, for instance, had suffered the regime's repraisals for their public use of a non-Castilian language.
2. There exists no common-use term for the whole of the languages spoken in Spain with the exception of (Castilian) Spanish. I will use *vernacular*, meaning just "the language used by a certain community as their first language," in the understanding that it will not apply to Spanish (which is the vernacular of its speakers, of course!).
3. The official institution for scientific research, both in the sciences and the humanities.
4. See also Polo; Entrambasaguas'sarticle is reproduced there, together with other articles on the need for and convenience of learning and speaking foreign languages.
5. "Nearly all stupid people value the knowledge of foreign languages exceedingly much. . . . The Jews, apatrids, provisionally stuck in so many countries, value polyglotism as much as money, their universal tongue." (Does anyone doubt that anti-semitism was a part of the ideology of Franco's regime?)
6. See the discussion in Siguan, for instance.
7. The most recent discussion of the real situation of the languages of Spain can be found in the contributions to Turell.
8. *Pujol, speak Spanish!* Jordi Pujol is the president of the Catalan Autonomous Community.
9. With the exception of Hebrew and Arabic, banned together with their speakers.
10. "Many people hold nowadays that Galician is fully adequate for poetry, but not for ideological or critical prose" (of course, Xesús Alonso rejects such an opinion). "Extremely few Catalans write poetry in Spanish: At the lyric proetry´s close distances, Catalan is the only language that is really possible."
11. "Arregi created unreal and mythified persons, persons who possessed or should possess all those virtues which were inherent to the Basque people: they were all sincere, hard-working, intelligent, home-loving people . . ." (www.argia.com/siglo/prota/20txomin.htm)
12. My country, my country / the country where I grew, / the orchard I love so much, / the fig trees that I planted. (This translation, as all others, is my own; I make no claims for their literary value.—EB)
13. Like a traveler on top of a hill / from where he can behold his dreamed land, / the old man sighs in tenderness: / and seeing it growing so green, so beautiful and pretty, / he watches, in love, the whole of it, / and young again, he feels his heart fly thence.
14. Equalitarianism can be applied to the human beings but not at all to the languages. Languages are essentially unequal objects; they are tools whose utility can be measured, and their conflicts must never be solved with the same methods used to solve conflicts among human beings.

15. The birth and present situation of Euskara Batua reminds me of the creation of Landsmål or Nynorsk in nineteenth century. Norway by Ivar Aasen: a completely artificial creation on the basis of a number of dialects. But nowadays Nynorsk is the mother language of a significant number of Norwegians, who usually acquire it at the same time as a regional dialect.
16. Fray Bernardino de Sahagún was in fact a bilingual writer in Spanish and Nahuatl, while Guamán Poma de Ayala used Spanish and Quechua. Writing in these (and other) American languages was therefore a real possibility. José María Arguedas did write some stories in Quechua.

Works Cited

Alonso Montero, Xesús (1973): *Informe—dramático—sobre la lengua gallega*. Madrid: Akal.

Bornaetxea, Adolfo R. (n.d.): "Euskara Batua: lengua vasca literaria unificada." *Diccionario Crítico de Ciencias Sociales.* (http://ucm.es/infor/eurotheo/diccionarioE.htm).

Entrambasaguas, Joaquín de (1952): "Poliglotismo y traducciones." *Revista de Literatura* I 2: 257–261.

Iturralde, Joxemari (2001): "El estado de salud de la literatura vasca." *Euskonews & media* 133.zbk (http://suse00.su.ehu.es/euskonews/0133zbk/gaia/13305es.html).

Kortazar, Jon (2000): "La literatura vasca al final del milenio." *Luke,* no. 10–11. (http://www.espacioluke.com).

Lorenzo, Emilio (1984 [1980]): "Breve historia de los departamentos de inglés en España." *Actas del IV Congreso AEDEAN* (Salamanca, 1980), 9–12. Salamanca: Ediciones de la Universidad de Salamanca.

Marías, Julián (1970 [1966]): *Consideración de Cataluña.* 2nd ed. In *Obras,* vol. VIII, 337–422. Madrid: Revista de Occidente.

Moreno Cabrera, Juan Carlos (2000): *La dignidad e igualdad de las lenguas. Crítica de la discriminación lingüística.* Madrid: Alianza.

Polo, José (1976): "Monoglotismo y poliglotismo. Cuatro opiniones en contraste." En: *El español como lengua extranjera, enseñanza de idiomas y traducción. Tres calas bibliográficas,* 117–124. Madrid: SGEL

Salvador, Gregorio (1992): "La esencial desigualdad de las lenguas." In: *Política lingüística y sentido común,* pp. 93–98. Madrid: Istmo.

Siguan, Miquel (2001): *Bilingüismo y lenguas en contacto.* Madrid: Alianza.

Turell, María Teresa (ed., 2001): *Multilingualism in Spain.* Multilingual Matters: Clevedon.

3

"José, can you see?"

Latin@ Responses to Racist Discourse

Ana Celia Zentella

"José, can you see?" is the punch line to a bad joke. José, a new immigrant, praises American hospitality because at his very first baseball game, he was sent way up to the best seat in the stadium. Just before the game began everyone stood up, turned to him—perched on the flagpole—and sang out, "José, can you see?" Jokes like this one, along with exaggerated imitations of a Spanish accent, as in, "Es no my yob," and "My ney José Jiménez"; racist labels such as spic, wetback, greaser, beaner; and public insults like J. Edgar Hoover's admonition that one need not worry if Mexicans or Puerto Ricans came at you with a gun because they couldn't shoot straight, but if they had a knife, watch out—are examples of the blatantly racist discourses that construct Latin@s in the United States as stupid, dirty, lazy, sexually loose, amoral, and violent. Linguistic anthropologists, notably Bonnie Urciuoli and Jane Hill, have analyzed the ways in which these forms of speech and evaluations of language succeed in constructing whiteness, with standard English as its voice box, as the unmarked, normal, and natural order in the United States. In her powerful study of language prejudice and Puerto Ricans in New York City, Urciuoli documents how the English of working-class Puerto Ricans and other racialized groups—in schools, workplaces, and all gatekeeping encounters—is intensely monitored for any signs of an accent, nonstandard grammar, pronunciation misfires, or vocabulary gaps. On the other hand, their use of Spanish is censored as out of place, even offensive, in any public domain except those that are clearly marked as "ethnic," like folklore festivals or restaurants in which Spanish is spoken. The normal bilingual practice of switching from one language to another is despised in all settings. Monitoring for linguistic signs of disorder may be carried out in the name of improved communication and national unity, but instead it creates levels of tension and insecurity that can effectively silence New York Puerto Ricans and others who are monitored in similar ways.

Jane Hill's work in the Southwest of the United States focuses on particular Anglo American uses of Spanish, which she calls "Mock Spanish." These include the insertion of Spanish words and phrases like *mañana, Ah-dee-os, macho man; Hasta la vista* (with heavy aspiration of the <h>), and the invention of words meant to sound like Spanish, like "*el* cheap-o" or "correctomundo," the latter spoken by Samuel L. Jackson as pathological murderer in the movie *Pulp Fiction*. The link between Mock Spanish and uncontrolled violence is underscored when movie killing machines such as Schwarzenegger's Terminator alien says "Hasta la vista, baby" before blasting a victim, and when the perpetrator who is trying to get away with seven heads in a bag mocks a Mexican bellhop with "I can't wait uno minuto, I have a plane-o to catch-o." If these usages seem innocuous or innocently humorous to most Americans, some of whom surely would warn us against adopting chilling attitudes of political correctness, Hill points out that the jocular key is deceptive because Latin@s are always the butt of the joke. As she explains, "in order to 'make sense of' Mock Spanish, interlocutors require access to very negative racializing representations of Chicanos and Latinos" (Hill 1999: 683). In my own analysis of the "*chiquita*-fication" process that is central to Hispanophobia because it reduces Hispanics to an undifferentiated and uncomplicated but huge and threatening mass, I cite examples of Mock Spanish, such as "no problemo," as indicators that Spanish is minimized and dismissed as a simple language. The implication is that all you have to do is add an *-a* or an *-o* to an English word and anyone, even alien terminators, can master it with little effort (after all, Latin@s speak it). Hill's main point, building on Urciuoli's work, is that both the monitoring of Latin@ speech and the use of Mock Spanish accomplish "the elevation of whiteness" (Hill 1999: 684) by indexing Latin@s indirectly as inept and disorderly—read "out of control and dangerous"—and therefore in need of linguistic and other controls, ranging from remedial English and Spanish classes to nationwide English-only laws. At the same time, those who monitor Latin@ speech and speak Mock Spanish are directly indexed as "in control" and therefore worthy of being in control of others. Moreover, they come across as knowledgeable and cosmopolitan, people with a good sense of humor, and with the best interests of the United

States at heart. Because they function as the "invisibly normal" (Hill 1999: 683), Anglos are allowed to do and say all kinds of things without appearing overtly racist. They can mispronounce Spanish with impunity, create a simplified grammar, and jumble English and Spanish together indiscriminately, yet all of that remains invisible. My Puerto Rican family would label this a classic example of *la ley del embudo* (the law of the funnel), ascribed to those who reserve *lo ancho* (the wide part) of the funnel for their own unfettered actions but force their lessers to struggle through *lo estrecho,* the narrow neck. In this example of *la ley del embudo,* Latin@s are visibly constrained by rigid norms of linguistic purity, but white linguistic disorder goes unchallenged; in fact, white linguistic disorder is *essential* to a congenial persona, and passes as multicultural "with-it-ness."

Urciuoli and Hill are to be applauded for their insights into the linguistic practices that define and sustain "white public space": "a morally significant set of contexts that are the most important sites of the practices of a racializing hegemony" (Page and Thomas, cited in Hill 1999: 682). While I concur with their analyses, I have been wrestling with some discomfort, even after I distinguish my sympathy for Anglos who genuinely attempt to communicate with immigrants in their rudimentary Spanish from my disgust with those who bellow "Comprenday, amigo?" I also admit that I find references to "the whole enchilada," the "Frito bandito," and "dropping the chalupa" less offensive than "hot tamales" and "grassy-ass," perhaps because I am not as sensitive as I should be to disparaging Mexican stereotypes.[1] But the root of my uneasiness lies elsewhere. I am most concerned about the fact that given the hegemony of racializing discourses, there seems to be no way out—that is, no way to subvert these racist practices, to escape the stranglehold imposed by white public space. *Me explico.* If we try to resist by not apologizing for—or not trying to change—our accents, or refuse to restrict our use of Spanish, or eliminate the other ways of speaking that the dominant society judges as disorderly, we end up entrenching damaging evaluations of us as dangerous and in need of control. On the other hand, the more we force ourselves to function within the limited linguistic space allotted to us—no accent, no switching, watching our *p*s and *q*s—or thetas (q) and *s*s—the more we confirm the notion that linguistic purity and compartmentalization are valid objectives and achievable goals, if only we Latin@s tried hard enough. And, consequently, we distance ourselves from those members of our communities, particularly immigrants, who cannot perform as if a bilingual were two monolinguals stuck at the neck, that is, with one tongue in control of two inviolably separate systems. Is there really no way out?

Certainly, the power of the dominant discourses is oppressive and destructive. After all, we cannot have it both ways—we cannot claim that a wave of Hispanophobia is sweeping the nation, but insist that Latin@s have resisted and emerged unscathed. Ever since the 1970s, when demographers began to predict that Hispanics would become the largest minority group in the nation in the early part of the twenty-first century, policies that restrict legal, educational, health, and employment services have been implemented at local, state, and national levels.[2] Those policies frustrated immigrant efforts to pull out of poverty, while an elite class amassed unprecedented wealth, based in part on the cheap labor of Latin@s and other immigrants. The resulting economic disparities constitute serious challenges to our democratic ideals of equality and justice, yet they receive much less attention than the English proficiency of immigrants. Between 1972 and 1999, the top 1percent of the U.S. population increased its income by 119 percent, averaging $516,000 per person after tax income, while most Latin@s remained among the poorest segments of the 20 percent of the population with the lowest income. This group suffered a 12 percent decrease in its earnings, and in 1999 its members averaged $8,800 after taxes (*New York Times,* September 5, 1999, p. 16). The backlash against remedies that have attempted to correct these inequities, including quotas, set-asides, affirmative action, and bilingual education, has led to the identification of working-class Latin@ bilingualism with unfair privileges, turning reality on its head. These prejudices are expressed openly or may be thinly disguised, as in the following joke (told to my sister, a teacher in a bilingual education program, by an Anglo teacher): "A Latin@ lifeguard is standing at the edge of the water, watching someone who is drowning. When concerned bathers ask why he isn't trying to save the victim, the lifeguard says he doesn't know how to swim. 'How did you get the job?' they ask, horrified. His huffy response: 'I passed the test, I'm bilingual.'" If my sister and other bilingual teachers do not laugh at jokes like these, they are accused of not having a sense of humor, of being too uptight. But if the bilinguals were to suggest that monolingual Anglos are not qualified to teach in a school in which most of the children are Spanish speakers whose parents do not speak English, their Anglo colleagues would not react kindly, and might accuse them of being anti-English, even anti-American. Monolingual English-speaking teachers who fear erosion of their job security have helped place bilingual education at the center of heated national debates. Instead of addressing those fears by underscoring the growing need for teachers of English as well as the advantages of bilingualism for all

American children, teacher unions and educational administrators have abdicated their responsibility by allowing, and in some cases encouraging, anti-bilingual education legislation. In this highly charged climate, research findings that prove bilingual education can work are rarely heard above the din of anti-bilingual jokes and diatribes.[3]

Immersed in depressing statistics and the sobering realities of contemporary Hispanophobia, it is easy to lose sight of the fact that racializing discourses do not go unchallenged. Missing from well-argued analyses of white public space is the response of the marginalized others, including poor whites, African and Native Americans, non–English-speaking immigrants from increasingly diverse regions of the world, and the distinct reactions of Latin@s from different countries and of different racial, class, and gender backgrounds. My research with Puerto Rican children in New York City's "Barrio" (East Harlem) and with Dominican, Cuban, Colombian, and Puerto Rican adults throughout the city reveals that Latin@s are not passive receivers or observers of racializing discourses. To begin with, they communicate in bilingual and multidialectal ways that resist hegemonic and racist notions of language. The children who were raised on *el bloque* (the block) in El Barrio between 1979 and 1989 acquired several dialects of English and Spanish, principally the New York Puerto Rican English (NYPRE) of the second generation (which is not limited to Puerto Ricans but is the way of speaking of most second-generation working-class Latin@s in the northeast), and the African American Vernacular English (AAVE) of their black friends. Some learned Standard English as foster children in middle-class homes in Long Island, while still others learned working-class Italian American English from the descendants of El Barrio's heyday as a predominantly Italian neighborhood. In Spanish, *el bloque's* children interacted primarily with working-class people who spoke popular Puerto Rican Spanish, although several residents who had high school diplomas from Puerto Rico also spoke standard Caribbean Spanish. In addition, some *bodegueros* (grocery store owners) spoke popular Dominican Spanish, and in the early 1980s unexpected arrivals from the Mariel boatlift added their *cubanismos* (Cuban expressions) to the bilingual and multidialectal mix. Since the late 1980s, a growing number of Mexicans from Puebla have been converting many *cuchifrito* (traditional Puerto Rican food) stands into *taquerías* (taco stands), and new Mexican–Puerto Rican mixes in families, foods, and language are underway. Growing up in communities like *el bloque* is not only a bilingual experience, it is also increasingly multidialectal.

Children learned to negotiate the linguistic diversity that surrounded them in keeping with the central Puerto Rican norm of *respeto* (respect), which requires that children defer to their elders. They tried to honor their interlocutors' choice of language by speaking what was spoken to them. Since most were in regular contact with monolingual Spanish and English speakers, they learned to switch rapidly from one language to the other. For example, in one interaction, a bilingual eight-year-old went into the local *bodega* with two other Puerto Rican children, one English-dominant peer and a toddler who was a Spanish monolingual. The bilingual told her friend that she was going to buy chips in English, paid the *bodeguero* in Spanish, asked her friend in English why the toddler was following them, warned the little one in Spanish to go home, and finally told her friend to leave with her in English—all in rapid-fire succession. This ability to switch seamlessly for different interlocutors is extended to in-group talk with other bilinguals, and it becomes their badge of authentic membership in two worlds. The move from switching at sentence boundaries to switching within a sentence draws upon the meanings and values of both languages and cultures for heightened effect, as when a seven-year-old recounted his father's reaction to the new baby's color: "I remember when he was born, *que nació bien prietito* [that he was born real dark], *que* [that] he was real black and my father said *que no era hijo d'el* [that it wasn't his son] because *era tan negro* [he was so black]." Much of the best Latin@ poetry and prose make use of the same inter-sentential switching rules and strategies that this little boy had acquired in his community.[4]

El bloque's children called their language switching "mixing" or "talking both," while Cultural Studies scholars who admire the phenomenon in bilingual songs and literature rhapsodize about "the vanguard of polyglot cultural creativity" (Flores and Yudice 74). But many more people disparage it as "Spanglish," implying a linguistic mongrelization. Sociolinguists have attempted to counter the notion that these bilingual speakers are linguistically and/or cognitively confused by replacing "Spanglish" and its southwestern equivalent, Tex-Mex, with the neutral, albeit anemic, linguistic designation, "code-switching," and by quantifying and explaining the complex grammatical and conversational rules that switchers command (Pfaff, Valdés 1976, 1981; McClure 1977, Huerta 1978, Poplack 1980, Sankoff and Poplack 1981; Woolford 1983, Lipski 1985; Zentella 1981a,b, 1982, 1997; Alvarez 1991). In *Growing Up Bilingual,* I quantified over two thousand switches by *el bloque's* children to prove that they honored the grammar of both languages simultaneously, adhering to the grammatical constraints that Poplack and Lipski found at work in the switching of Puerto Rican and Mexican adults respectively. This approach is aimed at de-stigmatizing switching in the minds of teachers and other gatekeepers, but I fear that the emphasis on proving that "*aquí no pasa nada*" ("nothing's wrong here") obscures the power and beauty of mixing various dialects of Spanish and English, and the positive statement it makes about embracing several languages and cultures. More and more young Latin@s are reflecting this positive stance by transforming labels like "Spanglish," "Nuyorican," "Chicano," and "Dominican York" through via the process of semantic inversion, and adopting them with pride.

Ironically, while academic discussions about multiculturalism advocate unity and understanding among different groups, all the while treating them as separate entities, the children of communities like *el bloque* live their lives in the midst of multicultural mixes. Many enter school with more inter-racial, cross-cultural, and multilingual experience than their teachers, but that knowledge goes untapped or is discredited. There is little room in recycled Dick and Jane texts, workbook drudgery, and classrooms that insist on Standard English only, for the multiple ways of what Auer, in an effort to call attention to the creative and contextually dependent construction of a bilingual's linguistic identities, refers to as "doing being bilingual." For Latin@s whose networks include speakers of several dialects of both English and Spanish, "doing being a Latin@ bilingual" has multinational and multiracial aspects that are communicated bilingually and multidialectally.

"Doing being a Latin@ bilingual" requires skills reminiscent of an expert basketball player or *salsa* dancer. When the rhythm and rules are acquired at an early age, even new partners share a wealth of moves and can follow each other without missing a linguistic step or dropping the conversational ball. A criticism like "Blanca be actin' big an' bad" in the midst of a bilingual conversation calls upon a shared understanding of African American models of tough or cool behavior as well as the grammatical meaning of habitual "be," just as the insertion of a "*Bendito*" a few seconds later conveys a traditional Puerto Rican lament about whatever is being discussed. Loanwords like *bipéame* (beep me), *jangueando* (hanging out), *el rosheo* (the rush/hectic pace), *un breiquecito* (a little break/slack), and *frontear* (to let someone down or act falsely, from AAVE "to front") reflect the incorporation of new technologies, lifestyles, and hybrid identities in the community's Spanish. *El bloque*'s bilinguals tap into a wealth of linguistic and cultural knowledge in defiance of the static boundaries around identities and languages imposed by monitors of white public space. Moreover, bilingual dexterity is such that it allows them to poke fun at their own semantic and grammatical constraints, to come up with goofy spoofs like *cuellando* (literally "necking"), or to adopt useful creations like *tu emilio* (your e-mail address). Writers and poets often exploit the humorous effects that can be achieved by relaxing the rules of Spanish, English, and their alternation. When Henry Padrón, who identifies himself as a "Rochesterican," laments the effects of a doubly stigmatized identity in a code switched poem, "*Dos* Worlds/Two *Mundos*," he demonstrates mastery of complex constraints, but he also violates several rules on purpose. In the following excerpts, the violations include switching a lone adjective (*mucho*) between a possessive pronoun and a noun (*tu* brain), and between a personal pronoun and verbs ("They *vienen* . . . they *van*):

. . . Trying to understand this system,
mejor dicho cystern,
[better yet]
can cause you *mucho* pain.
[much]
Puede causar un tremendo strain *en tu* brain . . .
[It can cause a tremendous . . . in your]
[. . .]
No saben from where they *vienen*
[They don't know . . . come]
Y no saben to where they *van*.
[And they don't know . . . go]

In my experience, Spanish and English monolinguals are thrown off, or put off, by the rule-governed and rule-breaking switches alike, especially when in written form, but bilinguals always know where to laugh or cry.

Young children seem immune to the comic or dramatic effects of code-switching, because they react with surprise when one of their switches causes comment. Part of their socialization, or learning "how to do being bilingual," involves the development of a sensitivity to code switching rules and an appreciation of the nuances that are communicated when those rules are broken. In a third grade bilingual classroom, children did not respond to the kind of linguistic creations that elicited loud laughter from sixth graders, for instance, when a single word contained morphemes in both languages, in violation of the bound morpheme constraint, as in "chalk*ita*" (little piece of chalk). The enjoyment of playing with language flourishes during teen years, when slipping in and out of two languages and several dialects enhances the multiple identities that Latin@ adolescents try on like new outfits for specific settings or situations (see Zentella, *Multiple Codes*).

Latin@ bilinguals can run circles around monolinguals with more than just code-switching; they also make use of time-honored bilingual strategies like calquing, when a word in one language takes on the meaning of a word in the other language, especially when the words look and/or sound similar (Weinreich, Otheguy et al). It is not uncommon to hear bilingual students talk about going to study in *la librería* (the bookstore), because *librería* has taken on the meaning of library and replaced the Spanish word for library (*biblioteca)* in their lexicon. Many calques go unnoticed among bilinguals, but some are designed to cause a chuckle or raise eyebrows, for example, when speakers play the English meaning of *embarrassed* against the Spanish word *embarazada* (pregnant). Perhaps the most fun is had with loan translations, which turn word-for-word translations into comic gibberish. A classic example, "Between, between and drink a chair, for the water zero is falling down" is the translation of "Entre, entre y tome una silla porque el aguacero está cayendo" ("Come in, come in, because there's a storm"). My personal favorites are the names of the famous Spanish singers, July Churches and Placid Sunday (Julio Iglesias and Plácido Domingo), and the precautionary statement, "For if the flies" (*Por si las moscas,* or "Just in case").

Latin@s demonstrate familiarity with the lexical and phonological features of varied Spanish-speaking regions that enrich their verbal repertoires in pan-Latin@ ways and that reinforce positive identification with other Spanish speakers. As a result of close contact with Puerto Ricans, speakers from beyond the Caribbean learn, sometimes the hard way, that they cannot jump up and point at an insect on a man's pants, shouting "*Qué bicho feo!*" ("What an ugly insect!"). In the presence of Cubans one is cautioned to ask for *fruta de bomba* instead of *papaya* when ordering that tropical fruit, and with South Americans one must be alert as to where normal uses of *coger* (to take) and *pisar* (to step on/in) are restricted.[5] Experiences that introduce Latin@s to other dialects' synonyms, especially the taboo terms, form part of the narratives of Latin@ adaptation to life in the United States, and those who form friendships outside of their national origin group end up swapping in-group jokes that rely on regional lexical items and stereotypical pronunciations. Anyone who has had extensive contact with Dominican immigrants from *el Cibao* hears many references to "hablar con la i" (to talk with an i), the lower-working-class habit (in that region) of replacing post-vocalic /r/ and /l/ with /i/, for example, *carne* > /kaine/, *doctor* > /doktoi/. Repeated exposure to this practice makes it easy to laugh along with Dominicans when they hear a joke about a *Cibaeño* who was taught to remember how to say his shoe size in English by recalling the word for frying pan: /saiten/= "size ten"< *sarten*. Some dialect jokes are applicable across several national boundaries because the features that are the basis for the wordplay are widespread in the region. In the Caribbean and along the coasts of several Central and South American countries, the aspiration and deletion of syllable-final /s/ is common, as are the hypercorrections that result from attempts to speak "correctly," as defined by standard bearers from other regions. Because *comerse las eses* (literally eating one's <s>s) is frequently criticized, self conscious speakers who are trying to pronounce every <s> may insert one where it doesn't belong. Some jokes reflect a community's awareness of the standard vs. local linguistic norms and poke fun at those who try too hard to avoid the local way of speaking. One Puerto Rican joke is about a small town mayor, eager to impress at his inauguration dinner, who responded to a waiter's query, "*Señor Alcalde, quiere Ud. tabasco?*" ("Mr. Mayor, would you like Tabasco sauce?") with "No graciaS, no fuSmo" ("No thank you, I do not smoke").[6] The emphasis on the end of *gracias* and the intrusive /s/ in *fumo* communicate a pedantic preoccupation with pronunciation, and the folly of it. In fact, aspiration and deletion of syllable final /s/ is frequent and expected, unless one is reading or making a formal presentation. In the Dominican Republic, where final *s* deletion rates are very high across all genders and educational levels, it appears with more frequency in the speech of highly educated females in formal situations, such as reading (Terrell 1983). Consequently, the repeated pronunciation of *s* at the end of syllables or words is popularly ridiculed in two Dominican expressions, *hablar fiSno* (*hablar fino,* with an intrusive *s* in *fino,* literally "to speak fine") and *comió espaghuettis* (s/he ate spaghetti). Males who speak with lots of final /s/ run the risk of being labeled effeminate. In this case, a regional feature that is criticized by purists, deletion of syllable-final *s,* is maintained because of powerful covert norms in its favor.

But how do Spanglish, calques, loans, loan translations, puns, and dialect jokes constitute responses to the racializing discourse Latin@s are subjected to by guardians of white public space? After all, the linguistic and cultural prowess that they require and the wit that they reflect are lost on monolingual speakers of English and cannot be expected to dislodge their negative attitudes. I think their power lies elsewhere. Spanglish alternation of several dialects of Spanish and English challenges the notion of bounded languages and identities so successfully that any effort to halt the crossing of linguistic boundaries seems as foolhardy as the proverbial finger in the dike. The collaborative and inclusive spirit of Spanglish wins out, even in the face of self-proclaimed Spanish language priests who strive to protect the purity of Spanish, and English watchdogs who patrol a fenced-in English. In addition, Spanish wordplay that crosses national and regional boundaries reaffirms the homeland's ways of saying things in the very act of sharing them with a wider audience. These practices are part of the linguistic glue that binds Latin@s from distinct communities to each other, fostering a pan-Latin@ consciousness that finds strength in differences as well as similiarities.

Other discourses that intensify feelings of *compañerismo* are those that reflect, manage, and resist Anglo dissing of Latin@s more directly. Many are variations on the ways of speaking that we have sampled above, but the specific configurations of anti-racist speech acts deserve to be studied. It would be useful, for example, to distinguish the form and content of the discourses of opposition that predominate in in-group Latin@ settings from those that occur when Latin@s are in the presence of Anglos, and when Latin@s address Anglos directly. When they are alone among themselves, what labels do Latin@s use for those who label them "spics" and "wetbacks"? I have heard many generic insulting descriptors attached to *gringo(s)* and *americano(s)*, for example, *estúpidos, hijos de putas,* and *cabrones* ("stupid sons of whores" and "ballbusters" or "cuckolds"), but I know of no study that documents the Spanish epithets that Latin@s in general, or particular groups of them, reserve for U.S. Americans. If there is none beyond "gringo," "americano," "gavacho" (Mexican), "bolillo" (Mexican), or "yanqui" (Caribbean), none of which packs the insulting wallop of "greaser," or "beaner," does it mean that Latin@s are less racist, or more respectful, or that they like and admire U.S. Americans too much to stereotype them with hostile cliches? The latter is unlikely, in view of the venom that can surface when Latin@s discuss their "gringo" teachers, bosses, landlords, and social service workers. Common experiences of being overworked, underpaid, and abused exist, even if unique terms to identify the perpetrators do not.

Counterparts to the racist labels that some U.S. Americans use for Latin@s may be hard to find in Spanish, but it is not difficult to encounter Latin@ imitations of English monolinguals speaking Spanish. They are a mirror image of mocking imitations of immigrant English, i.e., they exaggerate the vowels and consonants that give Anglos trouble because they differ or don't exist in English, or mock the incorrect gender endings that are common errors in Anglo Spanish. For Latin@s, "*no problemo,*" a stock bit of Mock Spanish, is an indictment of Anglo ignorance about the complexities of Spanish grammar.[7] And just as some English monolinguals make fun of Spanish speakers' difficulties in distinguishing *sheet, cheat, chit,* and *shit,* some Spanish speakers deride the Anglo inability to produce either the flap or trilled /r/, for instance, *el carro caro* and *pero el perro* ("the expensive car," but "the dog") become "el carRow carRow" and "perRow el perRow." Even young children know that imitating an English speaker's Spanish can communicate feelings of superiority, and get a laugh for being pretentious. An eight-year-old from *el bloque* who wanted to keep a friend from her bag of candy acted like a haughty lady by turning "*Espérate, no toque*" (Wait, don't touch) into "usPEAR-uh-ta, noh touch-a." Reducing the unstressed vowels to "uh" sounds (technically schwas) and rendering all the other vowels as diphthongs, as native English speakers do, successfully communicated arrogant ownership. Evidently, becoming bilingual includes becoming capable of appropriating Anglo pronunciations of Spanish, for comic relief and to exercise control.[8]

Finally, there is some evidence, probably apocryphal, that Latin@s may use Spanish that sounds like English to force a supercilious English monolingual interlocutor to become an unwitting participant in an insult. In one such example, the Latin@ asks an arrogant Anglo something that is meant to sound like a Hispanized version of "Do you speak English?"—"*A Ud. le pican las ingles?*" ("Do your gonads itch?")—and in another, the question "Are you an American citizen" is rendered as, "Are you a *maricon* [homosexual] citizen?" In both cases, a proud yes answer to both questions makes Latin@s roar with satisfaction at having duped an insufferable gringo.

Latin@s have a good deal of fun at the expense of gringos, and language play is at the heart of their defense against their marginalization, exploitation, and stigmatization. But most of this opposition is expressed in closed Spanish quarters. Anglos may believe that Latin@s are talking about them when Latin@s switch to Spanish in their presence, but usually that is not the case. When working-class Latin@s come face to face with English monolinguals, the imbalance of status and power that is customary in those situations makes conversation on an equal footing impossible. Even the bilinguals—and more than 80 percent of the nation's Latin@s speak English—find themselves incapable of holding their own or defending themselves adequately in gatekeeping situations in which only they can be the losers, for example, at parent-teacher conferences, in housing and job interviews, and at welfare and social security offices. But some have begun to fight back, even risking their jobs, when the restrictions become unbearable, for example, when they are forbidden to speak Spanish to co-workers by employers who nevertheless exploit their language skills for the benefit of customers. I refer to these cases as examples of "hired for speaking Spanish, fired for speaking Spanish," more than a dozen of which have been challenged in court over the last decade (Zentella 2001). More important, many bilinguals have known for a while—and monolinguals are catching on—that bilinguals are winners at language games that confirm their virtuosity and sophistication. If this kind of self-respect, along with pity for the monolinguals who can't play, were more widespread and admitted more openly, it might have the effect of loosening the gates. Some gate-crashers have an international flavor—that is, the word play requires interpreting Spanish as if it were another language—as in the following examples:

> Fujimori's Minister of Housing is Tikito Tukasa ["Te quito tu casa"= I take your house]
>
> Bus in German is *Suben estrujen majen bajen* ["Get on, crush, smash, get off"]

Whether it is used as a comic gloss on international languages or as a proud national flag, Spanish is the voice of home and neighbors in Latin America. In U.S. cities, it is transformed in collaboration with English. The result is both the coat of arms and armor of bilingual Latin@s—every José's defense against bad jokes that take him for a *tonto*. When mocked with, "José, can you see?," he can respond, "Seguro que yes, yo veo bien claro. Y tú?"

Notes

1. Mexicans may react more negatively to Frito-Lay's "bandito" and the Taco Bell Chihuahua than Puerto Ricans and others (Alicia Pousada, personal communication). I was raised by a proud Mexican father, but I am more offended by the objectification of Latinas as sultry or silly sexpots, e.g., hot tamales, Chiquita Banana, Muriel cigars. An investigation of national-origin and gender distinctions in Latin@ responses

to racialized discourse undoubtedly would uncover significant interrelationships between ethnic and gender attitudes.

2. An English Language Amendment to the Constitution proposed in 1981 would have eliminated bilingual ballots and other bilingual services. The English-only law passed in California in 1986 led to conflicts about the use of other languages in libraries, hospitals, homeless shelters, and schools. Nevertheless, twenty-three states have passed similar "official English laws" and a federal version passed the House of Representatives in 1996. Similarly, California's efforts to eliminate health and educational services for undocumented immigrants and to dismantle bilingual education in the late 1990s were duplicated in many other states.
3. Consult the webpages of the National Association for Bilingual Education and the Center for Applied Linguistics for continuous updates on bilingual education policies and research.
4. This child was from a New York Puerto Rican community in the Bronx, not El Barrio. Children in working class Puerto Rican, Mexican, and other Latino communities across the United States acquire similar linguistic abilities.
5. A common term for insect, *bicho,* is the word for the male organ in Puerto Rico, *papaya* is the female organ in Cuba, and *pisar* and *coger* are synonyms for the sexual act in distinct regions of Latin America.
6. Small-town a*lcaldes* in Puerto Rico are the frequent butt of jokes because in the past many were better known for their faithfulness to their political party's line than for their intellectual or administrative abilities.
7. English "no problem" is "*No es ningún problema*" in Spanish. *Problema* is one of the few masculine nouns that ends in *-a*.
8. This has important implications for second- and third-generation speakers who sound like Anglos, and may contribute to their reluctance to try to learn their heritage language.

Works Cited

Alvarez, C. 1991: Code switching in narrative performance: Social, structural and pragmatic functions in the Puerto Rican speech community of East Harlem. In C. Klee and L. Ramos-García (eds), *Sociolinguistics of the Spanish-speaking World: Iberia, Latin America, the United States.* Tempe, AZ: Bilingual Press. 271–98.

Auer, P. 1984: *Bilingual Conversation.* Amsterdam: John Benjamins.

Durán, R. P. (ed.) 1981: *Latino Language and Communicative Behavior.* Norwood, NJ: Ablex Press.

Flores, J. and Yudice, G. 1990: Living borders/buscando América: Languages of latino self-formation. *Social Text* [24], 8(2), 57–84.

Hill, J. 1993a: Hasta la La Vista, Baby: Anglo Spanish in the American Southwest. *Critique of Anthropology* 13:145–176.

———. 1993b: Is it really No Problemo? *N SALSA I: Proceedings of the First Annual Symposium about Language and Society-Austin.* R. Queen and R. Barrett (eds). Texas Linguistic Forum 33: 1–12.

———. 1999: Language, Race, and White Public Space. *American Anthropologist* 100 (3):680–689.

Huerta, A. 1978: *Code switching among Spanish-English bilinguals: A sociolinguistic perspective.* Unpublished doctoral dissertation, University of Texas, Austin.

Johnston, David Cay, Gap between rich and poor found substantially wider, *New York Times,* Sept. 5, 1999:16.

Lipski, J.M. 1985: *Linguistic Aspects of Spanish-English Language Switching.* Tempe: Arizona State University, Center for Latin American Studies.

McClure, E. 1977: Aspects of code-switching in the discourse of bilingual Mexican-American children. In M. Saville-Troike (ed.), *Linguistics and Anthropology,* Washington, DC: Georgetown University Press, GURT, 93–115.

Otheguy, Ricardo. 1993. A reconsideration of the notion of loan translation in the analysis of U.S. Spanish. *Spanish in the United States: Linguistic contact and diversity,* Ana Roca and John Lipski (eds), Berlin: Mouton de Gruyter.

Padrón, H. 1982: Dos worlds-two mundos. *Hermanos Latinos,* 13, 2. (SUNY Binghamton).

Page, H. and B. Thomas. 1994: White public space and the construction of white privilege in US health care: fresh concepts and a new model of analysis. *Medical Anthropology Quarterly* 8: 109–116.

Pfaff, C. 1975, December: Constraints on Code Switching: A quantitative study of Spanish/English Paper presented at the annual meeting of the Linguistic Society of America.

Poplack S. 1980: Sometimes I'll start a sentence in Spanish y termino en español: Toward a typology of code-switching. *Linguistics,* 18, 581–616.

Poplack, S. and Sankoff, D. 1988: Code-switching. In U. Ammon, N. Dittmar and K.J. Mattheier (eds), *Sociolinguistics: An international handbook of language and society,* Berlin: Walter de Gruyter.

Terrel, Tracy D. 1983: *Relexification en el español dominicano: Implicationes para la education. El español del Caribe,* Orlando Alba (ed.) Santiago, República Dominicana: Universidad Católica Madre y Maestra.

Urciuoli, B. 1996: *Exposing Prejudice: Puerto Rican experiences of race, class, and language in the U.S.* Boulder, CO: Westview.

Valdés, G. 1976: Social interaction and code switching patterns: A case study of Spanish-English alternation. In G. Keller, R. Teschner and S. Viera (eds), *Bilingualism in the Bicentennial and Beyond,* Jamaica, NY: Bilingual Press.

———1981: Code switching as a deliberate verbal strategy: A microanalysis of direct and indirect requests among Chicano bilingual speakers. In R.P. Durán (ed.), 95–108.

Weinrich, U. 1968: *Languages in Contact*. The Hague: Mouton. (First edition published 1953)

Woolford, E. 1983: Bilingual code switching and syntactic theory. *Linguistic Inquiry*, 14, 520–36.

Zentella, A. C. 1981a: *Hablamos Los Dos. We Speak Both: Growing up bilingual in el Barrio*. Unpublished doctoral dissertation, University of Pennsylvania, Philadelphia.

———1981b: "'Tá bien, you could answer me en cualquier idioma": Puerto Rican code switching in bilingual classrooms. In R.P. Durán (ed.), 109–32.

———1982. Code switching and interactions among Puerto Rican children, IN J. Amastae and L. Elías Olivares, eds. *Spanish in the United States: Sociolinguistic Aspects*, London: Cambridge University Press.

———1995. The 'chiquita-fication' of U.S. Latinos and their languages, or Why we need an anthro-political linguistics. *SALSA III: the Proceedings of the Symposium about Language and Society at Austin*. Austin, TX: Department of Linguistics.1–18.

———1997: *Growing up bilingual: Puerto Rican children in New York*, Malden, MA: Blackwell.

———1998: Multiple Codes, Multiple Identities: Puerto Rican Teens in New York City. *Kids Talk: Strategic language use in later childhood*, Susan Hoyle and Carolyn Temple Adger, eds. Oxford University Press.

———2001 "English-only on the Job: A Comparison of Racial and Ethnic Attitudes toward the Right of Employers to Restrict Employee Language Rights." Paper delivered at the American Anthropological Association annual meeting, Washington, D.C.

Part II

Places

4

Nueva York, Diaspora City

Latinos Between and Beyond

Juan Flores

I have a good friend whose brother, a jazz pianist, died recently at an early age. When sitting with my friend to express my condolences, I asked about his brother's music, to which he responded by offering me a CD. As soon as I got home I put the music on to listen, and was intrigued to hear prominent features of Afro-Cuban percussion, a clave-based rhythmic structure, and even some wobbly montuno on the piano. I then noticed on the jewel box that several of the musicians are well-known Latin performers. The next time I saw my friend, whom I always assumed to be a straight-up African American, I asked him about his brother's incursions into the Latin idiom.

"Well, K never made the connection through the spoken or written language, but he did it through the language of the music."

"What do you mean?" I asked.

"Oh, I guess I never told you," he answered, "my mother is Puerto Rican." He paused, then added, "And the funny thing is, is that it was moms, not my father, who always made sure that we spoke English, only in English."

New York magazine has been renamed Nueva York, at least for a week. The Spanish word on the cover of the September 6, 1999 issue is an eye-catcher for readers of the popular weekly, and attests to the currency of things, and words, "Latin" among the contemporary public in the United States. The theme of Nueva York, after all, is "The Latin Explosion," those words emblazoned in bold yellow and white lettering across the half-exposed midsection of Jennifer Lopez. The Nuyorican actress, singer, and pop idol is surely "Miss Nueva

York" in our time: her shapely body, a large crucifix dangling suggestively above her conspicuous cleavage, provides the cover image, and the feature article, entitled "La Vida Lopez" (calling Ricky Martin to mind), sets out to explain "Why Jennifer Lopez, Puerto Rican Day parade marshal, girlfriend (maybe) of Puffy Combs, inspired by Selena, aspiring to be Barbra Streisand, and owner of America's most famous backside, might be the celebrity of the future." Before you know it, all New Yorkers, and all America, will be "living la vida loca" on the streets of Nueva York!

With the new millennium upon us, Latino fever is gripping U.S. popular culture at a pitch unprecedented in the protracted history of that continental seduction. Hardly a week passes without still another media special, and hardly an area of entertainment and public life—sports, music, movies and television, advertising, fashion, food—untouched by an emphatic Hispanic presence. Visibility is of course not new to the "Latin look" in American pop culture—think of Carmen Miranda, Ricardo Montalbán, or Desi Arnaz—nor is the Latin "flavor," the salsa y sabor, a new ingredient in the proverbial melting pot, be it musical, sexual, or culinary. But those passing crazes and that subliminal sense of otherness have become in the present generation a veritable saturation of the pop public sphere, the "Latin" way attaining to a ubiquity and prominence that has converted it into an active shaper of contemporary tastes and trends.

Underlying this spectacular cultural ascendancy are of course major demographic and economic changes, which have resulted in the incremental growth and enormous diversification of the Latino population in the United States, such that nearly all the Latin American and Caribbean countries are now present in substantial numbers in many settings, especially in the global cities of Los Angeles, Miami, and New York. By the early 1990s New York Newsday titled a lengthy supplement "The New Nueva York," and with that phrase capsulized the momentous increase and dramatic recomposition of the city's Latino community since the seventies. The swelling influx of Dominicans, Mexicans, Colombians, Ecuadorians, and numerous other Latin American nationalities has meant that "Latin New York," for decades synonymous with Puerto Rican, has become pan-ethnic, to the point that Puerto Ricans, while still the most numerous group, have come to comprise less than half the aggregate. By 1999, then, it was high time that New York become Nueva York, and that its burgeoning population of Spanish-language background be given its day in the glitz.

Visibility, though, can do as much to obscure as to illuminate, particularly when it remains so preponderantly concentrated in the image-making of the commercial culture. In the case of U.S. Latinos, celebrity status and ceremonial fanfare is clearly one of those mirages, serving effectively to camouflage the structured inequality and domination that accounts for their diasporic reality in the first place, and deflecting public attention from the decidedly unceremonious and unenviable social status of the majority of Latino peoples. The spectacular success stories of the few serve only to mask the ongoing reality of racism, economic misery, and political disenfranchisement endured by most Latinos, who moved northward from their homelands only because of persistent inequalities at global and regional levels.

But the Latino avalanche has given birth to the "sleeping giant," a demographic and cultural monster whose immense commercial and electoral potential has only begun to be tapped and who, if roused, could well upset some of the delicate balances necessary to the prolongation of the "American Century." Typically, awe and fascination mingle with a sense of foreboding, an alarmism over the imminent threat Latinos are perceived to present to the presumed unity of American culture and to an unhampered control over the country's destiny. An integral component of this nervous prognosis, repeated with mantra-like predictability when public discussion turns to the "browning of America," is the identification of Latinos as the country's "fastest growing minority," the group whose numbers are on pace to exceed that of African Americans as early as the first decade of the new millennium. The fear of an "alien nation"—the title of a recent xenophobic book on immigration—veils but thinly an even deeper phobia, the fear of a non-white majority. And this does not mention the next sleeping giant: the "brown peril" is soon to be eclipsed by another "yellow peril," as Asian Americans are poised to outnumber both blacks and Hispanics by mid-century.

Such calculations, however, beg more questions that they answer when it comes to assessing the cultural and political relations which prevail in contemporary society. Most obviously, they take for granted the sociological equivalence of the various "minority" groups, in this case Latinos and African Americans, as though a diverse set of immigrant and colonially conquered populations occupy the same historical position, and constitute the same kind of collective association, as a group unified, within the United States, on the basis of their common African ancestry and history of enslavement. Of course African Americans, like all other groups, have long differed along class, gender, color, regional, and other lines, but the seams in the Latino patchwork stand out as soon as we go beyond the media hype and wishful census counts and undertake comparative analysis of any degree of rigor. Even the obvious commonalities like language and religion, for example, turn out to be deceptive at best in light of the millions of Latinos who are neither Spanish-speaking nor of the Catholic faith. But beyond that, it is certainly a spurious sociological exercise to conjoin in one unit of discourse Puerto Ricans and Mexican Americans on the one hand, whose position in U.S. society is fully conditioned by legacies of conquest and colonization, with on the other hand immigrant and exile nationalities of relatively recent arrival from varied national homelands in Latin America. Differences along the lines of economic class and educational and entrepreneurial capital are striking, as are those having to do with issues of race and national cultures.

At least one of the spokesmen cited in Nueva York voices a sensitivity to the pitfalls of this pan-ethnic labeling process. The Dominican writer Junot Díaz is skeptical about any and all ethnic generalizations, stating about "Latinos" that "I'd rather have us start out as fractured so we don't commit the bullshit and erasures that trying to live under the banner of sameness entails." The most obvious of these erasures for Díaz, aside from the internal differentiation among the varied "Latino" groups, is the reality of racism—being called a "spic" and reacting to that denigrating denomination. "And rare is the Latino kid who hasn't been called a spic." Discrimination in educational opportunities and in the criminal justice system, for example, is what unites Latinos beyond the multiple cultural variations, along with the strategies developed to confront these social inequalities. "This is a nightmarish place," Díaz concludes, "for people of color."

What is not mentioned in the pages of Nueva York, by Junot Díaz or any other commentator, is the most consequential of the "erasures" involved in pan-ethnic naming—the relation of Latinos to blackness, and to African Americans in particular. While the Latino concept does generally indicate otherness, "people of color" and non-white, the history of social categorization has selectively equivocated on the issue, and many media representations allow for or foster a sense of compatibility with whiteness; the Latino faces shown for broad public consumption, whether belonging to Daisy Fuentes, Keith Hernandez, or Chita Rivera, tend to be decidedly from the lighter end of the spectrum. The unspoken agenda of the new Latino visibility, and of the imminent surpassing of African American as the largest minority, is the ascendancy of a non-black minority. To mollify the fears of an invasion from south of the border is the consolation that at least their presence does not involve dealing with more souls of more black folk.

Yet social experience tells us otherwise. The rampant "racial profiling" and waves of police brutality are directed against both African American and Latino victims, with no color distinctions of this kind playing a role. For the fact is that, in many inner-city situations, there is no such difference, and it is not possible to "tell them apart." What the hegemonic, consumer version of Latino ethnicity obscures is that many Latinos are black, especially according to the codes operative in the United States. And what is more, while this version tends to racialize Latinos toward whiteness, much in tune with the racist baggage of Latin American and Caribbean home cultures, on the streets and in the dominant social institutions, "brown" is close enough to black to be suspect.

In Nueva York in particular, where the prevalent Latino presence and sensibility remains Caribbean, this counter-position to blackness is often disconcerting at best, and among many Puerto Rican and Dominican youth the response has been to reaffirm a sense of belonging to an African diaspora. Indeed, in the case of Puerto Ricans this perspective entails not only an emphasis on Afro-Boricua heritages but, because of the decades-long experience of close interaction with African Americans in New York, an identification and solidarity with American blacks perhaps unmatched by any other group in the history of the "nation of immigrants." Cultural expression in all areas—from language and music to literature and the visual arts—typically illustrate fusions and crossovers, mutual fascinations and emulations, that have resulted in much of what we identify, for example in the field of popular music, as jazz, rock and roll, and hip-hop. Collectively, and as a reflex of broader social experiences, this demographic reality and this conjoined cultural history put the lie to any wedge driven between Latino and black life and representation.

This Latino "double consciousness" among Puerto Ricans and other Caribbeans goes back generations, in intellectual life to the contributions of Puerto Rican collector and bibliophile Arturo Alfonso Schomburg during the Harlem Renaissance, in music history at least to the 1940s with the beginnings of Latin jazz, and in literature to the writings of Jesús Colón in the 1950s and Piri Thomas in his 1967 novel *Down These Mean Streets*. In our own times, Latino youth find themselves in tight league with young African Americans in forging the constantly shifting currents of hip-hop and other expressive styles. In a frequently cited poem, "Nigger-Reecan Blues," the young Nuyorican writer Willie Perdomo addresses once again the interracial dilemmas first articulated by Piri Thomas thirty years earlier, and concludes with the dramatic lines,

I'm a Spic!
I'm a Nigger!
Spic! Spic! No different than a Nigger!
Neglected, rejected, oppressed and depressed
From banana boats to tenements
Street gangs to regiments . . .
Spic! Spic! I ain't nooooo different than a Nigger.[1]

In a similar vein, the spoken-word artist "Mariposa" (María Fernández) objects to being called a "Latina writer," as present-day literary marketing would classify her, reminding her audience that "I myself feel more in common with my sistahs [African American women writers] than with, say, Chicana poets like Sandra Cisneros or Lorna Dee Cervantes."

Yet Mariposa does not consider this intense affiliation with African Americans to stand in any conflict with her Puerto Rican background. On the contrary, in her signature poem, "Ode to the DiasporRican," she signals her "pelo vivo" and her "manos trigueñas" as evidence of her national identity, and rails against those who would deny it:

Some people say that I am not the real thing
Boricua, that is
cuz I wasn't born on the enchanted island
cuz I was born on the mainland. . . .
cuz my playground was a concrete jungle
cuz my Río Grande de Loiza was the Bronx River
cuz my Fajardo was City Island
my Luquillo, Orchard Beach
and summer nights were filled with city noises instead of
coquís
and Puerto Rico was just some paradise that we only saw in
pictures
What does it mean to live in between . . . ?[2]

Mariposa thus gives voice to the sentiments of many young Puerto Ricans, and of many Latinos in general, in their defiance of a territorially and socially confined understanding of cultural belonging. Place of birth and immediate lived experience are not wholly definitive of cultural identification, which in this view has more to do with political and social experience, and with personally chosen ascription. "No nací en Puerto Rico," she exclaims in the poem's refrain, "Puerto Rico nació en mi."

As these instances show, present-day social identities press simultaneously in varied directions, linking individuals and groups along lines that would appear mutually exclusive according to their representation in commercially and ideologically oriented media. Nueva York, New York magazine's momentary interlude as a Latino-focused publication, dwarfs the cultural horizons of Latino experience by postulating its categorical differentiation from blackness, and also by disengaging Latino culture in the United States from its moorings in Latin American and Caribbean realities. Not only are the featured Latino celebrities treated as interchangeable in their collective background, but in the entire issue no mention is made of Mexico, Puerto Rico, Cuba, the Dominican Republic, or Colombia except as potential extensions of the U.S. market. What is more, there is no discussion of the massive migrations from those home countries, nor of the historical relations with the United States, which have generated modern migratory movements, as the transnational origin and setting for the very presence and position of Latinos in U.S. society.

Today's global conditions impel us beyond these tidy, nationally constricted views of cultural identity, which might well be referred to as "consumer ethnicities." The Latino community is if anything a process rather than a circumscribed social entity, and its formation entails complex and often converging interactions with other, purportedly "non-Latino" groups such as African Americans and American Indians. But the idea of the pan-Latino necessarily implies the trans-Latino, the engagement of U.S.-based Latinos in the composition of cultural and political diasporas of regional and global proportions. The interdependence of old and new "homes," and the constant bearing of U.S. policies and practices on the life circumstances in Latin America and the Caribbean, propel more and more Latinos across the hemispheric divide and resonate loudly in the everyday lives of all Latinos. But beyond those direct geopolitical ties, awakened cultural heritages and congruencies also engage Latinos in more abstract but no less pronounced diasporic affiliations, notably transnational indigenous and "Black Atlantic" trajectories of identity formation.

The "new Nueva York" is rich with these innovative cultural possibilities, and as the newfound home of so many people from so many Latin American countries it now serves as a seminal ground for the rethinking and reimagining of America. One hundred years after the prophetic ruminations of José Martí about the contours of "nuestra América," we are now in a position to conceptualize "América" itself in its world context, and the multiple lines of an "American" identity as coordinates of radical transnational remappings. The "Latin explosion" receiving so much coverage in the United States today, the hyperboles and hypes generated by "la vida loca," are but one index of a pervasive change in human affairs, leaving all of us asking, with Mariposa, "What does it mean to live in between?"

[This piece was written for the catalogue of the exhibition "Territorios Ausentes" ("Absent Territories"), curated by Gerardo Mosquera, which opened in Casa de América Museum in Madrid, January 2000].

Notes

1. See Willie Perdomo, *Where a Nickel Costs a Dime* (New York: W. W. Norton, 1996), pp 19–21.
2. See "Ode to the DiaspoRican" by Mariposa (María Fernández) in *Centro Journal*, vol. 12, no. 1, Fall 2000, p. 66.

5

Crossing Town

Montreal in Translation*

Sherry Simon

Anne Carson is an internationally renowned poet and classical scholar who lives and teaches in Montreal. Like many of us, she often reads bilingual texts, and she's picked up a professional tic. When she finds a text puzzling, she automatically moves her eyes to the left-hand page, searching for the original, for clarification. The reflex kicks in, she says, even when the words are not translated. The writing might be awkward or opaque, but looking left yields no results. It is like looking for the "place before the zero."

To live in Montreal is often to live in a world of right-hand pages, of mixed and confused expression. English is infiltrated by French, French tries in vain to resist incursions from English. Translation is called upon to play the role of regulator, to keep languages separate. But when two languages intermingle, as they do in Montreal, translation is put to the test. This is not the proficient dispatching that runs multilingual organizations or countries, not a benevolent act of hospitality toward a guest from a distant land. Translation is a relentless transaction. It is the condition of living in a city with a double history, a city somewhere between Paris and New York, between Quebec City and Toronto, between Iqualuit and Miami, where, on the sidewalks, you hear teenagers start their sentences in one language and finish in another, where graffiti send out truly mixed messages.

How does this double consciousness play itself out in daily life and in creative practices? We have learned in our French department not to ask students what their mother tongue is. If they are immigrants or children of mixed marriages who may have gone to high school in French and college in English, they won't know what to answer. We prefer to ask then which is their *stronger* language. And we hope that they won't say they are equally good in both. This is almost always a bad sign, especially if they want to become translators. The many specialists who are constantly trying to count up *who* speaks *what* in Montreal are also now finding that labels like Anglophone and Francophone are inadequate. These categories don't account for increasingly fluid usage patterns that mean that you might speak one language at home and another at work, and in the evening switch according to which set of friends you're with. A new term has recently come into favor: language of public use. It has the advantage of avoiding categories of identity entirely. If mother tongue is the language one possesses intimately and entirely, it exists for many a goal as remote—Montrealers as an ideal—as the place "before the zero."

Montreal today is a French-language city, and French is the matrix of its social and cultural life. Yet Montreal was once, not so long ago, a British colonial city and its cultural relations were precisely represented by its geography: an English-speaking sector in the west, a larger French-speaking sector in the east, and a narrow corridor between them occupied by immigrants, mostly Jews. The spatial arrangement was a faithful model of the divisions that ran through Montreal's social life. When psychiatrist Karl Stern arrived as a refugee in Montreal in the early 1940s, he described the city as parcellated, frozen into different time zones, living in separate histories. Looking down on the city from the lookout on Mount Royal he saw "frontiers of distrust." To translate across those borders was a challenge which few took up then.

In Leonard Cohen's 1963 novel *The Favourite Game,* Lawrence Breavman is a teenager who lives in English-speaking Westmount. One Saturday night he and his buddy travel across Montreal for an escapade in a downtown dancehall. Their night ends, somewhat predictably, with a brawl. The boys were out to be rebellious. They find themselves in a throng of Francophones, to whom they relate only through stereotypes. Neither side has much of a vocabulary that could produce any real communication. Dancing and roughhousing are about it, and they allow for a kind of meeting across divides.

Cohen himself no longer lives primarily in Montreal and the geometry of the city has loosened up a great deal since the sixties. It is his work that crosses the city now in the form of translation, and the territories it crosses speak the many languages of a mixed and cosmopolitan metropolis. Last year Cohen's collected poems were turned into French as a gesture of friendship by Quebec poet and playwright Michel Garneau. Cohen didn't like the version done in

France. *Stranger Music* had become *Musique d'ailleurs* in France. Garneau turned it into *Etrange musique étrangère*, accentuating the double strangeness of the original title rather than referring to the vague elsewhere the Parisian title gives. Garneau brings Cohen back to the city he wrote from, to the nexus of language relationships he wrote out of. This translation across the city, avoiding the detour via Paris, makes cultural sense. It also makes good literary sense—the match between translator and author is good. But such good sense does not always prevail, since the publishing industry in France often gets to dictate the terms of exchange.

Garneau and Cohen were neighbors, when both lived in the former immigrant area, which is Montreal's most mixed neighborhood. At the border, contact is vigorous, and the interface between languages becomes a creative space. Garneau is not a newcomer to translation. During the 1980s, he became one of the first Quebeçois playwrights to take on Shakespeare, translating *Macbeth, Coriolanus,* and *The Tempest* into his own version of "joual," Montreal's urban slang. Garneau's translations were innovative—some would say deviant. His "joual" was archaic, and heavily accented, not the imitation of everyday language in the manner of popular playwright Michel Tremblay. His versions, surprisingly, were picked up by Robert Lepage and used for a successful run in Montreal and in Europe, including France. Lepage is Quebec's most intensely international theater director and he is not generally known to use the vernacular.

Garneau's Shakespeare was a remarkable moment in the history of language crossings in Montreal. Competition between languages was turned to the task of cultural renewal. Writing "against" a powerful language and literary tradition became a means of moving "toward" emergent forms of expression. His French versions of Cohen, some twenty-five years later, show none of the tension of his Shakespearean texts, none of the aggressive desire to "write back," but also display little of the extraordinary energy that made Garneau's translation one of a series of founding texts for a new dramatic tradition. This may be because poetry has less dramatic potential than theater. Or it may be because that particular nationalist moment has passed, along with its absolute faith in the cultural and political power of language.

Here's another story of translation in Montreal. Gail Scott is a novelist. Her books, *Heroine* and *Main Brides,* are both set in Montreal. In an essay called "My Montréal: Notes of an Anglo-Québécois Writer," she takes an American friend on a tour of the city. She walks him through the various neighborhoods, shows him the cafés and the bars that define versions of Montreal identity, and listens to the languages around them. She wants to explain why it is essential for her to write English "with the sound of French" in her ear. And "why an Anglo writer of my generation must, in order to express the Québec of this last quarter-century . . . participate in . . . two often clashing, but also mutually nourishing cultures, simultaneously" (7). For Scott, to live "in translation" is more than the daily experience of living in a multilingual city. For her, it is the basis of her creative project.

To grasp the pulse of the city, Scott wants her English to be "punctured" by French, so that it becomes a local, minor language, demoted from its world status. It is not a broken English, not the equivalent of slang or joual, but a stylized idiom reflecting the influence on Scott of her Francophone precursors in Montreal: Nicole Brossard, France Théoret, and others. Scott has translated the impulses behind their work into her own, creating a language-centered writing. This is not a situation of exile, nor is it Kafka in Prague. "I have the impression that French language and culture in a sense also *belong* to me; it is part of my cultural background." It is interesting here to contrast Gail Scott's position with that of Nancy Huston as she describes it in *Nord perdu,* both having arrived in their respective cities as young adults, Scott to Montreal from Ontario, Huston to Paris from Calgary. Living in Paris, Huston defines herself as an "expatrié" in constant tension with the linguistic security of the "impatrié," or native. Absorbed by her new culture, which is aggressively monolingual, she abandons English and sets out to speak and write in perfect imitation of the French. Scott is equally passionate about Francophone Quebec culture, but she won't try to pass. Montreal does not make her a foreigner, does not relegate her to a position outside any charmed center. And she wants her writing to reflect a position neither outside nor inside.

R. W. B. Lewis says of Dante that . . . "Florence was not merely his birthplace; it was the very context of his being." This sentiment could describe those of many Montreal writers. Erin Mouré, for example, is a prominent poet and translator, experimental and exuberant in her use of language, who has recently published a volume of what she calls "TransElations." Mouré has also translated Nicole Brossard. The points of contact between the feminist and experimental writer Brossard and her translators are especially intense. It's as if her work demands translations that are as innovative as the originals. Brossard herself uses translation idiosyncratically. *Mauve Desert* (1988) is a well-known example. The novel is the story of a translator, from Quebec, who discovers a book written about the desert of Arizona. The novel tells us about the imaginary encounter of the translator with the author, about her thoughts as she translates the book, and then gives us the translation itself. The three parts of the book—the story, the commentary, and the new version of the story—are all in French. What Brossard gives us then is a rewriting within the same language, the fiction of a translation. Brossard stops short of introducing a real second language into her work, preferring the idea of translation to the practice itself. *Picture Theory* (1982) is also driven by a translation-like paradigm, Deleuze's thinking about serial systems and "surfaces of sense" (58). Barbara Godard, another of Brossard's translators, has taken this connection and made it the productive model of her own writing, which is associated with her translation of Brossard, diaries, criticism, and translation theory based on the Deleuzian notion of the fold. These writings form a constellation, giving translation strong generative powers.

One might expect that in such a context some writers would be tempted to cross over to the other language—to convert, so to speak. But though contact between languages in Montreal is intense, literary institutions and traditions remain separate and few writers seem to want to desert their home language. Nicole Brossard's reticence in actually including English in *Mauve Desert* is surely reflects a political as well as an aesthetic decision. The boldest experiments in mixing come today from the English side. Among the few who have converted is the poet Agnes Whitfield, who called her first collection of poetry "translations without originals." These are very precisely the right-hand pages mentioned by Anne Carson, crossover texts expressing a double sensibility but with no left-hand source.

I have been talking about the way language interference in Montreal encourages deviant forms of translation, which go beyond the mandate of exchange and transmission, operating above or below the norm—sometimes as resistance and appropriation, sometimes as mixture and hybridity.

These transactions don't go on only between English and French; they also operate in triangular relationships with the more recent languages of immigration. One of the most unusual and unexpected reroutings of recent cultural history involves a language from Montreal's past, Yiddish. During the first decades of the twentieth century, Montreal was the site of a remarkable literary culture in Yiddish. Translations into English were common. Not so translations into French. In fact, until recently, they were nonexistent. The anthropologist, historian, and literary scholar Pierre Anctil, a French Canadian, not Jewish, made an unusual decision some twenty years ago: He decided to learn Yiddish. He has now translated a substantial body of work—poetry, memoirs, labor history, and novels—from Yiddish into French.

What does this act of translation mean? Yiddish was the language of the Jews who arrived as immigrants in Montreal in the early twentieth century. They lived in a "triangulated" city, dominated by English. French Canadians and Jews had little significant cultural contact, though they lived side by side. Both Yiddish and French were at the time minor, "identitary" languages, and there was little common ground for communication. Anctil's translations changed these conditions. To move from Yiddish to French, avoiding the pivot of English, is to create a new circuit of communication, activate a contact between two languages that hardly existed before.

But there is more. The translations signal a shift of intellectual territory. The history of Jewish Montreal, like the history of other immigrants, was until the 1980s considered the exclusive purview of Anglophone historians. Beginning in the 1980s, Francophone social scientists began to pay attention to these histories and began to integrate immigrants into their work. Anctil's translations, prepared with great scholarly care, join a number of other translations that expand the range of Francophone Quebec culture.

These translations give us a new example of the age-old ambiguity of the translational gesture. To enclose Yiddish in the embrace of French: is this a transaction that should be viewed as a gift or is it, despite the excellent intentions of the translator, the mark of a new cultural regime exercising its influence? Pierre Anctil will explain, much as Gail Scott did in relation to Francophone culture, that the poets and thinkers of Yiddish culture "belong" to a common Montreal history. That to translate these poets into French is to re-embed them in their city, much as Garneau did for Cohen. All this is true. It is also true that if French translations of Yiddish writers were not done before now, if they did not seem possible or relevant, it was because French did not have the authority of a translating language. Translation is possible now because French no longer has to compete with the other histories on its own territory: It can absorb them.

As a curious footnote on the subject of Yiddish, let me mention a highly symbolic translation *from* joual *into* Yiddish. This is the production of Michel Tremblay's "joual" classic "Les Belles-soeurs," performed in the early 1980s by Montreal's Yiddish Theatre Company. This was very much a one-time affair, one not likely to have the kind of continuity and influence that translations from joual into Glaswegian have had. The encounter of joual and Yiddish produced an eerily strange music, the music of the "never been" and the "never to be." It is a monument to a past that never was, one in which Jews and French Canadians could have spoken a common language.

To map out the back and forth movements of translation in Montreal is to gather material for a cultural history of the city, highlighting the different directions and intensities of exchange, cooler at the extremities, more volatile at points of contact. The closer to the borders where communities meet, the more translation exceeds its conventional role, expands into mixed forms, becomes an active participant in cultural history.

Like other cosmopolitan cities, the sidewalks of Montreal are alive with the languages of migration and globalization. But many of these languages have only limited engagement with the city. It is the patterns of translation that will tell us which languages count and which languages are excluded from full citizenship in public life. To fill out this picture, we would have to take account of translation done under legal obligations, the "Francisization" that continues to make French a viable language of work, the obligatory dubbing of American movies that is one of the ways in which American popular culture is turned into French (and which means that the Simpsons speak Quebeçois, and that even the rapid-fire dialogue of "The West Wing" can be heard in French on TV). In the background of all these activities stand the pervasive, neat, matching paragraphs of official bilingualism. The federal government and its cohorts of efficient professionals provide this display of symmetry, the plaques and brochures ensuring that the government—not necessarily the people—speaks with double voice. This tranquil image of simultaneity and equality is necessary to the existence of Canada as a political confederation, coast to coast. To live in Montreal is, however, to experience daily the irregular shape of translation, its gains and losses, its differing cultural objectives and meanings. Here one experiences translation as a permanent condition in which languages are always unsettled and precarious.

This condition informs academic life as well. It means a double frame of reference, and the noise of sometimes unwanted feedback as concepts are heard in stereo. Is "métissage" the translation of hybridity? Is "francophonie" the equivalent of postcolonialism? Or, to recall an earlier era, Is a "phallogocentriste" the same as a male chauvinist? To hear these concepts in reverberation is to be reminded that concepts are linked to intellectual traditions, and that responsible translation involves what Antoine Berman called "translation," which might be correctly rendered as "thick translation." In the same way, models of translation theory emerge out of specific sites and are not universally applicable. I am thinking in particular of the way in which theories dominated by notions of "étrangeté" in France and "foreignness" in the United States are unable to account for the situation of proximate differences that I am describing in Montreal. To move from a cross-national frame onto the streets of cosmopolitan cities is to introduce a new angle of perception, to uncouple translation from its very long association with the nation.

Does a city like Montreal provide the definitive experience of modernity where at each moment one is aware of another language behind the mother tongue, the experience of what Alexis Nouss calls the "outre-langue," a ghostly reminder of what is always lost or imaginary in language? Montreal has many features in common with the Trieste of Joyce's day, a city whose authors, Joyce, Svevo, and Saba, were important creators of the modernist sensibility. Both cities are animated simultaneously by a nationalist and a cosmopolitan spirit. Both have a polyglot sensibility, in which languages compete publicly for recognition. In the Trieste of the early twentieth century, this tension provided extraordinary stimulus for literary creation.

The Montréal Jewish poet A. M. Klein was a fervent admirer of Joyce. Like Joyce, Klein turned his fascination with languages to literary use. In 1948 he wrote a poem called "Montreal" in which he used invented words combining English and French. In it Montreal is a soundscape, where "multiple lexicons are uncargo'd," where "double-melodied vocabulaire . . . bilinguefact your air." Admiring the spiral staircases of the city's triplexes, he speaks of "escaliered homes," and rows of maples become "grandeur erablic." Klein's poem evoked the Babelian confusion of postwar Montreal and gestured toward a possible utopian fusion of languages. How would it be written today? In French, no doubt, but in a French unsettled by English and by the other languages of the city, perhaps in a performance of spoken word poetry, a genre that has become popular in Montreal at the intersection of many influences. Or in a mixed language yet to be imagined, by a poet like Anne Carson.

Carson is not often seen as an emblematic Montreal writer. Her translations are from classical Greek. Yet she embodies Montreal's translational sensibility, using translation as a form of composition, continually creating encounters between the mythical and the modern. By mixing idioms and transforming original texts, her writing mirrors the relentless meeting of differences in Montreal. Speaking of two authors as she might speak of two languages, she shows how confronting one reality with another "keeps attention from settling." The purpose of the conversation she imagines between the fifth-century B.C. Greek poem Simonides of Keos and the Holocaust survivor Paul Celan in her recent essay *Economy of the Unlost* is to place two writers, two realms of thought, "on a surface on which the other may come into focus" (viii).

At its most negative, language consciousness in Montreal creates an experience of linguistic impoverishment, a fraying of the substance of idiom as it comes constantly in contact with the other; it nourishes an obsession with duality and a preoccupation with the *one* other to the exclusion of real and vivifying foreignness. At its best, this double consciousness is a source of linguistic energy and experimentation—a kind of mental vigilance kept sharp through the continual shock of hybridity. It encourages an easy familiarity with small or proximate differences. Like the imaginary encounter of Carson's two authors, the languages of Montreal are "with and against" each other, "aligned and adverse" (viii). The city is a multifocal surface that keeps attention from settling.

Notes

* This piece was originally presented at the MLA Presidential Forum, December 2001 and was published in *Profession* December 2002.

Works Cited

Anctil, Pierre. *Le rendez-vous manqué*. Québec: Institut québécois de la culture, 1988.

———. *Tur Malka. Flâneries sur les cimes de l'histoire juive montréalaise*. Québec: Septentrion, 1997.

Ara, Angelo et Claudio Magris. *Trieste. Un'identità di frontiera*. Torino: Einaudi, 1982

Berman, Antoine. *John Donne: Pour une critique des traductions*. Paris: Gallimard, 1990.

Brault, Jacques. *Poèmes des quatre côtés*. Québec: Éditions de Noroît, 1975.

Brossard, Nicole. *Picture Theory:* Montreal, Nouvelle Optique, 1982. Trans. Barbara Godard, Montreal Guernica, 1991.

———. *Le désert mauve*. Montréal: L'Hexagone, 1987. *Mauve Desert,* trans. Susanne de Lotbinière-Harwood. Toronto: Coach House Press, 1990.

———. *Installations*. Trans. Erin Mouré and Robert Majzels. Winnipeg: The Muses Company, 2000.

Carson, Anne. "ATranslation and Humanism." Lecture, Liberal Arts College, Concordia University, November 29, 2000.

———. *Economy of the Unlost. Reading Simonides of Keos with Paul Celan*. Princeton: Princeton University Press, 1999.

Cohen, Leonard. *The Favourite Game*. Toronto: New Canadian Library, McClelland and Stewart. 1970 (1963).

———. *Stranger Music: Selected Poems and Songs.* Toronto: McClellard and Stewart, 1993. Trans. Michel Garneau, *Etrange musique étrangère.* Montreal L'Hexagone, 2000.

Garneau, Michel. *Macbeth de William Shakespeare.* Traduit en québécois. Montréal: vlb éditeur, 1978.

———, trans. *Coriolan de William Shakespeare.* Montréal, vlb éditeur, 1989.

———, trans. *La Tempête,* Montréal: vlb éditeur, 1989.

Godard, Barbara. "Deleuze and Translation," *Parallax,* 2000, vol. 6 no. 1, 56–81.

Huston, Nancy. *Nord Perdu.* Paris: Gallimard, 1999.

Klein, A. M. *Complete Poems.* Toronto: University of Toronto Press, 1992.

———. *Le Deuxième Rouleau.* Trans. Charlotte and Robert Melancon. Montréal: Boréal, 1990.

Lewis, R. W. B. *Dante.* Viking, 2001. p.12

McCourt, John. *The Years of Bloom: James Joyce in Trieste 1904–1920.* Dublin: Lilliput, 2000.

Medresh, Israel. *Le Montréal juif d'autrefois.* Trans. Pierre Anctil. Québec: Editions du Septentrion, 1997.

Moure, Erin. *Sheep's Vigil by a Fervent Person. A Transelation of Alberto Caeiro/Fernando Pessoa's* O Guardador de Rebanhos. Toronto: Anansi, 2001.

———. *Montréal, l'invention juive,* Groupe de recherche Montréal imaginaire, Université de Montréal, Département d'études francaises, 1991.

Nouss, Alexis (with François Laplantine). *Métissages.* Paris: Pauvert, 2001.

Segal, J. I. Poèmes Yiddish. Trans. Pierre Anctil. Québec: Chanbly Editions du Noroît, 1992.

Scott, Gail. "My Montreal, Notes of an Anglo-Québécois writer." *Brick* no. 59, spring 1998, pp. 4–9.

———. *Heroine.* Toronto: Coach House Press, 1987.

———. *Main Brides.* Toronto: Coach House Press, 1993.

Majzels, Robert. *City of Forgetting.* Toronto: Mercury Press, 1997.

———. *My Paris.* Toronto: Mercury Press, 1999.

Stern, Karl. *The Pillar of Fire.* New York: Harcourt Brace & Co., 1951.

Tremblay, Michel. *The Guid Sisters.* Trans. William Findlay and Martin Bowman. Toronto: Exile Editions, 1988.

Whitfield, Agnes. *O cher Emile, je t'aime.* Traduction sans original. Ottawa: Hearst, Le Nordir, 1993.

———. "Entre les solitudes," *Francophonies d'Amérique* no. 10, Presses de l'Université d'Ottawa, 2000.

6

Introduction to Tetraglossia

The Situation of Maghrebi Writers

Réda Bensmaïa

In a speech given at the First Algerian National Colloquium on Culture, M. Lacheraf, a Maghrebi historian and former minister of national education, addressed the question of minimal requirements for the development of a Maghrebi culture, asking the following question: "At what level already or yet to be reached, does a national culture cease to be mere entertainment, and become as basic as the bread one eats and the air one breathes?" In the context of postcolonial Maghreb, it is clear that this kind of "culture," as M. Lacheraf realized, was first of all a goal "to be attained." That is why in his speech he subordinated this question and the answer it might receive to a much more radical one. He wrote: "To search for an answer to this . . . is once more to ask ourselves if a given terrain can usefully accommodate a culture that is also given; and whether such an operation does not necessitate that this terrain, that is to say, the mass of people, should first of all be in a position to respond, both to the cultural needs which fuel them and to the demands made on them by a small group of their fellows who are better equipped to satisfy these needs?"

Thus the first thing one should notice is that the situation inherited by Algeria at the time of independence is a catastrophic one: in the foreground a deculturation of the popular masses such that the very notion of a public seems like a luxury, or at best a difficult goal to reach; in the background a number of writers, artists (among them filmmakers) and intellectuals too few in relation to the "needs" and for the most part "acculturated." So not only are the "products" (and the producers) lacking, but also so is the "terrain" itself where such products might grow and assume a meaning, above all the material and objective conditions for an audience or a "public." At the time of independence, cultural problems are never addressed in universal and abstract terms of expression and production, but necessarily always in regional and concrete terms of territorialization or re-territorialization, based on the spiritual and material fragments that the country has inherited, in order to found a new and coherent cultural background. It is a question of attempting to create from scratch, but without improvisation, a new "collective subject," something like a national "entity," on the "debris" of a social and cultural community that has avoided disaster and total dismemberment *in extremis.* And at this level, every decision, every commitment becomes clearly a question of life and death. To create or re-create a "terrain," to define something as a national "characteristic," to re-territorialize, are all well and good, but with what basic elements does one start?

The forgotten past? The ruins of popular memory? Folklore? Tradition? In fact, none of these things carries as yet enough force and cohesion to allow the anchoring of a national culture. Better still, to believe in the possibility of a re-territorialization through folklore, the past, tradition, or religion would mean believing in the existence *sub specie aeternitatis* of a Maghrebi norm or essence that 135 years of colonialism would have left absolutely intact; it would also imply a belief that to sweep away the "leftovers" of this rule would mean recovering the "spirit" of the Maghrebi people in its pristine form. Obviously, neither this norm, nor this essence, existed on Independence Day: "To what norm can one return," wrote M. Lacheraf, "if it is not to the fleeting aspects of an essentially defunct universe, of which only illusory folkloric vestiges remain, and which would only reconstitute the past in its inoperative nostalgia?" What must be assured first of all "is the continuity of a past linked to the present by *new sociocultural facts,* by tangible and sure acts of resurrection more than of survival." If such a thing as a "national character" does exist, it is yet again a far off goal in constant dialectic with whatever "living" and "active" component is left in the past, not simply based on the past.

This said, even when phrased in this way, the questions are not very clear and the problems remain abstract, because whether it takes place through folklore, the past, tradition or anything else, the re-territorialization of a particular, authentic culture should first manage to solve the problem of medium or mediation through which all this might come about: "What language should one write in? In what language should one make films? In what language should people be allowed to speak and write? In what places? At what time? Or still, in

French? Arabic? In Berber? In Kabyle? In literary Arabic? Problems as concrete and vital as these explain the acuity of tensions, contradictions and difficulties facing every artist in Algeria. For the writers to write, for filmmakers to make films, is a question of life and death, as each one of their gestures, each one of their choices is a foundation. In every case it is a matter of delineating a "terrain" and to find, at any cost, one way out of the labyrinth of tongues and languages. In the words of Gilles Deleuze and Félix Guattari, in their fascinating book on Kafka: "To write [one could add "to film"] like a dog in his hole, a rat digging his burrow. And thus to find one's own point of under-development, one's own dialect, one's own Third World."[1]

These concrete conditions explain the complex mechanism by which it is historically the theatre, and not literature or even the cinema, for example, which will reach the goals expected of a 'renaissance' of Maghrebi popular culture: to be the vital medium which allows a people to recognize within itself a national "character"—that is, a certain *identity* in the diversity of languages and local cultures, a certain *unity* in the multiplicity of ethnicities and mores, and last but not least, an active *solidarity* in the disparity of towns and rural settlements.

What I would like to attempt here, as quickly as possible, is to analyze certain theoretical and practical difficulties that Algerian literature in French has encountered in creating, in spite of the obstacles inherited from the colonial dismemberment, its own "language," elaborating a "terrain," and encountering a "public" (three concepts, which I have tried to show, are absolutely inseparable in this context.

For a long time one thing impeded any approach to the problem of literature in French (falsely termed "of French expression")[2] and of its literary status—both aesthetic and ideological—in relation to French literature: namely, the illusion of believing that after independence there were only two possible antinomical ways open: re-territorializing either through literary Arabic or through bilingualism (French for science and technology, literary Arabic for the "soul," identity, roots). In the meantime, *vernacular languages*, still very much alive, found themselves literally shut off: in particular the so-called dialectal or *spoken* Arabic and Kabyle. Such a limited and narrow view of the linguistic question led, on the one hand, to the misunderstanding of an essential part of national cultural life, and on the other hand, to the impossibility of reflecting the real practice of writers, artists and the masses.

Indeed, to limit ourselves simply to the world of arts and culture, what was the situation of Maghrebi writers? All of them, whether French or Arabic leaning, found themselves face to face with a de-territorialized language, without deep social and cultural roots. This was, in any case, the lot of Francophone writers who, writing in the language of ex-colonial power, found themselves in a no-man's land. They found it *impossible not to write* because from their point of view as writers—"the national consciousness, uncertain and long oppressed, ought to be expressed through literature" (Deleuze and Guattari, 30)—and *the impossibility of writing in anything other than French* was for them both the sign of a limit and an irreducible distance from what they could only fantasize and dream about: "a primitive Algerian territorialization," which they had the feeling of betraying constantly. Finally, *the impossibility of writing in French* was also, for the Algerian writer, the fated inability to translate the idiosyncratic traits of one's society, in this case a society where several languages were competing for hegemony. The problem facing writers was then clearly drawn: How to live in several languages and write only in one?

Maghrebi writers, as we know, have addressed this in different ways, according to temperament, preoccupations and ideological and political commitments. Some simply stopped writing; others tried to come to terms with their acculturation by continuing to write in French, with the ambition of "mistreating" it (*le mettre dans tous ses états*), but making it say what it was not in principle "unable" to say; still others tried to write in literary Arabic and some in spoken Arabic. But it is worth noting that neither of the last two managed to solve the problem I raised earlier, that is the creation of a relatively homogeneous cultural "terrain," or should we say "melting pot" and to meet with a "public," in short, to anchor their works in a homogeneous cultural "terrain." The important thing, then, is that, contrary to what Albert Memmi[3] thought, a return to Arabic—including dialectical Arabic—was not at all sufficient to solve the contradictions which appeared, to fill in the void which separated creators from the public; whatever medium they chose, in a way writers ended up in the same impasse. Many reasons were invoked to account for this postcolonial phenomenon: deculturation, lack of material and human means, but all of them seem to me subordinate to one essential element—namely that the dichotomy between "high" and "low" popular languages, or rather the false dilemma between Arabic on the one hand and bilingualism on the other, does not help us understand what is really going on in the realm of Algerian culture.[4] An important sociolinguistics is missing here, one that might have concretely reflected what was actually happening in the country.

What a certain number of Maghrebi writers understood very well, without always however assuming its practical (and political) consequences, was that in the cultural era in which they had to produce literary or poetic works, they were not dealing with a single language, or even with two, nor were they dealing with high or low languages, but always, no matter what language they chose, with at least four types of well-differentiated languages:[5]

1. A *vernacular language*, "local, spontaneously spoken, made less for communicating than for communing," consisting essentially of a multiple "play" of languages: maternal languages of the community or of rural origin, including spoken Arabic, Kabyle, and Touareg for example—but also a certain deterritorialized usage, nomadic or typical of a language that is neither French, nor Arabic, nor Kabyle; a language made up of "bits and pieces," alive with sounds stolen, mobilized, emigrated from one language to another: a heterogeneous and disparate mix of proper French, Arabic dialect or Kabyle as spoken in the towns: *"Ouach rak bian?"*[6] ["So, are you all right?"]. We will return to this later.
2. A *vehicular language:* "national or regional, learned by necessity, aimed at communication in the cities," long monopolized by French but that has progressively tended to be replaced by Arabic on a national level or in certain sectors (commerce, industry, international relations) by English. The vehicular is thus the urban language of political and economic power or, in the words of F. Tönnies (in *Gemeinschaft und Gesellshaft*), the language of *Gesellschaft*. But what is worth noting here is that we find ourselves facing a new "play" of languages: classical Arabic, French and English.

   One more important observation on the subject: Because it wants to be universal, as Gobard clearly demonstrates, this kind of language "tends to destroy vernacular languages, whatever their sociolinguistic proximity or their genetic roots." Thus, whatever language it proceeds from, the vehicular is always a form of linguistic imperialism, a linguistic Attila: Wherever it passes "the affect of communities, says Gobard, carried by the vernacular (territory, way of life, cuisine, nomenclature, etc.) dries up and perishes in the long run. The vehicular is also a language of primary de-territorialization: As it is universal, it wants to be a "neutral," "objective" language of "everyone" and "anyone." Some politico-linguistic "malaise" stems from the confrontation or the clash between these two types of languages.[7]

3. A *"referential language"* that "acts as an oral or written reference, through proverbs, sayings, literature, rhetoric, and so on, and is destined *normally*, in "non-dislocated" societies, to carry out a cultural re-terrritorialization. Here, we find once again all the languages of the vernacular, each carrying in its own way a few notations, or fragments of the past, as well as the two main vehicular languages: Arabic (the poems and texts of the Emir Abdelkader for example or Ibn Khaldoun) and French (the works of Francophone writers, historians, as well as the Archives, etc.).
4. Finally, a *"mythic language"* "which acts as a last resort, a verbal magic whose incomprehensibility is seen as irrefutable proof of the sacred." (Henri Gobard, 44). It is mainly expressed in literary Arabic, as the language of spiritual and religious re-territorialization.

We must note, after Gobard, that all these plays of language do not share the same spacio-temporal terrain: Indeed, the *vernacular* is the *here and now* of regional and maternal language; the *vehicular* is the *everywhere* and *the later on* of the language of cities, at once centralizing and prospective; the *referential* is *the over there* and *the yesterday* of national life; finally the *mythic* is the *beyond* and *the forever* of the sacred.

As I said earlier, the fundamental thing is the medium—the language—and not the expression. But that is too abstract. We must ask ourselves what kind of expressive machine can take into account this multiplicity of languages without exploding? What machine can integrate, without crushing or reducing them to an abstract totality, all the functions performed by these various languages? Indeed, what machine is capable of embracing at once so many different terrains and heterogeneous temporalities?

If we think of the works of scholars such as Edward Said, Homi K. Bhaba or Mikhail Bakhtin for example, what immediately comes to mind is that it is the novel that can best fulfill this "demand." But in the sociocultural conditions of "dis-location" which I have described, the novelistic or narrative "take-over" could not be easily effected. It is only in the "integrated" countries, that is to say in the countries, which have not been subjected to colonial "dismantling," that this kind of fictional take-over could be exercised. I am thinking, here, of what José Carlos Mariátegui, for example, wrote in his *Seven Interpretive Essays on Peruvian Reality:* "In the history of the West, the flowering of National literatures coincided with the political affirmation of the Nation. It formed part of the movement which through the Reformation and the Renaissance, created the ideological and spiritual factors of the liberal revolution and the capitalist order."[8] It is only in the West that we can say without major risk that "the novel, as a literary form, like journalism, has been "one of the conductors of the essential force that preceded the emergence of Nations and of Nationalism, and remains an important part of this phenomenon."[9]

In the context which I have provided, it is not the novel, but the theatre which would play a role in "the formation" of a national, popular culture. What the writer Kateb Yacine and the playwright Abdelkader Alloula understood very well is that while the poet and the "traditional" writer, often stumble on a word, an idiolectal expression, a "national" (trans-individual) trait, the producers of popular theatre know virtually no obstacles. Because it is an oral art, the theatre can "stage," can set in motion all that is necessary and play on various registers: speech, gestures, mime and music which, even if they are "regional" or local, will be able to merge the accents and the sayings, tales, stories which will contribute to "narrating" the Nation. It is true that this kind of "mixing" will be done with more or less success, talent or genius, but still with a certain ease, which poets and writers—limited as they are by one language—can only dream about. Blessed are the men and women of the Maghrebi theatre who can express themselves in all of the country's languages, which run through them and nourish their artistic talents. These are languages in which it would be possible to express, even in a confused way, the national "sentiment."

There is, indeed, a difference between writing: "Krrr! Krrrr!" as in Kateb Yacine's *Nedjma,* which does not mean much to a francophone reader, in spite of the translation at the bottom of the page, which informs us that this expression means "Confess!"—and hearing an actor say it or scream it in a play.

In turning towards the theatre and in returning to "orality," Kateb Yacine and Abdelkader Alloula searched less for a linguistic anchor in spoken Arabic, than for a nomadic shift of de-territorialization which would allow them to adapt French to Arabic and also to mobilize all the languages of everyday life, and to provide the means to experiment with popular affects, sentiments, representations, etc. In this sense, there is some Kafka in Kateb Yacine, the Kafka who was interested in Czech or Yiddish popular theatre. There is perhaps, at the same time, an uncanny reminder of Artaud, the theoretician of the *Theatre of Cruelty,* who reflecting upon his relationship to language, says:

> As for French, it makes one sick
> It is the great sick one

Sick with a disease, a fatigue
Which makes one believe that one is French,
That is to say accomplished
The accomplished![10]

Kateb eventually became sick of French, "this great sick thing," as he put it, this potion for the sick which tried to make Maghrebis believe that they were none other than French, that is to say, incomplete (undone).

For Kateb, as for Artaud, it was a question of "vanquishing French without leaving it;" Kateb, too, had held French in his tongue for fifty years, while all the time he had "other languages under the tree": French, Arabic, and Berber. He does not hesitate to use these three languages, to obtain what Artaud expected from the theatre: "A chant that is stressed, secular, non-liturgical, non ritualistic and non Greek, between Negro, Chinese, Indian and French."[11]

If postcolonial Maghrebi literature, and Algerian literature in particular, had been confined only to the production of theatrical works, the problematic of language would have been solved and it would be unnecessary to question it further. Contrary to what Albert Memmi has predicted, the three countries of the Maghreb have restricted themselves neither to the production of theatrical works in spoken or literary Arabic, nor to literary works in classical Arabic. If these writers have used much of their time and energy producing and writing theatrical works, with the exception of Kateb Yacine and Malek Alloula, the majority are known, after all, as novelists. It seems paradoxical that it is as novelists that Khatibi, Farès, Djebar, Meddeb, Dib, Béji, and other great Maghrebi postcolonial writers have placed themselves in the literary scene as "authors"! In spite of the alienation the French language represented and the contradictions caused by this situation of "deterritorialization," each of these writers has been known, first of all, as author of poems, novels and essays.

We know today that all these de-territorializing movements are inseparable from the problem of language: There are Francophone intellectuals in a country that soon opted for Arabization; Arabophone writers in a country which is 85 percent illiterate and where French dominates in administration, universities, and towns; there are the Kabyles, the Mozabites and the Touaregs, who must abandon their language when they leave the country or the desert; there is also dialectical Arabic which everyone speaks but few people, with good reason, read or write. What can be done with this linguistic mush? Or as Deleuze and Guattari put it: "How do you become the nomad, the emigrant, and the gypsy of your own language?" How can one account for what is "specific" to the Maghreb when one can only write in the language of the former colonizer? And most of all: which social status will be given to Algerian Francophone writers in a "nation" which is in the process of switching into Arabic? Kafka said: "To snatch the child from the cradle, to dance on a tight-rope." And that is what it is like: to write, to think in a foreign language "like thieves" to submit the dominant language to the craziest of uses, to the wildest of transformations: "L'enter'ment di firiti i la cause di calamiti!"

"To snatch the child from the grave": to redirect French from its first mooring in order to define and create one's own situation. There too, for the Francophone writers of the Maghreb, there were only two possible roads: either one would artificially enrich French, stuffing it with all the resources of a delirious symbolism, onirism and allegory, as in the works of Mohammed Dib, Rachid Boudjedra, and to some extent, Farès; but such efforts imply "a desperate attempt at symbolic re-territorialization, based on archetypes of sex, blood and death, which only accentuates the break with the people." (Deleuze and Guattari, 34). Or one could opt for the ultimate in sobriety, and poverty; towards "white" writing or the zero degree of writing—that of the Algerian writer Rachid Boudjedra in *L'escargot entêté,* Mohammed Dib's poems, Mouloud Mammeri's Novels or Assia Djebar's "The White of Algeria": "For if," says Farès, "in these novelistic moments, I appear to be a wandering zero, I must say that the meanders of this zero seem mysteriously active. If only some event were to trigger the activity of this zero, the multiplication of the zero's capabilities would emerge immediately" (Farès, 59).

I hope to have shown how and why the Francophone writers of the Maghreb have to count with tetraglossia in every step of their work. It is the condition that makes it possible for the people of the Maghreb to connect with the multiplicity of facets of their culture.

Notes

1. Gilles Deleuze and Felix Guattari. *Kafka, Pour Une Literature mineure.* Les Editions de Minuit, Collection "Critique," Paris, 1975, p.33.
2. Jean Déjeux. *La Littérature algérienne Contemporaine.* P.U.F., Collection "Que sais-je?". Deuxième partie, "La Littérature des algériens," Chapitre Premier, "Littérature algérienne de langue Française," Paris, 1975, p.75.
3. Albert Mémmi. *The Colonizer and the Colonized.* Boston: Beacon Press, 1965. Trans. Howard Greenfeld from *Portrait du Colonisé précédé du Portrait du Colonisateur,* NRF, Gallimard, 1961. See the sections entitled: "The school of the colonized," "Colonial bilingualism and the

situation of the writer," and the following passage in particular: "The colonized writer is condemned to live his renunciations between maternal and colonial languages to the bitter end. The problem can be concluded in only two ways: by the natural death of colonized literature; the following generations born in liberty will write spontaneously in their newly found language. Without waiting that long, a second possibility can tempt the writer to decide to join the literature of colonizing country. Let us leave aside the ethical problems raised by such an attitude. It is the suicide of colonized literature; in either prospect (the only difference being in the date) colonized literature in European languages appears condemned to die young" (p. 111).

The problem is not to say that Memmi was mistaken, but we must note that the most important Maghrebi Francophone writers were born after independence, and that we continue to see more new, talented Francophone writers.

4. We could apply the same analysis to the other countries of the Maghreb: Tunisia and Morocco.
5. In what follows, I will rely on the works of Gilles Deleuze and Félix Guattari, op. cit, and that of Henri Gobard, *L'aliénation linguistique, Analyse tétraglossique* which is also cited by Deleuze and Guattari in *Kafka,* note 10, p. 44.
6. An expression in which we have words in French and words in Arabic, and a pronunciation (or an accent?) that is supposedly "Kabyle."
7. See Nabile Farès, *Un Passager de l'Occident:roman.* (Paris: Éditions du Seuil, 1971). I am referring here specifically to the little "allegory" that Farès gives us to meditate about on page 32: " . . . It is now that the Kabyle suffers from an unfathomable malaise: it is what we call the malaise of the fig-tree. There exists even a song which one can pronounce with the tip of one's lips to show that one can speak but does not want to be heard. A song so precious and so intimate nowadays! . . . Thus, this song says that "our fig-tree was always invaded by mushrooms "and that "the coming of the people of the plains has corrupted our orchard" and that "if the fig-tree does not speak anymore, it is because its friend, the hedgehog, has been stolen," etc. All of the context (and the rest of this apologue) shows Farès's acute consciousness of what Memmi called the "linguistic drama." The punctuation and italics are by Farès.
8. Cited by T. Brennan, "The National Longing for Form" in *Nation and Narration,*" edited by Homi K. Bhabha, Routledge, London and New York, 1990, p.68, note 14.
9. Anthony Barnett, "Salman Rushdie: a Review article," in *Race and Class,* Winter 1985, p.68. Cited by T. Brennan in *Nation and Narration,* Ibid.
10. Cited by Paule Thévenin, "Voire/Entendre/Lire," *Tel Quel,* no. 42–43, Automne, 1969 p. 58.
11. Ibid.

7

Bilingualism, Quechua Poetry, and Migratory Fragmentations in Present-day Peru*

José Antonio Mazzotti

Introduction

Within the complexity of Latin American cultural cartographies, the Peruvian space has been distinguished by an accelerated process of diversification during the last two decades. When referring to some of the aspects that affect literary production, it is essential to mention the marked increase in internal and external migrations, a phenomenon accompanied by an unprecedented exacerbation of political violence. Literature, and specifically poetry, on which I will here focus, has undergone these processes, reacting to and questioning this context, to the extent that we could well speak of a "poetics of flow" (*poéticas de flujo*) to characterize Peruvian production during the 1980s. In this "flow" the bilingual condition of some of its protagonists manifests itself through transits of subjectivity that compromise not only the autonomy of two languages in a diglosic situation (Spanish and Quechua), but also, as we will see, the stability of the most prestigious national narratives.

To speak of a "poetics of flow" requires, however, some explanation. The concept refers to the transfer in formal terms that "learned" poetic language has undergone in Peru, a transfer influenced by the two aforementioned social phenomena that were most radically made manifest during those years. Without considering both migration and violence, it is easy to lose sight of what comprises the contribution by one of the most valuable sectors within the abundant poetry published at that time.

Even so, the poetics of flow cannot be strictly defined as a function of the migratory movements or the breaks, deaths, and physical and psychological torments provoked in civil society by the armed, political activism of partisan groups or by the official state itself.[1] Of special interest here are the textual pleats by which such phenomena, external to the poem, originally transform themselves, taking into account each author's usage of poetic language *sui generis* within a long and prestigious tradition.

Despite the temptation, I will not refer here to the better known trajectory of Castilian "learned" poetry that has reached a certain international dissemination. Rather, I wish to consider that other tradition, not less longstanding or important, Quechua poetry and its translations.[2] I am interested in demonstrating how all of the existent literary systems in Vallejo's country are continually invaded by what Sánchez de Biosca has called a "grammar of fragmentation" and an evident disorder from utopia to dystopia.[3] Although said changes are more frequent in a Western or Creole tradition, they do not keep from tarnishing the sum written production in indigenous languages, enriching the literary institution despite the fact that a part of its components tries to undermine it and question the hegemony of the Spanish word.

Let us begin, then, with the subject at hand. Within the graphological reductions practiced since the sixteenth century in a language as rich in expressions and meanings as is Quechua, texts remained that in some way gathered the general characteristics of a verbal art comparable to what is understood as poetry in the Western sense of the term. In many cases, the traditional forms were re-created until a new type of discourse emerged, thus founding a long, extremely rich tradition of poetry written in the principal Andean language.

I will not dwell too much in describing the written poetic tradition in Quechua during the viceroyal period and the first decades of the Republic.[4] However, the early signs of Catholic missionary hymns in the first viceroyal decades are worth recalling, as is the discourse of the indigenous nobility, which by way of a tone, apparently vindictive toward the indigenous population as a whole, nostalgically defended, in fact, the lost privileges of the Incan noble class and its descendents during the viceroyal period. This was especially so in Cuzco, the central focus of this corpus. Examples such as the *Usca Paucar*, and the Quechua poetry of Lunarejo or the "Garcilasian myth," which fostered Incan nationalism in the eighteenth century, are complemented by a third type of written Quechua discourse, that of migrants, whose still-current situation and whose renovating spirit of ancient myths must be accounted for as a clear bet on its enduring validity and vitality.

This migrant discourse and its present-day manifestations is thus understood as parting from the premise that "the reason for being of written, Quechua poetry can be found in the decomposition and recomposition of the Andean world," as Noriega points out (*Buscando una tradición* 127). With this established, such a discourse hardly constitutes a fossilized and anachronistic object, but rather is part of a cultural transformation that challenges the unity and homogeneity of a strictly "cultured" literary system written in Spanish. Therefore, in the twentieth century, modern written Quechua poetry is "a literature of compensation and redemption" (*Buscando una tradición* 134). Toward the end of the sixteenth century and the beginning of the seventeenth century, this had also been the original motive for the composition of "indigenous" and mestizo versions of an Andean past such as the ones gathered by Guaman Poma, Pachacuti Yamqui, Cristóbal de Molina, and the Inca Garcilaso.[5] The viceroyal cases efficiently serve to enrich the reading of modern Quechua poets such as Andrés Alencastre, José María Arguedas, Dida Aguirre, William Hurtado, José Tamayo Herrera, Lily Flores, Eduardo Ninamango Mallqui, Isaac Huamán, Porfirio Meneses, and Teodoro Meneses, who constitute the central nucleus of written, contemporary Quechua poetry. It is a poetry that has "little or nothing to do with contemporary Peruvian poetry in Spanish, but which also does not follow the tradition of sung poems" (Lienhard, "Pachakutiy taki" 180). To appreciate the novelty of this writing in all its dimensions, let us see how its basis is already to be found in some way in Arguedas's poetic work as far back as the 1960s, work to which I will now refer briefly. Finally, I will establish a comparison with the most recent work of another notable poet who writes in Quechua, Eduardo Ninamango Mallqui, so as to conclude a brief look at the displacements occurring within said system according to the perspectives expressed by subjects of dystopic writing in the 1980s.

The Arguedian antecedent

The parallel continuity of a Creole tradition in the face of a Mestizo tradition is complicated by the overall work of José María Arguedas, and particularly with his poetry, written directly in Quechua. This part of Arguedas's production represents an enigmatic problem in itself and a serious challenge to Andean studies. Even so, the existing bibliography on Arguedas's poetry is relatively stark, as is his inclusion in broader studies and in anthologies of contemporary Peruvian poetry. This is due in part to the fact that the original versions of Arguedas's poems are all in Quechua. But the lack of criticism may be due to the poems' ambiguous form and genre, even in the Spanish translations Arguedas himself provided. The seven texts that compose *Katatay,* Arguedas's only book of poems, comprise a form that continues to escape conventional classifications of the genre.

To intensify the problem further, the complexity of Arguedas's poetry seems to be additionally related to spheres of knowledge much greater than those strictly of a linguistic, literary, or political nature. Perhaps the enigma could be resolved in part by further developing what some critics have already begun to unravel in relation to the mythical dimensions these texts contain.[6] I, for my part, wish to suggest a "stratographic" reading that could contribute to the explanation of the sacred and cosmogenic dimensions of this poetry. By the concept of "stratographic" reading I refer to the theoretical frame that recent historiographers such as Arnold Bauer ("The Colonial Economy" 19) and Ladurei (*The Territory of the Historian* 79) use to explain layers or levels of production and social practices, thatcoexist but are superimposed within a same region or country. Similar to the Genettian concept of "palimpsest," a "stratographic" approach facilitates the study of discursive strategies that Arguedas gathered from Quechua and Hispanic traditions, thereby re-creating in his own writing the invading flow of migrant Andeans into the coastal capital. I wish to emphasize both the analysis of a migrant subject in the social, economic, and cultural spheres of Peru in the 1960s, as well as the appropriation of the "learned city" that Arguedas himself practiced by writing in Quechua and then in Spanish. By way of this approach, I hope that the archeological, mythical, linguistic, and literary strata will be made more obvious as a whole, despite the fact that the translations can come to reflect little of the original semantic density.

The first edition of *Katatay* appeared in 1972, three years after Arguedas's suicide on December 3, 1969. The book contained six poems, four of which had been published between 1962 and 1966.[7] Years later, in 1984, Humberto Damonte and Sybila Arredondo, Arguedas's widow, published a second, more complete edition, containing a total of seven poems. Although almost all of Arguedas's novels contain fragments of Quechua songs and poems by an external author, *Katatay* is the only collection of poems originally written by Arguedas.

Arguedas's conviction that Quechua was much more suited to the genre of poetry than was Spanish, explains his preference for Quechua as the language for his poetry. He stated this on more than one occasion: "Quechua, when compared to Spanish, is a language much more powerful in its expression of the spirit's many critical junctures, and, especially, moods [. . .] Quechua words contain, incomparably intensely and vitally, the substance of man and of nature and the intense bond which, fortunately, still exists between the two" (*Katatay* 59).[8]

The fact that Arguedas considered Quechua the poetic language par excellence is not gratuitous. Diverse specialists have pointed out that Quechua is a radically grammatical language, as opposed to a lexical language, since meaning depends on a limited number of suffixes. In Spanish, in contrast, the spectrum of meanings depends on lexically charged expressions. Ferdinand de Saussure already showed us, a little over a century ago, that in lexical languages the arbitrariness between signifier and signified is more difficult to control than in grammatical languages. Therefore, languages such as Quechua are potentially more "motivated" (Lienhard, *Cultura andina y forma novelesca* 66) and can better express tonalities and affects without depending entirely on an extensive vocabulary.[9]

Arguedas's poetic conception remains fully concentrated in the book's opening poem, "Tupac Amaru kamaq taytanchisman" ("To Our Creator Father, Túpac Amaru"), to which I will primarily refer. As in traditional prayers to Andean divinities, Arguedas reassumes the invocation of a highly prestigious figure such as Túpac Amaru. The name can correspond to both the last rebel leader in exile, executed in 1572, as well as to the chief of the Great Rebellion of 1780–88, also decapitated by Spanish authorities in Cuzco's central square. In both cases, be it Túpac Amaru I or II, the notion of an indigenous resistance against a Western power prevails. But Túpac Amaru is also described as a divinity, as the son of Amaru, the two-headed serpent of Andean mythology. Túpac Amaru is "made of the Salqantay's snow" (*Katatay* 11), the snowfall that is visible from Cuzco, where ancient tradition locates one of the residences of the god, Wiraqucha (Lienhard, *La voz* 351). Not only is Túpac Amaru identified with Wiraqucha, but a relationship between Túpac Amaru and Pachakamaq is also made clear, given that in the title of the poem Túpac Amaru is referred to as "kamaq" or "one who brings or gives life." In this way, the historical character has been definitively transformed into an *axis mundi,* one of whose symbolic manifestations over more than two hundred years has been the figure of Inkarrí.

The poem offers two alternate rhythms. One is presented in long paragraphs and normal font in which the poet addresses the divinity and describes his characteristics in a racing, "prosaic" manner, in the manner of a "river during the rainy season," as Lienhard states ("Pachakutiy taki" 181). A second, less hurried rhythm is composed of short verses and is printed in italics. In these latter verses, the poet meditates on the indigenous population's orphaned and impoverished condition, clamoring for an immediate transformation. Both rhythms contain numerous references to a movement of descent, from the mountain range to the coast, and, more specifically, toward Lima, "the city of Lords" according to the poem (*Katatay* 15). This descending movement is two-fold: It is destructive when carried out by Western agencies, and constructive or redeeming when in the hands of the Andean migrants. For example, the poem states:

> bullets are killing
> machine guns are bursting open veins,
> iron sables are cutting through human flesh
> *[. . .] over the top of the hills of Cerro de Pasco*
> *in the cold plains, in the heated valleys of the coast*
> *[. . .] in the deserts*
> (13–15; italics in original)

The descent marks an oblique movement, from east to west (Cerro de Pasco/cold plains/ heated valleys /deserts), imitating the sacred direction taken by Wiraqucha toward the sea, even while bleeding. But further on, Arguedas also adds, "from the movement of the rivers and the stones [. . .] we [the migrants] drink powerful blood" (*Katatay* 13). This new, migrant agency is thus nourished by the forces of nature that emanate from the ground and the subsoil, while destruction and exploitation belong to the sphere of aerial elements. William Rowe has noted that the translation of "yawar" is not always "merry" when it appears isolated as "blood," for in this case, it is divine blood "a sacrificial product which creates fertility, as occurs, for example, in ritual Andean battles" (Rowe 80). Three of the poem's semantic fields, in its original version, those of "yawar" (blood of the god, Amaru), "kallpa" (his transformation into a human force) and "hatariy" (uprising or fight against oppression), are intimately tied to a vertical progression that leads to a fourth concept, that of "lloqlla," which relates to the flooding of a river or to a mudslide (Rowe 83–84), a frequent phenomena in Andean geography.

Related to a mythical idea of vertical movement, the worship of Pachakamaq originates and antecedes the existence of the Inca and marks a similar mythic and foundational route. In 1903, Max Uhle became the first to notice the similarity of beliefs among the high plateau culture of Tiawanaku, on the shores of Titicaca, and the coastal settlement of Pachakamaq, located south of present-day Lima. Uhle observes that the lowest level of the temple of Pachakamaq contains friezes that represent the same figure found in the Puerta del Sol of Tiawanaku (Uhle, *Pachacamac* 45–48). Many archaeologists propose that the divinity represented in Tiawanaku is Tunupa, god of the lightning bolt, storms, rain, and fertility, and that one of its representations was the two-headed serpent (Demarest, *Vivcocha* 51–52). According to Juan de Santacruz Pachacuti and other sources, Tunupa is an ancient name for Wiraqucha, who would have possessed the same attributes, characteristics, and powers.

Luis Guillermo Lumbreras explains the coincidence between the god Tiawanaku and the representations of the temple in Pachakamaq by proposing that the Tiawanaku culture (which reached its splendor in A.D. 700) created enclaves of commercial colonies along the Andean territory (*Los orígenes del Estado en Peru* 99). The dominion of different regions allowed inhabitants from Tiawanaku access to different layers of soil, essential in order to satisfy increasing demands for agricultural products and animals. One of the most important enclaves would have been the urban center of Wari in the environs of Ayacucho. Wari flourished around A.D. 900, adopting the same divinities, agricultural methods, and customs of its mother culture, Tiawanaku.[10] In turn, Wari created its own enclaves in other regions of the Andean territory. One of those enclaves must have been Pachakamaq, which would become one of the most important commercial and religious centers of the central coast in the tenth century (*Los orígenes del Estado en Peru* 99).

The journey of the high-plateau Wiraqucha, from his origin in Tiawanaku to his splendor in Pachakamaq, according to myth, meets a civilizing function. In accordance with numerous chroniclers, Wiraqucha appeared at Titicaca and created humankind. He then descended by way of the Collao plateau, stopping in a few places where he either punished his enemies or taught his followers agricultural and metallurgical skills. Finally, he descended to the coast and disappeared into the ocean. Some versions indicate that he disappeared at the locust of present-day Puerto Viejo, in Ecuador. Others say that he did so precisely in the place where, centuries later, the ceremonial center of Pachakamaq would be built.[11] It is precisely in this area of the coast, that Pizarro would found the Ciudad de los Reyes, at the shores of the Rímac, one of the three main rivers that were part of the Pachakamaq enclave.

Arguedas's poem reproduces this vertical and horizontal movement, re-actualizing the "life matter" by means of exclamatory, meditative, descriptive, prophetic, and performative expressions that bring to mind, through their vigor and power, a true verbal "landslide." Arguedas had already explained this in the final notes to *Katatay:* "The indigenous Peruvian is warmed, consoled, illuminated, blessed by nature: his hate and his love, when unleashed, precipitate themselves, precisely because of that, with all of that matter, and also with his language" (*Katatay* 59).

As is evident, such a "landslide" of nature, symbolized by the verbal downpour that this poetry materializes, constitutes an irruption in the institutionality of Peruvian arts. The landslide's destructive effect is symmetrically opposite to Pizarro's attitude when founding Lima in 1535, since the latter represented the imposition of a new architectonic and symbolic order on an ancient, sacred space. But the fact that Arguedas symbolically covered the modern, Western city with textual mud and "life matter" can be even better appreciated by recalling one of Pachakamaq's principle attributes: his power over earth tremors and earthquakes, constantly mentioned in the chronicles of the sixteenth and the seventeenth centuries.

Katatay, which means "to tremble," becomes then an aggressive act on the part of the migrant subject, who no longer conceives of himself as a "waqcha" or orphan, a passive and isolated subject vulnerable to assimilation. Although migration implies not only a geographic and temporal relocation, but also a linguistic one, for Arguedes it is the only means capable of assuring cultural survival and counterconquest. Arguedas's poems, primarily published in magazines during the 1960s, announced a social mobilization whose cultural thorns can still be felt thirty years later in the capital's clubs where migrants from Peru's different departments gather, and in phenomena such as "chicha" and "teknocumbia," which have definitively reconfigured, in the manner of an Andean-Castillian landslide, the Hispanized and archaic face of Ciudad de los Reyes.

Approaching to the sum of Arguedas's work, in a sense, Cornejo Polar ("Condición migrante . . ." 103–104) had pointed out that migrant subjectivity does not necessarily imply an adaptation to the new space (the place of attraction) or a rejection of origin (the place of expulsion). Nor is its opposite implied. The Andean migrant subject tends to move, rather, in both worlds without necessarily fusing them together. The result is the counterpart of the *mestizo,* conceived as national desideratum that would amalgamate the two elements and would therefore forge a homogenous nationality, a dialectical solution to the contradictions deepened by the Spanish Conquest. The Andean migrant is, on the contrary, living and prolonged proof of the failure to integrate two cultures, not one characterized as lacking, as a defective condition in the face of collective identities that were originally forged from nation-states obeying other historical circumstances.[12] Rather, this "double conscience"(to paraphrase W. E. B. Du Bois), is the sign of a tormented fulfillment (oxymoron withstanding) that greatly exceeds the mere de-centering of the Western subject in the postmodern crisis, and that at the same time announces the possibility of a respectful coexistence of contrast.[13] Even so, let us not forget that the Arguedas of *Katatay* presents at times a tone of homogenizing confidence and optimism that allows him to be identified with the desire for national unity and purification, not yet showing traces of deterioration at that time, but not necessarily placing bets on *mestizaje* either. For example, in the same poem to Túpac Amary, he states that "We should transform it [the city of Lords, Lima] into a city where people will sing the hymns of the four regions of our world, into a merry city, where each man can work, into an immense city that will not hate, and that will be clean as the snow of the god-mountains where the pestilence of evil never reaches" (*Katatay* 17).

The "merry city," far from evil, is the bet on a socialist future joined to the revindication of the Quechua world, a way to reconstruct the Incan empire or "the four corners of our world," an allusion to Tawantinsuyu, which literally means, "the four corners of the world joined to each other." The migrant subject's own fragmentation, to which Cornejo Polar alludes, finds in passages such as the one quoted above the affirmation of one of its poles of attraction, as also occurs in the *Katatay* poems to Cuba and Vietnam, which similarly betray the peculiar modernizing lens of its author.

Twenty Years Later

The constant migration of written Quechua poetry has been defined along at least two diverse currents: the aforementioned one from Cuzco, more aristocratizing, and represented by the cacique Andrés Alencastre; and the Arguedian one, initiated by the author of *Los ríos profundos* with his first publication of poetry in 1962, and "continued [especially] by three new poets: Dida Aguirre, Eduardo Ninamango and Isaac Huamán Manrique" (Noriega, *Poesía quechua* 30). Although it will be impossible in the space of these pages to discuss in depth a relatively autonomous circuit of poetic expression, a look at the vast corpus of written Quechua poetry reveals the recurring theme of journey, in its different dimensions, in almost all of the poets belonging to both currents. The journey is thus presented as the "objective correlative" of a transit of subjectivity, which no longer leads to the migrant's resounding triumph over the stolid modern periphery that is the capital, but rather to a multiple and disenchanted splitting, without visible signs of any utopia whatsoever. This loss of meanings could well relate to the state of *asimbolia* that Kristeva describes in the contemporary melancholic subject (see *Soleil noir* 9). Or perhaps, once the mists of that first slanderous *asimbolia* have dissipated, this loss of meaning could relate to the painful and progressive certainty that we live "in a secular and contingent world, [where] homes are always provisional (Said, "Reflections on Exile" 365) and the entire condition of existence is exile itself.[14]

The break with an origin of fulfillment perhaps inscribes itself in its most rigorous and transcendental dimensions in Eduardo Ninamango Mallqui's 1982 book, *Pukutay / Tormenta*. Beginning with the title, a climactic and emotional condition is alluded to, but one of much greater dimensions than the usual usage of the word for storm in Spanish, *tormenta,* connotes. Among mythical-allegorical categories of diverse Andean traditions, a storm is a time of transit (indeed, it marks the passage of seasons, from dry to wet and vice versa). It's a sacred time of doubt and (greater) definition. Illapa presides as an entity that groups together the three elements of lightning (lightning bolt, flash, and thunder). This divinity's trajectory and prestige goes back to times too remote for the discipline of literary criticism. His transformations have led to processes of pictorial syncretism (as in the paintings of Gonzalo Mataindios, surrounded by bolts of lightning or harquebusier archangels, or with swords of fire in hand) and to sporadic apparitions from the chronicles of the sixteenth century on, sometimes in confusion with the names of Tunupa and Wiraqucha.[15]

In Ninamango's case, the storm affects the whole community that the poetic voice addresses. The book's initial verses state, "Pain is coming to the towns/ like a blood-storm." In addition, the pain is identifiable with "the draught that befalls the towns" acquiring the condition of an inverse rain. Animals, trees, and grass die "with man unable/ old designer of stories/ of clay/ to detain the rain's fire (*Poesía quechua* 431). In this way, fire antecedes real rain, as numerous mythic narratives had so attributed to the god Wiraqucha during his transit through the Andean territory.

But this fire that falls from the heavens does not exclude the possibility of transit toward a wet season. The poems in *Pukutay* thereby indicate a temporal correlative depending on climactic changes. The "rain storm," which lets fall "arrows of fire," turning "the eagle's eyes" into "burning ashes" (the second poem of the first section in Noriega, *Poesía quechua* 433), also fosters hope in the fecund aspects of this same rain:

> the earth will again be ours
> because the rain storm is already on its way
> the rain storm comes
> to our town
> bringing golden fish, celestial
> as the sky where our ancestors dance
> (third poem, section 1, *Poesía quechua* 435).[16]

The *hanaq pacha mayu* (the River of the Upper World, the Milky Way, from where lakes and rivers originate) touches the *kay pacha* (the earth's surface,) bringing gifts. It represents the foundational moment of the passage of elements from the upper world to the world below, cosmofying (*cosmoficando*) the chaos by doing so. The "golden fish [are] celestial as the sky." They descend "to our town," confirming the omnipresence of the first person plural in this part of the book, overwhelmingly predominant over the "I." A time of plenty has been fulfilled: The sky rains fish, the ancestors are consecrated, the individual is an abstraction melded into fraternal identities, social alliances, and strongly rooted systems of reciprocity. The world is apparently complete.

Let us consider the two contradicting dimensions of the storm, given that in addition, the dialectic of fire/water is not foreign to the general attributes of Wiraqucha. According to some chronicles, humanity is devastated by the "unu pachacuti" or the destruction of the world by water (see Sarmiento de Gamboa, *Historia Índica*, ch. 6), so that the same divinity may then establish order and once again create human beings (cf. also Pease, *El dios creador andino*, ch. 1). Mythical destruction can, therefore, also occur by means of a flood.[17]

In the case of a contemporary poet such as Ninamango, however, these categories do not completely explain a continuous deterioration, despite fire and rain. As the reader progresses through *Pukutay*, he or she becomes conscious of the circularity of mythic time that cannot continue to function in a secularized world. The poetic voice begins to shift from doubt and hope to the certainty that the reunion with the community will no longer be a re-actualization of primordial time. Somewhere along the transit from the first to the second section of the book, a journey has taken place. The second section thus begins with an evident preeminence of the "I." The first text of this section reads, "My shadow is not in these places today/ I no longer see my parents today/ I also don't see/ the corn fields/ the wheat fields/ or the great hill." The poet can no longer identify his place of origin. The journey has been in vain. The coordinate elements of a totality can no longer be recognized. Man's fall occurs with the spread of the fragmentation of the social body that constituted the marrow of the individual "I." The poet (inevitably writing from a fragmented space) opts for total dissolution, in the way of an ontological suicide that also constitutes a negation of Western time:

> there
> they cry out my name
> they ask the wind
> the rain
> that is why
>   I would like to lose myself
> that is why
>   I would like to turn to stone.
>
> (first poem, section 2, *Poesía quechua* 437).[18]

To wish to lose himself, to "turn to stone," refers the reader back to the regression of fundamental symbols. To pass directly from the human to the mineral state (without even dwelling in the animal or plant kingdom) proposes, on the one hand, an inverse journey to that of the divinities in the form of stones who turned to warriors to help the young prince of Cuzco (later, Pachakutiq Inka) in the war against the chancas.[19] On the other hand, it also implies the memory of sacrifice for others in order to facilitate conquest or foundation. This is the case with Ayar Cachi, who turns to stone on the summit of the hill, Huanacaure, so that his brother Ayar Manco (or Manco Capac) may continue with the foundation of Cuzco, foreseen according to the foundation myth of the Ayar brothers (see Cieza, *El Señorío de los Incas,* ch. 7). Stone, then, has broad dimensions, but always in relation to a divinity's state.

It is curious that at the end of this section the stone appears linked to a return to the river, and in relation with images of blood or torment. Ninamango surely availed himself of his readings of Arguedas, for in the second section of *Pukutay* an implicit dialogue takes place with the "stone of boiling blood" from the first chapter of *Los ríos profundos.*[20] "I'm returning to your heart of blood/ old river," reads the fourth poem of the second section (*Poesía quechua* 443). The poem continues: "Death reverberates/ in your waters/ the work of men/ who seek their own death/ and sow/ the eternal absence of those already parted" (443). The intensity of the Incan stones in the vision of Ernesto from *Los ríos profundos* moves away from this stony but nonetheless alive vortex. Death and absence are compared. The return to childhood or adolescence is even less possible. If the Ernesto from *Los ríos profundos* was fourteen years old within the time of the novel, the poet of *Pukutay* is much further removed from the maternal lap. The second section of the fifth poem finishes with, "I look for my childhood/ eternal/ more eternal than your waters [River]/ more eternal than your waters, sweet/ as when I was born among alder trees and brooms" (*Poesía quechua* 445). The search is constant, despite the contamination of the *deletéreas* river waters by the time of absences. Childhood, too, is eternal, but not inhabitable, nor present. Like the river waters, it has already passed on to the realm of memory. In few instances can the Heraclitean adage be better applied. *Post*-erior time is not only the time to come. It is also a time to question foundations: "'post,' as in 'post-modernism,' is also the 'post-' that challenges earlier legitimizing narratives," states Appiah ("Is the Post- in Postmodernism. . ." 353). The loss of faith in the coexistence of languages and cultures produces a vision that paradoxically continues to manifest itself in a bilingual format.

A regressive stone and a river of blood are the two sides of the coin of *migrancy*.[21] The simultaneous centripetal and centrifugal movements divide the poet, transfiguring him as it does his environment. The losses are therefore multiplied. "My sorrow is a river's weeping," begins the first poem of the third and last section (*Poesía quechua* 447). The loss of the beloved magnifies the cosmic solitude. Images of nature (butterflies, pigeons) are not enough to reestablish a unifying tie. The loss is accepted, and in spite of it, the poet emerges unscathed. The section's last poem celebrates the loved one, but leaves her "the sweet blood of my absent heart." As can be seen, this poetry has managed to combine semantic fields as well as some of the rhythms of the Quechua tradition, together with the resources of an animist neo-avant-garde. It does this, while avoiding the traditional rhetoric of "street language" and the false cosmopolitanism of assimilation found in translations of other Western traditions. The poet's own name implies this truly transcultural tension: Nina (fire and word)/ Mango (Mankhu, the name of the first Inca) / Mallqui (sacred mummy, seed, and tree). Destruction, foundation, death, birth, and growth cyclically and successively inhabit not the poetry, but the poetic subject, as the former is outdone by the avalanche of changes in the Peruvian social milieu, where utopia, as this voice suggests, is not only impossible, but unspeakable. The avalanche, unlike Arguedas's, is no longer the unleashing of a utopia, but rather the measuring stick of the dystopia of a perpetual exile.

Conclusions

In the twenty years that have transpired between the first poems of *Katatay* and the appearance of *Pukutay*, an evident movement of deterioration and fragmentation has occurred that exceeds the dimension of subjectivities. It is true that this practically underground circuit that constitutes written Quechua poetry reveals the same blow suffered by the more official "learned" poetry written in Spanish. Precisely because of this, it is advisable to retrace the cultural maps beginning with the entrance of neoliberalism, in its third-world incarnation, in Peru, and the sinister face of violence and poverty that it has left in economic as well as artistic spheres. It is also advisable to reflect the backdrop that is bilingualism, and its concrete manifestation as a discriminating diglossia (or multiglossia, if we consider the seventy-two languages that live in the Peruvian territory under the dominance of Spanish).[22] In a recent study, Andrés Chirinos ("Las lenguas indígenas. . ." 264) proposes that Quechua was the maternal tongue of 16.6 percent of the Peruvian population in 1993. The chilling projection for the period between 2003 and 2008 is 13.2 percent. And it's to be expected that this slight decrease in numbers will grow larger in the decades to come. Even so, it's important to remember also, as Alberto Escobar et al. (*Perú, ¿país bilingüe?* 98–103) warned in 1975, that if in percentage terms there is a tendency toward a diminishing number of monolinguals in Quechua and Aymara, it is not so numerically.

The concept of a "cornered nation" that Mannheim proposes ("El arado del tiempo" 15) for the Quechua people increasingly manifests itself concretely. The gradual, although relative, loss of language also constitutes a loss of ethnic identity, as Smolicz explains for cases outside the Andean region. In this sense, as Grosjean ("The Bilingual as a Person" 41) points out, the prejudices that dominant monolinguals hold over bilinguals, or monolinguals of non-dominant languages, are powerful factors in the distribution of social hierarchies and spaces of power. Similarly, it is enough to observe the multiple effects of a non-standard accent on the standard speakers of any language whatsoever, as Hamers and Blanc (*Bilinguality and Bilingualism* 222–38) maintain, to come to understand that the history of linguistic discrimination in Peru, where dominance over Quechua is additionally tied to factors of race and social class, is unfortunately far from over.

Perhaps bilingual poetry in Quechua and Spanish, despite the greatly limited number of able readers of both languages, may be one of the last attempts to check this progression. In spite of everything, the deterioration of subjectivities and their fragmentation continues to appear in its rich bilingual craft.

Although it is impossible to give a complete panorama of Peruvian poetic production during recent decades in the format of an article such as this one, I hope that the examples of Arguedas and Ninamango provide a sense of the complexity of the problem and the urgent necessity to approach it while considering heterogenous, subaltern, and bilingual conditions, not always triumphant but without which any cartography of national, Andean literatures, would remain, to paraphrase Vallejo, "in its majority, invalid" of criticism.

Notes

*. Translated by Cintia Santana.

1. The painful toll of more than twenty thousand deaths and of at least three thousand "disappeared" is just one of the visible results of the ascending cycle of violence lived through until 1992 (see Manrique). Since the capture of the Shining Path leader, Abimael Guzmán, in September of that year, political violence has continued to manifest itself, although more sporadically and with lesser intensity. On the other hand, daily violence in the form of delinquency and gratuitous violence has continued to rise as a norm of life. These phenomena, parallel to the failed expansion of the neoliberal model (with its subsequent economic growth for private business and transnational capital, but not for the subaltern sectors) is also studied in other Latin American contexts in the recently published *Ciudadanías del miedo (Citizenships of Fear)*, edited by Susana Rotker. With this mention, I want to pay homage to this notable intellectual who passed away prematurely. It also not superfluous to mention that nearly 60 percent of the Peruvian population lives below the international poverty index (*Dimensiones y características de la pobreza en el Perú* 7), which explains to a great extent both political violence and migratory flow. It is calculated that at least a million people have been displaced as a result of internal warring during the successive governments of Fernando Balaúnde, Alan García, and the first period of Alberto Fujimori's leadership between 1980 and 1995 (*Migraciones internas en el Perú* 43). For urban growth in the 1980s, see Matos Mar. The works of Teófilo Altamirano, listed in the Works Cited, are extremely useful for information about the migration of Peruvians to countries abroad.
2. In a more extensive work, *Poéticas del flujo: migración y violencia verbales en el Perú de los 80* (see Works Cited), 146, I refer to other

currents within Peruvian poetry of the 80s, although not of a bilingual nature. Among these currents I make a distinction between poetry written by women, the renovations of the poetics of the 1960s, and that of members of the group, Kloaka, who proposed neo-avant-garde experimentation and total break with the literary institution. This present article, with necessary format reductions, forms part of the volume's first chapter, dedicated to the hardly new but more extensive phenomena of bilingual poetry in Quechua and Spanish.

3. Although the twenty-second edition of the *Diccionario de la Real Academia de la Lengua Española* published in 2001 does not register the word *distopía,* its ample use has been recognized as far back as 1958 by Martín Alonso in his *Enciclopedia del idioma. Distopía* is there defined as a "bad place," which is to say, "the bad state of an organ" (Alonso 1585). More recently, Manuel and Manuel (6) point out that a dystopia functions as the world opposite of a utopia—that is to say, a place where chaos, social fragmentation, and injustice reign without a solution in sight.
4. For a detailed, historical recount of the "domestication" of Quechua to the Roman alphabet, and the first written, poetic manifestations, see Noriega, *Buscando una tradición* 1–24. The panorama's variety is greater if we only consider the first attempt to catalogue the written pieces in Quechua and Aymara carried out by Paul Rivet and Georges de Créqui-Monfort in 1951–56, which registers 485 entries composed of documents, catechisms, pamphlets, and other texts between 1540 and 1875, and in which the major indigenous languages are transferred once and again to the alphabet code, almost always with ends most convenient to Western domination, although admitting paradigmatic cases of resistance and accommodation such as that of Guaman Poma, who, for example, included numerous passages in Quechua within Spanish writing, which is itself highly Quechuasized.
5. Along that same line of compiling popular compositions, including those of a sung nature, the collections offered by Farfán, Escobar and Escobar, the Montoya brothers, and Jorge Lira, among others, are essential (see Works Cited). See also the indispensable works of Jean-Philippe Husson on the general characteristics of pre-Hispanic Quechua, as well as recent studies by Julio Mendívil and Bruce Mannheim.
6. The studies by Cornejo Polar, Huamán, W. Rowe (77–89), Rebaza-Soraluz and Espezúa (107–23) are important. Lienhard, however, contributes most to the understanding of the mythical aspects of Arguedas's poetry (*La voz y su huella* 348–55).
7. These were "*Tupac Amaru Kamaq Taytanchisman; haylli-taki.* To Our Creator Father Tupac Amaru; a song hymn" (Lima: Ediciones Salqantay, 1962); "*Jetman; haylli.* Ode to the Jet" (*Zona Franca* magazine, Caracas, 1962); "*Katatay;* To Tremble" (*Kachkaniraqmi*

magazine 2, Lima, 1966; *Alcor* magazine 39–40, Asunción, 1966); and "*Huk doctorkunaman qayay.* A Call to Some Doctors" (*Dominical* supplement of *El Comercio,* Lima, July 3 and 17, 1966). More information can be found in *Katatay* 59–60.

8. He had affirmed this since 1938: "Quechua surpases Spanish in the expression of certain feelings [. . .]" (Arguedas, *Canto Kechwa* 16).
9. For a detailed description of Quechua morphology and grammar, refer to Cerrón-Palomino, especially chapters. 5 and 9. Huamán has also observed that the Spanish versions of Arguedas's poems prove more "diluted" (58) because of the necessary connectives and the cultural paraphrases that the original version does not need. In addition, the poems in Quechua have a "music [that] is present in the rhythm at the textual level, an untranslatable aspect which has to do with the phonologic qualities of Quechua, rich in fricative and trilled sounds, in the reiteration of desinences and roots, and its fixed accents"(57).
10. In effect, the relationship between Tiawanaku and Wari has already been put forth by Urteaga (chapters 1–5), Zuidema (193–218), and Lumbreras (96–99), which coincide in extending the link as a cultural antecedent to the Inca.
11. This also recalls the regional version of the manuscript of Huarochirí on the descent of Cuniraya Wiraqucha in pursuit of his beloved Cavillaca and her small son, who submerge themselves in the sea and precisely become the two small islands in front of the present-day ceremonial center of Pachakamaq (see Arguedas, trans., chapter 2). Schölten maintains that the transit toward Puerto Viejo is due to reasons of political justification for the Incan expansion into provinces that today constitute Ecuador.
12. In Cornejo Polar's own words, "the migrant's condition, if it is lived in a present that appears to amalgamate much previous rushing about, is in some way contrary to the syncretic eagerness which dominates the mestizo's nature. [. . .] The migrant stratifies his life experiences and [. . .] neither can nor wants to meld them because his discontinuous nature places emphasis precisely on the multiple diversity of these times and spaces and on the values or the deficiencies of one and the other. Fragmentation, is perhaps, then, his norm" ("La condición migrante . . ." 103–4).
13. The term "double consciousness" originated in the United States in the nineteenth century and was used by the African-American intellectual W. E. B. Du Bois at the beginning of the twentieth century in order to refer to the double condition of the African American population under the white democracy's pretended, but actually discriminatory, pluralism. Postcolonial theory has served theoretically to support multiculturalism and the respect for different ethnic and linguistic differences of populations that have been traversed by numerous migrant groups of diverse origins. See Sommer for a detailed

explanation of the term and its contemporary applications. See also Bhabha (49–51) for a theorization of the postcolonial subject's splitting of identity in other contexts.

14. For a critique of exile as an ontological condition in Said, refer, to Ahmad, *In Theory*, chapter 5.
15. Some samples of blazing and harquebusier angels can be seen in the appendix of illustrations of Mujica Pinilla. Also in Gisbert 108–10.
16. The original quechua reads: "allpan ñoqanchikpa uqtawan kanqa / paranchiksi qamuchkanña, / chaynas llakinchikpas qamuchkan / qori kausay challwata apamuspa / machu taytanchikuna / qaway pachapi uqtawan tusunampaq" (in Noriega, *Poesía quechua* 434).
17. Whether it be a creator god similar to the Christian god, or a simple trickster, Wiraqucha tends to appear in almost all of the chroniclers' accounts with similar attributes in terms of his climactic manifestations. See Urbano for a reading of one of Wiraqucha variations as a "fibber."
18.In the original quechua: "Chaypis / sutillata qaparispa qayanku / wayratapas, paratapas tapuspa. / Chaysi / Chinkakuyta munayman / Chaysi / rumipi kutiriyta munayman" (first poem, section 2, *Poesía quechua* 436).
19. Although they maintain, contrary to almost the entire set of Andean chronicles, the Quipucamayocs of Pacaritambo (36) and Inca Garcilaso de la Vega (I, IV, XXI-XXIV), that such a prince was the future Wiraqucha Inka.
20. In addition, we can recall that Ninamango's *licenciatura* degree thesis at the Universidad de San Marcos precisely concerns the poetic work of the author of *Los ríos profundos: Katatay y la poética quechua de José María Arguedas* (Lima: UNMSM, 1982).
21. The ontological and epistemological de-centering that migration sometimes provokes, and that can be coined with the term *migrancy*, acquires more concrete manifestations since the onset of a galloping globalization and its deterritorialized movement of capitals and labor (see Trigo and Chambers for a broader definition of the concept of *migrancy*). Therefore, migration (the physical act of the relocation of the body and of personal goods) has been studied as a potential cause of a central fissure in the psyche of the subject that relocates (Grinberg and Grinberg 129–45). Such a fissure conditions many perspectives assumedly fixed in the country or region of origin; if the migrant returns, especially temporarily, he or she begins to find himself or herself alienated in practices and gestures in which he no longer recognizes himself. The effect of the unusual, of the strangeness of the reencounter with the familiar that has become strange is thereby created, an experience that Freud tries to define in his now classic "Das Unheimliche" in 1919, translated into English as "The Uncanny."
22. The very same concept of bilingualism is in itself ambiguous and lacks a coherent theoretical foundation, as Hamers points out: "From the

vast number and variety of definitions of bilingualism given by different scholars it appears thus, that bilingualism can no longer be viewed as an all-or-none concept but is relative in nature and this on a number of dimensions; one can for example analyze bilingualism in terms of the relationship between language and thought, of the competence reached in both languages, of the age of acquisition of each language, of the relative socio-cultural status of both languages or of a combination of two or more of these factors" ("Psychological Approaches" 29–30). The number of languages/ethnicities that exist in the Peruvian territory is cited in the *Mapa etnolingüístico oficial del Perú,* published by the Instituto Indigenista Peruano in 1994. For an even more up to date compilation, see Inés Pozzi-Escot's *El multilingüismo en el Perú.*

Works Cited

Ahmad, Aijaz. *In Theory: Classes, Nations, Literatures.* London and New York: Verso, 1992.

Alonso, Martín. Enciclopedia del idioma: Diccionario histórico y moderno de la lengua española. Madrid: Aguilar, 1958.

Altamirano, Teófilo. *Los que se fueron. Peruanos en Estados Unidos.* Lima: Fondo Editorial de la Pontificia Universi-dad Católica del Perú, 1992.

———. *Éxodo: peruanos en el exterior.* Lima: Fondo Edito-rial de la Pontificia Universidad Católica del Perú, 1992.

Appiah, Kwame Anthony. "Is the Post- in Postmodernism the Post- in Postcolonial?" *Critical Inquiry* 17, 2 (1991): 337–57.

Arguedas, José María. *Canto Kechwa. Con un ensayo sobre la capacidad de creación artística del pueblo indio y mestizo.* Lima: Cía. De Impresiones y Publicidad, 1938. (New edition: Editorial Horizonte, 1989).

———. "La soledad cósmica en la poesía quechua." *Idea* 48–49 (1961): 1–2.

———. *Katatay.* Lima: Editorial Horizonte 1972, 1984.

———. *El zorro de arriba y el zorro de abajo.* Madrid: Archivos, [1972] 1990.

Arguedas, José María, trans., and Pierre Duviols, ed. *Dioses y hombres de Huarochirí: Narración Quechua recogida por Francisco de Ávila* [¿1598?]. Lima: Instituto Francés de Estudios Andinos / Instituto de Estudios Peruanos, 1966.

Bauer, Arnold J. "The Colonial Economy." In *The Countryside in Colonial Latin America.* Louisa Schell Hoberman and Susan Migden Socolow, eds. Albuquerque: University of New Mexico Press, 1999. 19–48.

Beardsmore, H. Baetens, ed. *Elements of Bilingual Theory.* Brussels: Vrije Universiteit Brussel, 1981.

Bhabha, Homi K. *The Location of Culture.* London and New York: Routledge, 1994.

Cerrón-Palomino, Rodolfo. *Lingüística quechua*. Lima: Centro de Estudios Regionales Andinos Bartolomé de las Casas, 1987.

Chambers, Iain. *Migrancy, Culture, Identity*. London and New York: Routledge, 1994.

Chirinos, Andrés. "Las lenguas indígenas peruanas más allá del 2000." *Revista Andina* 32 (1998): 453–80.

Cieza de León, Pedro de. El Señorío de los Incas. Segunda parte de la Crónica del Perú. Madrid: Historia 16, 1985.

Cornejo Polar, Antonio. "Arguedas, poeta indígena." In *Recopilación de textos sobre José María Arguedas*. Juan Larco, ed. La Habana: Casa de las Américas, 1976. 169–76.

———. "Condición migrante e intertextualidad multicultural: el caso de Arguedas." *Revista de Crítica Literaria Latinoamericana* 42 (Lima and Berkeley, 1995): 101–10.

Demarest, Arthur. *Viracocha: The Nature and Antiquity of the Andean High God*. Cambridge: Peabody Museum of Archaeology and Ethnology, Harvard University, 1981.

Dimensiones y características de la pobreza en el Perú, 1993. Lima: Instituto Nacional de Informática y Estadística y Fondo de Población de las Naciones Unidas, 1995.

Escobar, Alberto, José Matos Mar, and Giorgio Alberti. *Perú, ¿país bilingüe?* Lima: Instituto de Estudios Peruanos, 1975.

Escobar, Gabriel, and Gloria Escobar, eds. *Huaynos del Cusco*. Cuzco: Editorial Garcilaso, 1981.

Espezúa Salmón, Dorian. *Entre lo real y lo imaginario. Una lectura lacaniana del discurso indigenista*. Lima: Universidad Nacional Federico Villarreal, 2000.

Farfán, José Mario Benigno. Poesía folklórica quechua: 117 poemas quechuas en el idioma original y tr. al castellano. Tucumán: Instituto de Antropología, 1942.

Freud, Sigmund. "The 'Uncanny'." In *The Standard Edition of the Complete Psychological Works of Sigmund Freud*. London: The Hogarth Press, 1955. Vol. 17, 217–56.

Genétte, Gerard. *Palimpsestes. La litterature au second degré*. París: Éditions du Seuil, 1982.

Gisbert, Teresa. *El paraíso de los pájaros parlantes*. La Paz: Plural Editores, 1999.

Grinberg, Leon, and Rebecca Grinberg. *Psychoanalytic Perspectives on Migration and Exile*. New Haven and London: Yale University Press [1984], 1989.

Grosjean, François. "The Bilingual as a Person." In *On the Bilingual Person*. Renzo Titone, ed. Ottawa: The Canadian Society for Italian Studies, 1989. 35–54.

Hamers, Josiane F. "Psychological Approaches to the Development of Bilinguality: An Overview." In Beardsmore: 28–47.

Hamers, Josiane F., and Michel H. A. Blanc. *Bilinguality and Bilingualism*. 2d. ed. Cambridge: Cambridge University Press, 2000.

Huamán, Miguel Ángel. *Poesía y utopía andina*. Lima: DESCO, 1988.

Husson, Jean-Phillipe. *La poésie Quechua dans la chronique de Felipe Guamán Poma*. París: L'Harmattan, Serie Etnolinguistique Amerindiene, 1985.

———. "La poesía quechua prehispánica: sus reglas, sus categorías, sus temas a través de los poemas transcritos por Waman Puma de Ayala." *Revista de Crítica Literaria Latinoamericana* 37 (Lima, 1993): 63–86.

———. "El caso de los textos de autores indígenas. Propuestas para una lectura en simpatía." In *Edición e interpretación de textos andinos*. Ignacio Arellano y José Antonio Mazzotti, eds. Madrid and Frankfurt am Main: Iberoamericana and Vervuert, 2000. 105–36.

———. *La mort d'Ataw Wallpa. Tragédie en langue quechua du milieu du XVIéme. siécle*. Édition critique trilingue quechua / espagnol / français. Traduction, commentaire et notes de Jean-Philippe Husson. Ginebra: Ediciones Patiño, 2001.

Kristeva, Julia. *Soleil noir: depression et melancolie*. París: Gallimard, 1987.

Ladurie, E. LeRoy. *The Territory of the Historian*. Ben and Sian Reynolds, trans. Chicago: University of Chicago Press, 1979.

Lienhard, Martin. "Pachakutiy taki. Canto y poesía quechua de la transformación el mundo." *Allpanchis* 32 (1988): 165–95.

———. Cultura andina y forma novelesca. Zorros y danzantes en la última novela de Arguedas. Lima: Editorial Horizonte [1981], 1990. 2a. ed.

———. La voz y su huella. Escritura y conflicto étnico-social en América Latina (1492–1988). La Habana: Casa de las Américas, Colección Premio, 1990.

Lira, Jorge A. *Himnos quechuas*. Lima: Universidad Nacional Mayor de San Marcos, Seminario de Historia Rural Adina, 1988.

Lumbreras, Luis Guillermo. *Los orígenes del Estado en el Perú*. Lima: IEP, 1972.

Mannheim, Bruce. "El arado del tiempo: Poética quechua y formación nacional." *Revista Andina* 33 (1999): 15–54.

Manrique, Nelson. "Time of Fear." *North American Congress on Latin America* XXIV, 4 (1990–91): 28–38.

Manuel, Frank Edward, and Fritzie Prigohzy Manuel. *Utopian Thought in the Western World*. Cambridge, Mass.: Harvard University Press, 1979.

Matos Mar, José. Desborde popular y crisis del estado: el nuevo rostro del Perú en la década de 1980. Lima: Instituto de Estudios Peruanos, 1984.

Mazzotti, José Antonio. *Poéticas del flujo: migración y violencia verbales en el Perú de los 80*. Lima: Fondo Editorial del Congreso de la República, 2002.

Mendívil, Julio. "El harawi histórico incaico y sus reminiscencias en los Andes actuales." In *La memoria popular y sus transformaciones. América latina y países luso-africanos*. Martin Lienhard, ed. Frankfurt and Madrid: Vuervert e Iberoamericana, 2000. 173–83.

Migraciones internas en el Perú. Lima: Instituto Nacional de Informática y Estadística y Fondo de Población de las Naciones Unidas, 1995.

Montoya, Rodrigo, Luis Montoya, and Edwin Montoya. *La sangre de los cerros/Urqukunapa yawarnin*. Lima: Centro de Estudios Sociales, Mosca Azul Editores y Universidad Nacional Mayor de San Marcos, 1987.

Mujica Pinilla, Ramón. *Ángeles apócrifos en la América virreinal*. 2d. ed. Lima: FCE, [1992] 1996.

Ninamango, Eduardo. "Pukutay" in *Poesía quechua escirta en el Perú. Antología,* Julio Noriega, ed. Lima: Centro de Estudios y Publicaciones, 1993.

Noriega, Julio. *Poesía quechua escrita en el Perú. Antología*. Lima: Centro de Estudios y Publicaciones, 1993.

———. *Buscando una tradición poética quechua en el Perú*. Miami: Centro Norte-Sur, 1995.

Pachacuti, Yamqui Salamaygua, Joan de Santacruz. *Relación de antigüedades deste Reino del Perú*. Ed. de Carlos Araníbar. Lima: Fondo de Cultura Económica, 1995.

Pease, G. Y., Franklin. *El dios creador andino*. Lima: Mosca Azul Editores, 1973.

Pozzi-Escot, Inés. *El multilingüismo en el Perú*. Cuzco: Centro de Estudios Regionales Andinos Bartolomé de las Casas, 1998.

[Quipucamayocs de Pacaritambo] Collapiña, Supno, and others. *Relación de la descendencia, gobierno y conquista de los incas*. Juan José Vega, ed. (also published as *Relación . . . de los khipukamayuq al gobernador Vaca de Castro*). Lima: Editorial Jurídica S.A. [1542], 1974.

Rebaza-Soraluz, Luis. "La poesía y la lengua quechuas como un espacio andino de narración nacional: José María Arguedas, Javier Sologuren y la subjetividad artística." In *Indigenismo hacia el fin de milenio. Homenaje a Antonio Cornejo Polar.* Mabel Moraña, ed. Pittsburgh: Instituto Internacional de Literatura Iberoamericana, 1998. 169–95.

Rivet, Paul, and Georges de Crequi-Montfort. *Bibliographie des langues aymara et kicua*. París: Institut d'Ethnologie [1951]–1956. 4 vols.

Rotker, Susana, ed. *Ciudadanías del miedo*. Caracas: Editorial Nueva Sociedad, 2000.

Rowe, William. *Ensayos arguedianos*. Lima: Universidad Nacional Mayor de San Marcos / Sur, Casa de Estudios del Socialismo, 1996.

Said, Edward. "Reflections on Exile." In *Out There, Marginalization and Contemporary Cultures*. Russell Ferguson, Martha Gever, Trinh T. Minhha and Cornel West, eds. Cambridge, Mass.: MIT Press, 1990. 357–365.

Sánchez de Biosca, V. La cultura de la fragmentación. Pastiche, relato y cuerpo en el cine y la televisión. Valencia: Textos de la Filmoteca, 1995.

Sarmiento de Gamboa, Pedro. *Historia Índica* [1570]. Madrid: Atlas, Biblioteca de Autores Españoles, 1960. Apéndice del vol. 135.

Schölten De d'Ébneth, María. *La ruta de Wirakocha*. Lima: Milla Batres, [1977] 1985.

Smolicz, J. J. "Language as a Core Value of Culture." In Beardsmore, 104–24.

Sommer, Doris. "A Vindication of Double Consciousness." In *A Companion to Postcolonial Studies*. Henry Schwarz and Sangeeta Ray, eds. Malden, Mass.: Blackwell, 2000. 165–79.

Trigo, Abril. "Migrancia: memoria: modernidá." In *Nuevas perspectivas desde/sobre América Latina: el desafío de los estudios culturales*. Mabel Moraña, ed. Santiago de Chile: Editorial Cuarto Propio / Instituto Internacional de Literatura Iberoamericana, 2000. 273–92.

Uhle, Max. *Pachacamac*. Introducción de Izumi Shimada. Philadelphia: University of Pennsylvania Press [1903], 1991.

Urbano, Henrique. "En nombre del dios Wiracocha . . . Apuntes para la definición de un espacio simbólico prehispánico." *Allpanchis* 32 (1988): 135–54.

Urteaga, Horacio. *El Imperio Incaico*. Lima: Museo Nacional, 1931.

Vega, Inca Garcilaso de la. *[Primera Parte de los] Comentarios reales [de los incas]* [1609]. Lima: FCE, 1991. 2 vols.

Zuidema, R. Tom. *Reyes y guerreros. Ensayos de cultura andina*. Manuel Burga, comp. Lima: / CONCYTEC / SHELL / IFEA, 1989.

8

The Transamerican Trail to *Cerca del Cielo*

John Sayles and the Aesthetics of Multilingual Cinema

Joshua L. Miller

Toward the end of John Sayles's *Lone Star* (1996), an African American bar owner's display of photographs and paintings intrigues his grandson. When the teenager asks, "He a black man or Indian?" Otis responds that he is "both" (Sayles, *Men* 212–13). Otis Payne narrates the history of the black Seminole soldiers who fought removal from Florida on the Trail of Tears before fleeing slavetraders to Mexico until the conclusion of the Civil War. After 1870, Otis continues, the Seminoles returned to Texas and fought with the U.S. Army. Otis explains that his interest in the subject of the black Seminoles is personal as well as historical: "These are our people. There were Paynes in Florida, Oklahoma, Piedras Negras—couple of 'em won the whatsit—Congressional Medal of Honor" (Sayles, *Men* 215). The shocked young man asks if he is Native American as well. His grandfather tells him, "By blood you are. But blood only means what you let it" (Sayles, *Men* 216).

The issues circulating in this brief exchange—historical excavation, unacknowledged racial and cultural mixture, ethnic identity, and individual agency—are central to Sayles's film about Tejano borderland identity. *Lone Star* depicts the fictional border town of Frontera, Texas, through three sets of parent-child relationships, Chicana, African American, and Anglo. Otis's suggestion that blood "only means what you let it" is one of the central arguments of the film. He means that one can actively construct one's cultural and ethnic ancestry in order to prioritize certain characteristics, or one can allow ancestry anxieties to overwhelm the present and the future. Either way, as the film's complex web of intergenerational conflict demonstrates, individuals must ultimately choose to construct their own identity by choosing among competing historical and epistemological positions. As James Baldwin once wrote, "you drag your past around with you everywhere, or it drags you" (Baldwin 773).

Lone Star has been the most significant commercial success of writer/director/editor John Sayles's career to date. For an independent director dedicated to low-budget films made with minimal studio intervention, *Lone Star* had the makings of a breakout movie, the project that could catapult Sayles into the wellspring of Hollywood studio funding and mainstream audiences. However, Sayles chose the moment of his greatest visibility and box-office muscle to advance a film that critics viewed as the quirkiest in his long career of unconventional choices, *Hombres Armados* [*Men with Guns*] (1997), a film in Spanish and Native American languages, with only a handful of English lines.[1] While the logic of this move may have appeared as either self-destructive or mere posturing (critics suggested both), in fact *Men with Guns* follows so clearly from the ethical imperatives of *Lone Star* that it is possible to interpret the two films as a nonsequential series, each of which articulates separate segments of Sayles's cultural critique.

Men with Guns marks a significant milestone for both film history and United States culture. It is the first film by a major U.S. director with non-English dialogue, or, to put it more precisely, Sayles is the most prominent American filmmaker to write and direct a film predominantly in a language other than English. As such, *Men with Guns* is a sign of things to come in the emerging field of transamerican cinema. This constitutes a growing body of intercultural work that includes Julian Schnabel's biopic of Cuban poet Reinaldo Arenas, *Before Night Falls* (2000). Both film and literature are engaging the aesthetic possibilities of multilingual, multiracial, transamerican cultures. Similarly, Ang Lee has depicted Asian/Pacific/American cultural crossings in his films, *Tui Shou* [*Pushing Hands*] (1992), *His Yen* [*The Wedding Banquet*] (1993), *Yin Shi Nan Nu* [*Eat Drink Man Woman*] (1994) and throughout his remarkable ouvre. Multilingual cinema throughout the world creates the opportunity to present alternative linguistic practices that challenge the status of imperial languages.[2] For example, Mathieu Kassovitz's *La Haine* (1995) depicts the lives of poor Parisian project-dwellers through their inverted French that intentionally subverts the "proper" language of Paris. The dialects and accents in the film were so challenging that it was shown with subtitles, even to some French audiences. At the same time, multilingual films such as *Men with Guns* open up new ethical and aesthetic possibilities by recovering the complexities of multiethnic subjectivity in the international and intranational borderlands of the Americas.[3] Unlike much recent bilingual cinema and literature, Sayles's films are set primarily in rural areas or in small towns. The communities he portrays are not composed of recently relocated immigrants, but the inheritors of long-standing cultural interaction.

Considering Sayles's two films in tandem as a transamerican project also highlights another provocative common theme: the irrelevance of the United States to the cultures of the Americas. One of the most radical propositions of *Men with Guns* is the striking unimportance of the United States (politically, culturally, militarily) and of Americans to the narrative. Similarly, *Lone Star* decenters Anglo America by making the Anglo family merely one of three confronting the central problematic of lost memories and willful ignorance.

I

The cultural and political contexts of Sayles's films and the aims of transamerican cinema need to be traced through the history of the English-only movement, the emerging multilingual aesthetics in literature and art, and the history of non-English language cinema in the United States.[1] Non-English language cultures have flourished within U.S. borders throughout the nation's history, and it would do the Spanish-language Hollywood films of the 1930s, to take just one example, a great disservice to emphasize contemporary expressions of Spanish-language U.S. culture without recognizing this as an on-going feature at every stage of U.S. history.[5] However, certain periods of significant cultural and demographic change through imperial expansion, migration, and immigration have also been the moments of most intense linguistic anxiety. This dynamic has produced cogent articulations of nativist English-only nationalism as well as innovative configurations of bi- and multilingual aesthetics in literature and film. The two most evident spikes of popular interest in U.S. language politics occurred before and after World War I and during the 1980s and 90s.

Multilingual authors have advocated a range of political responses to English-only exclusionary ideologies, throughout the nineteenth and twentieth centuries. The most cogent appeal for transamerican identity was formulated by Cuban revolutionary, critic, translator, and poet José Martí in his 1891 manifesto, "Nuestra América" ("Our America"). Martí gave voice to Latin American visions of an equitable hemispheric alliance that would not be dominated by U.S. interests: "It was imperative to make common cause with the oppressed, in order to secure a new system opposed to the ambitions and governing habits of the oppressors . . . the pressing need of Our America is to show itself as it is, one in spirit and intent, swift conquerors of a suffocating past" (Martí, *Reader* 116, 119). In tandem with his political writings, Martí also made urgent appeals for a transamerican cultural network that would acknowledge both the indigenous and the transplanted influences: "Literature is simply the expression, form, and reflection of the vital spirit and natural setting of the people who create it. How, then, could our indigenous literature run counter to this universal law, and lack the beauty, harmony, and color of the American scene?" (Martí, *On Art* 202) In this review, written in English for *The Hour*, Martí argued for an intertwined American culture respecting the previous inhabitants of the continent: The "American intelligence is an Indian headdress. Is it not yet apparent that the blow that paralyzed the Indian, paralyzed America? Until the Indian marches again, America will limp" (202).[6]

Bilingual cultures flourished in both mid- to late-nineteenth-century realist and regionalist literature and experimental interwar modernism; however, Cold War pressures swept aside such subversions, and it was not until the post-civil-rights period that bi- and multilingual cultures found institutional support and receptive audiences.[7] In keeping with the historical logic that both monolingual and multilingual ideologies tend to cohere around similar historical trends, it comes as no surprise that both reemerged in the 1980s and 90s, with particular emphasis on Latino/a and Asian American cultures.

In 1980, the first federal English-only legislation in U.S. history was introduced by Sen. H. I. Hayakawa.[8] The decades since have produced the most feverish activity on the language legislation front since the 1920s.[9] During the 1980s and 90s, twenty-one states passed English-only laws, some with restrictions so severe that even the Rehnquist Supreme Court has found them unconstitutional. The Republican party has attempted to capitalize on the popular support for such measures by dusting off the plank in its party platform supporting a national language amendment to the Constitution. The popular obsession with the symbolic capital of language demonstrates, in Pierre Bourdieu's phrasing, "that the legitimate language is a semi-artificial language which has to be sustained by a permanent effort of correction, a task which falls both to institutions specially designed for this purpose and to individual speakers" (Bourdieu 60). Thus, coercive linguistic acts great and small constitute the "innumerable acts of correction" implemented by legislatures and grammarians that have led to conditions of widespread rights violations among both citizens and undocumented aliens. Accent and language discrimination suits have sprung up, filed by workers who have been dismissed for, in one case, simply speaking Spanish on their lunch break.[10] As Bourdieu indicates, aside from ideological and legal battles, this has also been a struggle waged at the institutional level, in public school curricula, workplace behavior rules, and labor standards. Carter Woodson pinpointed the oppressive elements of educational institutions in his landmark 1933 study, *The Mis-Education of the Negro,* as did W. E. B. Du Bois in articles and sociological research. More recently, anthropologists, sociolinguists, and cultural theorists such as Bourdieu, Paulo Freire, and John Guillary have described institutional mechanisms as indicative of ideological conflict over the symbolic meaning of language in the formation of cultural and ethnic identity.

Debates in both academic and popular media over multiculturalism in the 1990s often deteriorated into vaguenesses and tokenism, as numerous critics have outlined, as a result of inadequate recognition of the historical conflicts at stake.[11] Sayles's critique of patronizing liberalism and tokenist multiculturalism suggests that significant taboos (incest, language and ethnicity boundaries, class and region distinctions) must be challenged in order to confront racism so systemic and so ingrained that it has become invisible to its perpetuators.

Monolingual initiatives of the 1980s and 90s have drawn on both cultural pluralist and universalizing assimilationist rhetorics to link U.S. national identity to an imagined "standard" U.S. English. By contrast, bilingual cultures have articulated alternative practices through arguments drawn from ethnic particularism and cultural pluralism.[12] Sayles's films, particularly *Lone Star,* draw out these ideological conflicts by portraying them through institutional strife over high school history lessons and public monuments. Sayles moves between ideology and institutional practice to indict facile multiculturalism and liberal misrecognition of structural injustices. What distinguishes his vision as transamericanist, rather than simply critically oppositional, is the fact that his critique comes within a positive argument for binational multilingual aesthetics. He does not provide such an aesthetics in final form, but the combined effect of the two films is to provide one path among many toward what José Martí described as the affiliations of Nuestra América. Like other multilingual authors of the past two decades writing in the period of globalization—Gloria Anzaldúa, Julia Alvarez, Teresa Hak Kyung Cha, Junot Díaz, Jessica Hagedorn, R. Linmark Zamora—Sayles does not provide a definitive aesthetic alternative o much as raise the stakes in the continuing exchange of cacophonous bilingual cultures.[13]

II

The "lone star" of the film's title refers both to a forty-year-old badge discovered with an anonymous skeleton and to an isolated contemporary sheriff who is out of place in his childhood home, as much as it does to the star on the Texas state flag. Sheriff Sam Deeds is already a lone star when the film begins, but his dogged pursuit of a legendary unsolved murder mystery further alienates him from the townspeople who prefer comfortable myths to challenging truths.

Lone Star has a murder mystery plot in a Western setting shot with neo-noir aesthetics and multilingual poetics. It is a testament to Sayles's manipulation of such diverse genres that the self-conscious commentary on cinematic history does not detract from the compelling stories at its core. He borrows and reconceptualizes elements from multiple cinematic traditions to critique earlier representations of Latin Americans and Chicano/a culture, while establishing his own brand of ethnic particularism—a developing set of aesthetics that he extends in *Men with Guns*.

In this context, I want to highlight the form that Sayles's transamerican multilingualism takes in his cinematic diptych. Distinctive aesthetic choices set these works apart from earlier U.S. films set in the Mexico–U.S. borderlands as well as from third-world cinema. Neither foreign nor domestic, both films test the limits of existing categories of cultural production. Sayles's films bring both types of subjectivity—U.S. embedded hierarchies and indigenous third-world narratives—into the same frame.

Bilingual expression in *Lone Star* often goes untranslated, though it rarely threatens to exclude English-only viewers. Unlike bilingual cultural expression that uses untranslated words from other languages to challenge and unsettle English-only readers, the Spanish in *Lone Star* serves as a less deterministic marker of cultural politics. The three sheriffs portrayed (Charlie Wade, Buddy Deeds, and Sam Deeds) display varying degrees of mastery over Spanish. Wade, for example, speaks Spanish to his victims just before murdering them. Buddy can order beer in Spanish, but we have no idea how much he knew of Chicano/a culture. On the other hand, some of the Chicano/a characters speak Spanish in the film in order to reprimand others for not speaking English. Bilingualism in *Lone Star*, then, is no signifier of an inclusive cultural politics; it is simply a fact of life in the borderlands, a fundamental element of the town's culture. But *how* each character uses Spanish emerges as very different: educative, murderous, disciplinary, exploratory. Language does not determine identity or set narrative conventions. Bilingualism is a continuous feature of life in Frontera, and what individuals make of the linguistic options shapes their position in the region's cultural politics.

The film opens with the discovery of the unidentified remains of a long-dead body and concludes with the identity of Sheriff Charley Wade's murderer. Between these two events, Sayles explores intergenerational conflicts among three sets of families in Frontera. Within the interconnected families—Chicano/a, African American, and Anglo—all members are forced to confront conflicts that they have evaded for most of their adult lives. Sam Deeds's investigation of his dead father forms the central storyline; he pieces together the facts of the murder with the expectation that his father, the legendary Sheriff Buddy Deeds, murdered Wade in order to take his office. If proven, this illegality would tarnish the reputation of the man whose fame had become synonymous with the identity of the town itself. When the truth emerges that Buddy was present at Wade's killing, but did not pull the trigger himself, Sam is left with a final choice: to make the truth public and end the career of the still-prominent citizen who killed Wade or leave the truth hidden and leave the allegations as part of Buddy's mystique.

Through investigating the mystery of Wade's disappearance, Sam encounters and scrutinizes a wide range of Frontera residents. Sayles presents these viewpoints as a tableau of competing epistemological and identitarian positions. In this manner, *Lone Star* presents several sets of competing interpretive frameworks for understanding history and cultural identity. Each of the main characters voices a method of reading ethnicity and understanding historicity. Through the characters' interactions, interethnic alliances form *within* each generation, rather than the racial and familial links that may seem more likely at the outset of the film. The shared visions of individual ethics, linguistic particularity, and complex overlapping collective identities lie at the heart of Sayles's transamerican cinema as an ongoing project to redefine "Americanism" outside of U.S. hegemony. What truly sets Sayles's transamerican vision apart from his predecessors is his claim that ethnic and racial hybridity is not a recent revelation, but simply an established fact of every generation that has become more accepted recently in its most intimate manifestations. In an interview, he pointed out that "it is not revisionism to include Mexican-American culture or African American culture or any of the many other different groups. If you're talking about the history of the United States, you're *always* talking about those things. . . . As Sam Deeds says, 'They were here first' . . . English-speaking culture is just one of many cultures. It has become the dominant culture or subculture in certain areas, but it's a subculture just like all the others. American culture is not monolingual or monoracial. It's always been a mix" (Sayles, *Interviews* 212–13). In the same interview, Sayles differentiated his position from that of much mid–1990s popular and academic multiculturalism. His point was not to portray historical changes in either demographics or culture: "it's not *increasingly* multicultural, it's always been so" (213). Instead, he charts the recognition and willingness to act on bilingual, bicultural, multilingual identities as generational, and this establishes *Lone Star* as a commentary on earlier cinematic treatments, such as *Touch of Evil* and *Chinatown,* as well as a bridge to more radically multilingual recent efforts, such as his own *Men with Guns.*[14]

One of the key cinematographic techniques that Sayles uses to argue for the porous boundaries of temporality and epistemology is his method of changing times and interior monologues without a cut. By not cutting between, for example, the present-day Sam and the young Buddy, Sayles dramatizes the weight of the past mercilessly pressing upon the relationships of the present. This technique is also a subtle comment on earlier filmmakers, since Sayles noted that Orson Welles, among others, used this method to collapse temporal divisions (Sayles, *Interviews* 204). Unlike the classic western or even film noir that depends on "geographical or manmade" borders as narrative frames, Sayles simply did away with the formal separations: "The purpose of a cut or a dissolve is to say this is a border, and the things on opposite sides of the border are meant to be different in some way, and I wanted to erase that border and show that these people are still reacting to things in the past" (Sayles, *Interviews* 212–14). Similarly, in disintegrating the expected aesthetic boundaries between characters' thoughts (several flashbacks begin in one character's mind and end in another's), Sayles portrays individuals as active inheritors of multiethnic legacies, not passive receptacles of static cultural identities. These non-cuts in temporality and interiority set the film's boundary-crossing aesthetics from the opening scenes to the taboo-shattering conclusion.[15]

The network of interethnic alliances that Sayles presents as constitutive of transamerican identities becomes clear through a survey of the epistemological position the characters of *Lone Star* hold. Of all the residents of Frontera, Mayor Hollis Pogue has the most to lose in Sam Deeds's excavation of the past. As Charlie Wade's deputy, Hollis killed Wade in an impulsive act of utter revulsion at having to watch the racist and thoroughly corrupt sheriff commit yet another murder. Buddy arrived just in time to witness Hollis shoot the unsuspecting Wade in the back. Instead of charging the young deputy with murder, Buddy helped Hollis cover up the crime and became sheriff himself. When the elder Hollis tells Sam at the beginning of the film that "Buddy Deeds was my salvation," only he knows just how literally he means those words. Hollis's interpretive position advocates leaving useful legends alone. Myths, he intimates, are worth keeping when they achieve a better approximation of justice than the truth would.[16] In the end, he suggests, "time went on, and people liked the story we told better than anything the truth might've been" (241). The invented story designed to explain Wade's disappearance without implicating anyone, paradoxically, turned out to be a more ethical—if dishonest—account than the truth.

In opposition to Hollis's insistence on the benefits of useful myths, Sam takes on the role of the truth-seeking detective who will use every tool of empirical research, including the latest forensic science, to determine what happened. Sam's interpretive position for the bulk of the narrative is that the truth will liberate him from the burdens of the past. He has forsaken a strategy of avoidance that is represented by his football-crazy ex-wife (played with relish by Frances McDormand); attempting to avoid his past only proved Buddy's continuing influence on his adult life. Sam's determination to solve the mystery is met with repeated warnings that the missing information may be dangerous or disturbing. This reference invokes the film noir convention of cautioning the protagonist against digging too deeply for forbidden knowledge, particularly important since classic examples of film noir make Latino/a and Asian American characters and settings central to their narratives. In a nod to *Chinatown* (1974) and more recent neo-noir narratives of race and cultural identity, Wesley Birdsong, a Kickapoo roadside merchant who knew Buddy before he became sheriff, tells Sam, "Gotta be careful where you're pokin'—who knows what you'll find" and jokingly shakes a skinned rattlesnake at him. The friendly advice that the truth may turn out to be poisonous is precisely the attitude Sam hopes to change by facing up to the actual chain of events.

In the end, Sam's assumption that the truth will liberate both himself and the town from Buddy's influence is tested by the fact that

Buddy did not kill Charley Wade. Sam undergoes another epistemological shift in the penultimate sequence of the film, choosing to leave the myth in place rather than to bring the facts to light. Knowing the truth proves necessary for him personally, but he determines that the desired ignorance of the townspeople does indeed serve a just purpose.

Mercedes Cruz, Pilar's mother, is the most politically and culturally conservative of the central characters. She is a prominent businesswoman who endlessly berates her employees for not speaking English. In fact, Mercedes appears in two very brief scenes whose only purpose is to establish her cultural politics: "*En ingles,* Enrique. This is the United States. We speak English" (165). The other scene simply shows Mercedes in her luxurious house observing men running past. She says to herself, "*Otra vez los mojados,*" and immediately calls the Border Patrol to report the mojados or "wetbacks" (182).

In addition to her material success, Mercedes has constructed a narrative of ethnic differentiation for her family. When another teacher refers to Pilar as Mexican, she replies half-mockingly, "*Spanish,* please! My mother would have a heart attack" (203; emphasis in original). However, the dubious construction of elitism entirely falls apart when the twin revelations emerge that Mercedes herself was a mojado and that she had a long and passionate affair with Buddy Deeds, of which Pilar was the result.

Mercedes's view of her own history is to maintain a resolute silence on all subjects that cause her shame. Her silence allows her freedom to construct a more desirable history and to work productively in spite of—or as overcompensation for—the formative lie. Through either shame or disassociation, Mercedes adopts the conservative anti–undocumented-alien Americanism, conveniently forgetting her own pathway to success was due less to a bootstrap individualism than the ten thousand dollars that Buddy gave her in the wake of Charley Wade's death (the missing money supported the impression that Wade had disappeared voluntarily, rather than having been killed). Mercedes's adoptive Americanism covers the shame of her actual origins to the extent that she is entirely indifferent, if not hostile, to her Mexican background. For example, when Pilar suggests a family trip to show her son and daughter where their grandmother grew up, Mercedes responds sharply, "You want to see Mexicans, open your eyes and look around you. We're up to our ears in them" (160). As this exchange makes clear, Mercedes does not even consider herself or her family Mexican. Her anti-ethnic particularist brand of assimilationism is a falsified universalism since it is based on the lies she has maintained over the decades regarding her own status and social position.

Otis Payne's son Del espouses a philosophy of individual agency that is analogous to Mercedes's. Colonel Delmore Payne's tabula rasa identity politics argues that identity is entirely what one makes of it, meaning hard work and individual ethical choices. However, the unintended meaning of this position is what Mercedes has made of her identity—that is, a highly productive falsehood.

The other two epistemological positions are those of the central characters whom the film ultimately valorizes: Pilar Cruz and Otis Payne. That the central argument of *Lone Star* is bifurcated into the perspectives of two characters who barely know one another is indicative of Sayles's notion of community.[17] Otis Payne, the African American bar-owner, suggests that individual identity is actively constituted through history and culture, not merely bloodlines. The other elements of the film's transnational identity politics are voiced by Pilar Cruz, a Chicana high-school history teacher who turns out to embody the very ambivalent hybridity that she teaches as characteristic of Texas history. In school meetings, family discussions, and moments of self-reflection, she advocates open recognition of the Mexico-Texas border region as a thoroughly bicultural, multilingual culture. This perspective, divided into the points of view of both African American and Chicano/a characters, demonstrates that the development of multiracial bilingual and bidialectical subjectivities is one of the central goals for transamerican cinema in the early twenty-first century. Both Otis and Pilar express the need for a new vocabulary that represents the shared concerns of, for example, black Seminole army veterans and Chicano-Anglo offspring. This vernacular eludes Sam, Pilar, and Otis, but each is searching for a more subtle relation between language and identity.

Texas's size, geography, and status as the only U.S. state to have once been an independent nation lead the border authorities to dramatize their importance even more, to enforce the borderland region with at times murderous zeal against those who would transgress either visible or invisible boundaries. As Cody, a redneck bartender, tells Sam, some see the very existence of society itself as dependent on the forceful maintenance of borders: "You joke about it, Sam, but we are in a state of crisis. The lines of demar*ca*tion has gotten fuzzy—to run a successful civilization you got to have your lines of demar*ca*tion between right and wrong, between this one and that—your Daddy understood that" (Sayles, *Men* 162; emphasis in original). The lines of demarcation that have been imposed by Anglo settlers, first militarily and later culturally, represent the archaic narrative that Pilar Cruz and Sam Deeds seek to confront in the service of a new narrative that is based on identitarian multiplicity and historicity, rather than mythology and hierarchy.

In the case of Pilar, the film portrays her teaching of grade-school history as activist scholarship, in providing Mexican perspectives on U.S. history to counter the conservative legacy of Anglo-Americanist histories of Texas. This figure of a Chicana educator provides an important contrast to Américo Paredes's novelistic account of 1930s-era education in the borderlands. In *George Washington Gómez,* Paredes described as neo-imperial the effects of the education in Texas through three characters: a sadistic teacher who tortured her Chicano students, a kind and earnest reformist teacher, and an Anglo college professor revered as a specialist in a border culture despite his ignorance of Spanish and racist views of Chicano/as. Paredes argued that the two kinds of grade-school teachers, either sadistic or empathic, limn a double consciousness in Chicano/a identity: "Consciously he considered himself a Mexican. He was ashamed of the name his dead father had given him. . . . But there was also George Washington Gómez, the American . . . George Washington Gómez secretly desired to be a full-fledged, complete American without the shameful encumberment of his Mexican race. He was the product of his Anglo teachers and the books he read in school, which were all in English. . . . But the Mexican side of his being rebelled" (Paredes, 147–48). The kindly Anglo teacher "prodded [him] toward complete assimilation," with the promise of acceptance in an inclusive society, according to Paredes. She was "the mother of the Mexicotexan's American self," but this ideal of nonpaternalistic democratic acceptance existed only ephemerally; in practice, Texan history textbooks forced the Chicano student to "put down in writing what he violently misbelieved" in order to pass the class (149). Thus, Anglo border educators in Paredes's novel rank among the most significant cogs of the Americanization machinery in the borderlands, embodying a democratic egalitarian rhetoric that the nation has never enforced. Sayles read Paredes's works before writing *Lone Star* and *Men with Guns,* and he specifically singled out *George Washington Gómez* and *With His Pistol in His Hand* as influential sources in his research (Sayles, *Interviews* 212).

Lone Star is suffused with generational tension, and Pilar Cruz is the inheritor of this legacy of colonial pedagogy. By contrast, however, Pilar's teachings aim at a more inclusive method of education that gives her Anglo, Chicano/a, and African American students multiple points of view to consider, even those not explicitly advocated by the school textbook. Scenes depicting Pilar's teaching are juxtaposed through Sayles's jump cuts with Sam's investigation into the murder of Charley Wade. In fact, in Pilar's first appearance on screen, she almost appears to be answering Sam's comment from the previous scene. He concludes his conversation with a forensics expert with the thought that although he does not know "if there's been a crime" yet, "this country's seen a good number of disagreements over the years" (112). Pilar's off-screen voice seems to respond, "We do the best we can here . . . but hey, public education these days is a bit of a battleground, " though she is actually speaking to a concerned parent about racial dynamics among the students. Later Pilar confronts a group of Anglo parents who are furious that "the way she's teachin' it has got everything switched around" (128–29). She suggests that she has "only been trying to get across some of the complexity of our situation down here—cultures coming together in both positive and negative ways" (130). At the sound of "culture," at least one parent seems relieved that "music and food and all" is Pilar's point, but providing "a complete picture" of the historical events is "what's got to stop."

In a more immediate way than Pilar Cruz and her educational predecessors as drawn by Américo Paredes, *Lone Star*'s familial dynamics revolve around generational changes and the hesitant, ambivalent sociocultural shifts they represent. The three sheriffs—Charley Wade, Buddy Deeds, and Sam—manifest salient differences in types of authority. Wade was "one of your old-fashioned bullets-or-bribe kind of sheriffs," according to his former deputy, Hollis Pogue, the present-day major of Frontera. Wade's corrupt methods of rule allowed him to "take a healthy chunk" of all business in the town in return. Legality was not Wade's concern; instead, he defined permissible acts as those that enriched him. When a young Otis Payne is running numbers behind his back, Wade warns him that any business run without his knowledge is "both illegal and unhealthy."

Buddy Deeds overturned Charley Wade's ruthless corruption with a new code of ethics that put political power ahead of personal financial gain. Compared to Wade's shakedowns, Buddy's exchange of law enforcement for electoral support came as a relief. Although the film does not depict Buddy as a lawman/legislator in its flashbacks, the contemporary reverence for his thirty-year career strongly implies that he lived by a more equitable ethical standard than Charlie Wade. On the other hand, Buddy was antagonistic toward interracial couples, particularly Sam and Pilar as teenagers, which proves to be either hypocritical or evidence of overcompensation, when his love affair with Mercedes Cruz becomes known to Sam (and us). Both the

Oedipal and the historical significances of Sam Deeds's taking over his father's office become more substantial as the radical implications of Sayles's borderlands drama come into focus.

By all accounts, Sheriff Sam Deeds is only a pale reflection of his mythic predecessors, and the film's generational argument turns on whether this is a positive or a negative development. The historical trends of demystification and deflation of myths is perfectly summed up by Minnie Bledsoe, widow of the roadhouse bar owner preceding Otis Payne. When Sam introduces himself, she replies without looking up, "Sheriff Deeds is dead, honey. You just Sheriff Junior" (146). Sam's problem for much of the film is that this is precisely how he views himself, in Buddy's long shadow. The office of the border sheriff in the mid–1990s has aged and lost its mystique as well. Sam acknowledges that it has turned out to be "not what I thought it'd be. Back when Buddy had it—hell, I'm just a jailer. Run a sixty-room hotel with bars on the windows" (178–79). As played by Chris Cooper, Sam Deeds is a laconic loner with a flair for wry understatement, hardly the stuff of mythic proportions.

This nostalgic view of institutional decline and cultural deflation is common to most of the Anglos in *Lone Star,* particularly among the older generations. Sayles's point of reference here is, among others, Orson Welles's mythic border sheriff Hank Quinlin in *Touch of Evil* (1958). Quinlin, like Buddy Deeds, is depicted as a legendary sheriff with an instinct for justice and injustice that does not have to meet the usual standards of evidence. When such giants fall, they leave a measure of ambivalence in even those most relieved by their departure.[18] Sam experiences this ambivalence as he struggles with the conservative narrative of Anglo decline that he hears repeatedly from the town mayor to the redneck bartender who frets for the future of "civilization" without clear lines of demar*ca*tion.

Sam counters the conservative defense of borders and the nostalgia for mythical, racist lawmen of the past with an attempt to develop a new kind of authority. He recognizes the diverse ethnic history and demographics of the region. When an older Anglo complains that it is "bad enough all the street names are in Spanish," Sam testily reminds him, "nineteen out of every twenty people in this town are Mexican" (117). As sheriff, Sam aims at a more ethical and representative form of law enforcement, and, as a detective of a forty-year-old murder mystery, he claims to seek only the truth, despite his quiet hope to sully his father's reputation with a belated murder charge.

The film concludes with a resolution that shatters one of the most durable social taboos: incest. Sam and Pilar have finally freed themselves from their parents' prohibition against their relationship, only to be confronted with the general ban against incest. In keeping with the paradoxical nature of the film's construction of identity, Sam and Pilar choose to reject societal restrictions on interethnic and intrafamilial sex. They articulate Saylesian individualism by rejecting all collective institutions in order to maintain their renewed love affair. This final scene takes place, appropriately for a film that catalogues the history of cinematic genre, in the abandoned lot of an old drive-in. Facing the ruins of what was once a movie screen, Pilar and Sam resolve to seek a new community that will allow their accept their transamerican union.

III

While *Men with Guns* shares many of the central themes, character types, and ethical dilemmas of *Lone Star*, it examines them through another cultural lens. *Men with Guns* is a sequel (or prequel, since Sayles wrote it first) only in the loosest of senses. The 1997 film reconsiders the ethics and aesthetics of transamerican cinema in a Latin American context, rather than the U.S.–Mexico borderlands region. This contextual move raised new sets of questions: What is the cultural logic of multilingualism as alternative cultural practice? What aesthetic choices are impelled by bilingual film?

Men with Guns takes the various themes of the earlier film—hidden cultural and historical complexities, racial and ethnic mixture, cross-cutting narrative structures, and a central organizing murder mystery—and boils them down to the one epistemological position that concerns him: willful liberal ignorance of the violence inherent within structural inequality. *Men with Guns* is allegorically vague about its setting, yet this layer of abstraction allows it to be more penetrating as a meditation on a particular ethical and political position, as a detailed portrait of a naïve liberalism that depends on strategic (if unconscious) ignorance. This inadequate political intervention is shattered by a belated realization of the tragic interconnectedness of race, class, and region.

As with *Lone Star*, the plot of *Men with Guns* is simple and revolves around the mysterious disappearance of a body, in this case several. The missing individuals are the medical students whom Dr. Humberto Fuentes trained in a special program, the "Ambassadors of Health," to practice in the outlying regions of their unnamed Latin American country. When Dr. Fuentes catches sight of one former student in the city, he confronts the young man. Fuentes is shocked to hear that many of the doctors have not been heard from and are presumed disappeared. He sets off to visit his students to assure himself that they are still alive despite (or because of) his advanced age and impending retirement. As he moves further from the city center, Fuentes sequentially loses his urban tools—his camera, hubcaps, money, tires, and finally his Jeep itself—as he loses his illusions regarding the state of life in the countryside. Like Sam Deeds, Fuentes disregards the warnings of friends and colleagues regarding his safety and the danger of the desired information itself. Fuentes's journey into the heart of darkness of his country's rural rebellion finally confirms the worst of his suspicions concerning the fate of his students and the state of his country.

The central metaphor, the men with guns, is incisive as a result of its plasticity. The various men with guns who have terrorized the residents of the towns in the countryside (filmed in the Chiapas region of Mexico) include guerillas, army soldiers, and mercenaries, among others. What Fuentes comes to understand is the paralyzing state of vulnerability in which the unarmed live. The film conveys this sense of constant threat by portraying the aftermath of great violence: starvation, fear, and deep mistrust of outsiders. In scenes that are gripping (as well as problematic in their portrayal of passivity) Sayles presents a Hobbesian natural state of cyclical violence and relentlessly predatory relations.

In the service of establishing a framework for transamerican film, Sayles's aesthetic choices regarding narrative form and language structure the arguments on individual identity. Strictly speaking, *Men with Guns* is trilingual; it contains three storylines that unfold in Spanish, English, and the languages of indigenous peoples. However, Spanish is the primary idiom of the film to such an extent that the others seem more like brief exceptions or interludes. Does this make the film "less multilingual"? On the contrary, the effects of bi- and multilingual narratives function in a variety of ways, but certainly not less provocatively, when one language predominates. This strategy, as used by authors such as Américo Paredes, Sandra Cisneros, Julia Alvarez, and many others, infuses the exceptional, supplemental, extraterritorial words with new meaning.[19] Just as *Lone Star* is primarily in English, with Spanish conversations regularized within, *Men with Guns* makes its linguistic choices seem unsurprising: Americans speak English, Latino/as speak Spanish, and Native Americans speak Nahuatl, Tzotzil, Maya, and Kuna.

The innovation is based not on what language each character speaks, but on how the film uses these forms of expression. Dr. Fuentes is surprised that his urbane Spanish is of no use to him in the countryside. Many of the townspeople he encounters do not speak Spanish, and those who do often ignore outsiders after their experiences with the hombres armados. Sayles begins and ends in the remote Cerca del Cielo. At the outset, the mother and daughter speak of Fuentes's arrival with foreknowledge. They know he will arrive, and they know that he is a doctor who "can put his hand on you and tell what your sickness is" (Sayles, *Men* 3). By opening the film from their point of view, Sayles aligns the urban doctor with the strange and foreign: "City people don't get sick like we do. They speak a different language, they wear different clothes . . . they don't look anything like us" (4). The following line, spoken in Fuentes's office, is the patronizing comment regarding the ignorance of the "common people." In both of Sayles's films, the imperial language can tell only a small part of the story at hand; indigenous, hybrid vernaculars are required to make sense of a more complete narrative.

In *Lone Star*, the formal discontinuities and linguistic juxtapositions consistently break down the notion of borders, both material and immaterial. *Guns* does not programmatically attack boundaries; if anything it maintains the linguistic borders faithfully, so much as to show these gaps to be permeable. As an Anglo writing a primarily Spanish-language film, Sayles was highly conscious that subtitles would take up the bottom of the screen. This demand for screen-wide sentences kept the dialogue brief, and the script conveys terse, fragmentary exchanges throughout.[20]

The subtitle effect also increased the allegorical elements of the narrative. Unlike *Lone Star*, which is grounded in historical and cultural specificity and whose plot is premised upon locating specific events in the past, Sayles intended to evoke a number of global conflicts in *Guns*. While certain moments hint at events in Bosnia, Rwanda, and Afghanistan, the transamerican context organizes the cultural and linguistic confrontations of the film. For example, Sayles could not write the original screenplay for the Mayan woman and girl who open and close the film: Their language, according to Sayles "had never been spoken in a movie before," and he did not speak a word of it (Sayles, *Interviews* 228).[21] By using native speakers for all roles and non-professional actors for a number of key characters, Sayles keeps the film's Latin American context foregrounded. As in *Lone Star*, Sayles's casting is as ethnically specific as possible, which forms another metacommentary on prominent U.S. films of the past, such as *Touch of Evil*, which features Orson Welles as a South Texas border sheriff, minus the twang. Even more spectacularly, Charlton Heston plays a Mexican officer, and Marlene Dietrich a mystical bordello madam with an unaccountable thick German accent. The elements of cultural specificity make *Men with Guns* an even more intriguing piece of the Sayles canon. Many of his films fall into the genres of the allegorical (*The Brother from Another Planet, The Secret of Roan Inish*) or the historically specific (*Eight Men Out, Matewan, Lone Star*). Most reviews treated *Men with Guns* as purely allegorical, but it actually suggests a new merging of elements from both categories. This technique of merging allegory with historical/cultural specificity bodes well for Sayles's project and for transamerican cinema in general.

The film opens with Dr. Fuentes giving a rectal examination to an army general. Metaphorically and literally, this proves to be the central problematic of Fuentes's life. Although extremely successful and highly admired by those near him, Dr. Fuentes has had his head up powerful men's asses for too long. He is a naïve citizen, one who prefers to believe government propaganda rather than the contrary facts all around him. He parrots phrases that he hears from officials without even considering what such statements mean; the general tells him that "the common people—love drama," as an explanation for the persistent "rumors" of rebellion (4). Fuentes later uses the same line with American tourists who have read of violent clashes in the countryside (18). Even the general notes this quality: "You're like a child, Humberto. The world is a savage place" (6). Soon after, one of his former students tells him bitterly, "You're the most learned man I've ever met. And the most ignorant" (13).

The irony in this exchange is that Fuentes's "Ambassadors of Health" program was intended as social and political intervention, as well as a medical program. The target was "ignorance [and], no one is immune to this disease," as he remembers telling his students in a grainy black-and-white, jump-cut flashback. This paternalistic assumption takes for granted that the poverty-stricken rural and indigenous communities are suffering as a result of their lack of knowledge, as opposed to more immediate needs. In a series of flashbacks, in which Fuentes recalls his own lessons, he comes to understand that ignorance was far from the greatest difficulty in areas rife with starvation, rape, and murder. In fact, Fuentes is the one most guilty of ignorance, a strategic and willful—if unconscious—desire to be unaware of the most painful aspects of his society. When Fuentes discovers the facts of just a few of the towns that have been devastated, he responds that "people should know about this," but of course, "they do know." Only Fuentes and those similarly shielded by long habit seem to have been blissfully ignorant. Such willed ignorance renders the liberal social reform that he views with pride as his "legacy" not merely useless, but irresponsible. Fuentes is doing politically what he would never do medically—that is, treating the symptoms while ignoring the structural malaise that generates the symptoms. His program is inadequate, but even more troublingly, it puts the doctors he has trained in harm's way without any adequate methods of defense or escape. Through the plot trajectory, Sayles argues for the political awareness, just as his aesthetic choices of a Spanish and Native American script and local actors urge linguistic particularism. The allegorical elements of the film should not confuse viewers/listeners into thinking that Sayles is presenting timeless, prescriptive, decontextualized readings of transcultural zones of contestation. On the contrary, his general, allegorizable point is a plea for the specificity—ethnic and cultural particularism—required of any reformist or revolutionary program. Vaguely liberal methods of social change will not succeed and may even come to do greater harm.[22] Like Sam Deeds, Fuentes finds that the knowledge he has strategically avoided alters the most basic set of assumptions by which he has lived.

As a result of the language and setting of *Men with Guns,* the narrative function of the two American characters would seem to be one part comic relief and two parts critique of American parochial view of the world beyond its borders as mere sites for consumerist tourism. Although these anomalous characters do provide these elements—nicely combined in the offhand question, "What's the word for *fajitas?*"—their general function in the narrative is actually much more complex. The husband and wife played by Mandy Patinkin and Kathryn Grody are not, as Sayles himself has pointed out, "ugly Americans" who trample and destroy all that they do not understand. In fact, they are more informed than Dr. Fuentes is about his own country. Their newspapers-and-guidebooks knowledge of the rural areas is cartoonish and insensitive ("Tell him about the book we have, with the people with their hands cut off"), but they are far closer to the truth than the serenely confident doctor who assures them that what they have heard of was either invented, because "Newspapers are businesses," or occurred "in another country. Not here" (17–18). They demonstrate the depth of Fuentes's inability or unwillingness to cone to grips with his country's conflicts.[23]

In addition to showing the extent of Fuentes's self-imposed ignorance, the American characters also demonstrate the strangeness of English in the transamerican linguistic universe. Sayles deliberately has the audience *hear* the American characters' English before seeing them, which emphasizes the dissonant foreignness of their words within a film filled with evocative Spanish. English is definitively decentered by the film. Rather than presenting English as either inevitable or even necessary to the plot, the American characters show English to be a distant third in importance. The Americans are nearly inconsequential to the plot, and their exchanges with Dr. Fuentes are the least informative of the film. This does not make them metonymic figures of U.S. imperialism so much as irrelevant. They are in the film to break with the rhetorics of U.S. exceptionalism and centrality by demonstrating the relative inconsequentiality of U.S. politics, institutions, and culture. The Americans' benign unimportance is the most radical statement Sayles can make about Americans in a Latin American Spanish-language film. This in itself contradicts a century of U.S. produced and financed cinema history in which Americans—whether heroic or malevolent—have consistently been treated as inherently influential.

IV

Sayles's subtle critique of twentieth-century expansionist cultural imperialism is in the service of a representative transamericanism through Latin American multilingual aesthetics and the range of ethical and epistemological positions on collective history and individual identity. Like earlier visions of hemispheric alliances, such as José Martí's call in "Our America" for a truly expanded Americanism, Sayles aims at an inclusive form that is responsive to multiple cultures and identities. This twenty-first-century project looks back to bicultural figures such as Martí who have articulated such visions of a non-Anglocentric Americanism that is not dominated by U.S. interests and concerns.

As recent events have made abundantly clear, an interconnected, technologically driven global system that pursues imbalanced and unrepresentative economic gain through willful ignorance of the political and cultural implications courts resentment and reaction. Linguistic specificity as an ethical component of ethnic particularism will not solve systematic structures of racist and gendered violence—it would be naïve and even dangerous to imagine so—but the project of transamerican cinema may provide a foundation for an ongoing discussion of the relation between cultural institutions and wide-scale oppression through innovative alternatives to paternalistic liberalism or vaguely constituted multiculturalism.

Notes

1. As a point of comparison, *Lone Star* grossed over $13 million in theaters, while *Men with Guns* grossed approximately $742,000 during its comparatively brief run.

2. In *An Accented Cinema*, Hamid Naficy details the linguistic and visual expressions of exilic and diasporic films. Naficy suggests that border films tend to be "hybridized and experimental—characterized by multifocality, multilinguality, asynchonicity, critical distance, fragmented or multiple subjectivity, and transborder amphibolic characters—characters who might best be called 'shifters.'"
3. Sarah Kozloff's study of filmic speech, *Overhearing Film Dialogue*, considers verbal expression in a variety of classic U.S. film genres. For the most part, non-English expression is outside the purview of her work, but she refers to the narrative "conundrum[s]" that "the presence of non-English speaking characters creates" for filmmakers. Historically, "strict realism"—having characters speak in other languages—"always loses out to the other demands on film speech. Thus, the foreign dialogue is generally minimized, and its import is nearly always made clear by context, cognates, or pantomime, or by having a bilingual character handily present to provide a translation" (80). Whether films use English to stand in for all languages (for example, in *The Hunt for Red October* [1990]), append subtitles (*Sophie's Choice* [1982]), or leave untranslated non-English dialogue as radically other (*The Deer Hunter* [1978]), Kozloff suggests that English retains its privileged position. My contention is that in recognizing linguistic privileging, Sayles renegotiates the role(s) of English through his structural and linguistic choices within the two films.
4. See Ana M. López, "Facing Up to Hollywood."
5. For example, during the 1930s RKO, Universal, and MGM produced *El presidio* (1930), *El tenorio del harem* (1931), *¿Cuándo te suicidas?* (1931), *Contra la corriente* (1935), *Alas sobre el Chaco* (1935), *El día que me quieras* (1936), and *La vida bohemia* (1937).
6. See José David Saldívar, "Nuestra América's Borders: Remapping American Cultural Studies" on the disciplinary challenges and opportunities of reading Martí in relation to American Studies.
7. On nineteenth-century transnational literary expression, see and Kirsten Silva Gruesz, *Ambassadors of Culture: The Transamerican Origins of Latino Writing*. Princeton, NJ: Princeton University Press, 2002.
8. See, and, on language legislation and its effects on bilingual education. See, and, on the history of both populist and elitist efforts to standardize language.
9. See, on the relationship between the 1920s English-only movement and multilingual ethnic modernism.
10. As a result of state English-only laws, there have been so many recent cases of accent and language-discrimination lawsuits that it is nearly impossible to catalogue them. For a sampling, see the following accounts: "Housekeepers Told to Speak Only English Get Settlement" (April 22, 2001, *New York Times*, p. A24); "Behind the Court's Civil Rights Ruling" (April 29, 2001, *New York Times*, Section 4, p. 4); "13

Who Spoke Spanish Win Discrimination Case" (September 20, 2000, *The Houston Chronicle,* p. A32); "Ex-workers Sue Hotel for Bias, Alleging English-only Policy" (22 June 2000, *The Boston Herald,* p. A18); "The Politics of Talking Shop: Are Polyglot Workplaces Good for Diversity and Profits, or Do They Contribute to Interethnic Tension?" (March 15, 2001, *Financial Times* (London), p. 15); "Don't Speak English? No Tax Break, Alabama Official Declares" (June 4, 1999, *The New York Times,* p. A24; "Watlow is Sued Over 'English Only' Rule" (March 12, 1999, *St. Louis Post-Dispatch,* p. C1).

11. See Gordon and Newfield, *Mapping Multiculturalism,* particularly essays by Wahneema Lubiano, Christopher Newfield and Avery F. Gordon, and Antonia I. Castañeda.
12. See Doris Sommer, "A Rhetoric of Particularism,"
13. On globalization and film, see Stam and Shohat, "Film theory and spectatorship in the age of the 'posts,'"
14. For an overview, see
15. In *The Art and Politics of Film,* John Orr examines the Hitchcock and Welles-influenced doubling of past and present in Pedro Almodóvar's *Live Flesh* (1997) and Bryan Singer's *The Usual Suspects* (1995): "The power of Almodóvar's film lies in its capacity to blend these [temporal] worlds so seamlessly together. The double flash-forward. . . . Situated action of course dominates these films but the relationship of the action-image and time-image is reordered in the diegesis. For it is the past which moves the present forwards, galvanizes it, interrupts it and gives it the urgency of its tragic rush towards violence and destruction." . Christopher Nolan has also contributed to this narratological tradition with *Following* (1998), *Memento* (2000), and *Insomnia* (2002).
16. Jack Ryan suggests that this penultimate scene, in which Hollis shoots the unsuspecting Wade in the back, and the film's mythology-deflating historicism shape the aesthetics of an anti-Western. In the generation depicted, the land has been tamed and appears "washed out, deliberately made unappealing"; rather than beginning the film with a master shot of epic scenery, *Lone Star* begins in an abandoned rifle field. Similarly, when viewers are introduced to Sheriff Sam Deeds, the most noticeable fact about him is that he is a lawman who does not carry a firearm (231).
17. In *Thinking in Pictures,* Sayles's account of the filming of *Matewan,* he notes, "One thing I've tried to do in all the movies I've written for myself to direct is have the world populated by more than one or two people, to present a community. The norm in star-vehicle screenwriting is to have couple of leads and the rest of the characters there only to provide background and plot advancement . . . I'm more interested in how individual or political acts affect communities of people." What links *Men with Guns* and *Lone Star* is this attention to

individual and political acts (which are often the same) as inherently consequential to the community at large.

18. In an interview, Sayles explains how Welles's film influenced his treatment of the "legend" handed down through stories: "Orson Welles's character is a legend in his own time, but the first time you see him he's this monstrous character. He's the kind of legend who didn't die in time, he's hung around and now he's going to ruin his own legacy."
19. Michael North points to some important parallels in Ken Saro-Wiwa's use of "rotten English" in *Sozaboy.* In Saro-Wiwa's, as in many other authors' inhabiting of English, the "English in question is not, however, the uniform and universally intelligible variety . . . rotten English is ruleless and lawless, an improvisation born out of the 'mediocre education and severely limited opportunities' of a vast, ethnically and linguistically miscellaneous urban population" (North 100).
20. Gerard Molyneaux notes, "In employing the several dialects, Sayles wrote his dialogue to fit the subtitle format of thirty-two characters per line. What evolved was a screenplay style he describes as part haiku and part catechism."
21. Molyneaux describes the linguistic "honor system" that developed, since "the Indians in the cast had to translate the Spanish script into their own dialects, then, if they fumbled their dialogue on camera, had to tell Sayles about their mistake."
22. In "Be-longing and Bi-lingual States," Doris Sommer relates bilingual culture to the tenets of liberalism and particularism, specifically the subversive role of bilingual within theories of ethics and aesthetics.
23. "What I said to Mandy Patinkin and Kathryn Grody was, 'You're not ugly Americans at all. You're actually pretty nice people. You're better informed, you're very adventurous tourists. . . . But you are the Teflon tourists. You have a confidence you should not have. You're in places that you probably should not be in in terms of safety, but you're Americans. And so you feel that nothing bad can come to you. . . . So they're parallel to Dr. Fuentes, who's taking the same geographical voyage . . . each time Fuentes sees them, they're the same— it doesn't affect them. But Fuentes is different."

Works Cited

Bailey, Richard W. *Images of English: A Cultural History of the Language.* Ann Arbor: University of Michigan Press, 1991.

Baldwin, James. *Collected Essays.* New York: Library of America, 1998.

Baron, Dennis E. *The English-Only Question: An Official Language for Americans?* New Haven: Yale University Press, 1990.

Belnap, Jeffrey Grant, and Raul A. Fernandez. *Jose Marti's "Our America": From National to Hemispheric Cultural Studies. New Americanists.* Durham: Duke University Press, 1998.

Berumen, Frank Javier Garcia. *The Chicano/Hispanic Image in American Film*. New York: Vantage Press, 1995.

Bourdieu, Pierre. *Language and Symbolic Power.* Ed. John B. Thompson. Cambridge: Harvard University Press, 1991.

Bourdieu, Pierre, and Jean Claude Passeron. *Reproduction in Education, Society and Culture*. 1977. London: Sage Publications, 1990.

Brickhouse, Anna. "The Writing of Haiti: Pierre Faubert, Harriet Beecher Stowe, and Beyond." *American Literary History* 13.3 (2001): 407–44.

Chion, Michel. *The Voice in Cinema*. Trans. Claudia Gorbman. New York: Columbia University Press, 1999.

Crawford, James. *Hold Your Tongue: Bilingualism and the Politics of English Only.* Reading, Mass.: Addison-Wesley, 1992.

———, ed. *Language Loyalties: A Source Book on the Official English Controversy.* Chicago: University of Chicago Press, 1992.

Freire, Paulo. *Pedagogy of the Oppressed*. 1970. New York: Continuum, 1986.

Gordon, Avery, and Christopher Newfield (eds.). *Mapping Multiculturalism*. Minneapolis: University of Minnesota Press, 1996.

Hansen, Miriam. *Babel & Babylon: Spectatorship in American Silent Film*. Cambridge: Harvard University Press, 1991.

Jameson, Fredric. *The Geopolitical Aesthetic: Cinema and Space in the World System*. Bloomington: Indiana University Press, 1992.

Kellman, Steven G. "Sayles Goes Spanish." *Hopscotch* 1.1 (1999): 24–35.

———, ed. *The Translingual Imagination*. Lincoln: University of Nebraska Press, 2000.

Kozloff, Sarah. *Overhearing Film Dialogue*. Berkeley: University of California Press, 2000.

Martí, José. *Jose Martí Reader: Writings on the Americas*. Eds. Deborah Shnookal and Mirta Muniz. New York and Melbourne: Ocean Press, 1999.

Martí, José. *On Art and Literature: Critical Writings*. Philip Sheldon Foner ed. New York: Monthly Review Press, 1982.

Miller, Joshua L. "Lingual Politics: The Syncopated Accents of Multilingual Modernism, 1919–48." Diss. Columbia University, 2001.

Molyneaux, Gerard. *John Sayles: An Unauthorized Biography of the Pioneering Indie Filmmaker.* Los Angelos: Renaissance Books/St. Martin's Press, 2000.

Naficy, Hamid. *An Accented Cinema: Exilic and Diasporic Filmmaking*. Princeton, NJ: Princeton University Press, 2001.

North, Michael. "Ken Saro-Wiwa's Sozaboy: The Politics of 'Rotten English'." *Public Culture* 13.1 (2001): 97–112.

Orr, John. *The Art and Politics of Film*. Edinburgh: Edinburgh University Press, 2000.

Paredes, Américo. *George Washington Gómez: A Mexicotexan Novel*. Houston: Arte Publico Press, 1990.

———. *With His Pistol in His Hand: A Border Ballad and Its Hero*. Austin: University of Texas Press, 1958.

Ryan, Jack. *John Sayles, Filmmaker: A Critical Study of the Independent Writer-Director.* Jefferson, NC: McFarland, 1998.

Sayles, John. *John Sayles: Interviews. Conversations with Filmmakers Series.* Ed. Diane Carson. Jackson: University Press of Mississippi, 1999.

———. *Lone Star.* Culver City, CA: Columbia TriStar Home Video, 1996.

———. *Los Gusanos: A Novel.* 1st ed. New York: HarperCollins Publishers, 1991.

———. *Men with Guns and Lone Star.* London: Faber and Faber, 1998.

———. *Sayles on Sayles.* Ed. Gavin Smith. Boston and London: Faber and Faber, 1998.

———. *Thinking in Pictures: The Making of the Movie Matewan*. Boston: Houghton Mifflin, 1987.

Shohat, Ella, and Robert Stam. *Unthinking Eurocentrism: Multiculturalism and the Media*. London, New York: Routledge, 1994.

Sommer, Doris. "Be-Longing and Bi-Lingual States." *Diacritics: A Review of Contemporary Criticism* 29.4 (1999): 84–115.

———. *Proceed with Caution, When Engaged by Minority Writing in the Americas.* Cambridge, Mass.: Harvard University Press, 1999.

Williams, Linda, and Christine Gledhill eds. *Reinventing Film Studies.* London and New York: Arnold and Oxford University Press, 2000.

Part III

Genders

9

Doña Marina and Captain Malinche*

Margo Glantz

The world of epic has little to do with women, although perhaps my statement pertains only to Bernal Diaz del Castillo's chronicle, better known as the *Historia Verdadera de la Conquista de la Nueva España* (The Discovery and Conquest of Mexico), the only text to which I will refer here.[1] The Conquest treated as a heroic affair concerns itself with women only as secondary characters, anonymous and collective. They belong to the spoils of war and soldiers make explicit use of them to satisfy their domestic and daily needs: food and sex.

After the Spanish triumph against the Tlaxcaltecs, Xicoténcatl the Elder tells Cortés the following, thus sealing their alliance:

> " . . . so that you may know more clearly our good will towards you and our desire to content you in everything, we wish to give you our daughters, to be your wives, so that you may have children by them, for we wish to consider you as brothers as you are so good and valiant. I have a very beautiful daughter who has not been married, and I wish to give her to you," and so Mase Escasi and all the other caciques said that they would bring their daughters, and that we should accept them as wives, and they made many other speeches and promises. Throughout the day Mase Escasi and Xicotenga the elder never left Cortés' immediate neighborhood. . . . . Cortés replied to them that, as to the gift of the women, he and all of thus were very grateful and would repay them with good deeds as time went on. (Bernal 197)

Obviously, this kind of pact is not unprecedented. It occurs even in the best of families. Iphigenia's sacrifice in Greek tragedy and epic can take place because Clytemnestra surrenders her daughter expecting her to be wed to a famous warrior. Even though Agamemnon is chief of the Acheans, the racial group to which both Achilles and

Iphigenia belong, the offer of a daughter as chattel allows for the comparison. Women in Mexico prior to the Conquest appear to be at the conquerors' disposal—Spaniards or Indians, Mexicas or Tlaxcaltecs. Given over to the Spaniards as bounty following the battle of Potonchán, the Malinche represents an exceptional case. Had it not to been for her meddlesome, riotous, and boisterous self, she would have been relegated to the same fate as all the other women—slavery's total anonymity. Chieftains' daughters were at the disposal of their fathers, a prime example being Xicontécatl the Elder's daughter, sister of Mozo, Cortés's enemy. Her father offers her up to the conquistador, who takes her and has her baptized along with the other young noblewomen surrendered to the invaders; she "was given the name of Doña Luisa, and Cortés took her by the hand and gave her to Pedro de Alvarado" (Bernal 155). Pedro de Alvarado was single and although he later married a Spanish woman, his children with Doña Luisa would join the ranks of the ennobled Spaniards. Curiously, after the Spaniards disband in Tenochtitlán, only the two indigenous women—La Malinche and Doña Luisa—survive. Bernal also mentions one other woman, a Spaniard, "named Maria de Estrada, who was the only Spanish woman in Mexico" (387).

Women are good for "producing offspring," as the Tlaxcaltec chieftain and later Moctezuma put it, or simply to satisfy a primal sexual urge in a world bereft of real women—European women, that is. The indigenous women are referred to disparagingly as *indias* and often, when part of the bounty, simply as "pieces," and branded with a special iron used to identify spoils obtained in the New World. The Indian women thus bore the letter *G* for "Guerra" (War) on their bodies: "Aquí se hubieron muy buenas indias y despojos," (173) adds Bernal when recounting a battle in which they triumphed, before Tenochtitlan was won. It bears mentioning that this treatment is universal when it comes to captured Indians. A prime example of this notion is when Bernal tells how several townships were punished, among them Zautal, Tepeaca, Iztacamextitlan, for sacrificing and eating some of the Spaniards who passed through there while their comrades, defenseless, were driven from Tenochtitlan by the Mexicas:

> When Gonzalo de Sandoval arrived at the town of Segura de la Frontera after having made the expeditions I have spoken of, we had all the people of that province pacified. So Cortés decided, with the officials of the King, that all the slaves that had been taken *should be branded* so that his fifth might be set aside after the fifth had been taken for His Majesty, and to this effect he had a proclamation made in the town and

> camp, that all the soldiers should bring to a house chosen for the purpose all the women whom we were sheltering, to be branded and the time allowed for doing this was the day of the proclamation and one more. We all came with all the Indian women and girls and boys whom we had captured, but the grown-up men we did not trouble about as they were difficult to watch and we had no need of their services, as we had friends the Tlaxcalans. (Bernal 332)

It is evident that these practices were common to all conquerors, whether indigenous or Spanish. The prime difference, however, was the method by which the prisoners were punished and sacrificed. For indigenous groups, prisoners were objects of religious sacrifice—they offered their prisoners up to the gods, removed their hearts and ate their flesh. In contrast, Spaniards shackled them and convert them into "pieces"—they were work instruments. It bears mentioning that there is a great difference between an enslaved Indian and an allied Indian. For Bernal—and undoubtedly for his fellow Spaniards—the Indian, not as an individual but as a human group, occupies a decidedly inferior category within the hierarchy configured by Europeans. Therefore, the greatest praise that could be bestowed upon him would be to consider him akin to Spaniards, although never quite their equal: "At that time, in Mexico, they had raised up [to the throne] another Prince, because the Prince who had driven us out of Mexico had died of Smallpox. He whom they now made Lord over them was a nephew or very near relation of Montezuma, named Guatemoc, a young man of about twenty-five years, *very much of a gentleman for an Indian,* and very valiant, and he was married to a daughter of Montezuma, *a very handsome woman for an Indian*" (Bernal 328). The paradigm by which the Indian is measured is relative; it forms part of a hierarchy and therefore of a classification. When subjected to its scrutiny, he or she is often raised practically to the height of the recently vanquished. Donning some of the European's defining characteristics, the Indian's intelligence, courage, and beauty reach a special gradation and particular wonder. Behavior or education, bravery or beauty is appreciated if they come close to the Western standard. Another passage shows the wonder caused by the Indian's capacity to understand some of Western culture's institutions: "for although they were Indians, they saw and understood that justice is good and sacred" (129).

However, during times of war, the Indian is but an object, an enslaved body at times resembling that of a beast. Returning to Bernal: " . . . and we seared the wounds of the others and of the horses *with the fat of the Indian . . .*" (Bernal 59).

Not once do the chronicles mention a similar operation being performed on the bodies of fallen Spaniards. However, descriptions like the following are all too common: "We dressed the wounded men, who numbered fifteen, with the fat of an Indian" (Bernal 127). Captive Indians lose their human status: Until recently, the copiously used unction, a type of lard, was provided by hogs.

But if the Indian can become an object, women are invariably objects, regardless of their high station. Even the daughters of the cacique, who wear "rich blouses of the earth," who bear gold pendants on their necks and hoops of that same mint through their ears and are waited upon by other Indian women, will nevertheless be spoils of war. Doña Marina, Malinalli, or Malinche escapes, in part, this objectification. Bernal mentions her habitually and despite the fact that her role as translator has earned her an entire chapter of acclaim, he still feels the need to praise her chapter after chapter despite the fact that she always appears accompanied by Jerónimo Aguilar. Bernal's esteem for Doña Marina is genuine and categorical, while he rarely applauds the skill or diligence of the Spanish interpreter. He says, for example, "Cortés answered him through our interpreters who always accompanied him, especially Doña Marina," (Bernal 204) and in an earlier part of the text: "Let us leave this and say how Doña Marina who, although a native woman, possessed such manly valor that, although she had heard every day how the Indians were going to kill and eat our flesh with *chili,* and had seen us surrounded in the late battles, and knew that all of us were wounded and sick, yet never allowed us to see any sign of fear in her a courage passing that of woman" (Bernal 135).

It is well known, as the Greeks knew, that the race of women is different to that of men. So when a woman conducts herself in a manner different from that prescribed by the cultural model codifying her, this exceptional conduct confers human status upon her—that is to say—transforms her into a man. Can it be that behind that admiration and urge to measure or identify her strength, her spirit, her courage, or her intelligence with that of men lies a certain unease or strange discomfort?[2] Difference becomes inscribed onto two parallel axes, contiguous or confused: the virile body's status and its relationship to the feminine.

And Above All the Body, the Virile Body, That Is

When we read Bernal attentively, one significant theme stands out: the omnipresence of the body. The Tabasqueños, says Bernal, "turned on us and met us face to face and fought most valiantly, making the greatest efforts, shouting and whistling and crying out . . ." (Bernal 50) Virile bodies inhabit the epic. Naturally, the act of conquest itself is tied to this notion in which the struggle is literally body to body: The blows tear the body open, swords wound it, lances penetrate it, cold burns it, and flints cleave it. Likewise, punishment threatens the corporeal integrity of those judged to be transgressors. Cortés orders that Spaniards caught stealing even a bit of bacon be flogged, or he has their hands or feet cut off. Dissidents are bought off with prebends or gold, and if he is unable to soften them up (a key image in the text) he has them hanged. Indian spies have their hands and thumbs severed, sending them as reprisal to Xicoténtcal the Younger, his enemy. Certain Spaniards suffer shameful diseases plainly articulated by the chronicler: "As some of our soldiers were suffering from pustules or running sores, their things pained them as they went down [to the great temple]" (Bernal 238). Others suffer from ridiculous back problems, their idleness on the island of Cuba leaving them ill prepared for the violent effort they must deploy during the Conquest.

In turn, Indians collect the corpses of their own dead, burying or burning them so they will not stink. They sacrifice their enemies, removing their hearts and eating their flesh. Bernal recounts how Cortés and his men visit the Templo Mayor led by Moctezuma. The almost intolerable scenes of coexistence with the cloven bodies and spilt blood are, nonetheless, contemplated and described by the invaders: "The walls were so clotted with blood and the soil so bathed with it that in the slaughter houses of Spain there is not such another stench . . . and the everything was covered with blood, both walls and altar, and the stench was such that we could hardly wait the moment to get our of it" (Bernal 220). Relationships with the body itself change as the Spaniards make their way through what will become New Spain, and this substantiation applies to the foreigners as well as the Indians. Racial differences play a decisive role, especially regarding the contrast between the hair covering European faces and the almost-hairless Indian features. Upon reading certain episodes, several facts merit reflection. In a skirmish between the Mexicas and some of Cortés' men who have been left holding the rear guard, the story of Arguello, a soldier, is told:

> In this skirmish a soldier named Arguello was taken alive. He was from León, with a very large head and a black, curly beard, very robust in appearance. To return to the facts. After the battle the Mexicans sent

> Montezuma the head of Arguello, who apparently died on the road from his injuries, for they took him alive. We know that when Montezuma was shown it, so robust and large, with such a long curly beard, he was terrified by it, and ordered not to offer it in any cue in Mexico, but only to the idols in other towns. (Bernal 179)

Moctezuma and Arguello's bodies are both virile, and yet the latter's is the one that causes disgust and above all terror to the monarch, just as the torn bodies, plucked hearts, and spilt and reeking blood are violently repellent to the Spaniards. Never before has the body's fragility come so sharply into focus. Moreover, never have racial differences provoked such rejection and checked such deeply rooted structures. Something comparable occurs when indigenous soldiers, bewildered by the unprecedented likeness of armed, bearded, and mounted men, are unable to recognize them as men, converting them into *teules,* gods or demons. It is necessary that Xicoténcatl the Younger capture a mare, gut her, and offer her up for sacrifice for his people to begin verifying their invaders' flagrant humanity, up to then feared for their resemblance to centaurs.

This same terror that Arguello's head causes in Moctezuma is experienced by the Spaniards when they see their companions slaughtered by the men of Texcoco and Mexico, sacrificed in a temple located in the province of Chalco:

> Much blood of the Spaniards who have been killed was found on the walls of the Temple in that pueblo, for they had sprinkled their Idols with it, and Sandoval also found two faces which had been flayed, and the skin for gloves, the beards were left on, and they had been placed as offering upon one of the altars. There were also found four tanned skins of horses very well prepared, with the hair on and the horse shoes, and they were hung before the Idols in the great Cue. There were also found many garments of the Spaniards who had been killed hung up as offerings to these same Idols, and on the pillar of a house where they had been imprisoned there was found written with charcoal: "Here was imprisoned the unfortunate Juan Yuste and many other whom I brought in my company." This Juan Yuste was a gentleman, and was one of the persons of quality whom Narvaez had brought with him. Sandoval and all his soldiers were moved to pity by all this and it grieved them greatly. . . . (Bernal 352)

Of another sort, since it is not apparently a sacrifice but a complete rejection of an imposed foreign culture, Melchorejo (one of the Indians who has served as translator in the expeditions towards Mexico and at Cortés's side) stages a ritual that should be taken into account. In order to understand the passage I am about to cite, it should be noted that the Indian translators, before acquiring their titles, had to be baptized and dressed in European clothing, as well as learn the foreign tongue that enabled them as translators: "The next morning Cortés ordered Pedro de Alvarado to set out in command of a hundred soldiers, fifteen of them with guns and crossbows, to examine the country inland for a distance of two leagues, and to take Melchorejo the interpreter in his company. When Melchorejo was looked for he could not be found as he had run off with the people of Tabasco, and it appears that the day before he had left the Spanish clothes that had been given to him hung up in the palm grove, and had fled by night in a canoe" (Bernal 54). The complication does not arise from the anecdote itself, which is from the Indian fleeing to join his people and fight against the aggressors, but rather in finding the way in which a society encounters the basis for its models. For the Spaniards, the interpreter is a mutilated body that becomes a rhetorical figure, the synecdoche, that takes a part for the whole, condensing his body into a single organ, the tongue. Despite the efficacy of its function, while at the same time and jarringly contradicting this symbolic operation, the body in its totality must incorporate another way of conceiving the body, another way of seeing, of encompassing it. The Indian must adopt the dress and religion of his master; when regaining his liberty, the slave recovers his true semblance, abandoning the garb that is denaturalizing him. "Spanish clothing" hung by Melchorejo in Palmar corresponds in reality, if we but look closely, to a sacrifice and can be compared to the Spaniards' clothing hung at the sacrificial altar, clothing added to the personal effects of those immolated in the province of Chalco. This fact is confirmed by a reading of the last part of this story: Melchorejo flees, dressed as an Indian, to swell the ranks of his brothers and advises them to fight the Spanish. He reveals their weaknesses, explains their tactics, and believes the Tabasqueños can overcome them. Cortés, however, wins the battle and Melchorejo is punished: "but we came to know that they had offered him as a sacrifice because his counsel had cost them so dear" (Bernal 64).

What is the Body of Tongues Made Of?

Curiously, the same does not occur to the bodies of the indigenous women who retain their original clothing. But even if their appearance remain unaltered, they must be baptized to become concubines to the captains or soldiers. Doña Marina is represented in the codices at Cortés's side always dressed in "the rich robes of the earth," as Bernal qualifies the indigenous women's typical garment, the *hipil.* Bernal shamelessly describes all the wounds and scars inflicted on the human body during battle in full detail; he also lists all the illnesses, the small everyday accidents—for example, how Cortés loses a sandal in the muck, thus diminishing his efficacy in battle, or how he is forced to impose a truce "porque estaba purgado el día antes, y purgóse con unas manzanillas que hay en la isla de Cuba." (188) And although he pays excessive attention to the bearing, countenance, and character of the men who will hold some weight later in the narration, as I have pointed out earlier and I will set out in greater detail later, when he speaks of women he simply notes whether they are fair or ugly—that is to say, their aesthetic assessment determines the measure of his desire. This rule applies equally to indigenous women and Spaniards. ("Anthonio de Villaroel was married to the handsome Isabel de Ojeda" explains Bernal, before the Conquest has been consummated [Bernal 292].) However, when characterizing Marina, he bestows moral as well as aesthetic qualities upon her. He states that she was of fair countenance, an excellent woman and good translator, as well as being meddlesome, uninhibited, and boisterous.

Upon the warrior's body, Bernal can assign the slightest minutiae; however, the woman's body remains invisible to discourse, or at the most, with a few adjectives he takes stock of her beauty or her lineage. In epic, the virile body configures a model of the masculine and is perceived in its most complete materiality, not as abstraction—fatigue, hunger, wounds are marked indelibly on distinct parts of the body. The women, whose bodies the soldiers enjoy and thanks to whom they are often able to eat, remain bodiless in discourse. If they do possess a body it is generic, abstract, destined for pleasure (and in turn chastely omitted from the description) or to "produce offspring"—a fact that, when it occurs, is declared as one that collapses under its own weight since women compose an anonymous mass, collective and multitudinous, that can be confused with the plunder, with the lavishly embroidered shrouds, the rough gold exquisitely and meticulously described even though it will be melted down, or with the chickens and other livestock. In the political terrain, modesty prohibits Bernal from naming the sexual act, intercourse with women taken as concubines, even if they are of noble descent, and must be baptized in order to legitimate the coitus.

This means that when we read Bernal or any other Spanish chronicler, mental processes more complex than the constant verification of antithetical categories must be sought out. The virile body, the warrior's body (that epic figure *par excellence*) is subject to mental processes, to textual constructions. The male bodies occupy a singular place in the tale, attest to their own heroism and engorge their presence, underscoring the bravery of a handful of men whose courage allows them to vanquish an innumerable amount of equally heroic soldiers. Each male body is worth its weight in gold and sets itself apart from the others through its singular specificity.

To recuperate the female body (which is in this specific case that of Doña Marina), to make sense of the silence observed in the text on this topic, or rather on what women mean in this war-torn, intrinsically masculine universe, I will have to turn to subterfuge, analyzing the recurring sequences in Bernal's discourse in which an individual male body is delineated. I begin this outline with the body of Jerónimo de Aguilar, impeccably described by Bernal: Cortés has heard that there are bearded—and therefore Spanish—in Yucatan and attempts to rescue them. After a few incidents Aguilar appears with five Cozumel Indians:

> When Andrés de Tapia saw that they were only Indians, he at once sent word to Cortés by a Spaniard that they were Cozumel Indians who had come in the canoe [. . .] Tapia soon brought the Spaniard to Cortés but before he arrived where Cortés was standing, several Spaniards asked Tapia where the Spaniard was? Although he was walking by his side, for they could not distinguish him from an Indian as he was naturally brown and had his hair shorn like an Indian Slave, and carried a paddle on his shoulder, he was shod with one old sandal and the other was tied to his belt, he had on a ragged old cloak, and a worse loin cloth, with which he covered his nakedness, and he had tied up, in a bundle in his cloak, a Book of Hours, old and worn. When Cortés saw him in this state, he too was deceived like the other soldiers, and asked Tapia: Where is the Spaniard?" On hearing this, the Spaniard squatted down on his haunches as the Indians do and said, "I am he." Cortés at once ordered him to be given a shirt and doublet and drawers and a cape and sandals, for he had no other clothes, and asked him about himself and what his name was and when he came to this country. The man replied, pronouncing with difficulty, that he was called Jerónimo de Aguilar, a native of Ecija. . . . (Bernal 45)

Bernal's account speaks to us indirectly of a social practice subject to a very advanced process of discursive elaboration, in which what is kept quiet becomes elucidated through what is said. In order to make sense of the silence reserved for women, whether or not it be about the starring Malinche, I will continue analyzing the recurring sequences where the Spanish body is defined as paradigm of the civilized.

Aguilar recounts what occurred with Gonzalo Guerrero, the Spaniard who preferred the culture of those who were later to become the defeated. I cite an extensive, well-known passage:

> Aguilar set out for the place, five leagues distant, where his companion Gonzalo Guerreo was living, but when he read the letter to him he answered: "Brother Aguilar, I am married and have three children and the Indians look at me as a Cacique and captain in wartime—You go, and God be with you, but I have my face tattooed and my ears pierced, what would the Spaniards say should they see me in this guise? And look how handsome these boys of mine are, for God's sake give me those green beads you have brought, and I will give the beads to them and say that my brothers have sent them from my own country." And the Indian wife of Gonzalo spoke to Aguilar in her own tongue very angrily and said to him: "What is this slave coming here for talking to my husband—go off with you, and don't trouble us with any more words." (Bernal 43)

Again the narrative describes bodies and their attire, Aguilar dressed as an Indian, but a poor Indian, like the Indians who come to seek an audience with Cortés, dressed in modest clothing and with blackened faces, an *embassy* that Aguilar and Doña Marina declare an insult. Aguilar has traded in his scant Indian clothing and slave's posture (slave among the slaves, since he is in Indian company) for a soldier's uniform that, although also precarious, allows him to function as a translator since he is dressed as a Spanish private.

Those interested in representations of the body within Bernal's text must not forget the following: that strict differences separating a European from an indigenous Mexican passed primarily through dress and body. Gonzalo Guerrero—whose name is somewhat oxymoronic since he is a warrior who does not wish to join his Spanish brothers in arms and therefore surrenders his good name—is now totally an Indian, and his countenance has undergone irrevocable transformations. Also, as Aguilar stresses, he abandons his religion, his culture, and his language for a woman—an Indian woman, to make matters worse. Moreover, this Indian woman appears to be more hardened than Guerrero, and the model of femininity proposed by the chronicle becomes inverted. Furthermore, just as Aguilar, Guerrero has assumed Indian gestures and body language, and as an Indian he asks for *rescates,* the green notes with which the Spaniards began their trade ceremonies with the natives. I repeat, this topic deserves a much deeper analysis; I leave it as it stands, in hopes of returning to it on another occasion. Now let us analyze, at last, the case of Doña Marina, our Most Excellent Tongue.

Doña Marina and Captain Malinche

I will be brief. I will sketch out an idea that I have already developed in a previous essay and would like to continue analyzing in the future.[3] I formulate a strange ambiguity, one produced by Bernal's text, specifically in the chronicle in which Doña Marina, despite traveling in *hipil* garb, on foot, always at the side of her master, who rides on horseback or seated on his folding chair, occupies center stage in the discourse next to Hernan Cortés, at least until the conquest of Tenochtitlán.

Cortés, in turn, mentions Marina only once in his *Quinta Carta de Relación,* an omission that defines the imposing category of the masculine as a foundation for the political. However, the text's silence should be supplemented by resorting to the figure of Malinali-Malinche-Marina in order to sketch the contours of an ambivalence toward virility, that most forceful of categories. It remains of utmost importance that this reflection takes place within epic—the chronicle of the "true history" of New Spain, which is imminently heroic—in which the masculine leaves traces of its important but nonetheless fragile status. Bernal, following the example of the Indians who also use the moniker, rebaptizes the conquistador Hernan Cortés in his chronicle as Captain Malinche. Indeed, the inexorable presence of Marina has altered his identity shortly after she becomes empowered as a translator. I transcribe the words of Bernal Diaz, which bluntly explain this transformation: "Before going on any further I wish to say that in all the towns we had passed through, and in others where they had heard of us, Cortés was called Malinche, and so I will call him Malinche from now henceforth in all the accounts of conversation which we held with any of the Indians. The reason why he was given this name is that Doña Marina, our interpreter, was always in his company, particularly when any Ambassadors arrived, and she spoke to them in the Mexican language. So that they gave Cortés the name of "Marina's Captain" and for the short Malinche" (Bernal 150).

The body of the conqueror has suffered a radical transformation—it has either been transferred to the Malinche's own body or confused with it. Furthermore, Bernal's vision has been contaminated, taking on the perspective of those conquered. The translator, or better yet, she who holds this office, Marina, the interpreter by antonomasia, bridges irreducible distances that separate women from the men on the basis of their social functions. Furthermore—and here the text takes a strange turn—the place of the discourse's recipient becomes fractured. That is to say, the Spanish recipient to whom the chronicle is addressed loses the solidity of his structure, because it is the vanquished Indian, the object and not the subject of discourse, who has the word, at least during this difficult and heroic phase during which the struggle between Spaniards and Indians has yet to be resolved. One final passage reinforces what was said earlier. Here Bernal recounts a skirmish between Spaniards and Mexicas, one of many such scuffles prior to the taking of Tenohtitlan by the Spaniards: "Our soldiers seeing that they could gain no advantage whatever, and that they could not hit on the road and causeway which was there before, because it was all covered with water, cursed the town and our profitless expedition, and were half ashamed because the Mexicans and townspeople shouted at them and called them women, and said that Malinche was a woman too, and that his only bravery was in deceiving them with stories and lies" (Bernal 357). Cortés-Malinche: a doubled body? The body of Doña Marina-Mallintzin, the interpreter, and that of Hernan Cortés become superimposed. Or are they perhaps a single unique body? For the indigenous people she is definitely the master of the discourse, and he, Cortés, Captain Malinche, chief of the Spaniards, is a man suddenly stripped of his virility, lacking a tongue because his words lack force—that is, the ability to be understood. Only the words emitted by a woman who masterfully fulfills her post as *lengua* (the ambiguities surrounding this term for "translator" are well known) actually reach the addressed: This operation of language acts on virility, clouding what should be a strict category, that of the masculine. Language games operate with a strange alchemy and transform the conqueror Hernan Cortés into a woman, because as the cited text reiterates, he is, like his soldiers, simply *another woman* . . .

In this exchange that disrupts the equilibrium between the masculine and the feminine, Cortés suffers the worst affront. He is incorporated into the Spaniard's most unspeakable, most feared, and despised sexual category, that of the invert, the sodomite. Let us finish with this fragment from Bernal, which I hope confirms what I've stated above:

> The Great Montezuma was about forty years old, of good height and well proportioned, slender and spare of flesh, not very swarthy, but of

the natural color and shade of an Indian. He did not wear his hair long, but so as just to cover his ears, his scanty black beard was well shaped and thin. His face was somewhat long, but cheerful, and he had good eyes and showed in his appearance and manner both tenderness and when necessary, gravity. He was very neat and clean and bathed once every day in the afternoon. He had many women as mistresses, daughters of Chieftains, and he had two great Cacicas as his legitimate wives. *He was free from unnatural offences. . . .* (Bernal 208)

Notes

* Translated by Joaquín Terrones and Emily Ludmir. All passages from the Bernal Diaz chronicle are taken from the classic translation into English by A. P. Maudslay (1908), reprinted in 1996 with an introduction by Hugh Thomas (New York: Da Capo Press, 1996). The italics are the author's, except as noted.

1. From the translation by J. H. Cohen. See: Diaz, Bernal. The Conquest of New Spain (London: Penguin Books, 1963).
2. See: Nicole Loreaux. *Les expériences de Tiresias,* Paris, Gallimard, 1989.
3. Glantz, Margo. "La Malinche, la lengua en la mano." In: Glantz, Margo ed. *La Malinche, sus padres y sus hijos,* México, UNAM, 1994.

10

Bilingual Blues, Bilingual Bliss

El caso Casey

Gustavo Pérez-Firmat

In a letter written toward the end of his life, Ivan Turgenev remarked that a writer who did not write only in his mother tongue was "a thief and a pig."[1] Although Turgenev did not explain the epithets, it's not difficult to figure out what he meant. Since a language is a form of cultural property, a writer who uses words that don't belong to him is a thief; and since his theft of the words of others entails the neglect of his own, he is a pig. As it happens, Turgenev wrote his letter in German, though apparently for him the use of other languages in correspondence didn't count as an infraction against his mother tongue. Indeed, it is revealing that Turgenev, in spite of his mastery of several foreign languages and his many years of residence outside Russia, never took advantage of the opportunity, or yielded to the temptation, of writing fiction in a language other than Russian. Once, when a reviewer incorrectly stated that Turgenev had written one of his novellas originally in French, an offended Turgenev pointed out—in flawless French—that he would never stoop to something so base.

Turgenev's attitude toward the Russian language offers an instance of the phenomenon that Uriel Weinreich has termed "language loyalty," that powerful, deep-seated attachment that many of us feel toward what we term our "mother" tongue.[2] Although in Western culture the sentiment of language loyalty goes back to ancient Greece, it's only recently that individual languages have acquired the pull and prestige that they now enjoy. As Leonard Forster has pointed out, for several centuries multilingualism was the norm rather than the exception among European writers.[3] A sixteenth-century neo-Latin poet felt few qualms about not using his mother tongue for literary composition;

and even writers who worked primarily in the vernacular also wrote, without apparent damage to their self-esteem, in other languages: Milton composed Italian sonnets, Garcilaso wrote Latin odes. It was not until the rise of nationalism in the eighteenth and nineteeth centuries that native languages became national languages, and thus a privileged cultural possession. This has remained true to this day. For most of us, as for Turgenev, the language that we speak is a fundamental component of our nationality and hence our sense of who we are. That is why, when we want to attack someone's claims about his nationality, we often take aim at his language skills: How can that guy be Cuban? He doesn't even speak Spanish. Or: Funny, you don't sound like an American.

In my own case I have always felt a mixture of regret and remorse that I have not done more of my writing, and my living, in Spanish. Sometimes I have even thought that every one of my English sentences hides the absence of the Spanish sentence that I wasn't willing or able to write. Why I haven't tried to work more in Spanish is something that I've wondered about, something that I'm wondering about right now, but that I don't entirely understand. I know of course the practical reasons for my use of English, but I also suspect that there may be other, more murky motives of which I'm only half-aware: resentment, anger, fear of failure, maybe even a little self-hatred. If you say "tomato" and I say *tu madre,* the code-switching expletive may be a symptom of the speaker's unhappiness with his mother tongue, with his other tongue, and most of all, perhaps, with himself. And if you say "latino" and I say *la tuya,* this expletive may reflect his unwillingness to accept the consequences of his switch in loyalties.

I wish rather to speak to you about another little-known and conflicted Cuban writer, a man with the unlikely name of Calvert Casey. Along with Guillermo Cabrera Infante, Edmundo Desnoes, Antón Arrufat, Heberto Padilla, Lisandro Otero, and some others, Casey formed part of the generation of writers and intellectuals that came into prominence with the triumph of the Cuban Revolution in 1959. During those heady days of the early sixties, Casey was everywhere—hobnobbing with visiting writers, making the rounds of book exhibits and cocktail parties, contributing to *Lunes de Revolución* and *Casa de las Américas,* and writing a couple of well-received books, *El regreso* (1962), a collection of stories, and *Memorias de una isla* (1964), a volume of essays. It was also during these years that he acquired the nickname of La Calvita, a punning reference both to his hairline and to his homosexuality. But in 1965, during a trip to Poland for the publication of the Polish translation of his stories, Casey decided not to return to Cuba, at least in part because of the revolution's persecution of homosexuals. Eventually settling in Rome, a city that for some reason that reminded him of Havana, he worked as a translator and continued to write stories. In 1967 Seix Barral published an expanded edition of *El regreso* and, a couple of years later, a new volume of stories, *Notas de un simulador*, which turned out to be his last. In May 1969, despondent over an unhappy love affair, La Calvita committed suicide by taking an overdose of sleeping pills.

For years after his death, Casey was nearly forgotten. In the eyes of the cultural commissars on the island, there had never been a Cuban writer named Calvert Casey. Like other exiled writers, he was of course not included in the important two-volume *Diccionario de la literatura cubana* published in Havana in 1980. Even critics of Spanish American fiction writing outside of Cuba tended to ignore him.[4] It was not until 1993, nearly a quarter-century after his death, that the Cuban journal *Unión* began his rehabilitation by reprinting several of Casey's stories as well as a dossier of critical and personal appreciations.[5] Two years later, a selection of his work appeared in Spain; and this was followed in 1998 with a volume in English of Casey's fiction.[6]

Several reasons account for Casey's lapse into obscurity. One is that he was an exiled Cuban writer at a time, the late sixties, when it was unfashionable to be an exiled Cuban writer. And what is worse, he was an exiled, homosexual Cuban writer. Another reason had to do with bad timing: In the decade when Latin American novelists were publishing big, booming novels, Casey was writing what he termed "notes," six- and seven-page miniatures without family trees or banana plantations. And Casey himself, because he had very mixed feelings about the value of his work, didn't help himself much by lapsing into periods of inactivity. As he once said, "mas silencio, menos corrupción."[7] But there is one more reason, I think, for Casey's neglect: He is one of those writers whom Turgenev would have considered a thief and a pig, since he wrote fiction in more than one language. Although the bulk of Casey's work is in Spanish, two English-language stories bracket his Spanish-language fiction; that is to say, both his first story and his last story were written in English. What is more, it is now generally agreed that Casey's single most powerful performance is his last story, a brilliant short monologue entitled "Piazza Margana" that he wrote in the months before his death. The Cuban critic Víctor Fowler has gone so far as to assert that this story is "nuestro supremo texto del goce."[8] It is striking—is it not?—that Cuban literature's supreme text of bliss would be written in a language other than Spanish; it is also striking that Fowler, who lives in Cuba, uses the possessive "nuestro" unselfconsciously, as if Casey's English were irrelevant to an assessment of his work's cultural location.

But Casey's case is complicated, because, if he was a thief and a pig, it's not clear which language he was betraying and which language he was stealing from. Born in Baltimore of a Cuban mother whose first language was Spanish and an American father, Casey grew up speaking English. By the time he was an adolescent, Casey and his mother had moved to Cuba, but some years later he returned to his homeland, the United States, where he lived for the next ten years. It was after his return to the States in the late 1940s that Casey began to write fiction; his first story, "The Walk," was published in the *New Mexico Quarterly* in 1954, when Casey was thirty years old.[9]

Then, a couple of years later, while still living in New York, Casey began sending notes and essays in Spanish to the Cuban magazine *Ciclón,* and in 1958 he moved back to Cuba. Although he spoke Spanish with an American accent, he made a determined effort to become a part of the Cuban literary scene, and he continued to write in Spanish until the last couple of years of his life, when—surprisingly—he launched into a novel in English, a language that he had not used for literary expression in fifteen years.

That Casey switched back to English toward the end of his life is all the more puzzling given that he had insisted for years that he was a Cuban writer rather than, as some people thought, an American who had emigrated to Cuba. Depending on his mood, he would rail at reviewers for mistaking him for an American, or lacerate himself because of his ambiguous name—"mi eufónico y despreciable nombrecito," as he once called it.[10] And yet not only did Casey choose English for this project, he also remarked to the Spanish critic Rafael Martínez Nadal that this work was his most personal: "allí estaba, al desnudo, mi íntima verdad."[11]

It turns out, then, that the same man who resented his anglophone name—"nuestro infecto nombrecito," he also called it[12]—resorted to English when the time came to write the "naked" truth about himself. But can a Cuban writer ever lose his clothes in English? Doesn't an intimate truth become less intimate when it is rendered in someone else's language? Paradoxically, even as the publication in Spain of Casey's two story collections, *El regreso* and *Notas de un simulador,* was introducing his work to a wider readership, Casey himself was holed up in a shabby Rome apartment making sure that those very readers would not have direct access to his intimate truth.

What I would like to do is try to understand Casey's equivocal striptease by looking more closely at the fragment of the novel that he left behind. What we know about the genesis of this work is this: In the summer of 1967, Casey fell in love with a young Italian named Gianni. At the time, Casey was in his mid-forties; Gianni was no more than twenty. The relationship was passionate but stormy, with rifts and reconciliations that Casey described as a cycle of "riñas, besitos, riñas, besitos."[13] Only a few months after meeting Gianni, Casey got the idea for a new book, which he described in a letter to his friend Cabrera Infante as "una maravillosa novela de amor, terrible, antropofágica, pues así es como suele ser el amor."[14] Calling the work-in-progress "Gianni, Gianni," Casey worked on it, on and off, for the next year and a half—that is to say, for the rest of his life. Less than a month before his suicide, he confided to Rafael Martínez Nadal that he had destroyed most of his novel because several friends, one of whom was Cabrera Infante, thought it unpublishable. The only part he saved, he said, was the seven-page monologue entitled "Piazza Margana." Handing it to Martínez Nadal, Casey explained why it was written in English: "Debí escribirlo en italiano porque en italiano está pensado y sentido, el italiano es su *habitat*, pero como no domino el idioma, y como en este caso particular el español no me servía, recurrí al inglés, mi segunda lengua."[15]

By suggesting that Spanish was not a suitable vehicle for the story, Casey is evoking the phenomenon that linguists term *diglossia*—that is, the use of different languages for different purposes. If a bilingual is someone who can handle two languages interchangeably, the diglossic individual is someone whose verbal bilingualism

is complicated by a bilingualism of thought or feeling, by the sense that objects, events, emotions come with words attached. Although we can't be sure what Casey meant when he said that Spanish would not do "in this particular case," "en este caso particular," what does seem clear is that Casey's choice of English—a preference already evident in his use of an anglicism, habitat, to describe the story's linguistic environment—was a matter to which he had given some thought. As many of his stories make clear, Casey realized that to speak a language was to occupy a place, to settle into a cultural habitat with its own history and contours. That is why he remarks, in one of the essays gathered in *Memorias de una isla*, that the user of a language becomes a spokesman for all those who have preceded him in that language. As, he puts it, to say *alpaca* is to let an anonymous Quechua Indian speak with our lips; to say *arar* is to become one with the voice of a Spanish peasant. For the writer the question then becomes: "Cómo perpetúo yo los movimientos de millares y millares de labios?"[16] But if this is what Casey believed, why did he choose to sever his ties with the historical community of Spanish speakers? And on behalf of whom was Casey speaking when he elected English as the habitat of "Piazza Margana"?

These questions are all the more relevant because "Piazza Margana" narrates the taking over of someone's body. Having already written written about *espiritismo* in "Los visitantes," Casey here takes the idea of possession to a literal extreme. This is how the story begins:

> I have now entered your bloodstream. I have gone beyond urine, beyond excrement and its sweet, acrid taste, and have at last lost myself in the warm recesses of your body. I am here to stay. I will never leave it. From my vantage point, where I have finally attained bliss, I see the world through your eyes, hear the most frightening and the most enchanting sounds through your ears, taste all tastes with your tongue, feel all shapes with your hands. What else could a man desire? Forever and ever "emparadised in thee." "Envejeceremos juntos, dijiste," and we will.[17]

In the paragraph that follows, Casey goes on to explain the background to this dramatic opening: One day, after he and Gianni had had a particularly bitter quarrel, Gianni cut himself while shaving. Dressing the wound, Casey felt tempted to drink his lover's blood and eat his flesh. But then he realized that a more definitive way of possessing Gianni was to lodge himself inside his body—which he proceeded to do. The act of possession completed, the rest of the story recounts Casey's marvel-filled exploration of Gianni's insides. Each organ is described in loving, sometimes delirious, detail: the brain, the ears, the nose, the mouth, the heart, the lungs, the large and small intestines, the testicles, the penis. This fantastic "safari," as Casey calls it, ends up—where else?—in his lover's rectum, where La Calvita has to dodge large, slow-moving shapes that threaten to crush him, or rather, *aplastarlo*. Finally finding a safe haven within the "forest of giants," Casey ends his journey, and the story, with the following words: "This is Paradise. I have found it. Unlike Columbus I will not be shipped home in a hold with bound feet. No Canossa for me either. I have entered the Kingdom of Heaven and taken proud possession of it. This is my private claim, my heritage, my fief. I am NOT leaving" (193). Perhaps we can now begin to see why Casey—*el Colón del colon*—decided not to write this story in his mother's tongue. Even though some of Casey's Hispanophone fiction anticipates "Piazza Margana," none of it comes close to it in the explicitness with which Casey expresses his desire for, and his enjoyment of, the male body.[18] Since the bulk of Casey's fiction was written in Cuba during the early 1960s, censorship or the fear of reprisal may well account for Casey's reticence in discussing homosexuality.[19] But this doesn't explain why, once he had left Cuba, he felt that he could not write "Piazza Margana" in Spanish. The issue here would be not censorship but self-censorship, a peculiar combination of reserve and exhibitionism that made it possible for him to state in one language truths that he could not utter in another. If the Hispanophone Casey is not quite straight, neither does he voice his pleasure with the relish displayed in "Piazza Margana."

George Steiner has suggested that for a writer such as Oscar Wilde, bilingualism may be an "expressive enactment of sexual duality."[20] Although the relation between language choice and sexual identity is surely more complicated than this, Steiner is right in pointing to their connection. And his reference to Wilde is certainly relevant here, for "Piazza Margana" is, in effect, Casey's *De Profundis,* but with two twists: the first is that, unlike Wilde, Casey elects to address his lover in a language different from that in which the relationship unfolded; the second is that Casey cries out not only from the depths of his soul—*de profundis*—but from the bowels of his lover's body.

Not only is the subject matter of "Piazza Margana" different from anything Casey had written before, but the style and diction of the story also set it apart from his earlier work. Casey's Spanish prose is spare, economical; it relies on dialogue and descriptions of Old Havana cityscapes. In contrast, "Piazza Margana" has no dialogue; in spite of the title the only locale is the pink bioscape of Gianni's insides; and the prose is dense and allusive. Let me give just one example: at the end of the story's first paragraph, Casey asserts that he has become "emparadised" in Gianni: "Forever and ever 'emparadised in thee.'" Though now archaic, the verb "emparadise" occurs with some frequency in sixteenth- and seventeenth-century English. In Book IV of *Paradise Lost,* for example, Milton describes Adam and Eve as "Imparadised in each other's arms"—a context of use consistent with Casey's. But the word also occurs in religious liturgy, and the phrase in Casey's story is actually lifted from a hymn by John Wesley, the founder of Methodism. Entitled "Come, Father, Son and Spirit," the hymn says in part:

> O wouldst Thou stamp it now on mine
> The name and character Divine,
>   The Holy One in Three!

Come, Father, Son, and Spirit, give
Thy love,—Thyself: and lo! I live
Imparadised in Thee.[21]

This quotation, which may be one of the rare moments in Casey's fiction that evoke his American childhood, injects into the story a motif to which Casey will return several times, that of the mystical union of the lover and the beloved, of the *Amada en el Amado transformada.* According to several of Casey's friends, one of the books that most impressed him during the last years of his life was Miguel de Molinos's *Guía espiritual,* a notorious seventeeth-century mystical work that was banned by the Inquisition.[22] Deep inside Gianni, Casey exclaims: "What infinite quietude, what peace" (192). Molinos's heretical doctrine, of course, was called *quietismo.* Thus, just as Casey literalizes the title of Wilde's *De Profundis,* he also gives a scandalously carnal meaning to the *camino interior* of mystical doctrine, which in this instance does not lead up to the godhead but down to Gianni's asshole.

Also enriching the story's texture is its latent and blatant multilingualism. The blatant part shows up in quotations from Spanish and Italian; the latent part arises from the proliferation of Latinate nouns, most of them anatomical terms that give Casey's English a decidedly "foreign" and even a "Spanish" feel. A quirky Latin lover, Casey delights in piling *latinajo* upon *latinajo:* "The thalamus, the thalamus! Where is the thalamus after the horrors of the claustrum, the lunar light of the globus pallidus" (190). Or: "I take to the depths: periosteum, outer table, diploe, inner table, sutures, calvaria" (190). Because these depths are not only physiological but lexical, the discoveries along the way are sometimes linguistic. The "calvaria" is the skull; but since "calvaria" is also the root of the Spanish *calvo,* Calvert, La Calvita, is making an onomastic pun; indeed, he's alluding to one of the nicknames he used for himself, "Calvario." Not only does Casey lodge himself inside Gianni's organs, he inhabits their very names with his own name.

Let me now cite a brief passage from Casey's other English story, "The Walk." Apparently autobiographical, "The Walk" describes the failed sexual initiation of an adolescent named Ciro, who is taken by his uncle to a brothel for the first time. Pronounced in English, the name of the protagonist already tells us what happens inside the brothel: zero. But this is how the narrator describes the rumor that Ciro is going to lose his virginity:

> It transgressed the limits of the household, trickled down the inner court to the neighbors, flowed past the iron grates of the balconies overlooking the streets and poured finally into the entire neighborhood.[23]

Here is Casey's own Spanish version of this sentence:

> Aquello cruzaba los límites de la casa, atravesaba el patio para infiltrarse en el de los vecinos, salía por la baranda del balcón y trascendía a todo el vecindario.[24]

The basic difference between the two versions is that the translation eliminates the fluvial metaphor: Instead of "trickled . . . flowed . . . poured," we have "atravesaba . . . salía . . . trascendía." The image of the spilling of a liquid—one charged with sexual connotations—disappears; and even the use of the imperfect tense in the Spanish version attenuates the sense of a tide or a flood that rises to a climactic outpouring. This is typical of the differences between Casey's English and Spanish. Compared to his English, Casey's Spanish is sparse, affectless—in a word, *seco*. Another change in the story: In the English original, when Ciro goes into the bedroom with the young prostitute, the black boy who works in the brothel breaks out into a fit of jealousy that the narrator labels a "torrent of words" (9). In the Spanish translation, the boy's jealousy disappears, and with it the verbal torrent. This process of semantic dehydration is carried into the smallest stylistic details: For example, in English the strong smell of Ciro's uncle's aftershave is described as "waves of cologne" (4); in Spanish, the waves evaporate and instead we read only about his "olor a colonia" (47); in English the black attendant's high-pitched voice is called a "thin stream of voice" (7), but in Spanish it becomes simply "la voz atiplada" (52).

My point is that what Casey suppresses in "El paseo," the Spanish-language title of "The Walk," is what he gives vent to in "Piazza Margana," which happens to be the account of a very different kind of *paseo*. From the very first sentence of "Piazza Margana"—"I have now entered your bloodstream"—the speaker inhabits a liquid world, a corporal geography of streams and eddies and channels and islands, one that perhaps will remind us—and that perhaps reminded Casey—of the Caribbean. Exploring Gianni's brain, Casey sucks up the moisture of the membranes; touring the bladder, he is nearly flushed out; drifting down a large artery, he gets "dragged by the torrent" (189); navigating the intestinal flora, he imagines himself traveling to the sources of the Nile. In Spanish, Casey reaches for dry land, for the stability and safety that he often associated with the words *sosiego* and *bienestar*.[25] Stories such as "El regreso," "Los visitantes," and "Mi tía Leocadia, el amor y el Paleolítico Inferior" record Casey's need for familial and communal connection. But the price of connection seems to be aridity, and the hydraulic imagery present incipiently in "The Walk" and lavishly in "Piazza Margana" all but disappears from his Spanish-language fiction. It's perhaps not a coincidence that the one Spanish phrase in "Piazza Margana—"envejeceremos juntos, dijiste"—refers not to the humid ecstasy of sex but to the milder and drier pleasures of companionship.

In English Casey is a different writer, and maybe a different man, than he is in Spanish. That's why he said, "en este caso particular el español no me servía." "Este caso particular" is also "este Casey particular," the one who oozes, who gushes, who goes with the flow even if it means drowning in the effluvia. If Spanish does not serve him, it's because, for Casey, Spanish is not self-serving. In the diglossic world of Casey's fiction, Spanish is the language of family, of community, of history, of the *sosiego* of social life and the *bienestar* of companionship; English is the vehicle for solitary self-assertion.

And here we finally reach the heart of the story, which is indistinguishable from La Calvita's own broken heart. Although he claims over and over to have lost himself—indeed, to have lost his self, his individuality—inside Gianni, the truth is that it's hard to imagine a more narcissistic performance than "Piazza Margana." From the very first paragraph, Casey insists on the first-person singular with self-serving fury: "I have now entered . . . I have gone beyond . . . I am here . . . I am not leaving." In the rest of the story, Casey's "I" will recur nearly one hundred times; even when he momentarily lapses into Italian, the language that he shared with his lover, it is to cry out: "Sono io, sono io!" "It is I, it is I." Only when he is talking about growing old does he refer to Gianni and himself as a "we"—as happens in that Spanish sentence at the end of the first paragraph, "envejeceremos juntos," where once again Spanish appears as the language of companionship. But *juntos* is what Gianni and Casey are not. In spite of his assertions, there is no togetherness here, no merging of identities, no meeting of body or mind, but only an isolated "I" straining after an inaccessible "you."

Feeling abandoned by his lover and betrayed by his country, Casey chooses a language that neither one will understand, a language that, in the words of the last sentences of the story, will be his "private claim," his "heritage," his "fief." No longer a resident of Havana or even of Rome, Casey becomes a citizen of the state of bliss, a homeland-for-one that exists only within his lush and lovely English prose. Toward the end of his monologue he says: "I have attained what no political or social system could ever dream of attaining: I am free, utterly free inside you, forever free from all fears and cares. No exit permit, no entry permit, no passport, no borders, no visa, no carta d'identità, no nothing!" (188–89). I read this sentence as a linguistic loyalty oath. If Casey is "utterly free," it's because his is a freedom in utterance. If he can come and go as he pleases, it's because the only borders that confine him are those of the page. And if he needs no ID card, it's because he is in the act of authorizing his own.

Emerson, who was never an exile, once declared: "utterance is place enough." Like many of Emerson's aphorisms, this one isn't really true, but it's true enough. When he has no other place to live, a writer must live in the writing; when he has nobody's body to settle into, he can always settle into his words. "I am here to stay" (187, 190), Casey repeats with the nervousness of a man who knows that he is in transit. "I can choose to settle on the right nipple" (189), he asserts with the willfulness of the helpless. In the end all that La Calvita could do was curl himself up inside his father's tongue. That's why the final sentence of the story is so moving: "I am NOT leaving," he says, knowing that Gianni has already left. "I am NOT leaving," he says, and then takes an overdose of sleeping pills. These words, La Calvita's last, would be pathetic were it not that, in reading them, we make them true. To whom is "Piazza Margana" finally addressed? Not to Gianni, who wouldn't have understood it, and certainly not to Casey's Cuban readers, who didn't have access toit. It is we, readers he could not have foreseen, *visitantes* he could not have anticipated, whom Casey is addressing. It is our brain he is licking, our skin he has gotten under. *We* are Gianni. Or rather, *you* are Gianni. Me, I'm just another English-speaking Cuban writer with water on his mind.

Notes

1. Ivan Turgenev and Ludwig Pietsch, *Briefe aus den jahren 1864–1883*, ed. Alfred Doren (Berlin: Im Propyläen Verlag, 1923), 147.
2. Uriel Weinrich, *Languages in Contact* (New York: Publications of the Linguistic Circle of New York, Number 1, 1953); see also Joshua A. Fishman, *Language Loyalty in the United States* (The Hague: Mouton, 1966); and Sumathi Ramaswamy, *Passions of the Tongue: Language Devotion in Tamil India, 1891–1970* (Berkeley: University of California Press, 1997).
3. Leonard Forster, *The Poet's Tongues: Multilingualism in Literature* (London: Cambridge University Press, 1970).
4. Two exceptions: in 1970, the inaugural issue of the Cuban-exile journal *Alacrán Azul* included a dossier of essays, poems, and fragments of correspondence by and about Casey ("Calvert Casey, In Memoriam," *Alacrán Azul*, 1:1 [1970], pp. 23–33); ten years later, the

Spanish journal *Quimera* in its December 1982 issue also published several essays about Casey, including Guillermo Cabrera Infante's influential "¿Quién mató a Calvert Casey?"

5. *Unión* 16 (1993) includes essays by Jesús Vega, María Zambrano, Italo Calvino, Severo Sarduy, Miguel Barnet, Luis Marré, Luis Agüero, and Humberto Arenal; the pieces by Zambrano, Calvino and Sarduy had already appeared in *Quimera.*
6. Calvert Casey, *Notas de un simulador,* selección y prólogo de Mario Merlino (Madrid: Montesinos, 1997); Calvert Casey, *The Collected Stories,* ed. Ilán Stavans (Durham, N.C.: Duke University Press, 1998).
7. Calvert Casey, letter to Guillermo Cabrera Infante, February 21 [1967], G. Cabrera Infante Papers, Princeton University Libraries.
8. Víctor Fowler, "El siglo XIX de Casey y el proyecto de Ciclón," *Unión* 25 (1996), 14; see also Fowler's perceptive reading of this story, "Piazza Morgana" [*sic*], in *La maldición: Una historia del placer como conquista* (La Habana: Editorial Letras Cubanas, 1998), 128–140. Jesús Vega labels "Piazza Morgana" "su fabulación más terrífica e impresionante" ("El último regreso de Calvert Casey," *Unión* 16 (1993), 31.
9. Although "The Walk" is considered Casey's literary debut, Ambrosio Fornet and Humberto Arenal mention a book that Casey supposedly published during the 1940s. Fornet, in the introductory note to Casey's selection in *Antología del cuento cubano contemporáneo* (Mexico City: Ediciones Era, 1967), states that Casey pseudonymously published "una apología de Martí que él mismo se encarga de recoger y de la que no queda rastro"; Humberto Arenal, in a reminiscence included in the *Unión* volume ("Calvert, aquel adolescente tímido, tartamudo y otras cosas más"), indicates that before leaving Cuba to resettle in the United States in 1946 or 1947, Casey published a novel entitled "Los paseantes." Like Fornet, I have not been able to find any trace of the Martí apology, but in 1941 there was indeed a "novela breve" published in Havana under that title by one "José de América." Given that the pseudonym could be confused with a reference to Martí, it is possible that Fornet and Arenal are talking about the same book. Casey's authorship of this novel, however, would be extraordinary—not only because in 1941 he was only seventeen years old, but also because the tone and style of the volume are quite foreign to anything Casey ever wrote. A sample: "Hortensias y gladiolos se agrupan en las veredas y están hoy más enamorados que nunca: ellas, rebosantes, satisfechas; ellos, altivos, con su aire de nobles caballeros; las moyas y las margaritas, hermanas, desnudan su entraña al sol, mostrando su matriz nieve y oro y la violeta de púrpura desmaya su delicada cabecita ruborizada de su prístina belleza" (*Los paseantes,* 8). It is difficult to believe that Casey, no mat-

ter how great his talent for *simulación,* could have written this; nonetheless, the title does evoke that of one of Casey's best-known stories, "El paseo."

10. Calvert Casey, letter to Guillermo Cabrera Infante, February 28, 1967, G. Cabrera Infante Papers.
11. Rafael Martínez Nadal, "Calvert Casey y notas a una lectura de Piazza Margana," *Quimera,* 26 (diciembre 1982), 85.
12. Calvert Casey, letter to Guillermo Cabrera Infante, May 15, 1967, G. Cabrera Infante Papers.
13. Calvert Casey, letter to Guillermo Cabrera Infante, November 12, 1967, G. Cabrera Infante Papers.
14. Calvert Casey, letter to Guillermo Cabrera Infante, undated (perhaps February 1968).
15. Martínez Nadal, 85–86. It was not until ten years after Casey's suicide that "Piazza Margana" was finally published in a Canadian literary magazine, *The Malahat Review* (July 1981); its Spanish translation, by Vicente Molina Foix, was published alongside Martínez Nadal's essay in *Quimera.* It is somehow apt that Casey's meeting with Martínez Nadal, during which he explained why he had switched to English, took place on April 23.
16. *Memorias de una isla* (La Habana: Ediciones R, 1964), 90–91.
17. I am quoting from Calvert Casey, *The Collected Stories* (187). Further page references are included in the text. Casey's use of two languages creates a curious editorial situation: *The Collected Stories,* a volume of English translations of his stories, also includes two stories in the original ("Piazza Margana" and "The Walk"); on the other hand, the recent collection in Spanish of his work, *Notas de un simulador,* includes Vicente Molina Foix's translation of "Piazza Margana" as well as Casey's own Spanish version of "The Walk."
18. In "El regreso," written a decade earlier, Casey anticipates the subject of "Piazza Margana": while describing his relationship with a man named Alejandro, the narrator states: "¡Ah, poder ser como Alejandro, poder *ser* Alejandro!" (*Notas de un simulador,* 82).
19. When Casey reprinted one of his early essays, "Notas sobre pornografía," in *Memorias de una isla,* he deleted several references to homosexuality that had been part of the original version of the essay, first published in *Ciclón* in 1956.
20. *Extraterritorial* (New York: Atheneum, 1971), 5.
21. John and Charles Wesley, *The Poetical Works of John and Charles Wesley* (London: Wesleyan-Methodist Conference Office, 1870), VII, 327.
22. Vicente Molina Foix, "En la muerte de Calvert Casey," *Insula,* 272–273 (julio-agosto 1969), 40; María Zambrano, "Calvert Casey, el indefenso," *Quimera,* 26 (diciembre 1982), 60. In a letter to Cabrera Infante, Casey wrote: "Aquí en Roma, todo deja de tener

importancia; estoy más cerca de ese quietismo nirvanesco que tú tanto odias y yo tanto ansío. Tres semanas busqué por Madrid las obras del Padre Mariana, el gran quietista español excomulgado por esa cocinera incansable que era Santa Teresa y su amiga [*sic*] o hermana [*sic*] San Juan de la Cruz, activistas insufribles" (May 15, 1967, G. Cabrera Infante Papers). Casey confuses Miguel de Molinos with Juan de Mariana.

23. Casey, "The Walk," in *The Collected Stories,* 2; the story was originally published in the *New Mexico Quarterly* (Winter 1954–55), 407–419.
24. *Notas de un simulador,* 45. Other page references are given in the text. Casey's Spanish translation of "The Walk," "El paseo," was originally included in *El regreso* (1962).
25. As he puts it in "El regreso," a story based on his return to Cuba in 1957: "¿y si regresara a los suyos, a amarlos a todos, a ser uno de ellos, a vivir aunque fuera entre los más pobres, entre aquellos que a pesar de su pobreza parecían tan tranquilos y contentos, tan sosegados. ¡Cómo le gustaba la palabra! Tan sosegados. ¿No le harían un lugar?" (*Notas de un simulador,* 90).

11

The Mother Tongue*

Benigno Trigo

Speaking another language is quite simply the minimum and primary condition for being alive.

—*Julia Kristeva,* Intimate Revolt

In an interview with the *New York Times,* Rosario Ferré says that she felt distant enough to explore the death of her mother in her writing only when she began to write in English. Before that, she says she found it impossible to deal with the subject because it was taboo in her native Spanish (Navarro 2). A year later she describes her novel *Eccentric Neighborhoods,* written in English, in the same terms. The novel is "an attempt to lay bare the relationships between mothers and daughters," an attempt, she says, to come to terms with the death of her mother in 1969 (Burch 31). In both interviews Rosario says that writing in English gives her a psychological distance that allows her to write about that loss. She describes writing in English "as if another person were writing" (Navarro 2). Writing in that other language makes her feel like a spectator, less vulnerable. She suggests that language is a contradictory boundary. On the one hand, it can be a distance between the writer and its subject. She compares English to a brush that mediates between the painter and the canvas. But language can also be a porous space of passage. Language, she says, meaning Spanish (her mother tongue), "is like your skin" (Navarro 2).

Rosario's reflections on writing, language, and loss raise three important questions. First, what makes writing about the loss of the mother difficult and even impossible for her? Why is writing about the death of the mother a taboo? Who or what makes it a taboo? Second, why is it so important and even necessary to write about that loss, to break that taboo? And third, what are the implications of breaking that taboo in another language? What does it mean that Rosario can write about the loss of her mother only by displacing her mother tongue, by losing her collective language, by shedding her own skin?

I. Dies Irae

In her book of essays, *Room for Eros* (*Sitio a Eros*) published in 1980, Rosario listens for an echo of the wrath that haunts her own writing. It is a sound, a ferocity, a furious tone also found in the writings of other women writers, an irascible sound that recalls the Wrath of the Lord in Mozart's *Requiem*. Following Walter Benjamin's dictum, she aims "at the single spot where the echo is able to give, in its own language, the reverberation of the work in the alien one" (Benjamin 76). Rosario translates into Spanish the wrath, fury, and irascibility of Mary Shelley, George Sand, and Virginia Woolf (among other women writers). She describes wrath both as a timeless negative light and as a spectrum of energies and wavelengths. She compares it to a constant radiation from an indefinite place that she sometimes locates outside, in the heavens, and at other times finds inside the body. She compares the radiation to both an ancestral universal force that gives birth to the stars, and to a fever that turns the body livid and eventually kills it.

The book is a collection of thirteen essays. They are for the most part brief pieces that Rosario has described as a series of *exempla* meant for young women (*Coloquio,* 108). The longest essay in the book, however, is an ambitious piece that reaches far beyond the "example." Entitled "The Kindness of Wrath" ("Las bondades de la ira"), it is a poetics of anger. In this polemical and unapologetic essay, Rosario demystifies women's writing, shattering the myths surrounding, imprisoning, and silencing its voice. She traces back the laws governing the irascible artistic creation of women writers like Sylvia Plath, Alfonsina Storni, and Delmira Agustini to an opaque acoustic and visual source: a phonographic negative, the inverse, the opposite, the other side of their own voice and light (*Sitio a Eros,* 99).

A negative placed on a positive, a silence imposed on a voice, these are Rosario's opaque and jarring images for the principle of writing. The origin and source of writing is an essential prohibition, a fundamental censorship, a primary exclusion, a terrifying negativity through which and against which voice, presence, light, and even joy express themselves. In her feminist essay, she identifies this primary censorship with the patriarchal order. She argues that the patriarchy builds myths around women writers like Sylvia Plath that are meant to tame and repress the threat contained in their writing. They are fortifications of the male self against the perceived threat of an other displaced outside its boundaries, and perhaps outside all boundaries. But male critics unwittingly unleash upon themselves the very forces they seek to keep outside their fortified egos by calling the work of women writers like Plath a hallucination, a hypnotic trance. By turning the irascible nature of their writing into the myth of the eternal feminine, male critics turn into monsters the forces they seek to silence and contain. Rosario reads Mary Shelley's novel *Frankenstein* as one example of this return of the repressed as a repugnant, mutilated monster, a living cadaver that explosively incorporates the homicidal wrath produced by the prohibition, repression, and exclusion of women and their experiences from the patriarchal social order.

And yet this repression is but a more manageable form of a deeper, far more troubling experience. In the first essay of her collection, "The Authenticity of Women in Art" ("La autenticidad de la mujer en el arte"), Rosario distinguishes between two fundamental problems that affect women: the problem of their external, material freedom, and the problem of their internal, psychological freedom. Of the two, Rosario finds that the second is by far the most difficult and dangerous. The internal problem is in turn divided into two parts: the psychological penalties or sanctions imposed by society on women through tradition and customs, and the penalties or sanctions women impose on themselves in the form of an anger turned inward, a terrifying guilt (Ferré 1980, 14).

In her book, Rosario argues that guilt is anger turned inward. The anger turned against the external forces that threaten material freedom produces cathartic works like Mary Shelley's *Frankenstein,* works that sublimate the prohibitions into vociferous symbols of struggle aimed at unjust social forces. But the effect of the inwardly turned anger is the production of irascible works aimed at the self, which can eventually lead to suicide. Paradoxically, this anger turned inward can also be a form of liberation for Rosario, even if it doubles as an extreme form of self-repression.

Thus Rosario describes the paradoxical effect of Plath's poetry as exposing and creating both a shelter and a suicidal melancholia. She describes Plath's poems as photographs of the absence of light, comparing them to a projection, an x-ray, a negative, of Plath's feelings. These negatives reveal a composite force both developing and already inside of her. The negatives reveal this force with a paradoxical "meridian clarity," perfect poetic pitch, mastery of technique, and blinding phoenix-like light. This composite of negative and positive forces is the complex and profound origins of a tyranny, echoed and doubled by the patriarchal order. This tyranny is at times described as a vampire of light gradually substituting and sucking the light out of Plath. Indeed, Rosario explicitly compares it to the maternal experience, and more specifically to the newborn's involuntary end of the mother's private experience and internal freedom. At other times, this composite of light and darkness, of shelter and self-destruction, is compared to an ancestral force: the tyranny of the mother and of her maternal forebears, the cumulative experience of women.

II. Lacrimosa

Rosario changes the tone of her voice to a minor key in her book *Fables of the Wounded Heron* (*Fábulas de la garza desangrada*), published in 1982. Composed as a negative (a metamorphosis) of the Requiem mass, *Fables of the Wounded Heron* seems rather an Assumption that transforms the opening *Introitus* of the triumphant Requiem into a *Valediction* (*Envío*) and the final *Communio* into an *Epithalamium* (*Epitálamio*). Indeed, as she later describes it, her book is a tempering series of ironic inversions not only of myth but also of her original irascible tone: "Antigone, Desdemona, Ariadne . . . have a very different end from the one they were originally assigned in history. They embody the historical conflicts of women: Antigone defeats Creon, the pater familias; Desdemona poisons Othello; Ariadne aborts the Minotaur" (*Coloquio,* 109; all translations are mine unless otherwise noted). Perhaps the most striking of these reversals is Ariadne's in a poem entitled "Requiem." In that poem, Theseus is revealed as the maker of the Minotaur. Theseus, convinced that the Minotaur is his destiny, exits the labyrinth and abandons Ariadne inside it, after performing the sexual rites that will conjure the monster. The poem ends with Ariadne left abandoned in the labyrinth's echo chamber, left to bear in solitude the consequences of Theseus's solipsistic and ritualized desire. Suddenly, she feels the warm wine of blood running down her legs as she begins the painful abortion.

Running blood, flowing tears, falling tissue, open vessels are the materials running through these poems. The material is an antidote to the fortifications of the male superego, the architecture against which Rosario raised the irascible voice of *Pandora's Papers.* Like Theseus, in "Requiem," man conjures the monster again in the poem "Fable of the Wounded Heron." He needs the monster's labyrinths, its echo chambers, and its towers of wrath for support. He needs a threshold, a hole, an opening, to be born. He will build the architecture for his entrance, and the dead mother is his lintel: "perfect lintel of the dead mother / her body is marked by movement" (*Fábulas,* 17). In his imaginary as well as in the social imaginary, the mother is conceived as a dead certainty, a fixture for movement. The fortifying operation is defensive, and being defensive it is relentless in setting the stage for the equally implacable return of the repressed. Man builds a psychic wall around a void to protect himself from the ambiguity of a shared desire and an equally intense separation and prohibition. Like Julia Kristeva's borderline subject, man builds an empty castle. "Constructed on the one hand by the incestuous desire of (for) his mother and on the other by an overly brutal separation from her, the borderline patient, even though he may be a fortified castle, is nevertheless an empty castle . . . haunted by unappealing ghosts—'powerless' outside, 'impossible' inside" (Kristeva, *Powers of Horror,* 49).

The voice of "Fable of the Wounded Heron" struggles against the efforts of this borderline subject to stabilize itself by fixing and silencing the object of its desire. But the voice also confronts the forces that led the borderline subject to its perverse fortifications in the first place, forces that now return with added strength to build a second layer of stronger, impermeable material. Like negativity itself, the voice furiously assaults the double walls around emptiness from inside. But the walls are tripled now, because they are also built as a defense by the "othered" self, the self turned cadaver, object. The walls are built not only by arrogant, vain man, or by the returning, repressed abject. They are also built by the voice of the book as a defense against "the fragrance of evil that pursues [her]," against the death that "inhabits and defines her," against the torture of her own breath (*Fábulas,* 16, 18, 19).

The voice must excavate itself out of this stifling prison working backwards, rebuilding itself through abjection. It gives birth to itself in rhythmic waves of sound, expelling, vomiting, aborting, liberating what it lost to the void where she is imprisoned. *Lacrimosa dies illa / Qua resurget ex favilla / Judicandus homo reus.* (Mournful that day / When from the dust shall rise / Guilty man to be judged). Regurgitating matter, flesh, bones, eyes, extremities, sex, she opens the gates, she lets the blood run, the tears flow, and finally voice emerges like a phoenix from its ashes, and with voice consciousness returns.

> weeping burns and revives her,
> she deliberately breathes in the ethyl smell;

she fastens it immediately to her underside
helping herself at the point of birth. (*Fábulas,* 21)

The mournful self-birthing or abortion is aided by a containing placenta-like material, a layer of tissue that envelops the emerging voice. The tissue, made from the flowing tears and gases of abjection, is a returning figure in Rosario's writing.

forcing them to touch the skin feeling its weight and shape,
spying the soul through the secret keyhole of the ear,
chasing her heart through the bogs of the womb,
listening to the murmur of desire in relentless flux
under the sealed eyelid of the navel. (*Fábulas,* 20)

The tissue is the imprint on the abject that keeps the subject alive, which gives life to the subject and preserves it. It is a flexible and porous surface that substitutes the encroaching fortifying walls in an effort to contain while permitting the passage of the abject in and out of the voice. The tissue mediates the recuperation of the being-in-process at the center of the "Fable of the Wounded Heron." It is an acoustic keyhole, a wet spongy surface, through which the fleeting soul and the racing heart are glimpsed, heard, and pursued. The tissue is like the skin of bound Prometheus. It is the merciful savior that keeps him alive in his torment and punishment. *Huic ergo parce, Deus, / Pie Jesu Domine* (Therefore spare him, O God, / Merciful Jesu, Lord). The delicate skin of the eyelid, the tender scar tissue of the navel, are the flexible nets catching the black enigmatic seed of being, and protecting it in its free-fall.

Rosario identifies the regenerating tissue, the imprinted, scarred skin, with language in general and with writing in particular. The poem ends with the Heron, veins open, still bleeding, a version of Alice returned from Wonderland, who raises itself triumphant on the other side of the fortified mirror as she writes. She screams, laughs, and "*writes her name with the still-flowing blood at the base of the fragments of the poem / to soothe her delayed vanishing*" (*Fábulas,* 22). The scene captures the essence of *Pandora's Papers:* an abjection (the angry scream, the blood) that turns into writing that imprints the poem and creates the writer.

But the poem also goes beyond Rosario's first book. In this poem, the transformation of the abject (the scream, the blood, the mother tongue) into language (writing) also soothes the Heron. This soothing effect is reproduced in the tone of the poem that sounds more like an elegy than a condemnation. *Dona Eis Requiem* (Grant them rest).

III. Papageno's Tone

We are now ready to answer the first two of the three questions posed at the beginning of this essay. Writing about the loss of the mother is prohibited because the loss of the mother is but a reference to an archaic loss that is necessary for the self and identity to emerge. The speaking self, the poetic voice, Rosario's identity as a writer—all identity, in fact, emerges as a separation, a flight, and as a defense from the material source of words, from the abject origin, from its destabilizing ambiguity. The taboo against writing about the loss of the mother is a defense against the effect of tracing back the loss to a matricide at the origins of the speaking voice. This defense is the thickest wall surrounding and supporting the ego and identity. Its symptoms are the controls and prohibitions Rosario assaults in her writings: the social (external) tendency to contain the threat of the abject by reifying the maternal experience while splitting women into irreconcilable opposites, and the psychological (internal) tendency of the writer toward self-violence as self-silencing and self-censorship.

Why is it so important and even necessary to break that taboo and write about the loss of the mother? It is necessary to break the taboo because to do otherwise is to struggle endlessly with the implacable return of the repressed maternal cadaver. In other words, despite its centrifugal impulse, the speaking subject never fully separates from the rhythms and archaic rumors of the maternal body. The subject's language, its writing, its second skin, is made from the material of the abject, and the speaking subject will communicate its sounds, like it or not. To ignore, deny, or repress those archaic sounds is to build a wall around subjectivity that eventually crushes it with monstrous force. The only way of short-circuiting that return is to listen to the sounds and to the rhythms of the abject as they run through the fibers of language. To do this, however, is impossible by definition. The subject emerges as a speaking subject, and to listen to the sounds of the abject is to listen to the sound of the negative of voice, the sound of unspeaking, of the unspeakable. Thus every attempt at writing what cannot be said (as Rosario titles one of her more recent essays) is accompanied by the realization that "one is inclined to censor precisely that which one desperately needs to say" (*Coloquio,* 106). With each liberating iconoclastic gesture comes the suspicion, if not the realization, that one is keeping something hidden from oneself. And with that realization comes the desire to revisit oneself in order to exceed oneself and overcome self-censorship.

The third question asked at the beginning of this essay is important in this context. What does it mean that Rosario can write about the loss of the mother only by writing in another language? For Rosario, writing in another language is a way of translating the abject mother tongue; it is a way of developing the second skin that is necessary to live. Not surprisingly, for her writing in another language is also identical with translating herself, and coincides with self-exile. She began to write and publish in English in 1986, one year after she moved her residence from San Juan to College Park, Maryland, where she earned a Ph.D. in Literature. In so doing, Rosario joins writers like Joseph Conrad, Vladimir Nabokov, and Calvert Casey, who wrote in a language other than their mother tongue. At that time she translated several works from *Pandora's Papers, Room for Eros,* and *Fables of the Wounded Heron,* which appeared in various publications. Since then she has published several novels in English that she has insisted are English versions of work first written or begun in Spanish. Interestingly, she has translated these Spanish "originals" (often fragments, drafts, or incomplete work) twice: once into English and then from their English versions back into Spanish. Thus, Rosario's work in English is also a circuitous return to Spanish, to her mother tongue.

In fact, her work in English is a version of, or a second look at, her work in Spanish, which then turns into a third version when it is re-translated back to Spanish. As has been noted, these translations and re-translations not only contain additions and cosmetic changes but are often ironic reversals of the original. Most ironic is the fact that Rosario's translations into English suggest that the irascible and liberating tone of her work in Spanish also covers over a self-censoring impulse that keeps something hidden even from herself. After writing the novel *Eccentric Neighborhoods,* for example, Rosario published an editorial in the *New York Times* in which she points to this haunting self-censorship and to the reversals necessary to overcome it. "Our two halves are inseparable; we cannot give up either without feeling maimed. For many years, my concern was to keep my Hispanic self from being stifled. Now I discover it's my American self that's being threatened" (Ferré, "Puerto Rico, USA").

The revelatory power of self-translation changes the tone of Rosario's writing both in English and in Spanish. After her translations into English, Rosario moves away from the irascible and mournful tone of her earlier writings. Her tone now becomes lighter, ironic to the point of mischief. Indeed, she displaces self-censorship with self-deprecation. Rosario's new tone is not unlike Papageno's self-mocking tone in Mozart's *The Magic Flute.* Rosario's mischievous translations and her work in Spanish similarly resist external and internal (self-imposed) prohibitions on voice.

Originally published in 1990, *The Bitches' Colloquy* (*El Coloquio de las Perras*) is a negative, or an inversion, of *Room for Eros.* It is an often-humorous series of literary essays in which Rosario journeys inward, not only to the works of Latin American writers but also to her own early work to comment on it. In the essay of the collection dedicated to translation, Rosario describes the experience of translating her work into English. Self-translation, she states, is both a disturbing betrayal and a mischievous second chance, which allows her not only to struggle against the self-censorship she finds in her own earlier work, but also permits her to fix mistakes and to live differently (Ferré 1991, 162–163).

The essay titled (in English) "On Destiny, Language, and Translation; or, Orphelia [*sic*] Adrift in the C. & O. Canal" begins with a dream in which Rosario is ready to leave Washington D.C. after a productive five-year stay in that city. She is prepared to return to San Juan, a place she ambivalently describes both in maternal and military terms. A matrix of cultural meaning, San Juan is, on the one hand, the source that nurtures Rosario's "hidden springs of consciousness"; on the other hand, the city is also a war zone to which Rosario returns as a "war correspondent" (Ferré 1991, 153, 54). Her dream changes the return trip to San Juan into an allegorical crossing from one shore to another of the C. & O. canal in Washington, D.C. When Rosario reaches the middle of the canal she hears a voice that warns her that she must take "all the precautions of language" because the water locks will open and the water level will rise (Ferré 1991, 154). Despite the warnings, or perhaps because of them, the menacing undifferentiated waters of the canal are transformed into "a water of words" that keeps Rosario afloat. Compared to a mirror from childhood that fuses opposites, the water of words both connects and keeps apart the shores of the C. & O. canal.

Rosario interprets the dream to mean that the water of words is an intermediary place where she must learn to live. That place is not only language for Rosario, it is also the place of translation, the place of the in-between: in between San Juan and Washington, D.C., in between Spanish and English.[2] But that intermediary place is not only the place of translation; it is also the unconscious, the place where the dream is found. The unconscious is a place that keeps separate the opposites that threaten to tear Rosario apart even as it connects them. But the unconscious is also the place where Rosario finds a force more menacing and stronger than the irreconcilable opposites of the canal. It is the sound of an impeding storm, its terrible rushing not unlike the rolling thunder and waterfalls of Mozart's Queen of the Night. *Ja, fürchterlich ist dieses Rauschen, / wie fernen Donners Widerhall!* (Yes, fearful is that rushing, / like the distant echo of thunder!) The unconscious is the meeting place with that oncoming and undifferentiated rush of water that threatens to overcome and drown Rosario. Indeed, the unconscious is the meeting point at the center of the unintended slip in the title of the essay. The unconscious is translated into "Orphelia": neither masculine nor feminine, neither the suicidal Ophelia nor the oneiric Orpheus, but the transformative meeting place of both. In fact, the unconscious is the place where the dream can change Ophelia into Orpheus. It is the place where the dream can change the deadly rush of water, the curse of the vengeful Queen of the Night, into a palpitating life-source.

The operating principle of the dream-work is the opposite of the water's rush. If the rush of water threatens to drown Rosario by condensing all difference into one undifferentiated mass, the dream-work keeps Rosario afloat by displacing water into words and also by displacing Rosario from shore to shore. In other words, the dream keeps Rosario alive by turning her into a floating signifier between cultures, languages, and meanings. The dream creates an unstable identity and a malleable self for Rosario. Through Rosario's displacement, the dream makes light of the threatening pre-linguistic rhythms and material without denying or repressing them.

In this third moment of Rosario's writing, she changes yet again the direction of her drive for self-definition. Rather than focus on transforming, imprinting, and mourning the ancestral rhythms of the abject, she now mischievously revisits and transforms the sound of her emerging voice as an indirect means of returning to and transforming the mother tongue. Rosario's dream-work, her self-interpretation, and self-translation are like Papageno's playful song, like the sound of his silver bells, or like the music of the magic flute. They keep Rosario's voice cheerful and light as she walks through death's gloomy night. *Wir wandeln durch des Tones Macht / froh durch des Todes düstre Nacht* (We walk by power of the music/cheerful through death's gloomy night).

IV. The Curse of the Queen of Night

Rosario's self-translation (her self-displacement and self-effacement) allows her to return to the mother tongue to work through (disturb, trouble, and transform) its ancestral rhythmic condensations. The angry sounds and forceful curses made by the Queen of Night against the daughter who betrays her (Pamina sides with Sarastro against the Queen of Night in Mozart's opera) must be disturbed and heard. *Verstoßen sei auf ewig, verlassen sei auf ewig, / zertrümmert sei auf ewig alle Bande der Natur.* (Outcast forever, abandoned forever, / destroyed forever be all ties of nature.) Like the musical notation to Mozart's music, the mother's curse must be translated into an other language. Transforming the curse of the abject mother tongue into an intelligible sound in turn lightens its heavy burden on the emerging self. By re-suturing its sound to voice or music, by re-membering and working through the abject, the nature of the subject can also change. No longer outcast, abandoned, and destroyed by the unspeakable curse, the subject can live again.

Indeed, Rosario's self-translations are to the mother tongue what analysis is to trauma in Freudian psychoanalysis. Like analysis, Rosario's self-translations perform a dangerous but necessary operation to overcome a destructive tendency contained in the material that constitutes her writing. Like analysis, Rosario's self-translations revisit and provoke the abject material of Rosario's writing. Like analysis, Rosario's self-translations open up an intermediary region between her original writing and its potentially dangerous effect on the psyche. They produce a facsimile, a version, an interpretation of the abject material contained in Rosario's writing that is the first step necessary to overcome and change the abject's dangerous and destructive effect on the psyche. By disturbing, troubling, interpreting the original material, Rosario gives voice to herself and to the abject. And yet, Rosario's self-translations don't inhabit the exact space of analysis either. Rosario's works in English are not translations but self-translations in which she analyzes, interprets, and transforms her own dreams. Unlike the scene of analysis, there is no qualitative difference here between the analyst who interprets and the analyst whose dreams are interpreted. In Rosario's self-translations, the analyst is the facsimile of an analyst. Indeed, Rosario's humorous works in English function as a simulacrum of the art of a successful jokester.

According to Freud, "a joke is a double-dealing rascal who serves two masters at once": one master tells the joke and the other listens to it (Freud 1905, 155). But the apparent circuit traveled by the mischievous joke is but the simulacrum of a circuit because the person who listens to the joke is actually doing the bidding of the person telling the joke. In fact, for Freud the listener is a kind of dummy or servant of the person telling the joke. The joker needs the dummy because its laughter allows the liberation of the repressed material in the ventriloquist. But the "dummy" and the joke's closed circuit are also insufficient. The joker's laughter and pleasure, the release of her repressed material, are only temporary and do not get to the root of the problem. Giddiness and a hysterical non-comprehending laughter could be the recurring symptoms of a melancholy that continues to haunt the joker. Rosario's *Eccentric Neighborhoods* is an example of this persistent haunting. On the one hand, it is an example of her ongoing effort to face and work through the matricidal impulse at the origin of the process of subject formation, now by translating the mother tongue into voice. On the other hand, it is also an example of the artifice at the center of her efforts to work through the abject, a simulacrum that calls for eccentric readings that interrupt and reinterpret Rosario's work.

Eccentric Neighborhoods is a constellation of works that includes the 1998 version in English as well as a shorter unfinished Spanish version published as separate chapters between 1989 and 1992. The self-translation changes the autobiographical references and instead tells the saga of two families, the Rivas de Santillana and the Vernets. The Rivas de Santillana are a landowning aristocratic family from the south of the island. The Vernets are a family of immigrants who become part of the island's cadre of professionals challenging the authority and ultimately supplanting the landowners. The novel is interlaced with references to the colonial history of Puerto Rico: the occupation of the island by two imperial powers (first Spain and then the United States). But the novel also tells the story of three generations of both families. Elvira is the narrator and the great-granddaughter who decides to break with family tradition: "'No Rivas de Santillana has ever gotten a divorce except for Tía Lakhmé, and everyone knows she's crazy,'" Mother said. "'If you do, your grandparents' ghosts will follow you around and push you down the stairs or in front of a car. Your aunts and uncles will be furious. The whole family will be up in arms. You must be out of your mind, Elvira'" (Ferré, *Eccentric Neighborhoods*, 333).

Elvira, Clarissa's daughter in the novel, threatens her mother (not her husband) with a divorce. She refuses to wear the mantle of self-sacrifice proudly worn by her mother, her aunts, and by her grandmother, in dutiful respect of a Stoic philosophy of life. The daughter's threat of divorce, or separation, the mother's sacrifice and curse, and the ghost's haunting are the materials that make up the novel. The mother, Clarissa, is a Rivas de Santillana, and she tries to teach her daughter Elvira the Stoic philosophy of the family. Emajaguas, the fortified family home, is an architectural example of both that philosophy of life and the borderline subjectivity that has so preoccupied Rosario in all her work. Like the borderline subject, the Rivas de Santillanas sublimate and repress the pain, the suffering, and the pleasure of the body into ascetic experiences. Emajaguas, the walled-in, fortified paradise where Clarissa and her sisters (Elvira's aunts) grow up, is an architectural example of that philosophy, and it hatches examples of borderline subjectivity. Compared to the Garden of the Finzi-Contini, Emajaguas stands as an arrogant claim to a self-sufficient spirituality founded on the denial of the body and sexuality, both of which are displaced on to an evil lurking outside its walls: poverty, revolution, death, the Caribbean Sea. The "Swans of Emajaguas," Elvira's aunts and her mother, sacrifice their dreams to the guiding principles of the Rivas de Santillana. But Emajagua's fortifications prove insufficient and they all lead miserable, unhappy, and frustrated lives.

Elvira knows better. She knows that her ancestor's stoicism, their fortifications, their denial of bodily pain and pleasure are insufficient defensive mechanisms against a ghostly energy that must be confronted, translated, appropriated, worked through rather than wielded as a curse. Indeed, this energy is the same negative spectrum described in Rosario's first book of essays. And Clarissa's death at the end of the novel confirms the spectrum's timeless reach, its effect on the mother even after her death. Clarissa dies a peaceful death only in appearance. "No wounds marked her body, no grimace of pain distorted her beautiful, cameolike profile" (*Eccentric Neighborhoods,* 338). But when Elvira cleans her mother's body in preparation for burial, she is horrified by a torrent of fresh blood that spills out of her mother's mouth like a curse from the other world. The image is a striking representation of the mother tongue and its silencing effect on Clarissa. Even after death, she chokes on the abject, on the maternal blood that overcomes voice, the blood that substitutes words. Clarissa's horrific "last words" return to haunt Elvira as a recurring nightmare made of untranslatable material that Elvira cannot understand. Eventually, however, the nightmare stops repeating and is replaced instead by the striking dream that ends the novel where Elvira hears the voices of her aunts as they swim against the current of Río Loco *(Eccentric Neighborhoods,* 340*)*.

Dedicated "To the ghosts who lent me their voices" the English version of *Eccentric Neighborhoods* is also a novel told by Rosario's familiar ghosts. They are the ghosts of the maternal ancestors (the mother, the aunts, and the grandmothers) whose haunting curses not only end but also begin the novel. In fact, the novel opens with the original version of the dream that ends it. In that memorable scene of Elvira's childhood, the overflowing and unpredictable, dangerous river is explicitly compared to Clarissa's moodiness and to her melancholy tears (*Eccentric Neighborhood,* 3–4). The dream, which places Elvira in the protective shell of the Pontiac, transforms Clarissa's tearful moods into the rushing waters of the Río Loco (the Crazy River).

If the Río Loco is haunted by the untranslatable sounds of dogs, pigs, and goats, *Eccentric Neighborhoods* is riddled with remnants of this ancestral curse fortified by social conventions. These remnants take the form of violent, homicidal ghosts like Blanca Rosa, Uncle Basilio, Chaguito's mother, Aztec sacrificial priests, and Aurelio's piano music (*Eccentric Neighborhoods,* 12, 36, 198, 299, 339). But like the dream-work, the novel also repeats, revisits, and displaces those sounds into words, into another language, into English (the language of adventure stories and impish humor in the novel). Through displacement, by writing in another language, Rosario changes the menacing rhythms of the mother tongue into protective shells like Clarissa's Pontiac. In English, Clarissa's river of blood is transformed back into words. In dreams, she becomes an agent both of her own and of Elvira's salvation.

Notes

* I wish to thank Kelly Oliver and Doris Sommer for their careful reading of this essay and for their helpful suggestions.

1. Julia Kristeva suggests that the speaking subject emerges by cutting off the maternal source of words, by stripping off the skin of the abject (*Strangers,* 16). In *Strangers to Ourselves,* she compares this painful cut both to a primal flaying and to a flight. "The word foreshadowed the exile, the possibility or necessity to be foreign and to live in a foreign country, thus heralding the art of living of a modern era, the cosmopolitanism of those who have been flayed" (*Strangers,* 13). The separation from the abject sets the subject in motion in two ways. On the one hand, the separation liberates and begins a new speaking subject. The skin of this new subject heralds exile and the subject emerges speaking a foreign language. On the other hand, the separation displaces, flays an earlier skin (language), substituting it for another that works defensively as an anesthesia. The foreign language, then, is like a permeable but soothing skin that substitutes the old skin (language), and covers over the exposed material. Since the old skin and material are not entirely gone, the speaking subject not only emerges speaking a foreign language, but

she or he also emerges questioning inconsolably (Kristeva, "Love of Another Language, 366).

Works Cited

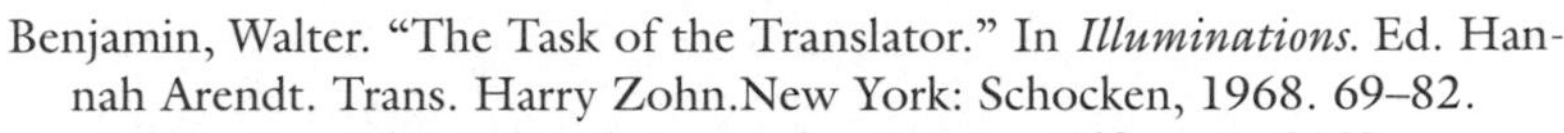

Benjamin, Walter. "The Task of the Translator." In *Illuminations*. Ed. Hannah Arendt. Trans. Harry Zohn.New York: Schocken, 1968. 69–82.

Ferré, Rosario. *A la sombra de tu nombre*. México: Alfaguara, 2001.

———. *Eccentric Neighborhoods*. New York: Farrar, Straus and Giroux, 1998.

———. *El Coloquio de las perras*. Mexico: Literal Books, 1992.

———. "Puerto Rico, USA." *New York Times*. March 19, 1998.

———. "On Destiny, Language, and Translation; or Orphelia [sic] Adrift in the C. & O. Canal." In *The Youngest Doll*. Ed. And foreword by Jean Franco. Lincoln: University of Nebraska Press, 1991. 153–65.

———. *Fábulas de la Garza Desangrada*. México: Joaquín Mortíz, 1982.

———. *Papeles de Pandora*. México: Joaquín Mortíz, 1976.

———. *Sitio a Eros*. México: Joaquín Mortíz, 1980.

Freud, Sigmund. *Jokes and Their Relation to the Unconscious*. Trans. and Ed. James Strachey. New York and London: Norton & Co., 1963.

Kristeva, Julia. *Powers of Horror: An Essay on Abjection*. Trans. Leon S. Roudiez. New York: Columbia University Press, 1982.

———. *Strangers to Ourselves*. Trans. Leon S. Roudiez. New York: Columbia University Press, 1991.

———. "The Love of Another Language." In *Intimate Revolt*. Trans. Jeanine Herman. New York: Columbia University Press, 2002.

Navarro, Mireya. "Bilingual Author Finds Something Gained in Translation." *New York Times*. Tuesday, September 8, 1998. Cultural Desk Section, p.2.

Oliver, Kelly. *Witnessing; Beyond Recognition*. Minneapolis: University of Minnesota Press, 2001.

12

The Novel as Cuban Lexicon

Bargaining Bilinguals in Daína Chaviano's *El hombre, la hembra y el hambre*

Esther Whitfield

A lexicon, if we look it up, has two principal meanings: (1) "a word-book or dictionary" or (2) "the vocabulary proper to some department of knowledge or sphere of activity; the vocabulary or word-stock of a region, a particular speaker."[1] In its first sense a lexicon translates; in its second, it delineates the sphere of those who already know. The two senses seem at odds, but they do not have to be; and when they come together in fiction they can wield cultural and commercial weight. The Miami-Cuban Daína Chaviano's *El hombre, la hembra y el hambre* (Barcelona: Planeta, 1998) is a lexicon twice over: published and sold in Spain, it is a word book of the particular "department of knowledge" that is Cuba's "special period in times of peace," the years of economic hardship, still in force, following the demise of the Soviet bloc. Ironically, playfully, and overtly, its characters and narrators conspire to translate the vocabulary and experience of this period in a bargaining bilingualism defined by Cuba's current place in an outside imaginary. Word-for-word translation, from a time- and place-specific Cuban vocabulary into a more standard Spanish, brings different cultural sites—late twentieth-century socialist Cuba on the one hand, and the rest of the Spanish-speaking world on the other—into dealings together. We are not too far removed here from the idea of tourism (itself an all-important player in the "special period"), and in a sense the word-book overlaps with another kind of book, the tourist handbook. For Chaviano's novel, ostensibly the tale of an art historian's decline into prostitution and into an imagined Havana of centuries earlier, is a guidebook to Cuba's recent history. The reader is a visitor, and the novel takes him or her by the hand, making the country's linguistic and sociopolitical landscape both comprehensible and inviting.

Just as tourism is an important economic program for today's Cuba, so there is a financial subtext to this particular lexicon or handbook. For it does not merely define words: It makes objects of them and trades them, we might say, in an international market. As words are offered up to foreign characters and readers, they take the shape of curiosities or mementos, and in a sense verbal exchange becomes a trading exchange. This objectification of words on the one hand parodies an officialist feigning of material production when there is in fact only processing: the novel mimics, and thereby denounces, Cuba's uncomfortable transition from production to service, represented by tourism overtaking sugar as the primary source of foreign income in 1994.[2] In a further step, however, the novel as a cultural product takes advantage of the tradable value of words as false objects. There is profit to be gained from commanding an esoteric vocabulary in the bicultural relations between Cuban and foreign characters, between guides and visitors, and, indeed, between text and readers. The parody, then, is a flawed one, for both the denounced—the government, or the Revolution—and the denouncer, the novel, deal in similar terms; a contradiction that raises questions about Cuba's status as a marketable cultural image.

Why the lexicon, we might ask? There is an answer toward the end of the novel when Claudia, the main character, dreams up an entry in an imaginary dictionary of the "special period": "El día que escriba un diccionario sobre el léxico de estos años, no podrá faltar *DIPLO (diminutivo de diplotienda). 1. Almacenes de mercancía donde la moneda oficial del país y la mierda son la misma cosa. 2. Ventana al mundo exterior que ayuda a quitar la depresión a quienes tengan la suerte de conseguir dólares . . .*" (Chaviano 286). This "diccionario de estos años" is being written through Claudia: It is *El hombre, la hembra y el hambre* itself. Just as the imagined dictionary would anticipate and accommodate interest in the period from those unfamiliar with its terms, so *El hombre, la hembra y el hambre* draws attention to the specificity of certain words and experiences—or their incomprehensibility to a certain readership—and provides translations accordingly. Perhaps the best way to approach the novel, then, is to play it at its own game and read it through an imaginary lexicon or dictionary. What follows is a handbook of words and phrases with a guide to reading them through the novel and its context.

The first entry is the title phrase:

el hombre, la hembra, y el hambre

This title is a trinity of empty signs, a hollow structure that gives a false impression of solidity. The three words begin with *h,* which in Spanish is written but not heard. It has an orthographical presence but it is phonetically immaterial; it is nothingness disguised as matter, and it is precisely this masking of nothingness behind a false physicality that the novel both censors and performs. Breaking down this nothingness into its constituents, we have our next three entries:

el hombre

El hombre links Daína Chaviano's novel to another tripartite title: Senel Paz's story "El lobo, el bosque y el hombre nuevo." *El hombre* would be *el hombre nuevo;* but to be more precise, *el hombre* signals the absence and failure in *El hombre, la hembra y el hambre* of Che Guevara's "new man," the worker and producer for the good of society introduced to Cuba in the 1960s. *El hombre* is the emptiest of three empty signs in Chaviano's title, and although it is a definition by negation (*el hombre* signals that there is no new man) this is partly the point—for the novel teaches us the creative power of negativity and necessity. There are no men to speak of in this novel: Claudia's two lovers abandon her and abandon the Revolution, leaving both without "producers." Che's essays "Socialismo y el hombre en Cuba" and "Papel de la mujer" famously assign production to men and supporting, processing roles to women; and the eradication of men from Chaviano's novel paves the way for a substitute, weakened production, as *el hombre* concedes his territory—as we will do now, in our lexicon—to *la hembra.*

la hembra

The woman is the sole player in this novel: It is all about Claudia, the art historian forced by poverty into both prostitution and communion with spirits, and she tells much of the text in the first person. This feminization of the action is, however, a double-edged move, for the very empowerment of woman represents a certain failing, and feigning, of production in its Revolutionary sense. The strong female voice is at the same time a victory over men and a parody of a failed economy. Claudia does not work in production but in servicing: She is a *jinetera,* defined by the novel as a woman who sells favors to tourists. She does not produce but rather reproduces, giving birth to a child who is a drain on her and on society. The failure of *el hombre* (*nuevo*) is projected onto woman, as production shifts to reproduction, recycling, and reprocessing (the basis, not coincidentally, of a tourist economy that promotes old cars, old buildings and revived music). *La hembra,* like *el hombre,* begins on an empty sign and becomes a sign of emptiness—but it is man's emptiness, not her own, that she signals.

el hambre

El hambre is where absence becomes presence, where pretending to produce solidifies into convincing production. Food is what this novel's "special period" is lacking and so, for its characters, hunger itself becomes sustenance. It is also through *hambre*—and through its association with biblical Creation—that we see words crystallize into physical and tradable entities, the most important metamorphosis in the novel. Claudia invokes *el hambre* in a monologue after the birth of her son: "Siento un hambre milenaria, de esas que corroen la bilis y el alma. Es un mal inextinguible que ya era mío antes de nacer porque mi madre ya lo padecía. No logro imaginarme cómo sería la vida sin este afán por devorar, por apoderarme de cada trocito del mundo y convertirlo en parte mía. Así comienza nuestro génesis: "En el principio fue el Hambre, y Su espíritu se deslizó sobre la superficie de los campos devastados, y fue el año treinta y cinco de Su advenimiento . . ." (41). Hunger has become the most grotesquely physical aspect of Claudia's life; a being so strong it corrodes her body and soul. *El hambre,* she tells us, is at the origin of life: it is Genesis, and specifically Genesis retold by St. John, in which Creation begins with the Word. Both *el hambre* and words create something from nothing; a practice to which official rhetoric (signaled by "el año treinta y cinco de Su advenimiento," the thirty-five years of Castro's rule), individual characters and the novel itself have recourse. This place is the "Paradise of Nada" into which Zoé Valdés's *La nada cotidiana,* an earlier novel of Cuba's "special period," has been translated.[3] Nothingness is a recurring theme.

Picadillo extendido, pollo de población and *carne de novena:*

Moving from the novel's title to its text, we stumble upon words marked by italics or inverted commas—words that, fortunately for the uninitiated, come with translations. One scene in particular is densely italicized, and it is here that the lexicon performs to the full.

Here, two female tourists, one Colombian and one Spanish, overhear Claudia and a friend (both guides at Havana's Museo de Bellas Artes) discussing their ration book food allowances. The *libreta de abastecimientos,* introduced in 1962 to regulate distribution of basic foods and materials to each Cuban citizen, has produced its own vocabulary, both directly and by popular designation. This vocabulary intrigues the foreigner visitors, and Claudia invents a game to taunt their ignorance, challenging them to guess the meanings of ration book phrases. The visitors translate wrongly, of course:

> —Supongamos que oyes decir que están vendiendo el *pollo de la población* que pertenece a una novena—le sugirió [Claudia] a la española—¿Qué pensarías que es?
>
> La mujer quedó pensativa unos segundos.
>
> —Pues que están vendiendo un ave que anda suelta en medio de cualquier poblao. Y una novena son los rezos, ¿no? Pero no sé qué tiene que ver un pollo con la iglesia.
>
> —¿No será un pollo que puede comer todo el mundo y que es la mascota en un juego de béisbol?—intervino la colombiana.
>
> Claudia y su amiga se morían de la risa. Lo mejor vino cuando mencionaron el *picadillo extendido.* La española pensó en <<un picadillo laaaargo como una longaniza>>, mientras que la bogotana, recién llegada de Miami, creyó que era <<una fuente de picadillo enorme, como esas que sirven en los restaurantes de La Pequeña Habana>> (118).

Claudia laughs at this linguistic incompetence, but not for long. As the tourists' guide and the reader's translator she takes its upon herself to explain, benevolently and magisterially, the intricacies of the ration-book lexicon:

> —Bienaventurados los ingenuos, porque no padecerán—murmuró Claudia.
>
> Y pasó a aclararles que el *pollo de población* era un pollo racionado para todo el mundo, al que llamaban así con la idea de diferenciarlo del *pollo de dieta:* una minúscula porción adicional que podían comprar los viejos y ciertos enfermos. La frase *picadillo extendido*—y aquí Claudia adoptó el tono catedrático apropiado—debía entenderse como un aporte del socialismo caribeño a las corrientes poéticas del siglo XX. Se trataba de una antífrasis, es decir, de una figura de la retórica que consiste en denominar las cosas de manera opuesta a su sentido original. En otras palabras, el *picadillo extendido* en realidad estaba <<recortado>> (119).

In translating *picadillo extendido* Claudia theorizes (or mock-theorizes) the performance of *el hambre* wherein, through words, nothing appears as something. In calling the performance "un aporte del socialismo caribeño a las corrientes poética del siglo XX," she attributes this creative use of words, this redefinition of nothingness, to a political system that tries to mask absence as substance. We might, however, want to think about what Claudia herself is doing with words; to look, that is, at her own position in the act of translating. She is, on the one hand, in authority as the holder of information: she adopts "el tono catedrático apropriado" because she is imparting knowledge to her curious disciples who have had no previous access to that knowledge. Importantly, though, she receives a reward for her translation: we are told that "las cuatro habían terminado en la barra del Floridita, cuando las periodistas las invitaron a unos daiquiríes" (119). She uses words to make the tourists feel comfortable but in a way, too, she bargains away her intimacy with the *libreta*'s language, selling words as curios of the Revolution and its "special period." We should bear in mind this exchange of words for rewards, between the inside informer and the curious outsider, as we turn to the last two entries in this lexicon. They are:

paladar and *jinetera*

Ironically, these two words are by now less part of an obscure, Cuban-only lexicon than something of frontier vocabulary—the sorts of "cubanismo" with which visitors to Cuba and even readers of travel magazines quickly become familiar.[4] In *El hombre,* though, these two are given careful definitions, as though they were not readily comprehensible; in a practice that has led Yolanda Sánchez to question the novel's familiarity with contemporary Cuba.[5] Unlike Claudia's lecture on *pollo de población* and *picadillo extendido,* these translations are neither acknowledged as such nor offered by a character; more surreptitiously, the text translates itself. The meanings of *paladar* and *jinetera* are couched in the narrative, unobtrusive and, indeed, accommodating to an outsider unfamiliar with the "special period." Weighing up her options for earning money, Claudia is reminded by a friend that "la gente se la busca de cualquier manera: pone un restaurante clandestino, un 'paladar,' o vende comida para la calle, o monta un taller de algo" (47). Claudia, who has lived all her life in Cuba, cannot be unfamiliar with *paladares.* Yet the word is set apart in quotation marks that signal difference, and its strangeness anticipated by the definition as "un restaurante clandestino." The simultaneous signaling of and compensation for lexical strangeness is even starker in the case of *jinetera.* Toward the beginning of the novel we are introduced to "una muchacha muy maquillada que parecía pertenecer a esa nueva generación de prostitutas que en la isla reciben el descriptivo y erótico nombre de 'jineteras'" (73). The *jinetera,* too, is within quotation marks, and the translation is almost unfeasibly long and solicitous. Moreover, to specify "en la isla" implicitly acknowledges another place outside the island and to eroticize ("el erótico nombre") is already to introduce a viewer and a viewed such that we cannot help sensing an unseen but fully intended recipient of the description. Put simply, there is no need to translate either *paladar* or *jinetera* in this novel unless the reader is assumed to be unfamiliar with them; and the fact that the narrator—not the character, this time—makes such an assumption brings us strangely close to the scenario we have just seen, where Claudia accomodates and informs the foreign tourists. If the narrator engages in this practice, then can we not see the novel itself as just such a cultural "translator"? This is a final question to append to our lexicon.

Appendix / Conclusion

The lexicon that is *El hombre, la hembra y el hambre*—and our reading of it—has guided us through the decline of "real" material production (as represented by *el hombre*) in favor of the feigned (re)production of *la hembra*. This same masking of insubstantiality as substance is "*el hambre,*" and it is taken up by the language of officialdom (by what Claudia calls "la corriente poética del siglo XX") but also, paradoxically, by Claudia herself. Claudia makes words into things that she can offer up, deal in, and be rewarded for. Words acquire a provisional objecthood and, like Marx's commodities, can be exchanged for other items of value, like drinks and money. Our last two lexical entries show the narrator mimicking Claudia in offering amenable, accessible translations to the foreign visitor. Shifting from the narrator who gives us *jinetera* to the novel as a product, we are faced with a much broader relationship between inside and out. We have a novel that translates Cuban—and Cuba—into a more standard Spanish and furthermore, maintaining this correlation between language and culture, into the language and codes of an international literary market. *El hombre* was written in Miami but published in Spain, where books win financial prizes (this novel, for example, won the 1998 Premio Azorín, which guarantees publication by Editorial Planeta). Because of the many idiosyncrasies of Cuban bookselling, few Spanish-published books are marketed there, and fewer still by Cuban authors in exile; *El hombre*'s target readers are in

Spain, Latin America, and the United States. These readers function as monolingual speakers of a "standard" Spanish vis-à-vis the esoteric vocabulary of the Cuban "special period," and in a sense the novel sells its words-as-products to them. In a moment when international interest in Cuba is soaring, *El hombre, la hembra y el hambre* promotes literary tourism to a troubled Cuba, making the outsider's experience pleasurable through a game, and a deal, with words. Closing our lexicon, we might reflect on the extraordinary currency, in many senses, of Cuba as a cultural icon and product and on the bilingual bargains—within the novel and around it—that bring such a product to the market.

Notes

1. Entry in the *Oxford English Dictionary*, on-line edition.
2. In 1992 gross revenues from sugar, in thousands of U.S. dollars, were 1,220.1; in 1993 they dropped to 752.5 and in 1994 to 748.0. Over the same period, gross revenues from tourism grew from 567.0 (1992) to 720.0 (1993) to 850.0 (1994), and have continued to grow rapidly since. Source: *La economía cubana: Reformas estructurales y desempeño en los noventa.*
3. Valdés's *La nada cotidiana* predates *El hombre, la hembra y el hambre* by three years but, like Chaviano's novel, it was published in Barcelona and is based in the hardships (and, in Valdés's case, sexual depravities) of Cuba's 1990s. The 1998 translation, by Sabina Cienfuegos, is titled *Yocandra in the Paradise of Nada.*
4. *Paladares* (small, family-run eating houses) were legalized in 1993 under law decree no. 141, passed to institute *cuentapropismo,* the operation of heavily regulated small businesses. *Jineterismo* (hustling with tourists) is illegal, but notoriously difficult to define. See Coco Fusco's landmark essay, "Hustling for Dollars."
5. See Yolanda Sánchez, "'Esta isla se vende': proyecciones desde el exilio de una generación ¿desilusionada?"

Works Cited

Chaviano, Daína. *El hombre, la hembra y el hambre,* Barcelona: Planeta, 1998.

Comisión Económica para América Latina y el Caribe (CEPAL). *La economía cubana: Reformas estructurales y desempeño en los noventa.* México: CEPAL/ Fondo de Cultura Económica, 2000.

Fusco, Coco. "Hustling for Dollars: *Jineterismo* in Cuba." In *Global Sex Workers: Rights, Resistance and Redefinition,* Kemala Kempadoo and Jo Doezema, eds. New York and London: Routledge, 1998. 151–66.

Guevara, Ernesto "Che." "Socialismo y el hombre en Cuba. "*El Socialismo y el hombre nuevo.* México: Siglo XXI, 1977.

———. "Papel de la mujer." *Escritos y discursos I*. Havana: Editorial Ciencias Políticas,1972.

Paz, Senel, *El lobo, el bosque y el hombre nuevo*. Mexico: Era, 1991.

Sánchez, Yolanda. "Esta isla se vende": proyecciones desde el exilio de una generación

¿desilusionada?" Eds. Janet Reinstädtler and Ottmar Ette, *Todas las islas la isla: Nuevas y novísimas tendencias en la literatura y cultura de Cuba*. Madrid: Iberoamericana and Frankfurt: Vervuert, 2000.

Valdés, Zoé. *La nada cotidiana*. Barcelona: Emecé, 1995.

———.Trans. Sabina Cienfuegos. *Yocandra in the Paradise of Nada*. New York: Arcade, 1998.

Part IV

Double-Barreled Canon

13

Pidginizing Chinese*

Yunte Huang

Let us imagine: Charlie Chan (a fictional Chinese American detective from Honolulu) meets up with Ezra Pound (an elite poet from Philadelphia) at an obscure limehouse tea shop. After the initial greetings, which are delivered in the most proper manner, the subject of their conversation comes naturally to one that concerns both of them deeply: the Chinese language. Only a few minutes into the topic some sort of disagreement seems to arise. The poet, apparently out of frustration, dips his right index finger into his tea bowl, draws out some tea water, and scribbles on the dark, smooth surface of the table. Where the trace of water stretches and shrinks, there appears a Chinese character, 信 (*xin*). Paraphrasing Confucius, the poet explains the meaning of the character, which happens to be one of his favorites: "Man stands by his word."[1] In response, the master detective dishes out a pidgin version of a good old Confucian witticism, as he often does in the novels and films: "Tongue often hang man quicker than rope. In like manner the gentlemen's brain-wrestling continues. . . ."

This imaginary scene, despite its apparent absurdity, helps to illustrate a simple but significant fact: American pop culture's creation of a demeaning image of the Orient—as in the case of Charlie Chan—was strikingly contemporaneous with modern American poetry's cultivation of a genuine interest in Oriental languages, as in the case of Imagism. Elsewhere I have described this interest as simultaneously poetic and ethnographic.[2] In this essay I continue to investigate Imagism's ethnographic enterprise, but in a different context. The "image" created by Imagism is but one of the many faces twentieth-century America has drawn for the Chinese language. Imagism's linguistic mimicry should, I submit, be understood in the context of

American pop culture's pidginization of Chinese, and both the mimicry and pidginization will be subject to countermockery in the work of Asian writers and Asian American writers such as John Yau. In all these instances, whether the writer means to idealize or demean, to mock or countermock, linguistic mimesis in its various formations remains a powerful tool of cultural description.

> *The secret is to talk much, but say nothing.*
>
> *—Charlie Chan in Earl Derr Biggers's Keeper of the Keys (1932)*

The genesis of Charlie Chan is a modern legend: One day, Earl Derr Biggers, author of the successful mystery novel *Seven Keys to Baldpate,* was basking in the sunlight of Honolulu when he came upon a report in a local newspaper about a Chinese detective named Chang Apana. Biggers had never heard of an Oriental detective, although he was, like everybody else at that time, familiar with Dr. Fu Manchu. A novel idea dawned upon him, and he started a new book called *The House Without a Key* (1925), in which an Oriental detective from Honolulu, Charlie Chan, made his debut. The book was an instant success, and Biggers produced, before his death in 1933, five more Charlie Chan novels, all of which, with one exception, were made into movies that still run today.

In both the novels and the movies, one of the objects of laughter is of course Charlie's stocky body. But what is more fascinating and ensures the character's popularity is the manner in which he speaks. Unlike Sherlock Holmes, who puffs and muses, Charlie is characteristically voluble. As he himself admits, "Talk is my weakness" (*Keeper* 177). He speaks Mandarin Chinese, Cantonese, English, Hawaiian, French, and who knows what else. His adroitness in shifting these linguistic gears is a big plus in his success as a detective. At times a short conversation with his Chinese informant, which sounds like only singsong and is therefore completely incomprehensible to the Anglo-Americans on the spot, can lead him to the essential clue to the murder case at hand. But nothing can compare with his mouthful, or stomachful, of half-baked fortune-cookie Confucian aphorisms, which he can dish out as the occasion demands. Let me provide a short list:

> Always harder to keep secret than for egg to bounce on sidewalk.
> Way to find rabbit's residence is to turn rabbit loose and watch.
> Some heads, like hard nuts, much better if cracked.

> Too late to dig well after honorable house is on fire.
> Mind like parachute—only function when open.
> Events explode suddenly like fire crackers in the face of innocent passerby.

What characterizes these witticisms is not the wisdom one can find in a wise man's saying such as Benjamin Franklin's "God helps those who help themselves." Charlie's proverbs are pidginized—the sentences lack subjects, the nouns lack articles, the verbs are not conjugated—and intended not to enlighten, but to baffle. In *Black Camel* (1929), for example, Charlie confronts a murder suspect by pulling out a spicy item from his proverbial stock:

> Jaynes pushed forward. "I have important business on the mainland, and I intend to sail at midnight. It is now long past ten. I warn you that you must call out your entire force if you propose to keep me here—"
>
> "That also can be done," answered Charlie amiably.
>
> "Good lord!" The Britisher looked helplessly at Wilkie Ballou. "What kind of place is this? Why don't they send a white man out here?"
>
> A rare light flared suddenly in Charlie's eyes. "The man who is about to cross a stream should not revile the crocodile's mother," he said in icy tones.
>
> "What do you mean by that?" Jaynes asked. (104–5)

Charlie knows very well the effectiveness of his talk, which is only half-comprehensible to most of his listeners. He enjoys getting people to ask, as Jaynes did, "What do you mean by that?" or "What does it mean in English?" although he *is* speaking English, if pidginized English. The psychological advantage he gains by baffling people is one of his hidden weapons in the sleuthing business. "The secret," as he tells a white colleague who is not good at talking, "is to talk much, but say nothing" (*Keeper* 137). But this talk-much-but-say-nothing business sometimes gets Charlie into trouble, especially when clear speech is needed. He is once publicly humiliated when appearing in court as the key witness:

> "I am walking down Pawaa Alley," he [Charlie] remarked. "With me is my fellow detective, Mr. Kashimo. Before us, at the door of Timo's fish shop, we perceive extensive crowd has gathered. We accelerate our speed. As we approach, crowd melts gradually away, and next moment we come upon these three men, now prisoners in the dock. They are bent on to knees, and they disport themselves with dice. Endearing remarks toward these same dice issue from their lips in three languages."

> "Come, come, Charlie," said the prosecuting attorney, a red-haired, aggressive man. "I beg your pardon—Inspector Chan. Your language is, as usual, a little flowery for an American court. These men were shooting craps. That's what you mean to say, isn't it?"
> "I am very much afraid it is," Chan replied. (*Charlie Chan* 133)

Partly because of the unsuitableness of Charlie's florid diction in court, and partly because Kashimo, his Japanese sidekick, lost the dice they had confiscated as evidence, the charge is dismissed and the three crap-shooters walk out free, much to Charlie's dismay. Hence the floweriness of his speech, which at times aids him, can become Charlie's stumbling block.

Charlie Chan and his nuggets of fortune-cookie Confucius will provide a good laugh only if we don't realize that they were all created by Biggers. It should be evident that this creation epitomizes a racist conception of the Chinese language and its speakers, for Charlie's metaphoric diction sounds all too familiar to readers of modern racist literature that depicts mysterious, inscrutable Orientals with their expressionless faces and slanting eyes. In this respect, Charlie's flowery and slippery speech resonates with the poisonous devil's tongue of Dr. Fu Manchu, an Oriental protagonist created by Sax Rohmer in an earlier series of equally popular detective stories. Under Rohmer's pen, Fu Manchu, a modern Satan from the East who designs an evil plot to take over the West, speaks in florid metaphors, as does Charlie Chan. What these two creations helped to fashion and substantiate in the early decades of the twentieth century was a stereotype of the racial Other's language and, more important, a stigmatization of the race.

Imagism appears to entail a very different conception of the same language. Two of the three principles put down by Pound in "A Few Don'ts by an Imagiste" stress directness and clarity in poetic diction: "1. Direct treatment of the 'thing' whether subjective or objective. 2. To use absolutely no word that does not contribute to the presentation" (*Literary* 3). And as I have argued, Imagism's aesthetic principle is closely tied to its encounter with the Chinese language from an ethnographic standpoint.[3] What especially attracted the Imagists was what Ernest Fenollosa saw as its "naturalness," or what Otto Jespersen called its "modernity." The naturalness, according to Fenollosa, is defined by, among other things, the clarity with which the language demonstrates, in its grammatical structure and in individual words, the transference of force from the agent to the object in the same manner that it takes place in nature (16). Compared with the floridity and nonsense attributed to Chinese in racist literature like the Charlie Chan series, Imagism's characterization of that language obviously ran the opposite course.

Identifying this incongruity between two contemporary conceptions of the Other's language has at least two corollaries. First, it becomes evident once again that just as the racist portrayal of the Orient in American pop culture was thoroughly ethnographic, Imagism's description of the language was equally so from the same perspective. Second, this incongruity testifies in part to the inadequacy of a kind of reductive contextualization that can be found in recent studies of "nativist" modernism. Walter Benn Michaels, for instance, asserts in his revisionist project *Our America: Nativism, Pluralism and Modernism* (1995) that American modernism is inextricably connected to American nativism. He makes a connection between what he calls modernism's identitarianism and the racist discourse of the same period, maintaining that modernist poetic terms are indistinguishable from the 1920s terms of racial identity, and that the promulgation of racial identity is made literally indistinguishable from strategies of literary narration. The stark contrast between Imagism and its contemporary racist literature in terms of how they project the image of the Orient belies this assertion.[4] However, to use Imagism's somewhat benign view versus the racist view of the racial Other's language as an example to undermine Michaels's argument is hardly my point here, because there is a far more important issue at stake. The weakness of Michaels's project lies not so much in his denigration of modernism as in his failure to grasp the significance of modernism's linguistic encounter with the Other.

Writing in a different context, Stephen Greenblatt identifies similar variations in attitude that one culture holds toward the language of the Other—in his case, the Old World's view of Native American speech. Greenblatt emphasizes two European beliefs that he finds to be equally colonialist: One was that Indian language was deficient or nonexistent, and the other was that there was no serious language barrier between Europeans and savages (16–39). The first view apparently corresponds to that presented in the Charlie Chan series, which deems the Oriental languages to be defective and inscrutable. The second, albeit not completely applicable to Imagism, may shed some light on our understanding of the radical ways American modernism has put to use its linguistic experience with the Other. Greenblatt suggests that the historical and philosophical reasons for the denial of the language barrier between the Old and New Worlds lie in that "embedded in the narrative convention [of the sixteenth century] was a powerful, unspoken belief in the isomorphic relationship between language and reality," a belief that in the seventeenth century grew into a search for a universal language (28). As I discussed elsewhere, this idea of a universal language found its way into nineteenth-century Transcendentalist philosophy, which, in turn, bore strongly on the work of Fenollosa, Pound, and Amy Lowell.[5] Yet the cachet of Imagism lay not just in identifying Chinese as a paragon of the universal language but more importantly in appropriating foreign linguistic signs into its own signifying practice. And in doing so, Imagism pushed the Western language project a step further while opening up a transnational route for "American" literature.

> Now don't you think my makeup's good?
> The man who fixed me said he thought
> I'd done it all my life. You should
> Have seen me put it on—I bought
> It down in the pawnshop row.
> I think we'll have a dandy show.
>
> —Sidney Toler, "Stage Fright"

When Sidney Toler wrote this title poem of his book of poetry (published in 1910), he could not have envisioned that his "makeup" would really be thought "good" two decades later by many who were enraptured by his "yellowface" performances as Charlie Chan on the silver screen. Indeed, in all the films made and remade from the early 1930s to the late 1940s, the role of Charlie was always played by white actors: Warner Oland, Sidney Toler, and Roland Winters. Whereas Toler needed a mask in order to look Asian, Oland, because of the mixed blood he inherited from Swedish and Russian parents, looked naturally Chinese.

In the novels, the racial masquerade is even more twisted. Not only does the author Biggers hide behind the puppet show, cooking his Confucius in Charlie's mouth, but Charlie himself often puts on a mask. In *The Chinese Parrot* (1926), for instance, Charlie has to disguise himself as a Chinese servant named Ah Kim in order to stake out a rich man's house and solve the mystery. Although Charlie's English is already a flowery pidgin, as Ah Kim he has to speak in a still less standard manner, saying such things as "Allight, boss." It is not a happy situation for him, as he complains: "All my life . . . I study to speak fine English words. Now I must strangle all such in my throat, lest suspicion rouse up" (70). But on other occasions he enjoys using the masquerade to trick others, the same way he uses metaphoric talk to baffle people. Here is an example from the same novel:

> "But listen, Charlie," Eden protested. "I promised to call my father this morning. And Madden isn't an easy man to handle."
>
> "Hoo malimali," responded Chan.
>
> "No doubt you're right," Eden said. "But I don't understand Chinese."
>
> "You have made natural error," Chan answered. "Pardon me while I correct you. That are not Chinese. It are Hawaiian talk. Well known in island—hoo malimali—make Madden feel good by a little harmless deception. As my cousin Willie Chan, captain of All-Chinese baseball team, translate with his vulgarity, kid him along." (78)

This is a case of double masquerading: The author masquerades as Charlie, who masquerades as a (speaker of) Chinese. Charlie's purpose in saying something in Hawaiian as if it were Chinese is to warn his listener not to make a natural error, such as presuming that he can be nothing but Chinese. In fact, Charlie is very ambiguous about his Chineseness. In *Keeper of the Keys*, comparing himself to Ah Sing, an old servant who has kept his Chineseness intact, Charlie says:

> It overwhelms me with sadness to admit it . . . for he is of my own origin, my own race, as you know. But when I look into his eyes I discover that a gulf like the heaving Pacific lies between us. Why? Because he, though among Caucasians many more years than I, still remains Chinese. As Chinese to-day as in the first moon of his existence. While I—I bear the brand—the label—Americanized. . . . I traveled with the current. . . . I was ambitious. I sought success. For what I have won, I paid the price. Am I an American? No. Am I, then, a Chinese? Not in the eyes of Ah Sing. (87)

Here, Charlie's confession sounds like an evangelical sermon on cultural assimilationism, a white man's sermon delivered through a masquerading yellow man's lips. Moreover, the stigmatized yellow man is pushed to confront the question of racial identity. But even as he is made to lament the loss of imagined pure Chineseness, his flowery, pidginized, and ultimately defective speech has already doubly bound him to a racial stigma. As a white police sergeant tells him: "You're all right. Just like chop suey—a mystery, but a swell dish" (qtd. in Hanke, 88).

Undoubtedly, Charlie Chan is an emblem of racial parody and his speech a pidginization of Chinese. In contrast, Imagism seems able to sever linguistic traits from a stereotyped racial identity, performing ventriloquism without parody. Here are some Imagistic poems in which ventriloquism is obviously at work. The first one, entitled "From China" (1919) is by Amy Lowell:

I thought:—
The moon,
Shining upon the many steps of the palace before me,
Shines also upon the chequered rice-fields
Of my native land.
And my tears fell
Like white rice grains
At my feet.

(*Complete* 204)

Here, the New England noblewoman sits in her Sevenel Mansion in Brookline, Massachusetts, and speaks through the mouth of a Chinese concubine from the countryside. With the moon and such phrases as "steps of the palace," "rice-fields," and "rice grains" embodying an evident literary Orientalism, the ventriloquism achieves its poetic effect without parodying the character. The same with another poem by Lowell, entitled "Near Kyoto" (1919):

As I crossed over the bridge of Ariwarano Narikira
I saw that the waters were purple
With the floating leaves of maples

(*Complete* 203)

What is being masqueraded here is a Japanese voice, one that even pronounces an untranslated Japanese name: Ariwarano Narikira. But again, the imagined "crossing over" of the racial "bridge" is not focused on the racial identity itself; instead, it only attempts to capture the somewhat clichéd motifs of Oriental poetry: bridge, water, floating leaves, maples.

In matters of linguistic mimicry, Pound is a master. He first tried his hand in Chinese ventriloquism in the four poems collected in the 1914 *Des Imagistes* (Imagist Anthology): "After Ch'u Yuan," "Liu Ch'e," "Fan-Piece for Her Imperial Lord," and "Ts'ai Chi'h." They are often read as creative translation but should also be read as linguistic mimicry, as in "After Ch'u Yuan":

I will get me to the wood
Where the gods walk garlanded in wisteria,
By the silver blue flood move others with ivory cars.
There come forth many maidens
to gather grapes for the leopards, my friend,
For there are leopards drawing the cars.

I will walk in the glade,

> I will come out from the new thicket
> and accost the procession of maidens. (43)

The poetic persona assumes the voice of the first Chinese poet, Ch'u Yuan, and walks with it—in today's parlance, he walks the walk and talks the talk. The odd, archaic sentence structure of "I will get me to the wood" corresponds to a scene exoticized with phrases such as "garlanded in wisteria," "silver blue flood," "ivory cars," "to gather grapes for the leopards," "leopards drawing cars," and so on.

Pound's *Cathay* (1915), which re-creates Chinese poetic motifs through translation, is the culmination of his Chinese ventriloquism, so much so that T. S. Eliot even called him "the inventor of Chinese poetry" ("Introduction" xvi). In "The Jewel Stairs' Grievance," for example, Pound identifies himself with the poetic voice of Li Po (Rihaku), who in turn identifies with the female "I" in the poem:

> The jewelled steps are already quite white with dew,
> It is so late that the dew soaks my gauze stockings,
> And I let down the crystal curtain
> And watch the moon through the clear autumn. (13)

It should be evident that the poetic "identification" here is by no means "identitarian," a feature Michaels claims to be crucial to modernism (*Our America* 141). For this is not a *racialized* masquerade; nor is the "transcreation" of features of the Chinese language intended as a mocking of its speakers. Instead, what lies at the heart of Pound's *Cathay*, of Imagism as a whole, is an effort to find a different "medium for poetry," as indicated clearly in the title of Fenollosa's essay—"The Chinese Written Character as a Medium for Poetry."

To say that race is not a crucial factor in the Imagists' ventriloquism is not to suggest that the Imagists were not racists, but rather to emphasize that their interest in linguistic traits has not led them to stereotype the racial identity that is often, as in popular racist literature, associated with a language. In *The Dialect of Modernism: Race, Language, and Twentieth-Century Literature*, Michael North argues that the mimicry of black vernacular provides white modernists with a "technical distinction" and "insurrectionary opposition" to linguistic standardization in English. He writes, "In fact, three of the accepted landmarks of literary modernism in English depend on racial ventriloquism of this kind: Conrad's *Nigger of the "Narcissus,"* Stein's "Melanctha," and Eliot's *Waste Land*. If the racial status of these works is taken at all seriously, it seems that linguistic mimicry and racial masquerade were not just shallow fads but strategies without which modernism could not have arisen" (v). What North conceives of as essential to modernism—the mimicry of black vernacular—is to a large extent analogous to Imagism's Chinese ventriloquism. And the analogy is even borne out by Pound's use of black dialect in his translation of Confucian Odes, as in this one:

Yalla' bird, you stay outa dem oaks,
Yalla' bird, let them crawps alone,
I just can't live with these here folks,
I gotta go home and I want to git goin'
To whaar my dad's folks still is a-growin'.

(*Classic Anthology* 100)

Or in this ode in which the translator/ventriloquist Pound adopts "the oldest cliché of the dialect tradition, the black freedman's nostalgia for the plantation" (North 99):

Don't chop that pear tree,
Don't spoil that shade;
Thaar's where old Marse Shao used to sit,
Lord, how I wish he was judgin' yet.

(*Classic Anthology* 8)

It should be obvious that what Michaels has called "identity essentialism" may not be a very accurate characterization of American modernism when it comes to the issue of language. The nativist approach that thematizes a period of literature as a search for racial identity often underestimates the slipperiness of cross-cultural appropriations and fails to identify signifying mechanisms in literary texts that stand on racial and linguistic boundaries. The pidginization of Chinese in Charlie Chan is indeed a racist stereotyping, but the poetic ventriloquism of Imagism constitutes an example of cultural translation by which "foreign" systems of meaning are appropriated so as to develop new ways of signification in the "home" culture.

I posed
as a cookie
fortune smeller

—John Yau, "Genghis Chan: Private Eye XX"

Whether looked at as the ideal Adamic language or as the poisonous Devil's tongue, Chinese continues to fascinate twentieth-century

America, and the representations of it remain varied. Whereas the Chinese as a race, according to Robert G. Lee in *Orientals: Asian Americans in Popular Culture* (1999), have at least six faces in American racist or racialist representations (the pollutant, the coolie, the deviant, the yellow peril, the model minority, and the gook), the Chinese language is also portrayed in multifarious images. Imagism and Charlie Chan provide but two extreme representations, both of which will compete with a throng of others and be subject to revision by them. Especially notable is the meticulous reconstruction of the "new" image of Chinese in the hands of Chinese American writers, whose work often absorbs the clichés about the language, but revises them and subjects them to double parody or countermockery. One salient example is the contemporary poet John Yau. Whereas Imagists ventriloquize Chinese without parody and Biggers parodies its speakers through pidginization, John Yau follows the ventriloquism by further ventriloquizing it and parodies the pidginization by further pidginizing it.

As a poet, Yau grew up in a cultural environment in which literary Orientalism collided with outright racism. His relationship to Imagism, for example, is a complicated one. In an interview, he once stated,

> Certainly the Imagist Pound is something I read quite carefully when I first discovered him, but I went on to read *Personae,* which contained his *Cathay* poems, and I was certainly intrigued by them. Pound's Chinese poems were very, very meaningful to me then. I just read them over and over again . . . and I was reading the anthology of Imagist poets that William Pratt had edited in the sixties when I was first going to college, and I used those two things to teach myself how to write a poem. I used those books to imitate, you know. So I would imitate John Gould Fletcher and T. E. Hulme and H. D. and all the others. ("Interview" 43)

With his declared indebtedness to Imagism, Yau composes poems that seem to imitate Imagist ventriloquism, but his imitation itself contains another layer of ventriloquism, as in this one, entitled "From the Chinese" (1979), which is oddly reminiscent of the aforesaid Lowell's "From China":

> I put on your gown, and was comforted by its blue
> Tigers curling around me, even though it was dark.
> Sometimes, even the stars are hidden by their dutiful glow.
>
> Sometimes, even the stars are hidden by their dutiful glow,
> As only the moon trundles down the mountain path.

But how was I to know why you got up, and stood by the
open window?

(Sometimes 54)

Compared with Lowell's poem, in which "I" directly assumes the role of a Chinese concubine, Yau's has a "you" standing between "I" and "the Chinese." And who is this "you"? Can it simply be an imaginary Chinese persona, since the scene is typically "Chinese," with blue gown, tigers, and the moon on mountain path? Or can it be a poetic persona, such as Lowell, who has imagined herself being in a "Chinese" scene? Or, in another poem, "Reflections," Lowell identifies herself with a woman in "a rain-blue, silken gown":

When I looked into your eyes,
I saw a garden
With peonies, and tinkling pagodas,
And round-arched bridges
Over still lakes.
A woman sat beside the water
In a rain-blue, silken garment.

(*Pictures* 27)

Both Lowell's poetic persona and this Chinese woman are in turn implied by Yau's "you": "I put on your gown, and was comforted by its blue." Yau seems to be mimicking Lowell's mimicking of Chinese, but his double mimicry in this case obviously lacks the parody permeating another series of his poems, poems that countermock Biggers's racist mocking.

This series is ironically entitled "Genghis Chan: Private Eye," collating Genghis Khan (the great Mongolian king who conquered half of the world in the thirteenth century) with Charlie Chan. And the poems themselves are also characterized by word collation and muddling, as in this one:

I posed
as a cookie
fortune smeller

I sold
the stale delays
your parents pranced to

(*Edificio* 87)

In response to the fortune-cookie Confucianism characteristic of Charlie Chan's speech, Yau plays with such characterization by muddling two phrases: "fortune cookie" and "fortune teller." Since the fortune cookie is an American creation attributed to the Chinese, in fact it is unlikely to tell fortune. Hence "I," seen as Chinese by "you" (recalling the "you" in "From the Chinese"), can only "pose," not as a fortune "teller," but as a "smeller." The identitarian masquerading implied in the word "pose" is also performed by the phonetic cross-dressing between "teller" and "smeller."

Sound play continues in another poem in the same series:

> Grab some
> Grub sum
>
> Sub gum
> machine stun
>
> Treat pork
> pig feet
>
> On floor
> all fours
>
> Train cow
> chow lane
>
> Dice played
> trade spice
>
> Makes fist
> first steps
>
> (*Forbidden* 102)

Marjorie Perloff, in her review of Yau's *Forbidden Entries*, has unpacked some of the word riddles for us, identifying puns and images that refer to the oldest of "Chinese" stereotypes: dim sum, chow mein, treated pork, the trained cow, the spice trade, the dice game, and the poor immigrant Chinese who must "Grab some/ Grub sum," "make fist," and slave in factories ("machine stun").[6] "Yau is calling attention," Perloff summarizes, "to the lingering orientalism of U.S. culture, the labeling that continues to haunt Chinese-Americans" ("Review" 40).

While Perloff is correct in her interpretation of the semantic force of this passage, there is another linguistic feature worth noting in

Yau's poetry: his play with pidginization. Sound and spelling approximations between *grab* and *grub, sum* and *some, sum* and *sub, treat* and *feet, floor* and *fours, chow lane* and *chow mein, fist* and *first* are all characteristic of the kind of pidginization by which Oriental languages have been portrayed in American racist literature. We may recall, for instance, Charlie Chan's "Allight, boss." The muddling of words clearly imitates the floweriness and inscrutability of Charlie Chan's speech. Needless to say, what is involved in Yau's poems is an intentional play, a countermockery of the mockery of Charlie Chan, just as the title of the series, "Genghis Chan," contains an explicit double irony. Better still, the format in which many poems in this series are composed also suggests a parody: short couplets or triplets, which may be seen as pidginized versions of Japanese haiku or Chinese classical lyrics. In this case, one cannot even tell whether Yau parodies only the racist stereotypes in American pop culture or if he also mocks, to paraphrase Perloff, the lingering U.S. *literary* Orientalism, in which the Imagists—or even maybe the earlier Yau who followed them—participated.

However, this distinction is not as important as what we have learned so far regarding racial identity and language. It is true that a language, especially in its pidginized form, may be tied to a stereotyped racial identity, and thus a literary work's concern with language may fall back on racial questions, as in the case of Biggers's Charlie Chan. Or as often seen in minority literatures, a strategy of associating a language or dialect with a racial identity promotes ethnic interests. However, the value of the latter lies in breaking from the dominant, standard language practice, rather than in creating another "natural" tie between language and identity. In fact, as in Imagism, the obsession with the racial Other's language stays inside the realm of linguistic culture, the *racial* association being rarely foregrounded. Yau's work, especially, through ventriloquizing Imagism's ventriloquism and pidginizing racist literature's pidginization of Chinese, problematizes rather than foregrounds language's ties to racial identity. And the countermockery and double mimicry in Yau's poetry further complicate the cross-cultural displacement taking place in language.

Notes

* Reprinted from *Transpacific Displacement: Ethnography, Translation, and Intertextual Travel in Twentieth-Century American Literature,* by Yunte Huang.

1. *Xin* is also the first Chinese character to have appeared in Pound's cantos (vide Canto XXXIV). In "Some Notes by a Very Ignorant Man," a supplement to the 1935 publication of Ernest Fenollosa's *The Chinese Written Character as a Medium for Poetry,* Pound interprets this character as "Man and word, man standing by his word, man of his word, truth, sincere, unwavering" (47).
2. See the first three chapters of my *Transpacific Displacement: Ethnography, Translation, and Intertextual Travel in Twentieth-Century American Literature* (Berkeley and Los Angeles: University of California Press, 2002), in which this essay constitutes part of chapter 4.
3. See note 2.
4. One may also, as Marjorie Perloff points out, think of many canonical modernist writers such as Ezra Pound, T. S. Eliot, H. D., Gertrude Stein, Djuna Barnes, and Wallace Stevens, who may not fit into Michaels's nativist paradigm ("Modernism" 100).
5. See my *Transpacific Displacement,* 12–15.
6. In his letter to the author, July 29, 1999, Yau wrote, "Sub gum machine stun=submachine gun (among other things). Didn't GI's always chew gum in the movies? And of course, in my childhood, the reruns of movies on TV that depicted World War II, and the Japanese, was one thread of music running through my mind."

Works Cited

Biggers, Earl Derr. *The Black Camel.* New York: Grosset & Dunlap, 1929.

———. *Charlie Chan Carries On.* 1930. Reprint, New York: Pyramid Books, 1969.

———. *The Chinese Parrot.* New York: Grosset & Dunlap, 1926.

———. *The House without a Key.* New York: Collier, 1925.

———. *Keeper of the Keys.* 1932. Reprint, New York: Bantam Books, 1975.

Eliot, T. S. "Introduction." *Ezra Pound: Selected Poems.* London: Faber and Faber, 1928.

Fenollosa, Ernest. *The Chinese Written Character as a Medium for Poetry.* Ed. Ezra Pound. New York: Arrow Editions, 1936.

Greenblatt, Stephen J. *Learning to Curse: Essays in Early Modern Culture.* New York: Routledge, 1990.

Hanke, Ken. *Charlie Chan at the Movies: History, Filmography and Criticism.* Jefferson, N.C.: McFarland, 1989.

Huang, Yunte. *Transpacific Displacement: Ethnography, Translation, and Intertextual Travel in Twentieth-Century American Literature.* Berkeley and Los Angeles: University of California Press, 2002.

Jespersen, Otto. *Progress in Language.* London: Swan Sonnenschein, 1894.

Lee, Robert G. *Orientals: Asian Americans in Popular Culture.* Philadelphia: Temple University Press, 1999.

Lowell, Amy. *The Complete Poetical Works of Amy Lowell.* Boston: Houghton Mifflin, 1955.

———. *Pictures of the Floating World.* New York: Macmillan, 1919.

Michaels, Walter Benn. "American Modernism and the Poetics of Identity." *MODERNISM/Modernity* 1.1 (1993): 38–56.

———. *Our America: Nativism, Pluralism and Modernism.* Durham: Duke University Press, 1997.

North, Michael. *The Dialect of Modernism: Race, Language, and Twentieth-Century Literature.* New York: Oxford University Press, 1994.

Perloff, Marjorie. "Modernism without the Modernists: A Response to Walter Benn Michaels." *MODERNISM/Modernity* 3.1 (1996): 99–105.

———. Review of *Forbidden Entries,* by John Yau. *Boston Review* 22.3–4 (1997): 39–41.

Pound, Ezra. *Cathay.* London: Elkin Mathews, 1915.

———. *The Classic Anthology Defined by Confucius.* Cambridge: Harvard University Press, 1954.

———. *Literary Essays of Ezra Pound.* Ed. T. S. Eliot. London: Faber and Faber, 1954.

———, ed. *The Chinese Written Character as a Medium for Poetry,* by Ernest Fenollosa. New York: Arrows Editions, 1936.

———, ed. *Des Imagistes.* New York: Albert and Charles Boni, 1914.

Rohmer, Sax. *The Insidious Dr. Fu-Manchu.* New York: McBride, Nast, 1913.

———. *The Mystery of Dr. Fu-Manchu.* London: Methuen, 1913.

Toler, Sidney. *Stage Fright and Other Verses.* Portland: Smith and Sale, 1910.

Yau, John. *Edificio Sayonara.* Santa Rosa, Calif.: Black Sparrow Press, 1989.

———. *Forbidden Entries.* Santa Rosa, Calif.: Black Sparrow Press, 1996.

———. "Interview with Edward Foster." *Talisman* 5 (1990): 31–50.

———. *Sometimes.* New York: The Sheep Meadow Press, 1979.

14

Found in Translation

Reflections of a Bilingual American

Julio Marzán

Does your child speak another language at home? To begin my daughter's education in a New York City public school kindergarten I had to answer this question, which really inquired if her parents spoke another language at home and also asked if those parents were of the kind who obstructed their child's capacity to learn in an English-speaking classroom. Of course, even though at home my daughter did speak Spanish—because it was her Ecuadorean mother's first language; because Spanish was another intellectual enrichment to impart and as a household rule my wife and I didn't celebrate ignorance, not even ignorance that passed for superiority—I answered "No."

My authority to read into that question came from having lived more than fifty years, since the age of four months, in polyglot New York City and having devoted, in one fashion or another, my professional biography to observing American culture as speaker and writer of English. For this reason, even though my written answer came as reflex, afterwards I found myself rewinding and playing back old introspection on my bilingualism only this time to better understand its effect on my daughter's future. I didn't want to endanger her ability to achieve in the classroom, but I didn't want her to grow unable to communicate with her cultural legacy. After all, lacking material wealth to pass on, I wanted to leave her the best I had gleaned. In the matter of languages, that meant I wanted to bestow on her the gift of literacy in two languages.

Good language management: Like her, I began learning it upon entering school and I refined it in the course of my education toward a writing career. Steeped in that education in Anglo roots back to Chaucer and Beowulf, at first I believed that my writing resulted by willing dormant the Spanish-informed part of my psyche. For the most part (or at least so I thought) I succeeded, except for moments of linguistic interference or lacunae of lore or common sayings that I would not have heard in my particular upbringing by a Puerto Rican mother and an American stepfather.

But even as I edited to pave those bumps on my career path, I began to appreciate them as external signs of the bicultural, unconscious threads I was weaving into writing my particular language. What I consciously expressed in English was experience also being filtered through my other language, which to some unknown extent I was translating.

In Jorge Luis Borges's story on the fictive titular planet, "Tlön, Uqbar, Orbis Tertius," the inhabitants practice the art of reproducing things, simply making a duplicate they call a *rhon*. The most highly prized reproduction has no original, being a reproduction "from inspiration, from hope." Borges's first intention may have been to parody human reproduction, a hallmark theme, but I realized that my poems were like those reproductions, translations from pure inspiration, and not just because I was bilingual but because all art is *rhon*. Looking to summarize this mysterious translation inside me, from Borges's metaphor I spun off my own as the title of my first poetry book, *Translations without Originals,* which contained no translations or poems having to do with being bilingual, the only linguistic connection being my given name, which suggested that I as a child spoke another language at home.

Over a decade later, while doing research for my book, *The Spanish American Roots of William Carlos Williams,* and therefore closely reading Williams' complete works for the first time, I stumbled on another antecedent in two poems titled "Translation." Combining my autobiographical condition and the universal condition of creativity, these figurative translations, like my own poems, were neither literally translations nor explicitly referred to any other language. Rather, their titles reminded us that they were translations from another Williams cultural persona. Reading on, I then came upon a third poem, "Hymn to Love Ended" (every Quevedoesque pun—Hymn/Him—is intended by Williams), whose subtitle was a gloss on his two poems titled "Translations": "Imaginary Translation from the Spanish."

Like Williams's, my own imaginary translations didn't need to dwell explicitly on translation as either subject or theme, as I am doing now, any more than a poet or novelist needs to verbalize that what he or she is writing is concomitantly a lesson on how to write a poem or novel. I simply wrote poems, at that time only in English, and asking what rang true, what clanged false in American culture. Among the latter, the most threatening to me as aspirant writer was the mythos through which the mainstream culture customized Spanish speakers or anyone perceived as one.

For according to that mythos's teachings, reliable narrators can be only ethnically nondescript monolingual writers or bilinguals whose other language English deemed prestigious. Any association with Spanish, even if I never spoke it, made me intellectually unreliable as narrator and implicitly as anything else, a pretension posturing as truth and proselytized as an upscale superstition. I have witnessed its power over the brains of graduate school professors, editors, and colleagues who, after admitting to some minor flattery, cleared their throats to assume pose of innate authority that they had nothing to gain by examining and that they felt compelled to celebrate with me as acolyte.

And so my writing as an American became like my being an American, an epistemological puzzle. For if someone whose mere name evokes Spanish could produce such absurdity, imagine the effect of a thick accent. In that language, of course: the key is prestige. In contrast, no such limitation attended the accents of Nixon's Secretary of State Henry Kissinger and Carter's National Security Advisor Zbigniew Brzezinski or the poets Joseph Brodsky and André Codrescu and Charles Simic. Against this cultural affront my parental duty was both to armor and arm my daughter.

Does your child speak another language at home? I must confess to having become functionally bilingual only after youthful years of being serially monolingual. Raised for most of my early childhood in a Spanish-speaking household, I still spoke a fluent Spanish before starting school. After that, school and the new gadget, television (which only my aunt owned), and even more influential, radio, changed my linguistic preference. By the age of ten, when I came under the tutelage of an *americano* stepfather, my de facto adoptive father, I had already begun willfully to forget my Spanish, a shedding that continued despite my growing up still hearing it at home and breezing through high school Spanish classes. This decline stopped in my second undergraduate year as an English major when, required to take a "foreign language," I took Spanish courses again and finally learned the grammar as if I had stepped out of a stupor. Then after graduating, inspired by the late sixties and early seventies, I submerged myself in revolution and Spanish, making it my political purpose to become as literate in it as I had become in English.

I must rush to clarify that the waning of my childhood Spanish was not owing to any bad influence from my dad, who as a lover of Puerto Rican culture had mastered Spanish and even how to dance like a Latin to Latin music. Upon my mother's marriage, in fact, we moved to Puerto Rico, where we lived for half a year. After a business deal fell through, we subsequently returned, this time to the North Bronx. So if my stepfather—born Jewish but a lapsed Christian Scientist; born Ashkenazic but more comfortable around Sephardim—did remove us from the immediate New York Puerto Rican community, he actually brought us closer to my family in Puerto Rico, which we visited often, and where my father worked tirelessly on naturalizing his Spanish. Ironically, because he worked in El Barrio as a furniture salesman, he was also our conduit to the latest Puerto Rican community's news, rumors, and musical releases. Years later, when I rescued my moribund Spanish, I had to credit the influence of his unwavering Americanness as my model for feeling comfortable about possessing Spanish and English unselfconsciously.

So not from my stepfather did I feel the original pressure to lose Spanish: That pressure came from my socialization as a Latino American kid. Brought in diapers from Puerto Rico, I am a first-generation cultural immigrant, whose story is the familiar one of learning to forsake one's parents' culture and also learning that true Americans are loath to speak a foreign language. Consequently, even though Spanish was the language of home, growing up here meant interpreting the world through English. Such has been the norm for immigrants whose home countries, for a myriad of reasons, had failed them, and despite being born U.S. citizens, culturally speaking, Puerto Ricans were no different.

Our post–World War II migration consisted mainly of hill people and urban poor strongly encouraged to leave the island by an industrialization initiative. When they were suddenly thrust into New York's hostile reception, the less than sophisticated response of some gave rise to stereotypes that distorted the public image of the gentle people that the majority had always been. Consequently, even though this community predated Miami's most recent wave of exiled Cubans, a working-class exodus, in retrospect it can be called Puerto Rico's Marielitos, whose presence clashed not only with New York bigots but also with the postindustrial culture of Puerto Rico.

An earlier, smaller Puerto Rican migration of skilled, educated workers—the generation described in Bernardo Vega's *Memoirs* had also encountered hostility, but its class and cultural resources made it possible to organize politically, whether working toward the island's independence or toward socialism. The great actor José Ferrer belonged to that demographic, if not to the New York community. Also the Afro-Puerto Rican Arturo Alfonso Schomburg, who, angered by his fellow islanders' racism, moved to black Harlem and devoted his life to writing and researching black history. His extensive library became the New York Public Library's Schomberg Collection. The socialist Vega himself was a fervent supporter of Italian Harlem's legendary Congressman Vito Marcantonio during F. D. R.'s administration.

But those of my generation had to come of age, get an education, and investigate much before we were to learn of that history and realize as well that our New York selves were as much emblems of class as of culture. The mainly cultured, if much fewer, among of the prewar Puerto Rican migrants, to illustrate, were put off by the new arrivals' *jíbaro* ways and the emergent youth-gang culture (its impact eventually romanticized in the musical *West Side Story*), prompting Vega to offer his inability to identify with the newcomers as the reason for leaving behind the struggles of the changed "Barrio Latino" and moving to Long Island. Unlike the more culturally secure Vega, however, as children, future *newyoricans* only had the gloomy images of their stigmatized and violently reactive community to defend against American culture's persuasion that they adopt English as the means of improving their lot by becoming something else.

I had the advantage of having spent almost every summer of my childhood back on the island, where for two months I was sheltered from New York's influence. Perhaps for this reason, no matter how humble my associations with Spanish and despite the allure of a world whose English I have no memory of having spoken, I also found it hard to warm up to a comparatively faded-color dullness about *americano* that made me gravitate to the tropical sheen and warm sensuousness of Caribbean Spanish. Nevertheless, my inner conflict continued its gestation as for ten months I was informed by New York, where I couldn't help stockpiling years of resentment toward Spanish's inexplicable inferiority passed on to me.

Many years later, when working for a bilingual education program, I asked a Puerto Rican boy his name. He answered "Efrem." I added, "Do you mean Efraín?" His answer took me back to when I was his age: "Don't speak to me in that horrible language!" Clearly, Efrem was angry, and he had yet to discover that when he grew up, savvier island-based, ostensibly fellow Puerto Ricans would dismiss him, flaunting a gold plumage of one-upmanship because they were not angry, because they had not passed through that baptism of self-doubt and were sure that they could address *americanos* eye-to-eye.

Behind them would parade equally deluded continental Latin Americans who immunized themselves from self-doubt by reasoning that Puerto Ricans, being *tropicales* to begin with, were naturally selected to find themselves in their pathetic social standing.

Does your child speak another language at home? The true answer would affix my daughter on a scale or grid or an index card, and from that point on any common English mistake that might routinely be said by any non-Hispanic, non-Asian, you know, American kid, out of my daughter's mouth would give the teacher license to wax anthropological, attributing my daughter's error to her problem of being able to speak another language. I thought back to the Irish priest, the high-school English teacher who gave me a failing grade, arbitrarily discounting accumulated scores. In our classroom argument he got tripped up by a rhetorical trap I had set and, frustrated, roared for all to hear that "Yes, I lowered your grade to what I thought you deserved." Days later, so blinded by his arrogance, he didn't realize what he was saying to my stepfather, whose riposte had no peer, when by rote he ascribed my deficiency as probably due "to the neighborhood [I] lived in." Dad let him know that our North Bronx neighborhood was considerably better than where this priest had ever lived.

I looked around the lunchroom in which I filled out the questionnaire. A few other parents sat at my table: a couple of Jewish parents, a few Latino mothers. Farther removed, separated from ours by two empty tables, Koreans were crowded together, laughing and chatting. Those parents had been waved over to that table in Korean by an officer of the strictly Korean PTA. For in this Queens elementary school, one of the city's best, the dominant cultural power had shifted in the past decade from Jewish to Korean. Korean clout was such that the parents ran their own PTA and, after bringing a civil rights suit against the city, managed to postpone testing for a year so that their children, who spoke only Korean at home, could improve their English and have a fair opportunity to enter the gifted-children's program.

Highly protective of the Korean identity of their children, those parents rarely allowed them to attend—or even answer invitations to—birthday parties. They hired Korean school buses to transport the children home or to Korean after-school programs. Their protectionism reminded me of my mother's early—although far more modest but comparatively just as Herculean—efforts to insulate me from the worst influences of Bronx sidewalks and keep me connected to island family.

Another important similarity between Puerto Ricans and Koreans was the emphatic message sent by Koreans—not only in this school but in their business and real estate practices throughout Queens—that, conveying more than a desire to gather around the hearth of the familiar promoted among them a mythos of the inadequacy of American culture.

To be fair, many previous immigrants have demonstrated the same ethnocentricism, and in certain matters Spanish speakers too address a superior air at Anglo America. My own sister was returned to an elementary school on the island to prevent her acquiring the looser morals of American girls. But unlike the more upscale Koreans, Spanish-speakers' snootiness only goes so far, undermined by an inevitable *realismo*. Then, reiterating José Enrique Rodó's trade-off, they admit the great material achievements of American culture while holding on to a claim of superior Latin humanism. Strengthened by this sort of balance, most Spanish speakers work to become good, socially mobile, bilingual American citizens.

But the pull to capitulate absolutely to English overwhelms a large number, like those Latino mothers who sat among us non-Koreans. Those women embodied a prevalent pattern among the handful of Latinas in this virtually suburban, small-town-like neighborhood in which, except for my wife, all were married to middle-class *gringos*—high-school teachers, middle-level managers and salesmen—and discouraged their children from speaking Spanish or mixing with children like mine who still did. This de-Latinization is paradoxically so Latino. Racializing their own culture in the intellectually lowest American tradition, mothers of a darker complexion than mine or my child's behaved as if getting too close to Spanish or someone associated with Spanish would culturally darken them even more. Of course, mothers whose complexion was no lighter than mine, mainly South Americans, reacted the same but not just because of Spanish: The gossip spread, I would subsequently learn, that the husband who had just moved in was the neighborhood's only "Puerto Rican."

In sum, with their *de rigeur* lightened hair, their unvaried, un-Latin dressing down in jogging clothes and sneakers, their redundantly repeating their children's polysyllabic mainstream-sounding given names (Jeremy, Christopher, Priscilla) these mothers seemed to live obsessively self-conscious of their repressed Latin identity, a persona kept alive by their vigilance that it not betray them. Sitting a few feet from each other, we were really miles apart. I can only extrapolate from their attitude that, besides whatever risible notion they had of my being Puerto Rican and a Latin male, the higher and more rationalized barrier between us was my still having a Spanish-speaking disposition as evidenced by my child, whom they heard converse with me. From my perspective, of course, the major differences were that I had long been where they wanted to take their children and, unlike me, they could answer truthfully that their children spoke no other language at home.

Does your child speak another language at home? How inspiring it would have been if the question were intended to profile the embarking kindergartner, so the school could provide lessons in literacy in that language, a recognition of that child's being linguistically gifted. But that intention would not have genuinely reflected real American linguistic attitudes. Instead, behind the doubtless high-toned reasons for asking—to better understand the child and to provide the necessary resources—the question was actually part of a hidden agenda to teach American children to want to understand only English.

The traditional argument for monolingualism is not altogether without merit: A country composed of diffuse European subcultures with a history of internecine warfare had to discourage other languages from hastening the nation's dissolution or sowing clashes of regional ethnocentricities. According to this Platonic argument, ever hovering above us is a national unity Idea more close to being attained at the moment that the country exclusively speaks English. Also implicitly argued is the notion that English-speaking communities become ethnically nondescript, American.

In reality, however, the nation is a coalescing of competing subcultures that preserve their ethnic identity even after adopting English. Among those subcultures, the "mainstream" is the mythically defined ethnicity to judge the Americanness of other ethnicities. For the mainstream, the symbol of national unity is a presumably unifying English, overlooking its historical proclivity to defame non-Europeans and prompt these groups to preserve their identity and heritage, creating today's fragmentation. Simply put, the argument sees nothing disharmonious about the collective self-portrait of the country starring its select cultural citizens supported by a cast of purely civic citizens whose exotic cultural lives they are free to exercise on a plane that neither changes nor informs the officially recognized blend called American culture.

The controversy, of course, is strictly limited to internecine group dynamics: The U.S. government offers information materials as well as a full range of services in other languages, especially acknowledging the demographic importance of Spanish. This cooperation takes place without either legally enforcing English as the national language or declaring the country officially bilingual. The government's practice partakes of an old tradition: Thomas Jefferson is known to have taught himself Spanish and on occasion in Spanish addressed the Congress. My purpose is not to attack English as the dominant language, nor am I advocating a bilingual country; I am juxtaposing American linguistic reality beside its long-sustained Anglophone myth. Jefferson did no less in addressing the issue with his contemporaries and in ordaining that Spanish must be taught at the College of William and Mary.

Unfortunately, Jefferson's linguistic openness was not passed down; Americans are conflicted about languages. A powerful monolingual tradition subverts modern educational curricula that pretend to teach foreign languages. In the late 1990s, to illustrate, New Jersey's newly elevated educational standards required that students pass a foreign language exam to graduate from high school. Given the fashion value attached to continental languages, we might imagine that if students are being made to study a language, French and Italian might be favorites. But if today, more than at any time, continental European iconography lines the major avenues and dominates the couture labels, French (which in parts of New York has been resuscitated by Haitian students) and Italian have been disappearing as available subjects in school curricula, in which the big ticket has been Spanish, whose culture enjoys neither pedigree nor prestige in the ears of English speakers.

The reasons why Spanish resoundingly succeeds in schools are legendarily two: (1) its phonetic consistency has earned it the reputation of being the easiest language to study, and (2) the large, domestic Spanish-speaking populations allow for the rhetoric that Spanish is eminently "useful." To these I append a third: As any foreign language goes against the grain of a culture that doesn't encourage such speaking, students forced to learn a foreign language they will never use, least of all to communicate with local Hispanics, have understood the language requirement to be largely ceremonial. Overwhelmingly and quite sensibly, therefore, students choose the language that will neither wreak havoc on their cumulative grade nor leave them traumatized.

In most schools, "taking Spanish" is a purely symbolic act. Teachers, schools, and the entire culture all collaborate to deliver that encoded wisdom surreptitiously by celebrating the ethnocentrism that keeps Spanish far away and foreign. For even though Spanish predates the arrival of English on North America by a century, is spoken across a third of the nation's landmass, and is either the first or second language of the nation's largest composite ethnic citizenry, it is still taught as the language of some other place.

That Spanish and that other place are kept distant from the too-familiar gibberish spoken in the popular anthropology about local Hispanics, whose neighborhoods students, who are taught about foods and music and lovely sights of places like Spain and Chile, would no more think of visiting to practice their skills than their teachers would dare make that suggestion, inducing an outbreak of parental hysteria.

One arguably understandable reason for this mental cordoning off is both the merely perceived or possibly real danger: Most "Spanish" neighborhoods are working-class, if not paradigmatic ghettos. Some are even infested with violent gangs. In all events, be they neighborhoods peaceful or violent, a complete demarcation from such "minority neighborhoods" defines non-Latino, white middle class identity.

Another arguably understandable reason for separating foreign from local is that the socioeconomic disparity between the respective cultural bases of English and domestic Spanish invokes in speakers of the former a Calvinist streak that subtly damns those usually poorer and therefore ordained Hispanic Others to their own impoverished figment nationalities. Hence the whiff of predestination that allows for routinely associating Spanish-speakers with "the help." Newly arriving, hipper middle-class Latin American immigrants, especially those more purely Euro-descended, rapidly know to avoid being confused with stigmatized "minority," often Caribbean if not Mex-type Latinos and, in extreme cases, with stigmatized Spanish itself. Consider: If this culture can convince native Spanish speakers to drop Spanish altogether, how should we expect non-Spanish speakers to be disposed to learning it?

And the greatest irony is that behind Anglo peacocking before Hispanic culture and the bluster against bilingual education, the mainstream posture toward Spanish is also a very effective, self-defensive canard. For however imbalanced the images evoked by the juxtaposed cultures, the fact remains that the United States's first and oldest Cold War has been over language and its Anglophone self-preservation amid the ubiquitousness and persistence of American Spanish. Thus the danger sensed in Spanish's resistance to fading into its speakers' "past," which it cannot do because it too is an American language of an American Hispanic present, whose Old Country is America itself. Bigotry, racism, superiority may have operated in English's traditional putting down of local Spanish, but ultimately it did so in the service of a historical consciousness trying to delimit a national identity against the threat of being swallowed up by its hemispheric American roots.

The long-running Anglo American superiority in just about anything one can name may have veiled this competition in a total wash, but at the end of the twentieth century that competition became increasingly visible with the voluminous increase of Latin American immigration at a time of Anglo American cultural decline. Today Latin America may still be "emerging," but it has evolved measurably. Tellingly, in the face of Latinos as both the largest minority and the newest politically influential ethnic block, a counterforce shrilly warns of a cultural invasion and cries out for the formalization of English as the national language. The criers may sound as if they know what they want, but what they produce is a question: what is American culture?

Does your child speak another language at home? Five years have passed since I encountered that question as portal to my daughter's schooling. Today she sits among gifted fourth-grade peers and no teacher has brought up the issue of her speaking another language. While, like their parents, her few Latino classmates seem to have set as the pinnacle of their formative achievement their becoming monolingual in English, she remains unimpressed. A voracious reader in English, from browsing through Spanish books in the house she taught herself to read Spanish phonetics and began writing notes to her grandmother in Spanish. She enthusiastically awaits our sitting down so we can start her with basic Spanish grammar—all this mimicking her older sister.

For the younger child's American rite of resisting Spanish was mercifully avoided as a consequence of earlier strategies plied on her now teenage sister, my stepdaughter, who at home resisted being made to answer in Spanish as much as being ordered to practice piano. Today she says she loves both although she formally studies high school French, which she has picked up with agility, as there was no point to her wasting time going through school Spanish, whose basic levels she had already come to know. French came into our lives as a byproduct of my shaking up her defiance against anything not English—the lesson she seemed to be getting throughout the school year from her peers—by our taking summer family trips to Quebec. When both girls were young, trips to Puerto Rico were helpful, but those trips got increasingly expensive. An economical way of widening the girls' linguistic horizons was visiting Montreal, where the older girl observed how different but familiarly "Latin" those Québécois were in their manners, taste in clothes, and, later, flirting.

Four years into French, out of the blue, she asked me when I could teach her Spanish grammar because she had made a decision to sound fluent and intelligent in Spanish.

My family's mentored bilingualism is, of course, an expression of who I am, but more than teaching them Spanish my objective was help them rise above an ultimately banal American socio-politico-racial discourse that sows self-doubts, wastes creative energy, and isolates one from the wider world. Both girls strongly identify with the United States as their country but are learning to discern its dimensions of greatness from its occasions of smallness, notably in its attitude toward Spanish. Personally, I can't help seeing their comfort with Spanish amid peer pressure to be monolingual as the legacy of my stepfather's Whitmanesque American consciousness, thanks to which they see no inner conflict in being American and speaking both Spanish and English.

Does your child speak another language at home? As I write this section it is two months to the day since New York's World Trade Center was toppled by terrorist airplane hijackers. The entire country senses a change, transformed by so many haunting images. Among them, striking a special chord in me, was the televised head-hunt by Attorney General Ashcroft, who announced immediate employment for native speakers of Arabic and Farsi. His appeal prompted public conversations on the importance of human over technologically gathered intelligence and the value to national security that its citizens learn foreign languages. Ironically, after a call for jihad drew thousands of Pakistani, Chechnens, and Chinese Muslims to resist the United States in Afghanistan, news reports described the movement of those linguistically diverse volunteer Taliban forces in trucks on each of which also rode a translator.

At first President Bush mistakenly described the coalition forces he had organized against the "forces of evil" as a "crusade," evoking the last Christian-Western effort to wipe out heathen-Eastern Islam. To correct this misnomer, subsequent propaganda underscored American determination to pursue certain Muslims for being terrorists but not for being Muslim. The news media also made us aware of the growing Islamic population on American soil, suggesting a future Islamic influence on American culture. Appeals were made to misguided citizens not to harm innocent American Muslims. Overnight we had all changed: One extreme interpretation of Islam resulted in mass murder and the destruction of those monumental twin metaphors forced the West to take stock of itself as a civilization.

Old, familiar conflicts were demoted in importance. On the day of the attack in New York, Fidel Castro offered to help however Cuba could. Within weeks the formerly outcast Westernized Pakistani leader was "persuaded" to cooperate against former fundamentalist allies. Also the new, West-looking Russia—fighting its own war with Islam in Chechnya—discovered how much it had in common with the United States. Later, as if loyal to battle lines drawn, Mexico and Russia refused to help OPEC, dominated by Saudi oil, to cut production and raise oil prices. Notwithstanding these acts as political posturings these were notwithstanding, they all wore the veil of Western solidarity. And throughout these two months a citizenry that had paid scant attention to international news now eagerly waited to hear from fraternal terrorist hunters in Germany, Spain, England, France, Italy.

In other words, Americans who had prided themselves in not having to know much beyond their sources of income discovered an international dependency that underwrote the peace that made possible their collective financial stability. The world once contained to the dimensions of a television screen was now directly connected to daily lives, and to protect ourselves from its human failing, we needed the services of foreign languages. Ashcroft's appeal to find Americans who also spoke Arabic and Farsi implied a change that would doubtless manifest itself in those school curricula that had been steadily eliminating foreign language classes.

Suddenly too the familiar xenophobia was replaced by another, this time at the level of civilization. Now at border crossings, where national security operated at the highest level alert, agents kept an eye out for a different kind of interloper. Mexicans entering the country illegally were no longer hard news. Surely the smuggler's trade continued unabated across hot dangerous terrain that no cell phone-carrying, car-renting terrorist would choose to endure. But Mexicans risk their lives to sell flowers or work in restaurants or dig ditches, not to harm Americans. Next to, unfortunately, the demonized Middle Eastern languages, even Spanish begins to sound downright like home.

This distracted mood, a transient wartime mood perhaps, seems rife with possibilities, auguring a new American regard for the world and its languages, even though the intuited, inner revolution of such a change seems to underlie the desire to return to normal, a nostalgia for an America gone with the wind, like New York's former skyline and the license to reassuringly, self-interestedly customize reality. That is why I fear that, even if unconsciously, for many rebuilding implies re-erecting familiar barriers, reinventing the isolationism that was part of pre-September eleventh peace. For now I will argue that since that momentous day I have witnessed that Americans are capable of seeing kinship where they once saw foreignness and demonstrated the capacity to see a gift in those who answer "Yes" to the question of whether one's child speaks another language at home.

1 5

Mixture's Speech*

Julio Ortega

Mixture in Latin America is a generous plant born of European seeds and American lands. Both the indigenous chronicler Guamán Poma de Ayala and the *mestizo* chronicler Inca Garcilaso de la Vega—each a product of Spain and its colonies—pause to note the wonders and abundance that this fertile hybrid yields. Indeed, the expanded tree is one of Jose Martí's preferred metaphors for affirming sum and difference: Nature becomes eloquent proof of cultural hybridity. Marti's tree is metonymic of the new American subject, its classical values and civic promise. Similarly, the intricate Argentinian *pampa* becomes ungeometric space, synechdocal of its border *gauchos* found in Sarmiento's catalogue of difference. Mixture is the production of difference, possessing no stable state in its boundless fluidity: Mixture is, in each subject, a principle of signification through difference. Thus, each of mixture's practitioners seeks to contextualize it and immediately articulate it for his or her own project. Guamán Poma proposed a bilingual subject—fluent in Quechua and Spanish—as agent of the world's "Andeanization," counseling his people to learn writing as a way to preserve the old and reappropriate the new. Writing appeared to him as a tool of mixture, and so he catalogued mixture's series as testament to a summed knowledge. Garcilaso de la Vega, on the other hand, discovered in his mother tongue the source for his universalization of the *Incario*. Quechua presents itself to him as a model of civility and humanist thought and Spanish as a graft to be reinterpreted and reordered. Garcilaso de la Vega was one of the first to understand bilingualism as cultural model and therefore political definition.

Grafting plants, along with the transport and sowing of seeds, is one of the principles of abundance documented by colonial chroniclers. The outcome of this fusion, however, is not simply the product of American and Spanish plants, but rather the fecundity that permits new growth. The notion of the new gestates in this practice within a cultural stage set by double series, by insertions and bipolarities. A parallel phenomenon occurs in the contact between two languages, not simply the linguistic borrowings to be expected from agglutinating indigenous languages imbricated by a discrete Spanish. Thus, several native languages increased their registers by appropriating new units or including their declensions in Spanish words. Bilingualism thus develops as an articulating attribute of the indigenous world: Quechua puts Spanish to the service of its own register. Conversely, Spanish practices an intense digestion of other languages into its own linguistic system, "castilianizing" names and expressions. In this manner, Peru arises from Virú and Lima from Rímac, a river. A different phenomenon is transcodification, the passage of a word or concept from one language to another, which affects its meaning. It occurs, for example, with the potato, perceived in Europe both as aphrodisiac and poison. Guamán Poma takes the term *India* to be composed of two words: *in* and *día,* the realm in or of the day, obviously Perú. Later on, Adam and Eve will become a single character in Andean mythology: Adaneva. On the one hand, in Spanish, we encounter a practice of forced adaptations; on the other, in Quechua, reappropriations and syncretism. Bilingualism is an intense inequality, a hybrid state devoid of a normative code.

The normativity of the Spanish language and the traditional values of its use do not recommend mixture and often dismiss hybridity as license or excess. For example, Joan Corominas, in his *Diccionario crítico etimológico castellano e hispánico* he cites Laguna while documenting the use of "melon" (1955): "the *melocotón* is in truth a bastard peach, because it is born of a peach and the *membrillo* grafted one onto the other."[1] The graft as bastard is a disqualification from both a natural order as well as a linguistic one ("truth" denigrates the product of mixture). Oliva Sabuco (seventeenth century) resorts to the same genealogical strategy (explaining an object by its origins) in order to sanction it: "We see children degenerate from their parents in turning out better and more virtuous, or turn out worse and more depraved, as the *melocotón,* results from peach and *membrillo,* and as the animal *crocuta* results from lioness and hyena."[2] In this space of control and sanction, the new in mixture can result only from excess: the opening up of an alternate scene. There, from graft to hybrid, transplant to *mestizaje,* the new proves to be the sum of the parts composing the American subject, fashioned in difference and strangeness. The new in America is an imminent form.

Abundance passes from wonder to excess, metaphor to hyperbole, becoming in the process a discourse fertile in and of itself. Abundance is autoreferential, occurring as sowing, transplantation, translation, and graft on the colonial stage; but soon it occurs in discourse, where it lavishes figures. A more classical notion is that of an abundance in common, shared by all in the New World. The idea of the sun as a communal model, its light collectively shared, is a topic of utopian humanism. Mexico's "eternal spring" is a wonder, but also a classical allusion.

When the native chroniclers pause in the descriptions of their own goods, they find other sources for their hyperbolic fecundity. Fernando Alvarez Tezomoc, grandson of Moctezuma, in his *Crónica mexicana* (1598)[3] pays more attention to the warriors' rich dress than to the war itself. Even Bartolome de las Casas's and Vasco de Quiroga's projects champion abundance's claims. The fourteen "remedies" that de las Casas recommends have as their goal to turn the islands "into the best and richest land of the world, all the while with Indians living in it." Abundance demands a subject. It will be, however, the poor man who is figured as the natural hero in an American Golden Age, a Golden Age that el Inca Garcilaso de la Vega believes to be a bettered extension of Spain. Guamán Poma, following de las Casas, holds discourse itself to be the remedy. In fact, he announces and anticipates it, saying "soon we will have a remedy."[4] He repeats his argument's central praise: Abundance travels the calendar with its fruits and herbs, as if time were an emblematic orchard. Gonzalo Fernández de Oviedo is perhaps the one who pays the most attention to flavors and sizes, sometimes even remembering the taste of a certain fruit while forgetting its name. Of the island fig groves he says: "they bear figs large as small melons."[5] And also: "There are also melons grown by the Indians, and they become very large, frequently measuring a half or a whole quarter or more; so large are some, that an Indian must carry one his back; and they are stout and white on the inside, and some yellow, and have graceful seeds almost in the manner of gourds . . ."[6] The comparison with the fruits of Spain sets the point of view, and thus the gourd, making the account more plausible In this manner, these fruits belong to the demonstrative category of examples, a humanist strategy of persuasion. However, they are examples that test the account's logic, exceeding cause and effect, potential and act, series and object. They demand the testimony of sight and taste, increasing their measure and worth.

Figs and melons, for example, are Spanish products that grow unchecked in the colonies. Comparable but for their scale, figs are like small melons, melons like enormous gourds, monstrous if not for the "graceful seeds" within. The seeds, that is, of a domestic fruit: the plausible. Examples become acts of faith, maintained by comparative accumulation and testimonial reiteration. Melons are an eloquent example, for here we have a generic term, surely involving several species. In this manner, the melon is an emblem of the transplant augmented by plurilingualism: a traveling name, beginning anew in the New World as an abundant syllable. (Covarrubias in his *Tesoro de la lengua castellana o española* rules that the Latin *melopepon,* "in rigor, stands for apple.") Everything tends towards the language of the Baroque; although when the Baroque arrives, it too is surpassed by this new language. As it is, the Baroque is a nominative splurge, prolonging subordinate clauses until the subject of the phrase almost disappears from view. In the Baroque, any circumstantial parenthetical becomes primary. In this way, the drama of abundance ceases to be a putting on as proof of the gaze and the name, becoming instead a sumptuous set of the art of seeing again and renaming. The Baroque subject is a child of bilingualism.

Jacinto de Carvajal (ca. 1567–ca. 1650), recounts in his *Descubrimiento del Río Apure*[7] Miguel de Ochogavia's 1647 expedition, in what is perhaps the most baroque of the so-called Orinoco Cycle. Lightly extravagant, with all the scenic tropes of the Baroque repertoire, the chronicle exalts a voyage down the Venezuelan river as if it were a mythic enterprise. Carvajal claims to be eighty years old, but his appetite for nature and its peoples is brought to life by the Baroque appetite for the world as a catalog of plurilingual plenties. He enumerates more than thirty types of fruit and thirty-five bird species using their regional names. He also offers ethnological information in his list of the Caribbean groups, designating seventy-two ethnic enclaves even though the vast majority are unidentifiable today.

Fruits he distinguishes by using the entire qualitative repertoire: color, taste, smell, size, shape, and resemblance to those found in Spain. These are fruits that exhibit the added value of their appearance: "Pammas, fruits the length of a coral tube, purple and very sweet." Their other value is in the pleasure of new names, that celebration of native language that resounds within the sensual language of the Baroque. Language and Nature coincide in their fecundity: *merecures, chivechives, cubarros, pachaccas, guamaches, yaguares, caramines, quebraderos, ojos de payara, manires, chares, muriches, guaycurucos, curichaguas*... He concludes: "Surplus of the mentioned fruits do the Indians enjoy, part from our own, and with such abundance as I was later to see and experiment" (242). Several other lists wind their way through this chronicle of Venezuelan sums, which is itself listed chronologically. The account reaches such great lengths that the chronicler informs us of the hours when he sleeps and wakes, when he conducts his prayers and attends religious services. The world is upheld by its names, reproducing itself in them, glittering and new, but also mutual and shared, as if a shelter secured by language. This appears to be a characteristic of the chronicle in question that gives an account of the Venezuelan plains, their botanical diversity, and their recent cities. It is a repertoire of the awe at a time of joy and promise, almost outside the shadow of the past. Even the most important Venezuelan poem of the nineteenth century, Andrés Bello's "Oda a la agricultura de la zona torrida," is a panegyric enumerating plants, joining those of Europe and America, as if they were all daughters of the grove and augmented language of the new nation. In his *Gramática,* Bello—humanist and translator, linguist and poet, philologist schooled by American catalogues—poses the shared memory of an oral civilization. He does not do so to conserve a norm, as has been readily suggested, but rather out of a modern and instrumental consciousness of language as an American abode.

Another chronicler overwhelmed by his subject matter's excess was Joseph Luis de Cisneros, a ware trader in the Guipuzcoana Company, the Basque enterprise awarded monopoly in Venezuela by the Spanish crown in 1742. Cisneros published a brief commercial treatise, *Descripción exacta de la provincia de Benezuela* (1764), salvaged and introduced by Enrique Bernardo Núñez. This succinct description of rudimentary economic geography is an inventory of the goods and products of some of the country's towns and cities. Here we have a curious treatise on abundance from the vantage point of commerce. To this end, the author needs only to provide a listing of the fruits, manufactures, and livestock of each region. His enumeration is animated by a faith in the exchange of goods as a display of public health and civic well-being.

The vantage point of commerce instates a public market of intermediations, in which negotiations and dialogue, production and consumption, take place amid impressive names—creole and native flavors—and well-stocked storehouses. Between wondrous nature and joyful inhabitants, the last part of the nineteenth century instates commerce's storehouse, a sort of modern day cornucopia distributed among rural spaces, the migration of European workers, and urban growth. (This storehouse follows previous instances of exchange, such as the *tambo* and the *pulpería.*) Meat is the most valued good in Caracas, according to Cisneros: "They stock this city with Cow Meat, which is the one consumed; since Mutton, is never weighed at the Butcher Shops."[9] The resonant names of townships are centers of production, and products themselves, herald the new fertile commercial discourse. Soon, this enumeration lends itself to designative hyperbole: "Veal, Good Mutton and Capons, are devoured and with abundance. Entran Pork Cold Cuts, Chickens, Hens, Turkeys and Duck arrive from the outlying Townships."[10] Cisneros writes from the public plaza, where the market is the center of a prodigious vision: products parade as if in a mundane allegory of wealth. As he elaborates, "white and brown sugar abound in excess." Flour accumulates so steadily as to be lost in storehouses. Even this loss, however, confirms that "we always find ourselves with abundance." This excess ending in overindulgence recognizes that consumption is free and that the Caracas citizen defines himself through his choice of one sweetener over the other for his cup of cocoa. When reviewing San Juan's capes, he is confident that in each cape "a whole shipyard could be built, cutting down the Wood of the proudest mountains next to the Valleys of the Yaracuy River."[11] This measure of desire seeks to transform nature under the new rule of industry. In a gesture worthy of dithyrambic empiricism, Cisneros ends by naming all the ports and coves on the coast, *sans* adjectives, since the geographic sum of the Venezuelan Caribbean is, if nothing else, as verbal a cornucopia as it is earthly.

Already in his *Grandeza Mexicana* (1604), Bernardo de Balbuena had made the city the center of his Baroque representation. Nature is a catalogue of goods for language to sort—not in the outside world or casual environment, but rather, in the urbane and courtly setting of the page, in that calm limpid lyric where the American subject travels the dictionary as if it were a map of Mexico. Balbuena moved from Spain to Mexico at about the age of twenty. His American apprenticeship fashioned him into an erudite poet, a formal classicist with a taste for the symmetries deployed by the Baroque. His project was not the specific difference of the "Mexican," but rather the inclusive difference of its language: The Baroque figure of American expansion occupies the present tense, devoid of limits, and so the Mexican becomes a fold in the fluidity of a Spanish universal. Like Gracian, he uses images of rare grandiloquence, whereupon the world's oddity places tension on the logic of representation. We see this is in the emphatic verse in which he states that Mexico City,

> Is heart and center of this great orb,
> Beach where highest rises and swells
> In its delight the sovereign wave.[12]

The city as heart and axis of the world imposes here a figure of equivalence. Mexico is a double center, geographic and corporeal, effective and allegorical, but also a border of the world where delights mount like waves. (Abundance, after all, comes from the Latin *unda*, wave.) And so, every word is something else; only the declaration "México es una ciudad deleitosa" (Mexico is a city of delights) would serve as implicit reference. The poem does not speak, although occasionally it sings. Mostly, it metaphorizes. It says one thing for another, increasing the register of verbal equivalences and descriptive hyperbole, a hymn too mundane to invoke the Muses. This "Epilogue and Final Chapter," declaring itself ciphered discourse, lingers even over a household's high rent (there is a house so arrogant, he says, that its rent is higher than the county's: "it yields from thirty thousand pesos, upwards"). His selection tends toward the generic; even the central market owes more to the catalogue than to the eyes:

> Whatsoever is craved by a varied taste
> And to the gift—treat and sustenance—
> July ripens and April blossoms,
> Towards its abundant market marches;
> And there craving meets thought,
> More than gluttony in asking hits its mark.[13]

Abundance becomes a literary citation, a rhetorical archive supporting the poem's authority. In truth, the "grandeza mexicana" lacks a subject: It is an adjectival phrase, a discourse in search of the enunciative act that would actualize the subject of abundance within the poem from outside itself. The poem ends with the following:

> Its illustrious people, full of nobility,
> Genial, sweet and mannered in their dealings
> Of a spirit without shade of paucity.[14]

This crowd is configured, therefore, from within abundance and against lack, in the urban plenty of its courtly lifestyle, and in opposition to disheartening poverty and the shadows it casts. Already in Balbuena, we can observe that where differences of a plurilingual mixture do not prevail, the hierarchies and exclusions of the monolingual are imposed. However, monolingualism implies more of a state than an actual subject.

If we move toward origins, we again encounter one of the originators of the very idea of American origins: El Inca Garcilaso de la

Vega. Max Hernández, in his suggestive psychoanalytic reading of the Inca's life and work, dedicates a chapter to "writing and power," in which he discusses in detail the fable of the Indians (all illiterate), the melons (which they take to their master's friend) and the letter (which reveals they have eaten half their errand). Let us pause for a moment over this plotting of nature and language, word and fruit.[15]

The owner of the grove where these first melons are grown bears the name Solar. In Spanish, the name invokes not only the sun—an indigenous deity—but a noble family's plot of land as well. Moreover, here we have a Spaniard who owns land in the indigenous religious center, since the melons are first grown in Pachacamac. Another scene runs beneath the surface of this account: the temptation of the forbidden fruit. Tasting it, says Hernández, is "to put the word to the test." He concludes that the word operates more as an instrument of repression than as a tool of knowledge. There is, however, a final irony, for, as Hernandez indicates, "the narrator of the written anecdote is himself an Indian. Through his pen, writing recuperates its liberating power." Hernández points to a chief mechanism of Garcilaso's account: transference, the permanent displacement of symbolic equivalences. Perhaps the Inca acquired this mechanism from a humanist tradition, through a reading of Petrarch, or perhaps even Dante. It is present, after all, in the symmetries and articulations of neo-Platonic discourse. Transferring the lost *Incario* to a political Utopis, possibly the greatest of all equivalences, permitted an articulation of the morrow. The humanist practice of narrating through *examples* constructs a sufficient proof, transforming history's truth into the present's lesson.

Acts are thus transferred onto modes of thought. Learning history implies refashioning the present. Garcilaso seems to have understood, from the onset, that his story would be intelligible and have a place within the larger history of Spain in the Americas only through this mesh of transferences and equivalences, in which each act and individual is projected as an example of an inclusionary tale, in which tallies are made to account for loss as gain, dearth as abundance, and the subject's displacement in his new written identity. The work of el Inca Garcilaso is that letter: knowledge passing into wisdom, memory into account, biography into history. The work itself is a palimpsest: Behind its writing lies orality; behind history, fable; behind the Indians, nature—their abundant mirror. Abundance's children are not, in the end, victims of the word but rather its best instance: The word that censures denies itself in discounting the Other. The word, proposes el Inca, is always of the Other. The hierarchical word, defining through exclusion, is counter to the new truth (Quechua and Castilian) rewritten by the fable as a more durable, intelligible letter. It is also due to this semantic polyphony that a transparent reading of the fable runs the risk of becoming literal. And yet, a system of *examples* whose mechanism is equivalence cannot be literal. Such is the case of proper names.

In another fable, the Inca gives the name of a castaway as Pedro Serrano. However, the anagram represents a transference: "la piedra de la sierra," the mountain's stone, a foundational emblem. Transferred to his American Isle, this castaway from humanism becomes an autodidactic American philosopher; in this particular case, a Spaniard who begins everything anew and learns how to live like a native. More of the same occurs with Pachacamac, the setting's name in the fable of the letter. The coincidence of the names Solar and Pachacamac (*pacha* is land; *camac,* sacred place) does not appear casual. Between their "sky" and "land," the Spanish melons are already American.

One of this fable's most anecdotal and narrative versions, "Carta canta" by Ricardo Palma (in *Tradiciones peruanas*)[16] adds details to the account. It is telling that while a historian such as Garcilaso relies on narrative devices, a narrator, Palma, attempts to document the fable. In the first version of the tale, Palma, evidently in line with the Inca, writes "the Pachacamac melon patch." However, in the second version (1883), he changes the setting to Barranca. It happens that Palma has discovered the *encomendero*'s story: "Don Antonio del Solar, by 1558, one of the most comfortably settled neighbors in this city of Kings [Lima]. Although he was not among Pizarro's brothers-in-arms at Cajamarca, he arrived in time to receive a good parcel of land during the redistribution after the Conquest. It consisted of a spacious lot in which to construct his house in Lima, two hundred leagues of fertile land in the valleys of Supe and Barranca, and fifty *mitayos* or Indians at his service." The first version read "twenty leagues" and "in the Pachacamac valley." Did el Inca Garcilaso change the setting to Pachacamac in order to endow the patch with mythic value? The fable of writing, by the same token, carries the open character, associative and indeterminate, of bilingual signs, implying myriad meanings, inexhaustible within a single reading. There is no better emblem for the causative force unleashed by this multi-writing of the New World, as well as for this American subject, which is so recent that writing begins by placing all his values in question. In the end, this is a telling *example* on writing's power—not only of its literal power against the Other, but also, more acutely, of its paradoxical power at the hands of the Other.

A fable of origins proves there are no origins, for the tale is in many places. It also proves that without Indians there would be no tale: their candor is that of the neophyte or illiterate, soon to be schooled and inducted. Through the "melons" he will appropriate the "Word." To wit, signs of the new in nature lead him to the new signs of exchange. This fable, ostensibly about dual tensions, is, in truth, about the erecting of triad, of an inclusive figure's three faces: the Indians, the *encomendero,* and the narrator; Spain, Pachacamac, and the melons; orality, writing, and power; censure, transgression, and apprenticeship. Its final lesson is that the fruit of abundance is shared through writing.

The emblematic character evinced by these products of abundance will develop its heraldic value and—as sign of the new times—economic and scientific summations of wondrous America nature. The case of quinine offers excellent proof. The quinine tree stands as emblem of vegetable abundance on the national Peruvian coat-of-arms. Its reputation as an American cure for fevers was legendary. Its diffusion within the royal European houses assured its place in the pharmacopoeia and Royal Apothecary. From 1634 until 1786, at least, quinine's fame transcended medical interest and botanical curiosity to reach literature. Joaquín Fernández Pérez, of the Universidad Complutense de Madrid, in his article "Las relaciones entre Linneo y Mutis. El problema de la determinación de los árboles de la quina," documents the history of the numerous and contradictory attempts to observe, classify, and study this tree, whose bark (*cascarilla*) was exported to Europe via Cadiz. Also known as Chinchona, the tree can be found in the mountains of Peru, Ecuador, and Bolivia. Linnaeus, who dedicated his doctoral thesis to fevers, displayed a vivid curiosity toward quinine. Thanks to José Celestino Mutis, originally from Cádiz and later installed in Nueva Granada, Linnaeus received a drawing of quinine bark, along with a sampling of dried leaves and flowers. He responded immediately, confiding that he "had never before seen" such flowers and that they "gave me an idea of this rare genus." Linnaeus baptized an American flower as Mutisia—in honor of his correspondent—of which he said, "Never had I seen such a strange plant; its leaf is clematide, its flower signesia."

For a naturalist such as Linnaeus, who had classified nature into a harmonious, symmetrical, and systematic order, these rare plants find their place in the specie *Plantarum*. Quinine, Fernández Pérez tells us, lies between *Bellonia aspera* and *Coffea arabia*—that is, coffee. Linnaeus baptized it Cinchona. The name remits us to Peru and another fable of origin, assuming a revelatory logic, that epiphany in knowledge of the new that characterizes these stories about the taste and knowledge of New World goods. Again, we owe the genealogy of this account that constructs itself as history to Ricardo Palma. In his "tradition" entitled "Los polvos de la condesa," Palma tells that the Viceroy Luis Jerónimo Fernández de Cabrera Bobadilla y Mendoza, count of Chinchón, had arrived in Lima at the behest of Phillip the Fourth. Shortly after his arrival, however, his wife fell ill, victim to a fever. Palma assures us that story takes place in 1631 and that, providentially, a Jesuit announced he had the countess's remedy. Not by chance, the remedy was initially known as "Jesuit's powder." But Palma includes another tale within his origin tale in a gesture characteristic of the philological fable (the more included, the more truthful it seems): "Besieged by fevers a Loja Indian, Pedro de Leyva, drank, to quench his ardent thirst, the waters from a pool, the banks of which housed quinine trees. Thus saved, he made others afflicted by the same illness drink flasks of water into which he had deposited roots of this tree. With this discovery he came to Lima to inform a Jesuit, who upon curing the viceroy's wife, performed a greater service for humanity than the priest who invented gunpowder." Fernández Pérez gives us, without mention of Palma, another explanation, not before noting that its character is more literary than factual: Around 1630 the corregidor de Loja suffered some paludal fever and a Jesuit, Juan López, gave him the remedy he had taken thanks to an Indian, Juan Leiva. In this version quinine is referred to as the "fever tree." The tale of the countess of Chinchón, Fernández Pérez informs us, comes to us from Sebastian Bado's book. Various medical historians believe to have proved that the countess never fell ill. Cured himself, Palma clarifies toward the end of a "tradition," so well documented as even to mention Linnaeus, that what he had attributed to the first countess in the initial version had, in fact, befallen the count's second wife. These philological fables require two wives in their genealogies of substitutions and equivalences. The fact is that the countess's story engendered a literary saga. In 1892, Jean de la Fontaine published a volume of verse entitled *Poema du Quinquina*, and the countess of Genlis popularized the story of quinine's discovery in her piece *Zuma o le decouverte du Quinquina* (1817), introducing the variant of a servant girl who keeps the remedy secret, at first taking it for poison. This polarity between poison and remedy is not rare, announcing the strangeness of an American fruit.

Fernández Pérez adds to this sum of versions a variety of names for the plant: *Pulvis Eminentísimo Cardinal de Lugo, Pulvis Lugones, Pulvis Cardinalis, Pulvis Patrum Scil. Jesuitarum, Pulvis Jesuiticus.*

These names, despite their Latin, evidently refer to distinct genealogies of mixture. Science on its own would later discover the various families of trees in this region of "cloudy forests," whose species—several of them hybrids—answer to new names. It was not long before commerce acclimated the best variety of quinine, *yungas,* outside Peru. The Dutch transplanted Peruvian quinine to Asia, achieving a specimen with a higher yield of tonic, says Fernández Pérez. This beneficial plant does not cease to provide textual complexity for all its emblematic nature, characteristic of its inclusion within the European repertoire, where American goods are deciphered as legendary genealogy. This representation also belongs to abundance's repertoire, to the family of laborious recondite objects (such as pearls, gold, silver, and other metals) that announce the potential state, still latent, of a furtive, secretive wealth. Gold, it was held, crept beneath the earth amid metals that sought each other out to fuse and become gold. This archaic, almost alchemical vision professes uncharted nature's wonders and the happenstance of its inexhaustible goods. Just as adventurous but more empirically based were the clandestine British alpaca rearing ventures in Australia and Africa, various countries' attempts at acclimating potatoes or *batatas,* and the aforementioned Dutch quinine enterprise.

Is abundance a tale that mimics American nature's fecundity, even if panegyric at its extreme? Or is it an account of accounts, a *trope*-graphy reproducing representation? The historical fact remains that productivity depends on available labor. The changing regime of property places accumulation and commerce above distribution and communality. But even the fertility of new goods on New World soil, that notion of a wondrous nature and prodigious fertility, sustains itself on a belief in communal sufficiency and the collective good. The anthropologist John Murra, while studying reports on population and tributes in the colonial Andes, describes these "libros de visita" as documenting a "vertical" agricultural system, according to which each community controlled various ecological levels between the cold highlands, warm climes, and coastal valleys. Thus, agricultural labor alternated periodically. Crops were farmed continuously throughout the year. This regime demanded a precise administration, guaranteeing the common good and avoiding hunger. But the *encomienda,* based on forced labor and exploitation, and the plantation, preserved through slavery, eroded community production, raising their own productivity over misery. When Guamán Poma de Ayala explains that in the Andean world the newborn already had an arable plot of land assigned, he is referring to a lost past even though this model of a common good still spurs him. Therefore, even those, such as Guamán, who most strongly denounce hunger still begin with the metaphor of abundance, a memory that contradicts the present. Father de las Casas threatens the *encomendero* with moral condemnation for profiting from the Indian's hunger. This intrinsic tension between dearth and abundance configures the very notion of a natural history of the Indies to the point that American subjects acquire their discourse from these intimate polar representations.

Next to this same latency and imminence of abundance as natural language that the subject manifest and unleashes, the stage of dearth arises, imposed by plague, barrenness, pestilence, violence, and hunger. Even so, the genealogy of the polar tropes remits us to the *locus amoenus* and a desert landscape, and its actuality is not only ideological, a dominant interpretation, but also constitutive and formative. That is, they are constructions that configure common spaces, the consensus of a possible veracious arena for the American subject. On the one hand, if the master gestures fecundity, it is the slave who gestates it. On the other, if the former suffers the misfortune of dearth, the latter embodies it with his misery and hunger. Indigenous black or poor subjects are champions or children of abundance when it is represented as a native garden or fertile grove, and its victims when abundance comes to be understood as gain and accumulation, whose mechanics are violent and disruptive. Paradise's inhabitant becomes slave to his own myth. Both representations often coincide and are juxtaposed. Their cultural history, however, does not simply confirm what we already know about colonial society and its systems of production: It also allows us to better observe the matrix of representations and interpretations that configure consensus, tropes, imaginary compensations, as well as disputes and demands of native, *mestizo,* and heterogeneous thought. The hero of abundance ends at the subject of dearth. Nevertheless, when it is his turn to speak, his appellative interlocution will be a project, often rehearsed, of rearticulating the word, translating into a Spanish diversified by regions and nations, by new migrations. The language of subjectivity will be, throughout the twentieth century, the pilgrimage of a cultural mixture bereft of social space. Modernity will leave traces of loss, ruins of language.

Social inequality has been, from the outset, a principle of authority. As John C. Super notes, "The fortunate times were those when an element of choice remained. In 1589, the viceroy from Peru responded to the measles and smallpox epidemic by enumerating the foods for the healthy and the sick. To give strength to the healthy he recommended foods of 'good substance,' mutton, and fowl, and goat; those already burning from fever had to settle for concoctions of barley, quinoa, amaranth, sugar, and raisins, dressed with vinegar and oil."[17] This example suggests without irony that abundance demands a privileged subject while paucity imposes poverty on another.

Not without a certain sense of drama, this unequal distribution of abundance's goods was observed by various chroniclers and writers. In the literature under the sign of the nation, which is already of a different consciousness, some balances sought to restore a sense of natural order. This is what occurs in Andrés Bello's praise of the banana tree in his "Ode to the Agriculture of the Torrid Zone." All chroniclers observed that there was an American variety of the banana or plantain. They also noted that the one brought from Spain reproduced ferociously, while continuously restating its ease to farm, its goodness, its various flavors and varieties. It was, shall we say, the most modest emblem of abundance. Bello adds a nuance indicative of his time:

> First, the banana tree,
> From which many beautiful presents bestowed
> Providence to the people
> Of the equator, happily with outstretched hand.
> No longer obliged by human arts
> The prize optimally conceded;
> It is neither the mower, nor the plow
> Debtor to its grapevine;
> Scarce industry suffices, which can
> Pilfer fatigue from enslaved hands;
> quickly it grows, and when exhausted it ceases,
> adult offspring in turn follows.[18]

Bello has abundance coincide with the natural subject. If nature produces this good without need for more labor, the slave can grow the plantain as if it were a small respite from labor. It is, as well, an instructive example of stamina and succession. Since society does not alleviate the slave's servitude, the banana, as first republican emblem, lessens his fatigue. In this poem, panegyric of all fruits, the setting announces a subject redeemed by abundance under the promises of a new order. This utopia of mixture heartens American cultural enterprises with all its sums and crossings, with its project of a subject capable of regaining the world thanks in no small measure to the languages that make it livable.

Notes

* Translated by Joaquín Terrones and José Falconi, including the Balbuena and Bello excerpts cited by the author.

1. Joan Corominas, *Diccionario crítico etimológico castellano e hispánico.* Madrid: Gredos, 1981, v. IV, 26.
2. Ibid.
3. See Fernando Alvarado Tezozómoc, *Crónica mexicana.* Anotada por Manuel Orozco y Berra. México: Editorial Porrúa, 1980.
4. Guamán Poma repeats "pronto tendremos remedio" in his *Corónica.* See Felipe Guamán Poma de Ayala, *El primer nueva corónica y buen gobierno.* Criticism by John V. Murray and Rolena Adorono; translation (from the Quechua) and textual analysis by Jorge L. Urioste. Mexico: Siglo Veintiuno, 1980, v.3.
5. Gonzalo Fernández de Oviedo y Valdés, *Sumario de la natural historia de las Indias.* Editing, introduction, and notes by José Iranda. México: Fondo de Cultura Económica, 1996, p. 214.
6. Ibid., p. 225.
7. Jacinto de Carvajal, *Descubrimiento del Río Apure.* Ed. José Alcina. Madrid: Historia 16, 1985.
8. Joseph Luis de Cisneros, *Descripcioón exacta de la provincial de Benezuela.* Introduction by Enrique Bernardo Núñez. Caracas: Editorial Avila Gráfica, 1950.
9. Ibid., p. 46.
10. Ibid., p. 47.
11. Ibid., p. 51.
12. Bernardo de Balbuena, *Grandeza Mexicana.* Introduction by Francisco Monterde. México: UNAM, 1963, p. 75.
13. Ibid.
14. Ibid., p. 76.
15. Max Hernández, *Memoria del bien perdido, conflicto, identidad y nostalgia en el Inca Gracilazo de la Vega.* Lima: Instituto de Estudios Peruanos, 1991.
16. Ricardo Palma, *Tradiciones peruanas.* Ed. Julio Ortega y F. M. Rodrigues-Arenas. Paris: Archivos, pp. 123–26.
17. J. C. Super, "The Formation of Nutritional Regimes in Colonial Latin America" in J. C. Super and Thomas C. Wright, eds. *Food, Politics, and Society in Latin America.* Lincoln: University of Nebraska Press, 1985, pp. 1–23.
18. Andres Bello, "La agricultura de la Zona Torrida," in *Poesias: obras completas,* vol. 1. Ed. Miguel Luis Amunategui. Santiago: Universidad de Chile, Editorial Nacimiento, 1925, pp. 81–92.

16

Kafka's Canon

Hebrew and Yiddish in *The Trial* and *Amerika*

David Suchoff

In "Before the Law," Kafka's most famous parable from *The Trial*, a humble man can spend a lifetime waiting for permission to enter the portals of official culture. The radiance of the Law beckons to him like the splendor of canonical language, much as the examples of Flaubert and Goethe, as Max Brod reminds us, called to Kafka.[1] Worship of canonical German, it seems often left Kafka like "the man from the country," seduced by the splendor of a canonical language that will bestow him with its distinction once and for all. Kafka admired Goethe, however, as Max Brod points out, with a "little note of mischief," and his worship was less a writer's seduction by high language than Kafka's need to define canonical German's limiting force.[2] The classics, as Josef K. complains, should be "accessible to anyone at any time." But canonical language tries to mark the difference between inside and outside: between those who possess elegant language, and its privileges, and those guilty outsiders "from the country," or elsewhere beyond the pale, and thus to separate the cultured from those who speak "other," lesser, or simply different tongues.[3] In this high cultural sense, it's worth remembering that *amoretz*, the Yiddish word for Kafka's "Mann vom Lande," with its older Hebrew source as *amha-aretz*, means the same as a "schlemiel," a fool. The man from the country is barred from the law not just for his supposed ignorance, but for the different languages he brings to the door of the Law.

Yet as my reference to Kafka's use of the Yiddish term *amoretz* suggests, canonical German was only one of the languages his texts speak.

Kafka's "reverential" regard for the German language underwent a pronounced change in his career, moving him far from any stance as a linguistic purist, as his absorption with the Yiddish theater in 1911 makes clear. During this early period, Kafka often felt trapped by the sense that "German was not really his language," according to Robert Alter, a canonical tongue that felt hostile to the Yiddish language and emotions Kafka began to recover while supporting Yitzhak Levi's Yiddish theater troupe in Prague.[4] "Yesterday," as Kafka put it on October 24, 1911, "it occurred to me that I did not always love my mother as she deserved . . . only because the German language prevented it. The Jewish mother is no 'Mutter.' . . ."[5] Before long, however, Kafka was using Hebrew and Yiddish sources throughout his narratives, in "The Judgment" and other works that Evelyn Torton Beck and other critics have rightly defined as Kafka's "breakthrough" texts.[6] Kafka soon began to permeate the canonical German that felt so closed to the Jewish mother, or feelings for "mamaloshon"—the Yiddish word for Yiddish is "mother-tongue"—with Hebrew, and Yiddish subtexts, even though his mastery of Hebrew, as Georg Langer attests, would not be complete for some years later.[7] In *The Trial*, for instance, Josef K. enters the "Cathedral" to hear the parable of the Law from a "priest": but his language echoes the Hebrew and Aramaic *aggadot*, or legends, which Kafka loved, transmitted in Hebrew as well as Yiddish, sources that he knew.[8]

The funny thing about this priest of High German culture is that Kafka has made his punishing protector of the purity of the Law a bilingual figure. This humor, as I will suggest, is integral to Kafka's view of canonical German and its relation to Hebrew and Yiddish, and has not been taken seriously enough in Kafka criticism, since it speaks to the more open view of canonical language and literary tradition that Kafka pursued. The more common reading is that Kafka was controlled by the serious, "othering" terms that German culture, according to Sander Gilman, tried to impose on Jewish languages as inferior, filthy tongues. In simple terms, Kafka was supposed to have been consumed by guilt for wanting to bring "the hidden language of the Jews" into his texts.[9] There's nothing humorous or affectionate in this view of Kafka's relation to Hebrew and Yiddish, and certainly no way to account for the playful feeling he demonstrated for the Jewish languages that he loved. Kafka's own reading of the first chapter of *The Trial*, by contrast—"he laughed so much that there were moments when he couldn't read any further"—suggests the powerful pleasure he took in the figures from the Yiddish theater who enliven his German text.[10]

Canonical German, of course, may have determined that this was the "crime," as Kafka wrote to Max Brod in 1921, of *mauscheln,* of writing official or "paper" German (*Papierdeutsch*) German with the accent of Jewish languages. While this created the "impossible" situation Kafka saw in Jewish writers who sought gain approval as "pure" German writers, Kafka himself was positively attracted to this "remnant of Jewish idioms and Jewish intonations," since it marked the long, flourishing life Hebrew and Yiddish had lived amid the German language.[11] "This is not to say anything against *mauscheln,*" Kafka insisted to Brod, rejecting the accusation that Jewish languages might be the mark of some kind of crime: "In itself, it is fine." But Kafka wanted to move beyond a Jewish accent, the idea of Jewishness as the "appropriation of someone else's property," and to use Hebrew and Yiddish as languages of his own.[12]

The breakthrough critics have seen in "The Judgment" of 1912 was described by Kafka himself as a new beginning in this direction. For him, the text was the start of his enjoyable integration of Hebrew and Yiddish into his writing, and his gradual removal of them from the verdict, or *Urteil,* that regarded Jewish languages as sources of shame. "The story came out of me like a real birth," he wrote in his diary shortly after composing it, "covered with filth and slime."[13] As I will show in the short readings of *The Trial* and *Amerika* that follow, the emergence Hebrew and Yiddish concerns in Kafka's major fiction becomes a way of taking pleasure in the Jewish language, and engaging the Jewish literary inheritance within his German text. Kafka began to acquaint himself with both Hebrew and Yiddish in practical terms in works of cultural synthesis like Fromer's *Organismus des Judentums,* with its Hebrew sections, the Yiddish theater performances he attended and produced, and Pines's *L'histoire de la litterature Judeo-Allemande,* a book he remarked that he read "with such thoroughness, haste, and joy as I have never yet shown in the case of similar books."[14] Kafka digested the history of Hebrew and Yiddish as languages of independent and specific integrity, with meanings that grew for him as he used their linguistic sources and took an increasing pleasure in bringing their concerns into his texts. "In German," Kafka wrote to Brod, in 1921, "only the dialects are really alive," and "can only be brought to life when excessively Jewish hands rummage through them." For the High German that seemed to exclude Jewish writers was in fact given a "semblance of life" by them: "That is a fact, terrible or funny as you like."[15]

At the beginning of Kafka's reception, Max Brod commented on this bilingual form of canonicity that Kafka's "paper" German had achieved.[16] "Without the word Jew appearing anywhere in his works," Brod observed in 1922, in a work entitled *Juden in der Deutschen Literature* (Jews in German Literature), Kafka's German managed to encompass, as Marthe Robert's classic paraphrase of Brod later put it, "the great themes of Jewish thought and Jewish literature."[17] In comparing Kafka's German to the Kabbalah, the varied schools of Jewish linguistic mysticism, Brod began a tradition of reading Kafka's German for what it does *not* say in so many Jewish words, recognizing the fact that Kafka often seemed to hide his cultural and linguistic sources from view. The difficulty of Kafka's writing, as Robert Alter observes, represents a constant "challenge to exegesis," since there is "something almost uncanny" about his use of Hebrew predecessors.[18] Kafka left Hebrew and Yiddish words out of his literary texts for the most part, but openly pointed his readers to them, publishing work in venues where their connection with the Jewish linguistic concerns of his era would easily come to light. Readers looking for Kafka's relation to the Jewish "tradition"—the literal meaning of the word *Kabbala*—have therefore always been obliged to look beneath the surface, and face the "kabbalistic" difficulty that his major critics have always noted, though the journals Kafka chose to publish in during his lifetime make this a hardly mystical task.[19] In 1917, for instance, Kafka published two stories in Martin Buber's *Der Jude,* in the same issue in which the modern Hebrew classic by S. J. Agnon, "Agadat Hasofer, as "Die Erzählung vom Torahschreiber" ("The Story of the Torah Scribe") would appear in German translation for the first time.[20]

Kafka took pleasure in making his German open to Jewish languages, as Gershom Scholem suggested in the advice he gave his students at the Hebrew University early in his career. In order to understand the Kabbalah, he said, "one had to read Franz Kafka's writing first, particularly *The Trial,*"[21] Scholem described this idea of a German text transmitting Hebrew and Yiddish ideas of tradition in a moment of playfulness, to be sure. But it was advice he later repeated, for it contained a serious truth that envisioned the German and Jewish traditions in a new way.[22] Scholem suggested that Kafka's closed German text could very well be understood as a "new Kabbalah," in which the German words opened up to provide access to the hidden traditions of independent Jewish languages that were hiding in plain sight in supposedly pure, canonically German works. Kafka's ability to "explode the conventional reading of well-known texts" thus means more than reading for the accents or ethnic flavor of "minor" languages, including Czech, in his novels.[23] Kafka's writing, as Yoram Ben-David's beautiful Hebrew phrase puts it, can be seen as exercises in "how to write Hebrew in German words."[24] In this bilingual spirit, the readings below measure Kafka's increasing success in examining the hidden openness of canonized traditions in general—the multilingual nature of apparently closed, canonical works. Kafka's canon shows us the open door of the law: that Hebrew and Yiddish as independent languages, with their own concerns, are alive and well within his canonical German text.

The Trial: The Emergence of Jewish Languages

Josef K.'s guilt, as readers recognize from the first line of Kafka's most serious novel, has been decided before his trial ever starts. As the guards announce, "our department . . . doesn't seek out guilt among the general population, but as the Law states, [it] is attracted by guilt, and has to send us guards out" (8–9). Students of Kafka's relation to Jewish languages have not faulted Josef K. as much as canonical German for the guilt that is written across the face of *The Trial.* Josef K, like Kafka himself, as Ruth Wisse explains, was not wholly to blame for the symbolic betrayal that seems to attract the court. "German," as she put its, bore its share of the fault, because the heavy canonical weight it conveyed as the "dominant language" of European language of culture, "would keep the non-German Jewish writer forever on trial," persecuting him and leaving him "condemned by the universal language in which he lives." If Kafka, like Josef K., does bear any fault, it is for having checked his Jewish languages at the door of his canonical German, which, as Sander Gilman puts it, tempted him with the lure of literary fame. In Gilman's formulation, Kafka's ambitious desire to place "himself in the framework of 'high' German culture" and its "striving for universals" led him to leave "Hebrew and Yiddish" outside his literary texts, and become "bilingual in everything but his writing." Josef K. is on trial, as Wisse argues, because he "inhabits German at the cost of everything else."[25]

A funny thing happens, however, on the way to Josef K.'s execution for excess fealty to the German tongue. The guards who carry the charge of his guilt into *The Trial,* as Evelyn Beck points out, are themselves dead ringers for two figures from a Yiddish play, Zygmund Faynman's *The Vice-King,* a play that Kafka recorded having seen in the original Yiddish on January 6, 1912. Their roles in the Yiddish original, as Beck notes, does indeed make them carriers of a serious accusation: they are charged with rooting out crypto-Jews and bringing them before the "high court" during the Inquisition.[26] The humorous aspect of a hidden Jew uncovered during the Inquisition may seem hard to find, despite Mel Brooks's in *History of the World, Part I,* and Beck herself warns us a bit too sternly against seeing the humor in Josef K.'s trial. "It is not to be thought," she cautions, "that Kafka transformed a piece of straight tragedy into a comic idiom," since both the hero of *The Vice-King* and Josef K.'s fortunes decline precipitously once their respective trials begin. The comic meaning of Josef K.'s guards, however, was already apparent in the original Yiddish Kafka heard. "Idiomatic asides," Beck tells us, "make the agents of authority look foolish, less threatening," and on stage, these agents of a punishing high culture were even more comic, especially from the German point of view.[27] The agents of this Inquisition, of course, themselves speak Yiddish in Faynman's play and are mocked by other servants, who present the Inquisition, as Brooks understood, from the Yiddish point of view.

Though "someone must have slandered Josef K." as the first line of *The Trial* has it, Kafka's guards—and one is named Franz—are also messengers who liberate the repressed linguistic perspective of Yiddish, and Hebrew, in the midst of this German text. The reason that the two lower-class guards who "looked a little like porters" (7), one with a "big nose," the other with a "traveling jacket," can enter the house so easily is because the assimilated Josef K., who works at a bank, has always known them in a sense. They stand for the "slandered" but mobile Jewish languages that enter the German of *The Trial* as soon as Josef K. opens the door, and allows their linguistic perspective into his house. I say "slandered" because Josef K., as critics have always noticed, never rejects these figures, though he tries to vilify their presence as an affront, if not an assault, "the wild horde which he himself is and with which he wants absolutely nothing to do."[28] The liberating effect of these guards on the banker's reserve is immediately obvious, for these are bumbling transmitters of guilt and punishment by design, the "laughingstock of Europe" at their best.[29] They eye his "undergarments," steal his nightshirt, and mock his banker's aplomb by forcing him to change his clothes: "He would have to wear a worse one now." Yet what Josef K. tries to take as the donning of prison garb, a "dressing down," as it were, is a chance to make a positive change in his attire, and to transform his upper class speech. The guards mock Josef K. but give him a more important chance to shed the linguistic "arrogance" critics have always noticed in different terms.[30] The beginning of his trial is thus the chance to talk with "these lowly agents—they admit themselves that's what they are," rather than down to them. Suddenly, Josef K. has the opportunity to engage in banter on an equal basis with fearfully common figures who prove crucial to his happiness after all. For these "Wächter" (13) give him the chance to *wake up* and change his haughty linguistic dress: "Perhaps all he had to do was laugh in the guards' faces and they would laugh with him."

The "agents" of Yiddish, as Kafka himself was, as he put it in his "Introductory Speech in the Yiddish Language" of February 18, 1912, "did not set out to punish," for they engage in foolish hijinks antithetical to the idea of a serious court.[31] They offer K. the chance to look more carefully at the schlemiel, the text's symbol of the Yiddish language, "whose defects have been transformed into a source of delight," though "K. knew that there was a slight risk someone might say later that he hadn't been able to take a joke" (7).[32] These guards are more than "doubles," the shadow figure as *schlepper,* carried along unwittingly, "that extension of the self which is visible to others though extraneous to its owner," and much more than "a little diaspora of truncated selves."[33] As representatives of the Yiddish theater in Kafka's canonical German, they stand for the "strangers" from eastern European Jewry, the "brothers" who spoke Yiddish, with its strong Hebrew element, that German-speaking Jews like Josef K., not to mention Kafka's own family, had tried so desperately to leave behind in their quest for *Bildung,* or German culture.[34] The "court" does indeed represent this kind of Literature with a capital *L,* a high culture that offers no reprieve once its subjects accept the judgment, issued before any trial has taken place, that "other" languages like Yiddish and Hebrew are a source of shame. "They are only proceedings," as even Josef K. realizes, "if I recognize them as such" (45). And though K. eventually has these guards whipped for the liberties take in the name of "court," they remain his "guards" in the classically comic sense of the schlemiel, giving the "foolish," scorned languages of the "ridiculous" and "ugly" a voice in high culture.[35] The laughter they provoke is thus not an assault on a wearer of the "cravat," to borrow Steven Aschheim's elegant term for assimilated German Jews, but an attempt to liberate him from the straightjacket of a German high culture that rejected the "caftan," sign of the "Kabbalistic" Jewish languages that proponents of canonical German had always despised.[36] In this regard, Franz and Willem are Josef K.'s "Wächter," or *watchers* in the most literal and figuratively authentic sense of shielding him from the narrow judgments enforced by German high culture against Yiddish and Hebrew, and from inflicting its judgment on its protectors, not to mention himself.

The tawdry nightshirt they've recommended (and opponents of Yiddish often referred to this garment as *gatkes,* or underwear) they know might bring on the wrath of official culture. As Y. L. Gordon wrote to Scholem Aleichem in 1889: "It would be a sin for you to educate your children in that language. It would be like compelling them to march down Nevsky Boulevard in undershirts, with their boots sticking out."[37] For the lower-class speech for which it stands certainly can result in painful scorn: "What are you thinking of, they cried. 'Do you want to see the inspector in your nightshirt? He'll have you soundly flogged and us along with you!'" (11). But these would-be haberdashers are far from sell-outs, and their dress-for-success doctrine is mildly comic, like a "fitted black jacket" that contains hidden things within, and thus is arrayed with "a variety of pleats, pockets, buckles, and a belt" (5). The guards recommend the "cravat," a style that looks formal and closed, but opens up to suggest the "caftan," the "traditional clothing" worn by speakers of Yiddish, whose "crucial component" was Hebrew, the holy tongue: "The guards smiled, but stuck to their words: it had to be a black coat" (12). This guardian humor gently chides Josef K. for being a stuffed shirt, *noodging,* as it were, this banker who prefers an "evening jacket" (11) to come off his high linguistic horse. "They might indeed grab hold of him," Josef K. worries, "and once subdued he would lose any degree of superiority he might still hold" (10). But the Josef K. who thought the "intellectual limitations" of these guards were "obvious," and lumped them together as "a crude joke [of] his colleagues at the bank" (6) soon begins to hear their claim to individual dignity and respect: "You haven't treated us as we deserve" (9). The strait-laced speaker of canonical German, who saw his arrest as a linguistic "farce" (7), begins to accept these figures from the Yiddish theater, even to depend on their standards of taste. "He grumbled," like someone acquiring a new style, "but he was already lifting a coat from the chair and holding it up for a moment in both hands, as if submitting it to the judgment of the guards" (11).

The "black coat" (*schwarzer Rock*) recommended by the guards is a general symbol of Kafka's mature, canonical prose, an elegant garment that contains other languages without losing any of its style. As representatives of what Gershom Scholem called "the strong light of the canonical" in Kafka's writing, they suggest that his German was neither wholly tragic nor a power that excluded Hebrew and Yiddish from Kafka's text.[38] *The Trial* is better not seen as a movement from "farce to tragedy," as its newest translator suggests, because Franz and Willem were indeed good actors from start to end.[39] Acting the role of high-cultural Inquisitors, Josef K.'s guards represent the perspective in *The Trial* that survive the power of the high court and preserves the most common sense and humane truths of all. From the "laughable" perspective of these servants, it is the "higher authorities" (8)—those who turn Block into a "dog" (195), and then blame him for acting like one—who are truly vulgar. As Josef K. notes in the Cathedral, "lies are made into a universal system" in the culture of the Priest, though they do not have to be believed (223). It is the "porters off the street corner," representatives of the Yiddish theater, who beg K. to resist that "system," end their flogging, and stand up for the dignity of the common against the punishing authority of the elegant court. Given the depth of these insights, the "old supporting actors" (226) [*untergeordnet*] who murder Josef K. with "nauseating courtesies" before the knife is ever plunged are a sideshow indeed. Kafka allowed this deeper "Franz," as it were, to survive and flourish, just as he permitted Josef K's guards to live beyond Josef K's demise. The Hebrew and Yiddish they represent find a place in *Amerika*, a novel that overlaps with *The Trial*, where, as befits languages transported to New York, Kafka's Jewish languages had already taken on an open, humorous, and surprisingly assertive life of their own.[40]

Hebrew in *Amerika*: A Future for Older Tongues

At the time he was beginning *Amerika* in 1911, Kafka attended a reading of perhaps the most canonical poem of the Hebrew national poet, Hayim Nahman Bialik. The version read by his friend Yitzhak Levi was in Yiddish, written by no less a figure than Bialik himself, and the fact that this master of high modern, literary Hebrew had deigned to offer his most famous poem in the *mamaloshon* gave Kafka no end of delight, despite the sorrowful subject matter at hand.[41] There was "no question of the primacy of Hebrew," for its status as the Jewish language of high culture had a biblical genealogy, while Yiddish, the language of the Jewish masses, was often despised by the advocates of the Hebrew renaissance as the lesser, vernacular tongue.[42] "The complete truth of all the reading" Kafka notes with satisfaction, refers to this "fall" from Hebrew to Yiddish, for it was this downward move from high culture to Yiddish (*herabgelassen*) that gave the event its emotional power. For the spell of the canonical had been broken. The creator of the Hebrew standard had been heard in the mother tongue, and the complete truth was that canonical language had gained "authority," as David Roskies notes, by expressing itself in and allowing itself to be ennobled by the more common tongue.[43] The most canonical Hebrew poet of his generation had in fact gained dignity by the fall of his High Language into the more common Jewish vernacular, and Kafka went home, as he put it, "with all my abilities concentrated," as if a major literary effort were about to start.[44]

In *Amerika,* Hebrew becomes the symbol for a monolingual form of high culture that Karl Rossman continually escapes. Banished to America after being "seduced" (26) by the Austrian maid who "pray[ed] to a wooden crucifix" in the kitchen (27), Karl must do everything possible to redeem his high cultural authority, an injunction this schlemiel seems to oblige, from trying to perfect his English, to taking the job with the most status in the Hotel Occidental—elevator boy—in Kafka's comic vision of the course of Latinate Western civilization as a *translatio studii,* the acquisition of ever more cultured languages that E. R. Curtius described as a progressive journey to the top.[45] The Bible that moves westward with Karl, packed into his luggage by his parents (101), symbolizes the torments of these high cultural expectations, since the Hotel Occidental is located in a city called Ramses, and the deeper glory of Karl's failures refer to Yiddish in this regard. No matter how large the letters in which high culture is written, Karl is like the "deaf" uncle, the wiser fool in Chelm, the traditional Yiddish city of fools, who reads, of course, but closes his ears to the demand that he join high culture. Or as the tale has it:

> Someone saw a Chelmite writing a letter in an unusually large hand and asked, "Why such huge letters?"
>
> "I am writing to my uncle, who is—may you be spared the like—very deaf."

As Ruth Wisse suggests, "the intellectualism of the culture is under attack *for* its . . . foolishness and innocence" in this version of dumb meets dumber, as it were. In the deeper sense, of course, the fools of high culture are being attacked for ignoring the possibility that the deaf uncle isn't *just* deaf, he just isn't interested in their *lettres,* no matter how *belles.* He stands for the Yiddish equivalent of "Feh—what do I need your big language for?" and turning up the intellectual volume to read Chelm as high culture, and the deaf man as the schlemiel who wins by losing, won't change the structure of the joke.[46] Instead of learning the new form of high culture, English in *Amerika,* Karl is a textbook schlemiel in this symbolically Yiddish sense, in that his canny failure to adequately understand, or even hear the foolish siren song of Western high culture is what saves him from linguistic destruction at its hands. A notorious bungler, Karl fails to fulfill this classically "Hebrew" pattern of high culture in *Amerika*, and those failures, because they preserve symbolically lower languages, become his most liberated and satisfying forms of success.

I say "Hebrew" in quotation marks because the biblical expectations enforced on this prodigal son are not, properly speaking, Hebrew at all. The biblical commands Karl fails to uphold are "Hebrew" only in the classically Western and assimilated sense in which success means attaining a canonical language that replaces an older tongue, figuratively absorbed without a disturbing accent or trace. The older Hebrew text, in this classic Western model of the canon, is supposed to be magically replaced by a newer language, or "testament," whether in Luther's version or the King James, when the new canonical language miraculously appears. Thus it is Karl's American Uncle Jacob, a "Senator," "who must have had his name changed" (26), as Karl observes, who himself quotes Luther's German Bible translation, intoning the "Signs and Wonders" *(Zeichen und Wunder)* (27) of New York.[47] In this model of Hebrew immigration, the old language is always an immigrant compelled to change its name, accept the onus of lower, narrower, "pharisaic" culture, and pass willingly and magically into the eloquence and capaciousness of the new. Before long, one scarcely remembers that Luther's translation, or the King James, is based on an older Hebrew text, for the newly canonical German or English has become the standard, high-cultural speech and soon attains "a sanctity properly ascribable only to the unmediated voice of God."[48] The reason canonical language becomes the object of such idolatry is that it is far from original, and only the kind of veneration Uncle Jacob demands for himself, and the English and riding lessons he imposes on Karl, can keep the immigrant's high cultural aura intact.

The writing desk Karl receives from Uncle Jacob symbolizes this American high cultural self. It is the site where English is to be studied, and where Karl's American identity it to be constructed, a high cultural meaning of the desk as the gift of canonical language that is transparent from the start. Given by Uncle Jacob, a European immigrant who has become Senator, the desk is the figurative and literal site where the language of home is supposed to pass eloquently into the language of the new canonical tongue. The prospects of success tied up with acquiring the canonical language, as John Guillory observes, have always seemed "transcendent" and boundless.[49] And American English, as symbolized by the desk Karl receives, is no exception to this rule: "It had a hundred compartments of different sizes, in which the President of the Union himself could have found a fitting place for each of his state documents." For all its serious intent, the desk. is actually Kafka's quite funny send-up of canonical language's long-standing failure to erase the "other" languages it contains in its many drawers. The "new apparatus" atop the desk. uncovers an older, more traditional text at the very site where the new canonical language is supposed to be learned, like Uncle Jacob himself, the Senator born in the old European home, and someone who "must have changed his name." It hardly surprising that uptight "Uncle Jacob by no means approved of this particular desk." For the gift of new writing he offers comically exposes him as an *arriviste*, like the biblical Jacob himself, who displaces his older brother, and canonical language as a latecomer as well, an imposition on an older scene of writing legible beneath the assimilated veneer. "Nowadays," as the narrator laconically observes, " these [desks] were all furnished with this new apparatus, which had also the advantage that it could be fitted to more old-fashioned desks without great expense" (41–42).

It should come as no surprise that the desk, as symbol of canonical language, recalls the false spectacle that attends all celebrations of "new" origin, for it reminded Karl of "the nativity scene" [*Krippenspiele*] which was shown to gaping children in the marketplace at home" (41–42). As I've suggested above, this model of canonical language is hardly just American, or novel, but canonically biblical and "Hebrew" in the sense that the new canonical language always stages its nativity, masking its displacement and incorporation of the older language that lives within its lines. In this regard, the writing desk. In *Amerika* is not the place where Karl will become "pretty certain of his English" (49), but where he begins to recover a comic sense of the Western cultural vocabulary that had already transfixed him as a child. Though it was certainly "not intended to remind him of such things," the American desk makes Karl think of the New Testament as an Irving Berlin construction, a "White Christmas" that signifies a pure origin but owes its existence to a representative of an older culture and its texts. Karl was thus "enthralled" by the different scene of writing and nativity the desk brings to mind, but more attentive to the older presence behind it. He "closely comparing the movement of the handle, which was turned by an old man, with the changes in the scene, the jerky advance of the Three Holy Kings, the shining out of the Star, and the humble life of the Holy Manger" (41). The "old man" pulling the strings, of course, signifies the comedy that reduces the drama of sacred origin to kitsch, and Karl's obliviousness to the lofty, canonical meaning of the scene does indeed make a comic point. Standing for the status of older languages in the Western tradition, the "old man" will always be laughable, in high culture's terms, as the "Hebraic," mechanical, older language that is mocking but lives within the text's sacred lines.

To move "up" as an elevator boy at the Hotel Occidental of course, Karl must deploy the "perfectly good English" (134) impressed upon him by his Uncle Jacob shortly after his arrival. And like all of Kafka's father figures, the successful immigrant Jacob banishes the son from the intimacies of the linguistic home. Karl then acts out his schlemiel's version of the motif of success as linguistic exile, acquiring his "uniform" to work in the Hotel Occidental in an allegory that extends well beyond the American scene. Social mobility in the Kafkaesque West means acquiring a "uniform" language that doesn't really fit: requiring the elimination, or in Karl's case, the laughably bad suppression, of "older" cultural tongues (42). Not surprisingly, Karl, like the Jews, whose European cultural history was marked by "internal bilingualism," in Max Weinreich's apt phrase, will only be a temporary guest in this Hotel.[50] Though he tries to follow the serious side of his new boss's immigrant example, Karl instead takes comic pleasure in her remembered attachment to the language of the old country. "When I think of the difficulties I had with my English!" she tells her countryman, more in enjoyment than lament (134). These are not guilty linguistic pleasures so much as they are pleasures in languages that are supposed to feel shameful and guilty in the high culture of Hotel Occidental as a whole. Unlike the "somber Chaplin clown" Northrop Frye saw in Kafka, Karl's comic failure to fit into high society is far from tragic—it is the pleasurable drama of the schlemiel who mocks official culture, breaking its spell and gesturing instead toward the silenced pleasures of immigrant speech.[51]

As with Schlemiel, who constantly tries to get to the capital where canonical Polish rules but always ends up back in foolish Chelm, Karl's attempts to become monolingual lead to a series of glorious defeats, pulling him toward his linguistic heart, even on the ship from Europe. An eloquent speaker of the Captain's "official" language on board, Karl would rather defend the "stoker" and so defends him before Uncle Jacob and the Captain. He stands up for this representative of "artistic failure" and defends the rights of lower class speech, for "the thought came into Karl's head: 'where am I likely to find a better friend?'" (5).[52] Not surprisingly, Karl becomes a wonderfully bad student of good English, the language he will need to move up in Ramses and that eventually snags him his job as elevator boy. He chooses reading material that will teach him a lesson but mocks the lofty demands of his new language and almost drives his teacher from the room. "He learned by heart many exclamations of pain in English," the narrator observes, "gasping them out to his English teacher, who always leant on a door" (46). Karl chooses immigrant companions who literally open up, or carry the suitcase he forgets on ship, containing the Bible his parents packed, as if Delamarche and Robinson carry the languages that he can never lose, and which they seem to be able to unlock magically from within. Though it seems Karl is unable to escape Robinson the Irishman and Delamarche the Frenchman who follow him in his American adventures, the fact is that Karl never really tries very hard to avoid their clutches. As American markers of European languages—one more repressed than the other—the Irish and Frenchman stand for ethnically marked tongues that Karl doesn't really want to leave behind. Like home languages, both feed and sustain him, breaking open the "Koffer" he brought from Europe—they eat his sausage—but has foolishly tried to ignore since his ship came in. They mock the linguistic hauteur of an Occidental culture that represents lower languages as filthy but, Karl knows, are vital to his health. "My friends are first-rate comrades," he announces at the door of the Hotel, "but they're not exactly clean" (123).

Happily, Karl fails to rise in the Hotel Occidental. Booted from his job as elevator boy, he finds the pleasure he seeks when he picks up his "trumpet" in the "Great Nature Theater of Oklahoma." The instrument stands for Kafka's German—it's a Western instrument, after all—but Karl is also raising a shofar, the Jewish ritual instrument, at least in a theatrical sense, since the scene reflects his immersion in company that, at least from the German perspective, seems frightfully low at the start.[53] Headed for Oklahoma instead of Prague, where Kafka helped produce a performance of Yitzhak Levi's Yiddish theater troupe, the "Great Theater" is in fact *shund*, a low-class affair, symbolizing Kafka's return to his parents' original spoken tongue. The process was one of painful fits and starts. "Yiddish was, after all, for a long time a despised language," Kafka told a Prague audience in 1912, about to watch the Yiddish theater production he had arranged.[54] To such an audience of refined, German-speaking Jews, Yiddish was nothing but a dissonant dialect, a feared marker of their lower-class past and the *mamaloshon* they'd left behind. *Amerika* registers the complex feelings of an eloquent speaker of German as he confronts the snobbery learned from his parents and rediscovers the dignity of what high culture regards as the repressed mother of Jewish speech. In the larger sense, Karl's subsequent reflections apply to the foolish intellectual or striving middle class of any culture who, as the Yiddish folktale has it, finally realizes that the linguistic treasure sought for an entire life lies buried beneath the front door. Karl had imagined, when seeing the theater, that "it was a roughly fashioned trumpet intended merely to make a noise," a *grayger* in Yiddish, "but now he discovered it was an instrument capable of almost any refinement of expression" (279).

The foolish aesthete in Karl was not entirely pleased, of course: "If all the instruments were of the same quality," he worries, "they were being ill used." From the perspective of a narrow view of canonical language, which restricts dramatic action to a single day or time and surely to a single language, Karl is undoubtedly right in his fears. This theater recruits on a "race-course" (280), runs on its own time, and has a repertoire and cast of its own that are constantly growing. As the recruiting poster declares, there is a "place for everyone!" (272), or as Fanny explains it to Karl, "it's an old theater, but its constantly being enlarged" (280). Exclusive, high literary expression is thus not the aim of this *company*, as we say in English, since the concerns of everyday speech and life have a place in it and are regarded, when the actors have their say, as more important than the noble claims of art. "No one wanted to be an artist," as the narrator explains, "but every man wanted to be paid for his labors" (272). The "Great" theater begins to please Karl precisely when such "low" motifs—like making a living—become artistically acceptable: when common people speaking different dialects and languages can blow their trumpets, as it were, without being accused of a grotesque parody of sublime artistic speech.

The crowds, to be sure, no longer believe that their inclusion in the theater will make any difference, jaded by the cant that surrounds the idea of minority literature itself: "There were so many placards; nobody believed them any longer" (272). Yet Karl begins to give up his aesthetic misgivings. The language of this drama company may be low, but it is willing to accept an immigrant with an accent like himself as having something important, if not crucial, to contribute to the exalted kingdom of art: "'Everyone is welcome,' it said. Everyone, that meant Karl, too . . . even if the great Theater of Oklahoma were an insignificant travelling circus, it wanted to engage people, and that was enough" (273). This traveling circus is not the meaty drama that Kafka's hunger artist will despise, and the denial of linguistic appetite is not the price of admission. For this theater, like Kafka's later tale, succeeds in making the self-denial of high art look. absurd. To the aesthete, its linguistic openness is a disruptive vulgarity and makes the artistic production seem "confused," not great, in Karl's telling phrase. The many trumpets signify the contrary truth:

that great art itself becomes vulgar, if not brutal, through the very posture of repressive condescension, and attains dignity only by accepting the "plebian" languages that lend the eloquence to high speech.[55] Karl moves from his distaste to a form of Adorno's insight that clashing languages are not a dissonant sickness, but the cure for the reified concepts of culture, and the secret of the art that breaks their spell: "he heard at once the noise of many trumpets. It was a confused blaring; the trumpets were not in harmony but were blown regardless of each other. Still, that did not worry Karl; he took it rather as a confirmation of the fact that the Theater of Oklahoma was a great undertaking" (273).

Coda: The Hidden Openness of Tradition

The doorkeepers of high culture have never agreed, always worried that the national language permits too many bilingual shenanigans: that it's allowed too many "trumpets," or words from beyond the pale, to become part of its sounds. Kafka addressed these concerns directly in a short piece called "The Cares of a Housefather," and it is with Kafka's general sense that bilingual games are crucial to all national languages that I'd like to conclude. The story, you'll recall, describes "Odradek," a creature of many different linguistic strands. Kafka published these "Cares" during his lifetime, placing the piece in the Prague Zionist journal *Selbstwehr*, in its Chanukah issue of December 19, 1919.[56] And Odradek becomes the object of the fathers' concern precisely because of his hybrid linguistic nature, with a name that suggests the Czech word for "stranger," "apostate," Kafka's own Jewish family history, and more.[57] From the point of view of the family man or "Housefather" who narrates the story, the question is whether the multilingual Odradek, "son" of the tradition, will permit the continuance of the House of Israel, or *Beit Yisrael*. But tradition, despite the "Hausvater's" anxieties, is strong precisely because it is composed of different strands. Some say the name Odradek itself "is of slavonic origin" (*stamme aus dem Slawischen*), while others "believe it to be of German origin, only influenced by the Slavonic" (*es stamme aus dem Deutschen, vom Slawischen sei es nur beinflusst*). Like Central European Jewry, influenced by both the Slavic (*Ostjuden*) and the German (assimilated German Jews), Odradek, despite being "broken" (*zerbrochen*), sustains his national character through all his travails. For though he is a "Spule" or spool for these various cultural strands "of the most varied type and color" (*von verschiedenster Art und Farbe*) he has collected along his way, his center takes the shape of a "Stern," or Star. And "one of the emanations" (*einer der Ausstrahlungen*) of that Star is quite visible, especially to the readers of a Zionist journal.

Tradition, in this collection of cultural strands, is "closed off in a certain respect," yet open to additions, closed but open to new languages and their views. Such a porous tradition sometimes seems to have vanished: Odradek is at times not to be seen for months and even appears to have moved, or assimilated himself into other linguistic houses ("Manchmal ist er monatenlang nicht zu sehen; da ist er wohl in andere Häuser übersiedelt"). But he always returns with the utmost loyalty to the people he remembers: "but he always comes faithfully back to our house again" (*doch kehrt er dann unweigerlich wieder in unser Haus zurück*). Though the cultural fathers constantly worry about his disappearance—"Can he possibly die?" ("Kann er denn Sterben?")—he's right there at the feet of future generations, of the House's "children and its children's children" in Kafka's evocation of different Hebrew prayers (*vor den Füssen meiner Kinder und Kindeskinder*), trailing his glorious and different linguistic threads behind.

Kafka's sense that traditions are radically open to other languages takes us back. to the man, sitting before the Law and waiting to enter. Bilingualism is part of the parable's very literary texture: The expression *Mann vom Lande* is Kafka's German translation of a Yiddish expression for "fool," which he derived from a Talmudic passage in Aramaic that treats the difference between common speech and ancient, priestly Hebrew. In ancient Israel, an *am ha-aretz,* was literally the individual from the country who did not understand the canonical, high literary language and ritual practice in Jerusalem.[58] In Kafka's modern version of the confrontation, the man waits patiently for admittance his entire life, is told by the doorkeeper he cannot enter, only to be told upon dying, when he finally spies a "radiance" emanating from the Law, that the door has been open all the time. Thus it is that the bilingual speaker seems to lose either way: Without entering the door, he remains marked by lower speech, and is deprived of the status of the canonical: He cannot enter the *Hotel Occidental.* Yet to enter means terror, the sacrifice of the vernacular, or home language, and obeisance before the "radiance" of high literary speech.

The parable, however, is not about an either-or choice between literary language and foreign others but the false structure of that choice. So the law of high culture has always behaved when faced with the bilingual truth. The doorkeepers of high culture will always try to make high language into a "law" closed to all, a "system," *langue* and not *parole,* something inaccessible, attainable only through loss of everyday speech with its taint of different homes. Yet only because, as the logic of snobbery would have it, the opposite case actually obtains. Language in Kafka, like tradition, is in fact "open" at all times, subject to illicit intercourse with the sounds that echo through its nation's doors, permeated with the sounds of "other" languages and what used to be common speech. Literature's doorkeepers always strive to give us the impression of its pureness and inaccessibility, of being finished instead of a work-in-progress, of being closed. The problem of the Law in Kafka's parable is not that "other" languages are excluded from its domain and must look. away in patient shame. That's the doorkeeper's problem and, to be sure, the dilemma suffered by those who take his word as the watchword of their literary faith. The simple truth is that other languages are present within the very tradition he guards, and that they're "capable of almost any refinement of expression": Even a schlemiel like Karl Rossman knows that. Bilingual games do not break the fetish of the canonical, but show us, much to the dismay of the doorkeepers, that its threshold had long been crossed. And that the most eloquent and high cultural scripture of them all, as Walter Benjamin put it in the final line of his translation essay, is the one that speaks a different language from the start.

Notes

1. Max Brod, *Franz Kafka: A Biography* (New York: Schocken Books, 1947). "To hear Kafka talk about Goethe with awe was something quite out of the ordinary," Brod reports . . . the love he felt for Goethe and Flaubert never changed in all the twenty-two years I was his close friend" (122, 51).
2. Goethe, as Kafka reminds us after his definition of "the literature of small peoples," can never be cited by an author without those within the hallowed halls of literary distinction marking the "dependence" of those outside its gates. Franz Kafka, *Diaries,* 1910–1923, ed. Max Brod (New York: Schocken, 1976), entry of December 25, 1911, pp. 148–152; on Goethe and "dependence," p. 152, and Brod, *Franz Kafka,* 122.
3. Franz Kafka, *The Trial,* trans. Breon Mitchell (New York: Schocken Books, 1998), p. 216, and *Der Prozess, Gesammelte Werke,* ed. Max Brod, Vol. 2 (Frankfurt, 1976), p. 182: "Das Gesetz soll doch jedem und immer zugänglich sein. . . ." Citations from *Amerika* will be taken, with slight modification, from Franz Kafka, *Amerika,* trans. Willa and Edwin Muir (New York: Schocken Books, 1974), and *Amerika, Gesammelte Werke,* ed. Max Brod, Vol. 1. References will hereafter be given parenthetically in the text.

4. Robert Alter, *Canon and Creativity: Modern Writing and the Authority of Scripture* (New Haven, CT: Yale University Press, 2000), p. 68.
5. *Diaries,* 87–88.
6. Evelyn Torton Beck, *Kafka and the Yiddish Theater: Its Impact on His Work* (Madison: University of Wisconsin Press, 1971), p. 5.
7. See Georg Langer, "Ma'shehu al Kafka" (A Few Words on Kafka), first published in 1941, later included in *Me'at Zori,* ed. Miriam Dror, (Tel Aviv, 1984), pp. 132–134. Versions of Kafka's acquisition of Hebrew are actually quite varied; for the standard account, see Hartmut Binder, "Kafka's Hebräischstudien," *Jahrbuch der detuschen Schillergesellschaft* 11, 1967, 526–556.
8. Heinz Politzer, in *Franz Kafka: Parable and* Paradox (Ithaca, New York: Cornell University Press, 1962), p. 174, was one of the first well-known American critics to point out this multilingual fact. One of Kafka's own sources for this linguistic history is a book much discussed in his diary entries of early 1912: Jakob Fromer, *Der Organismus des Judentums* (1909), pp. 64–65. Ritchie Robertson gives an extensive account of Kafka's Yiddish sources in *Kafka: Judaism, Politics, Literature* (Oxford: Clarendon Press, 1985).
9. See Sander Gilman, *Jewish Self-Hatred: Anti-Semitism and the Hidden Language of the Jews* (Baltimore and London: The Johns Hopkins University Press, 1986), 282–285, and the section of *Franz Kafka: Jewish Patient* discussed below.
10. "When Kafka read aloud himself, this humor became particularly clear. Thus, for example, we friends of his laughed quite immoderately when he first let us hear the first chapter of *The Trial.* And he himself laughed so much that there were moments when he couldn't read any further. Astonishing enough, when you think of the fearful earnestness of that chapter. But that's the way it was." Brod, *Franz Kafka,* p. 178.
11. Max Weinreich, *History of the Yiddish Language* (Chicago and London: University of Chicago Press, 1973), p. 282.
12. Franz Kafka, Letter to Max Brod, June 1921, in *Letters to Friends,* 286–289, and *Briefe,* 334–338.
13. Franz Kafka, *Diaries,* 1910–1923, ed. Max Brod (New York: Schocken, 1976), Entry of February 11, 1913, p. 214.
14. Franz Kafka, *Diaries,* Entry of January 24, 1912, p. 173.
15. Franz Kafka, Letter to Max Brod, June 1921, in *Letters to Friends, Family and Editors,* trans. Richard and Clara Winston (New York: Schocken Books, 1977), pp. 286–289, and *Briefe,* 1902–1904, ed. Max Brod (New York: Schocken Books, 1958), 334–338.
16. The term has a long history in Kafka criticism, centering on the question of whether Kafka's German was in fact pure, denuded of any dialect, tinted and perhaps tainted by other languages and idioms, or a canonical or "major" literature inflected with a minority perspective, in Deleuze and Guattari's terms (*Kafka: For a Minor Literature,*

trans. Dana Polan [1975; University of Minnesota Press, 1986]. For the initial position, using the same term "papiernes Deutsch" in 1918 that Kafka used in the 1921 letter to Brod, and on the relation of Prague German to other languages, dialects, or accents, see Fritz Mauthner, *Errinerungen* (München, 1918), pp. 51 ff. For a still helpful framing of the issues, see Peter Demetz, "Noch Einmal: Prager Deutsch," *Literature und Kritik,* 1:6, 1966, 58–59.

17. Max Brod, "Der Dichter Franz Kafka," in Gustav Krojanker, *Juden in der Deutschen Literature* (Berlin: Welt-Verlag, 1922), p. 60, and Marthe Robert, *As Lonely as Franz Kafka,* trans. Ralph Mannheim (New York: Harcourt Brace Jovanovich, 1982), p. 3.
18. Robert Alter, *Canon and Creativity: Modern Writing and the Authority of Scripture* (New Haven, CT: Yale University Press, 2000), p. 64. As Karl Grödzinger notes, Kafka's texts and personal denials of Jewish knowledge operated according to a kind of "Verstellungstrategie," or strategy of dissimulation. Comparison of the Hebrew and Yiddish sources of the Kabbalah and Kafka's accounts of them in his diary and literary works, Grödzinger shows, demonstrates an impressive carrying over of Hebrew and Yiddish material in what remains a linguistically German text. See Karl Erich Grödzinger, *Kafka und die Kabbala* (Frankfurt: Fisher Taschenbuch Verlag, 1994), p. 12. Kafka's diaries and notebooks, as scholars know, contain many open references to Hebrew and Yiddish sources, and by the time the eighth Oktavo Notebook was written, fifty-eight of the seventy pages were filled with Hebrew vocabulary. Unfortunately, the discussion of how much or how little Kabbalah Kafka knew has drawn attention away from how many of Kafka's Hebrew and Yiddish concerns are transparently discussed in German terms.
19. Harold Bloom, *The Strong Light of the Canonical: Kafka, Freud, and Scholem as Revisionists of Jewish Culture and Thought* (New York, 1987): " . . . what most needs and demands interpretation in kafka's writing is its perversely deliberate evasion of interpretation," p. 7.
20. *Der Jude: Eine Monatschrift,* Zweiter Jahrgang, 1917–1918. Kafka's pieces were "Report to an Academy" and "Jackals and Arabs." In 1919, Gershom Scholem would publish his translation of Bialik's Hebrew essay "Halakha v'Aggada," which would become the centerpiece of Walter Benjamin's interpretation of Kafka's work.
21. Gershom Scholem, *Walter Benjamin: The Story of a Friendship,* trans. Harry Zohn (Philadelphia: Jewish Publication Society of America, 1981 [1975]), p. 125: "I am reminded of one of my own statements . . . that students of mine used to quote. Apparently, I told them that in order to understand the Kabbalah, nowadays one had to read Franz Kafka's writings first, particularly, *The Trial*").
22. See, for instance, Aharon Appelfeld, a student of Scholem's in the 1950s, and his statement that the traditions of the Hasidism and the Kabbalah came through much more strongly to him in Kafka's Ger-

man than in the original Hebrew and Yiddish texts. Aharon Appelfeld, *Sipur Khayav* (The Story of a Life) (Jerusalem, Ketev, 1999), pp. 132, 134. For a perspective on the interrelatedness of German, Hebrew, and Yiddish for Kafka and for subsequent German letters, see Amir Eshel, "Von Kafka bis Celan: Deutsch-Jüdische Schriftsteller und ihr Verhältnis zum Hebräischen und Jiddischen," forthcoming.

23. David Biale, "Gershom Scholem's Ten Unhistorical Aphorisms on Kabbalah: Text and Commentary," *Modern Judaism* 5:1 (February 1985), p. 69. Kafka's ability to "explode the conventional meaning of well-known texts and reveal their secrets," as David Biale puts it more fully, "must have reminded Scholem of the Kabbalah," but also indicates a larger model of an open literary and cultural tradition. For Kafka's "new Kabbalah," see *Diaries,* January 16, 1922, p. 399, an entry composed after both *The Trial* and *Amerika*. On Kafka and Czech, see Scott Spector, *Prague Territories: National Conflict and Cultural Innovation in Franz Kafka's Fin de Siecle* (Berkeley: University of California Press, 2000), 217–232.
24. Yoram Ben David, "Kafka K'Talmid L'ivirit: . . . u Ekh Lichtov Ivrit b'Milim Germaniyot" [Kafka as a Student of Hebrew: . . . Or, How to Write Hebrew in German Words], *Kafka v'Dimiyotav: Beyn Yahadut Nisteret L'Sgida L'Lo-ya'ad* [Kafka and His Figures: Between Hidden Judaism and Subtle Devotion], (Jerusalem: Tzur-Ot, 1998), 71–102.
25. Ruth Wisse, "The Logic of Language and The Trials of the Jews: Franz Kafka and Yosef Haim Brenner," *The Modern Jewish Canon: A Journey Through Language and Culture* (New York: The Free Press, 2000), pp. 74–75 ff, and Sander Gilman, *Franz Kafka: The Jewish Patient* (New York: Routledge, 1995), 39–40. In Gilman's less forgiving terms, Kafka can produce only "stereotypes of the Jew." The presence of authentic Hebrew and Yiddish sources in Kafka's German, and his sympathetic portryal of them, belie precisely such Jewish stereotypes, including the Nordauesque myth of the deracinated Jewish intellectual on which Gilman's reading is based.
26. Beck, *Kafka and the Yiddish Theater,* 156–159. As Beck summarizes the initial action, they "announce" to the protagonist of the Yiddish drama that "they have been sent to arrest him on suspicion of being a secret Jew."
27. Advocates of German, as Dan Miron points out, "vilified Yiddish as a linguistic hodgepodge . . . nothing more than disfigured German blended with disfigured Hebrew." *A Traveler Disguised: The Rise of Modern Yiddish Fiction in the Nineteenth Century* (Syracuse, New York: Syracuse University Press, 1996 [1973], pp. 35–36.
28. Marthe Robert, *As Lonely as Franz Kafka,* p. 181.
29. Miron, *A Traveler Disguised,* p. 36.
30. *The Trial,* p. 7. On K's arrogance, see A. E. Dyson, "Trial by Enigma: Kafka's *The Trial,*"(1972), in Harold Bloom, ed., *Modern Critical*

Interpretations: Franz Kafka's The Trial (New York: Chelsea House, 1987), p. 70.

31. Franz Kafka, "An Introductory Talk on the Yiddish Language," February 18, 1912, in Mark Anderson, ed., *Reading Kafka: Prague, Politics and the Fin de Siècle* (New York: Schocken Books, 1989), p. 266.
32. Enid Welsford, *The Fool, His Social and Literary History* (Gloucester, Mass, 1966), p. xi. Quoted in Ruth Wisse, *The Schlemiel as Modern Hero* (Chicago and London: University of Chicago Press, 1971), p. 4.
33. Ruth Wisse, *The Schlemiel as Modern Hero,* p. 16, and Marthe Robert, *As Lonely as Franz Kafka,* p. 180. This idea of a "shadow" self or discourse is not part of the Jewish schlemiel tradition, which, to paraphrase the French, is much more comfortable in its own linguistic skin. On Heine's earlier use of the schlemiel as a figure for autonomous Yiddish and Hebrew "counter-narrative" in the German text and tradition, see Willi Goetschel, "Rhyming History: A Note on the 'Hebrew Melodies,' *Germanic Review* 74:4 (Fall 1999), 279 ff.
34. See Steven E. Aschheim, *Brothers and Strangers: The East European Jew in German and German Jewish Consciousness 1800–1923* (Madison: University of Wisconsin Press, 1982).
35. According to Northrop Frye, most comedy is a "low mimetic mode," following Aristotle, who defines comedy in the *Poetics* as "the imitation of people who are worse than average" (1449A). Sholem Aleichem's humor, as Meyer Wiener defines it, is closer to Kafka's sense in that it involves a "conquest of fear of the tragic in life," claiming "nobility" for languages that seem low from the perspective of high culture, but have a dignity of their own. See *Anatomy of Criticism: Four Essays* (Princeton, NJ: Princeton University Press, 1957), p. 34, and Meyer Wiener, "On Sholom Aleichem's Humor," first published in 1941, "Vegn Sholom-Aleykhems humor," v. 2 of Wiener's *Tsu der geshikhte fun der yidisher literatur in 19tn yorhundert* [On the History of Nineteenth Century Yiddish Literature], (New York, 1946), 281–381. The passage from Meyer is quoted from *Prooftexts* 6:1 (January 1986), 41.
36. See Steven E. Aschheim, "Caftan and Cravat," in *Brothers and Strangers,* 58–79. On pp. 14–15, Aschheim cites Jacob Fromer's Introduction to *Solomon Maimons Lebensgeschichte* to show how the Caftan, the Kabbalah, and Hebrew and Yiddish were linked in Kafka's period. In fact, Kafka recommended this specific edition of the work, which he possessed and wrote about in his diaries, to his friend, Felix Weltsch, in his letter of December 1917. Franz Kafka, *Letters to Friends, Family, and Editors,* trans. Richard and Clara Winston (New York: Schocken Books, 1977 [1958], p. 173.
37. Quoted in Emmanuel S. Goldsmith, *Modern Yiddish Culture: The Story of the Yiddish Language Movement* (New York: Fordham University Press, 1997), p. 53.

38. Gershom Scholem, Aphorism 10, in Biale, "Gershom Scholem's Ten Unhistorical Aphorisms on Kabbalah," 88. For contemporary readers, Scholem declares, Kafka's texts have something "von dem strengen Glanze des Kanonischen—das Volkommenen, das zerbricht."
39. Breon Mitchell, "Translator's Preface," p. xxi: "*The Trial* begins as a farce and ends as tragedy."
40. Kafka finished working on the novel in late 1914 and finally abandoned it in 1915 or 1916. Hartmut Binder dates the composition of the final chapter, "The Great Nature Theater of Oklahoma," as the second week of October 1914 and Kafka's beginning of the first chapter of *The Trial* as the second week of August 1914. See Malcolm Pasley and Klaus Wagenbach, "Datierung Sämtlicher Texte," in Jürgen Born, ed., *Kafka Symposion* (Berlin, 1965), pp. 62–63, and Hartmut Binder, *Kafka Kommentar zu den Romanen, Rezensionen, Aphorismen und zum Brief an den Vater* (München: Winkler Verlag, 1976), pp. 5–6.
41. Levi had read "In the City of Slaughter" ["In Shkhite-Shtot"], the Yiddish version of what was already a Hebrew classic, "Ba'ir haharegah." the work. which made its author the leader of the "Generation of Bialik," as writers in this period of the revival of Hebrew as a modern literary language came to be known. Dan Miron, *Bodedim b'-Moedam: L'Dyokana Harepublika Hasifrutit Haivrit b'Thhilat Hamea Haesrim* [When Loners Come Together: A Portrait of Hebrew Literature at the Turn of the Twentieth Century] (Tel Aviv: Am Oved, 1987), p. 125 ff.
42. On Hebrew's cultural authority, see Benjamin Harshav, *The Meaning of Yiddish* (Berkeley: University of California Press, 1990), pp. 21–22.
43. See David G. Roskies, "The Pogrom as Poem," *Against the Apocalypse: Responses to Catastrophe in Modern Jewish Culture* (Cambridge: Harvard University Press, 1984), p. 91.
44. Franz Kafka, Diary Entry of October 20, 1911, *Diaries,* pp. 80–81, *Tagebücher* 1910–1923, p. 78.
45. Ernst Robert Curtius, *European Literature and the Latin Middle Ages*, trans. Willard R. Trask (Princeton, NJ: Princeton University Press, 1953), p. 29.
46. "A Hearing Aid," in "Tales from Chelm," Irving Howe and Eliezer Greenberg, eds., *A Treasury of Yiddish Stories* (New York: Penguin Books, 1953), p. 672, and Ruth Wisse, *Schlemiel as Modern Hero,* p. 11.
47. [*Luther Bibel,* 2 Moses 7:2], Kafka, *Amerika,* ed. Max Brod, p. 28
48. Luther's Bible is thus conventionally known as the originator of High German, the "first work of art in German prose." The King James Bible similarly acquires its divine and foundational status only through a de rigeur forgetting of the intervening Hebrew text. Harold Bloom is correct in his statement that "Freudian memory," or where the repressed returns, "is Jewish memory," but only in the

sense that Freud revises an overly monolingual vision of Western thought. See *The Cambridge History of the Bible,* ed. S. L. Greenslade (Cambridge: Cambridge University Press, 1963), v. 3, pp. 103, 168, and Harold Bloom, *The Strong Light of the Canonical,* p. 36.

49. John Guillory, "*Canon,*" in Frank Lentricchia and Thomas McLaughlin, eds., *Critical Terms for Literary Study,* second edition (Chicago and London: University of Chicago Press, 1995), 231–244. Karl's writing desk, is not at "school," for as Guillory notes, "the school brings the written text into contact with spoken language" and thus would cast a shadow on Uncle Jacob's transcendent linguistic dream for Karl (p. 240).
50. See "Internal Jewish Bilingualism," in Max Weinreich, *History of the Yiddish Language* (Chicago and London: University of Chicago Press, 1973), pp. 247–314.
51. Northrop Frye, "Tragic Fictional Modes," *Anatomy of Criticism* (Princeton, NJ: Princeton University Press, 1957), p. 42. In fact, Frye drew on Max Brod's earlier comparison of *Amerika* to the Chaplinesque and reversed Brod's interpretation of Kafka's pleasurable comedy. See Max Brod, "Nachwort zur ersten Ausgabe" [1927], *Amerika* (Frankfurt: Fischer, 1976), p. 262.
52. "Die Unfähigkeit des Heizers ist letzten Endes ein künstlerisches Versage." ["The stoker's incapacity" to speak canonical language, according to Sokel, "is in the final analysis an artistic failure."] Walter Sokel, *Franz Kafka: Tragik und Ironie* (Frankfurt: Fischer Taschenbuch Verlag, 1976), p. 353.
53. The scene suggests Kafka's immersion in the Yiddish theater, as Evelyn Beck. observed long ago, as the central concern of his life in 1911–12. See Beck, 126 ff.
54. Franz Kafka, "An Introductory Talk on the Yiddish Language," February 18, 1912, op. cit., p. 264.
55. Theodor Adorno, *Aesthetic Theory,* trans. C. Lenhardt, ed. Gretel Adorno and Rolf Tiedemann (London and New York: Routledge & Kegan Paul, 1984), 340: "Whenever art has succeeded in taking its bearings from the plebian moment—and not in a tongue and cheek way, but seriously—its weight or gravity increased."
56. Franz Kafka, "Die Sorge des Hausvaters," *Drücke zu Lebzeiten,* ed. Wolf Kittler et al, II, 349, and I, 282–284.
57. For an account of these different meanings, see Hartmut Binder, *Kafka-Kommentar zu Sämtlichen Erzählungen* (München: Winkler Verlag, 1982), p. 232.
58. Kafka's source for this linguistic history is a book much discussed in his diary entries of early 1912: Jakob Fromer, *Der Organismus des Judentums* (1909), pp. 64–65.

17

Igor Guberman

An Exile's Art of Punning

Greta N. Slobin

Born in Moscow in 1936, Igor Guberman belongs to the generation that came of age in the post-Stalinist thaw of the late fifties. Guberman graduated from the Moscow Institute of Transportation Engineering in 1958 and worked in his profession for the next twenty years. In the 1960s he publishes books on psychology, brain research, and cybernetics, and writes articles for the popular science magazine, *Znanie-sila* (Science is knowledge), one of the most interesting journals of the time. He also works as a ghost writer for members of the Writers Union, although he himself is not a member. Guberman is actively involved in dissident and samizdat activity, and becomes well-known for his satirical rhymed quatrains, later named "*gariki*," whose compact form becomes a venue for a free-spirited voice that speaks of love, life, and life's ironies.

His later quatrains become more political and target the repressive Soviet state. The 1970s are a period of intense Jewish activism and a wave of immigration to Israel. Guberman contributes to an underground dissident journal, *Evrei v Rossii* (Jews in Russia), and applies for an exit visa in 1978. He is arrested in 1979 on false charges and spends a year and a half in a Siberian labor in the Irkutsk region, followed by three and a half years of exile in the settlement of Borodino, 200 kilometers east of Krasnoiarsk, where his wife and children join him. Soon after his arrest, an international campaign begins in his defense, and he is made a member of the International PEN Club.

An early collection of Guberman's quatrains, titled *Bumerang*, a paranomastic transposition of the poet's name, is published in the United States in 1982 through the efforts of his friends and the

Guberman Rescue Committee. The brief note on the back cover states that this is the first collection published under the author's name. This marks a shift in his status from a dissident to a published author. *Bumerang,* with drawings by David Miretsky, opens with a brief preface by the author about writing poems and smuggling them out from the camp. The collection includes fragments from his "Prison Diary," "Poems of Different Years," and "From Old Verse." The poems in this early collection are rhymed quatrains, a form that is to become his trademark, a brilliantly compact poetic unit with a witty punch line able to carry great semantic impact of philosophical and political significance. The poems are a sharp political satire of the repressive state and meditations on the dual identity of Russian Jews as a despised minority, both topics laced with sexual imagery.

Punning and word play are the mainspring of his verse as in the following lines from the prison poems: "Ia—v strane, a dusha—v moem tele—oba terpim ot vnutrennikh organov" (I—in the country, my soul—in my body—both suffer from internal organs, 20). The double meaning of "internal organs" also as a reference to the KGB members who will return in later *gariki.* The opening line of another quatrain, "Umom Rossiiu ne spasti'" (Russia cannot be saved by reason, 21), a paraphrase of a famous opening line of the nineteenth-century poem by Tiutchev "Umom Rossiiu ne poniat'" (Russia can not be understood by reason), will reappear in another paraphrase in later verse.

Guberman's poetic diction in the early poems draws primarily on the classical tradition, with occasional unofficial lexicon and *mat* (obscenity). In "Poems of Different Years," the chapter title and the first poem's opening line are a parody of an official state song "Broad is my motherland" (Shiroka strana moia rodnaia), combined with strong expletives and swear words, "gde ne tknis', to suka, to mudak" (whatever you bump into, there is a bitch or a motherfucker, 48). The effect is resonant in its transgressiveness.

In addition to political satire, the section "From Old Verse," in the collection contains an early example of Yiddish-Russian pastiche, a mock-heroic parody of Russian folk songs about folk heroes, in which Sten'ka Razin, the leader of the seventeenth-century peasant rebellion, becomes "Sen'ka Raizman" (118). The use of Yiddish names and jargon (slang) here is reminiscent of Isaac Babel's *Odessa Stories* and his Jewish hero, the gangster Benia Krik.

The Jewish theme is central in the earliest publication of Guberman's *samizdat* verse, collected in manuscript by various hands, under the title *Evreiskie datzybao* (The Jewish datzybao), appears with the pseudonym "Igor' Garrik" in Jerusalem in 1978, and then in 1980. The collection is published again in Jerusalem in 1988, the year of Guberman's immigration. It now bears the author's name and a new title, *Gariki,* retaining the subtitle *datzybao,* with cover drawing by E. Sarni and A. Okun'. The quatrains now named *gariki,* after the poet's childhood nickname given by his grandmother, are a verbal amalgam that combines high poetic diction and quotations of classical Russian verse, from Pushkin onward, with substandard prison slang and *mat,* sprinkled with Yiddish jargon. This strategy is doubly transgressive—the shocking proximity of "dirty" or "low" words, forbidden by the Victorian Soviet standards, to the almost sacred classical lines that represent the national heritage, serves to undermines the ideological underpinnings of the system with epigrammatic wit and word play.

The subtitle *datzybao* is a reference to the "big character newspaper" in the early years of the Chinese Cultural Revolution. It was a public wall paper, on which any citizen was free to write in brush hand his opinion or criticism of a leader, an uncensored venue that gave voice to the people and which had Mao's approval, although gradually it became more controlled. Guberman's appropriation of the genre signals his choice of an unofficial channel or *samizdat,* in which he can voice his independent opinion and criticism of the existing social order, for which there was no other venue at the time.

The titles of individual chapters of *gariki* here, as in subsequent collections, are rhymed aphoristic couplets. The book opens with a cycle devoted to Russia "There Is No Tale in the World More Capricious/ than the Tale of Caprices of the Russian Conscience" (Prichudlivee net na svete povesti,/chem povest' o prichudakh russkoi sovesti, 7). In this anticivic verse, Russia appears as a mother who eats her own children, as a land of misbegotten ideas, where someone is always imprisoned—"some for spirituality, others for materialism" (30). Guberman reiterates motives familiar from nineteenth-century literature, such as Dostoevsky's Russian Devil (*russkii bes*), and the country's predilection for oppression and excessive patriotism. He attacks the Soviet leaders, Lenin—a dried up "mummy, considered more alive than all the living" (25)—and Stalin, whose genius invented the prison regime and personality cult.

Guberman's first extensive collection, *Gariki,* is significant for the period of political repression and conveys his double consciousness, that of a dissenter who is also a Jew. Along with political satire, the Jewish theme appears in the cycle with the ironic title "God Made a Wild Joke, / When He Made Up the Story of the Jew" (Gospod' likhuin shutku uchinil, / kogda siuzhet evreia sochinil), with poems that speak of the Jew as an outsider and an exile, "a scapegoat" whom "nobody loves and everyone loves to hate" (127), hence the source of Jewish laughter (115). Guberman predicts that Jews will pay a terrible price for their role in Russian history, especially their involvement in Russian rebellion or "*Russkii bunt*" (139). The poems are at once a self-conscious comment on the Jewish minority and its status, as well on the less than glorious state.

The serious tone of the quatrains gathered here gives way to spirited humor of the verbal pastiche in the second cycle, whose title "Obgusevshie lebedi" (Russified or Goosed Swans) is a phonemic pun containing a stereotypical Jewish mispronunciation of a Russian "r," which sounds like "g." This single sound transforms the phrase "russianized swans," which is funny enough to a ridiculous "swans turned into geese," whose absurdity is a comment on "assimilation." This is an example of the bilingual pastiche of Yiddish-Russian, whose economy of means has an immediate comic effect as the language of exile, of a repressed minority in a great empire. Another favorite device consists in the appropriation of a classical poem, such as Lermontov's well known "The Lone Sail Whitens" (Beleet parus odinokii), which in this version, with Jewish names and puns, has a parodic, lowering effect.

Another source of humor is in mock-heroic Jewish travesties of popular folk songs and epics depicting glorious events in Russian history and their heroes. Thus Lermontov's famous narrative poem, "Borodino," whose title refers to a decisive battle with Napoleon in the war of 1812, here becomes "Borodino under Tel-Aviv." The Egyptian Port Said on the Suez Canal is punned as "Pots Aid" or "Jewish Prick" (150). Another mock-epic poem, titled "Montigomo, the Indestructible Kogan" (Montigomo, neistrebimyi Kogan), is a brilliant pun on a well-known children's adventure tale by Mayne Reid (translated in Russian as "Montigomo, iastrebinyi kogot"). Guberman's poem describes a tribe of primitive Jews "on the banks of the Amazon" with hilarious names based on phonic puns or sound play: Orangutang—Aron Gutang or Kolumb—Aid (Columbus, A Jew), with Tamagavker and Bumerang. Another poem, with a title familiar from war poetry, "Pro tachanku" (About a Machine Gun Cart), is a parody of the Civil War stories and, especially, of Babel's *Red Cavalry,* in which general Budenny's brave Cossacks are replaced by Jewish fighters with stereotypical comic names, like Srul' and Moishe.

After his release in 1984, Guberman begins work on a major prose project, *Shtrikhi k portretu* (Sketches for a Portrait), a semi-autobiographical documentary novel of a search for the lost history of a remarkable man, N. A. Bruni, a representative of the Russian cultural renaissance, a typical member of the intelligentsia who falls victim to Stalinist purges and is shot in 1938. This effort to preserve the memory and history of the 1930s seeks to document the purges from the perspective of someone who went through prison experience in the 1970s. In the afterword, Guberman explains that he took down stories heard by fellow prisoners (*zeki*), that is, eye-witness accounts. The novel was written "for the drawer" at the end of the 1980s. Guberman returns to it to prepare the book for publication in 1994.

Guberman immigrates to Israel in 1988 and has been living and working in Jerusalem since then. He works on the Russian radio program and in the Russian press, and performs public readings. His prison memoir in prose, *Progulki vokrug baraka* (Walks Around the Barracks), an understated, detailed eyewitness account of everyday prison existence, is published in the United States that year. In a 1997 review in *Literaturnaia gazeta,* Bulat Okudzhava calls the book "a quiet confession."

A major collection of Guberman's verse, *Gariki na kazhdyi den'* (Gariki for Everyday), is published in Jerusalem in 1989 and reprinted the following year, with a Moscow edition in 1992, and along with *Shtrikhi k portretu* in Ekaterinburg in 1999. The author's introduction to his anti-authoritarian, philosophical verse is a tongue-in-cheek series of admonitions that makes fun of didactic Soviet advice to readers. The author suggests that "this book ought not to be read all at once and in order, but better a bit at a time and from different chapters as suits the mood," and that it ought not to be read "as a source of incontrovertible truth, since that does not exist in nature." The last page of the book, as of subsequent publications, is left blank, marked "for the reader's reflection." The two volumes (each with ten chapters) that constitute the collection are thematically organized, including chapters V and VI of volume II from the 1988 *Gariki,* devoted to the Russian and Jewish themes.

Guberman's satire of the Soviet system is rife with skepticism of the received truths of Soviet ideology and includes a consistent philosophical critique of the belief in social and scientific progress. The quatrains are marked by a complex web of poetic reminiscences of nineteenth-century poetry from Pushkin to Lermontov, Nekrasov, Fet and Tiutchev, but also of early twentieth-century poets, Blok, Bely, Tsvetaeva, and Mandelstam. What is strikingly new in this collection that renders the quatrains a truly original poetic genre is the extensive use of substandard, unofficial lexicon of *mat* on par with high poetic diction.

As in the first collection of *Gariki,* chapter titles here are witty aphorisms in rhymed couplets which announce the debunking of every sacred institution, the State and its prisons, Science, Family, and Matrimony. For example: "It is simple to take away freedom from people: just simply entrust it to the people"; "Family is given to us by God, it is a substitute for happiness"; "He who is tormented by spiritual thirst, must not await the love of his compatriots." Sometimes, just one letter in a homonym changes the expected meaning, as in the slogan-like parodic paraphrase: "V bor'be za narodnoe delo/ia byl inorodnoe telo" (in the battle for the national cause/I was the unnational/foreign body," where *narodnoe/inorodnoe* (national/foreign) and *delo/ telo* (cause/body) play off each other.

The poems provide verbal equivalents of the toppling of official monuments after 1989. Poems reiterate the skepticism of the twentieth century which "revealed the imperfection of human construction," (konstruktsii liudskoi nesovershenstvo), thus postponing "hope for universal bliss" (92). The deformation of the human organism is the result of a life of ideological excess, as in the title of chapter five: "Esli zhizn' izlis'ne delovaia / funktsiia slabeet polovaia" (If life is excessively businesslike/the sexual function weakens). One of the quatrains posits a creation of a new, hermaphrodite homus sovieticus through fear: "novyi variant gemafrodita: plot'iu muzhiki, a dukhom—bliadi" (a new variant of a hermaphrodite: male by sex, and whores in spirit). The title of chapter seven states declares that "uvy, no istin—bludnitsa, / Ni s kem ei dolgo ne lezhitsia" (truth is a whore/she cannot lie with anyone too long)

Guberman uses a variety of verbal devices that telegraph subversive meaning: word play; phonemic punning, in which one sound can change the meaning of the phrase; parodic paraphrase of patriotic verse; unofficial lexicon with strategically placed obscenity. The penultimate chapter nine uses obscene invective in a sarcastic, blatantly blasphemous condemnation of Mother Russia, and its brutality and violence. Titled "Davno pora, ebena mat', /Umom Rossiiu ponimat'" (It's time, fucking mother/to understand Russia with a brain), it is to be read against Nekrasov's civic verse, familiar to every schoolchild, as well as the Symbolist poetry of Blok, Bely, and Briusov, devoted to meditation on Russia after the 1905 revolution. The cycle title itself is a variation of an earlier poem in *Bumerang:* "Russia cannot be saved by the mind," a parodic paraphrase of the famous Tyutchev poem, "Umom Rossiiu ne poniat'" (Russia cannot be understood by the mind), cited earlier, that mythologized Russia's particularism. In Guberman's verse the tradition of mystical nationalism is ridiculed and, indeed, reason rather than emotions is invoked. In this example of the economy of means in Guberman's approach, a triple transgression is accomplished in a single line. First—an unpatriotic, blasphemous swearing at Mother Russia; second—parodic paraphrase of a well-known high poetic line; third—the ironic suggestion of the line implies that another body part had been involved, whose unspoken identity is clear from the semantic context.

This poetic shorthand is one of the main devices in Guberman's linguistic revolution. The opening quatrain of the ninth chapter is justly famous. In a verbal counterpart of the Sots Art of Komar and Melamid, with its debunking of symbols of the omnipotent Soviet state, it represents a familiar statue of a bronze man of power, but with a difference—"under a small fig leaf hides an enormous member of security [ogromnyi organ bezopasnosti]." This adds yet another semantic dimension to the term "organ." Guberman's philosophical skepticism of the Enlightenment and the idea of progress that underlies Marxism are clear: "the twentieth century revealed [or rendered naked] the imperfection of human construction." He is also skeptical about the human striving for perfection: "with age I understood, how dangerous is/the creation of universal bliss;/the imperfect world is so beautiful, that god save us from perfection." A distinct role is given to art which can save the world with the trinity of "image, harmony, and form," stating that all besides poetry will disappear after death without a trace.

Guberman goes on to publish three consecutive books of *Erusalimskii dnevnik* (Jerusalem Diaries) in Israel between 1991 and 1995, that present a continued meditation of Jewish identity and history. A partial collection of *Erusalimskie gariki* I and II, dedicated to the poet's friend, the artist Aleksandr Okun', with his drawing on the cover, appears in Moscow in 1994. The entire series of the Jerusalem Diaries is published in 1996 in Jerusalem and in the Nizhnii Novgorod edition of Guberman's *Collected Works*. Guberman writes of his double identity, of belonging to two nations. The poems present a continued meditation on Russia now seen from abroad, as in the title of the opening chapter "Seeing Russia at a Distance,/No Longer Sad About Parting" (Rossiiu uvidav na rasstoianii, / grustit' perestaesh' o rasstavanii). The poems also reiterate earlier motifs of Jewish identity and history, now tinged with postcommunist nostalgia for the "poisonous, stinking, and powerful breath of the immense empire" (9). With characteristic irony, Guberman titles the second notebook with a rhymed aphorism "Russia for the soul and the mind is like first love and like prison," noting that once the Jews left, "the empire immediately fell apart" (105). Firmly ensconced in the historic Jewish homeland, Guberman remains a Russian.

The next major collection, *Zakatnye gariki* (The Sunset Gariki), a philosophical contemplation of maturity and the changes in perspective that it brings, appears in Jerusalem in 1998. A video recording of his life and work in Jerusalem, entitled "Igor Guberman s utra do vechera" (Igor Guberman From Morning to Evening) is released in 2000. It features the poet in his apartment, filled with paintings of his favorite contemporary Russian artists, and accompanies him on walks around Jerusalem, which he calls "not a city, but a place, which is very well known to God," referring to the Jews as "not a nation, but a way of being." He speaks of himself as a man of Russian culture and Jewish soul.

The postcommunist 1990s bring fame and star status to Guberman as he becomes a bi-local writer, giving pubic readings to wide Russian audiences not only in Israel and the United States, but also in the former Soviet Union, Germany, Canada, Australia and all over Europe. In his prose memoir *Pozhilye zapis ki* (Notes of Mature Age, 1996), Guberman remembers thinking to himself on the first flight back to Russia: "Where am I going? . . . Am I flying to my country or from it?" (148). The book addresses the reader in familiar, conversational tone, speaking about his family, a beloved grandmother, and friends who shared his fate of a dissident and a prisoner in the Soviet Union. Guberman travels to Russia about twice a year and performs in public readings in the capital and provincial cities to enthusiastic audiences. He is a best-selling author, with numerous editions of his work published in Moscow, Ekaterinburg, and Nizhnii Novgorod, where a four volume set of his *Collected Works* appear in 1996 and again in 1997. His poems have been put to music by M. Brenner, with a compact disc released in Moscow in 1995. A video recording of his performance in the Kremlin Concert Hall in Moscow on March 18, 1997, and conversations with friends is produced in 1998. His astronomic rise in popularity in Russia and the former republics is referred to as a "Guberman phenomenon" in the media.

Guberman has been called the Omar Khayyam (a twelfth-century Persian poet, widely popular in the west) of his times, and has been compared to François Villon, a celebrated fifteenth-century French poet, also known for his prison verse. Many lines of Guberman's poems have become part of Russian folklore. In an interview conducted in 1998 for the Belorussian Business Paper, Sergei Shapran writes: "There is a simple explanation for Igor Guberman's popularity: it is very difficult to coach complex thoughts in four lines of verse." As ever ironic, Guberman comments on the brevity of his *gariki* in *Pozhilye zapiski* : "four lines are sufficient for me in order to express and say everything—to the last drop . . ." (129). In *Gariki na kazhdyi den'*, Guberman provides an understated description of the form as "a joke baked in banalities" which lies like "a hot water bottle on the belly/ aching from undigested reality" (438). While he also denies the music that permeates his poems, "It is not music that lives in my verse," it is in fact its distinguishing feature.

Guberman's acutely witty epigrammatic rhymed quatrains represent a complex and saturated poetic unit, whose most pronounced feature that contributes to the immediacy of its reception is intonation. The pervasive music of the poems is keyed to the classic iambic line that echoes nineteenth-century poetry, dear and familiar to every educated Russian. It creates a complex echo-chamber within which reverberates the clash between the music of the line and the strident *mat*. This feature, combined with the punning and mixing of lexical levels of language, creates a linguistic revolution in verse able to telegraph multiple layers of signification in Guberman's transgressive quatrains. A fellow Russian writer living in Israel, Dina Rubina, remarks on the Guberman Internet site for 2000, that the brief quatrains manage to "tamp down" central postulates of the philosophy of life and death in their eternal struggle with each other.

Guberman accomplishes this with a heady mix of mutually exclusive elements in *gariki* that taps into vast reservoirs of collective cultural and historical memory, including the classical poetic tradition, anecdotes, folksongs, and popular Soviet songs of the post-war period. By combining the high poetic diction of Russian classical verse with substandard Soviet prison slang and the unofficial *mat*, as well as with Yiddish jargon, Guberman creates a brilliant hybrid that at once lifts political, cultural, and sexual repression. The semantics of his double-voiced, bilingual verse as the source of humor and acerbic wit in *gariki*, contain a heady "sexual turn": "In the years of stagnation, lies and fear/the sphere of the permissible is narrow:/Forbidden are jokes below the belt/And thoughts above the prick" (393). Guberman deftly manipulates the semantics of this double-voicedness as an amazingly effective poetic shorthand which explores the disparity between the idealist line of nineteenth-century verse, especially the civic poetry of Nekrasov, and the social critique of *gariki*, whose punch line reveals a stridently different reality and the hypocrisy of the Soviet system.

The shock value of obscenity in Guberman's verse works to condemn the deformed Soviet social organism and repressive ideology.

In his memoir *Pozhilye zapiski*, Guberman devotes a chapter to the eighteenth-century censored poet, Ivan Barkov, who used obscene sexual language that Guberman considers an important part of the treasure-house of Russian. In a conscious departure from the Victorian standards that prevailed in the U.S.S.R., Guberman understands its semantic potential: "Russian obscenity is a unique phenomenon, and speaking of it I feel something like national pride (166). Thus Guberman employs "unofficial," or censored, language, with substandard lexicon and slang, including the forbidden and rarely used terms for body parts and sexual organs in printed Russian. The effect of the breaking of prohibition is doubly transgressive, because the blasphemous verse speaks directly to the reader or listener as it brings a release of repression, both political and sexual, and a recognition of something deeply familiar that has just been revealed.

Guberman probes the potential of laughter as a means of destabilizing power in the satirical tradition of the early Soviet writing of Zoshchenko, Zamyatin, and Ilf and Petrov. His laughter has the capacity to break through the edifice erected by the omnipotent Soviet state and with a word or phrase clear the space for free expression. In public performances registered on video recordings, one can observe listeners explode as Guberman delivers his lines with a straight face. His verse addresses the audience whose memory of the painful past and the heavy legacy of repression are tinged with postcommunist nostalgia and anxiety about the future. The laughter is not only cathartic, it is also therapeutic and enabling. By taking aim at repression and sexual anxieties, it makes way for optimism, which, as he notes, is missing among his compatriots. Guberman's poetic gift and brilliant verbal wit enable him to keep the pulse of the times for succeeding generations. His verse continues to touch the nerve of Russian Jews and Russians, and the people of the former Soviet Empire, wherever they may be.

Works Cited

Books by Igor Guberman

Lokomotivy nastoiashchego I budushchego. Moscow: Znanie, 1963.
Tretii triumvirat. Moscow: Detskaia literatura, 1965.
Chudesa i tragedii chernogo iashchika. Moscow: Detskaia aliteratura, 1968.
Pobezhdennoe vremia. Moscow: Politizdat, 1975.
Bekhterev: Stranitsy zhizni. Moscow: *Znanie,* 1977.
Evreiskie datzybao, as Igor Garik. Jerusalem: Agasfer, 1978, 1980.
Bumerang. Ann Arbor, MI: Hermitage, 1982.

Gariki (datzybao). Jerusalem: Agasfer, 1988.
Progulki vokrug baraka. Tenafly, NJ: Hermitage, 1988.
Gariki na kazhdyi den. Jerusalem: Agasfer, 1989.
Kamernye gariki (Tiuremnyi dnevnik; Sibirskii dnevnik; Moskovskii dnevnik). Jerusalem: Leksikon, 1991.
Erusalimskii dnevnik I. Jerusalem: Leksikon, 1991.
Kamernye gariki. Jerusalem: Leksikon, 1991.
Erusalimskii dnevnik II. Jerusalem: Agasfer, 1993.
Erusalimskii dnevnik III. Jerusalem: Agasfer, 1995.
Erusalimskie gariki. Moscow: Politekst, 1994.
Shtrikhi k portretu. Moscow: Molodaia gvardia, 1994.
Sobranie sochinenii v chetyrekh tomakh. Nizhnii Novgorod: Izdatelstvo "Dekom," 1996.
Gariki iz Erusalima I, II, III. Jerusalem: Agasfer, 1996.
Erusalimskie gariki. Nizhnii Novgorod: Izdatelstvo "Dekom," 1997.
Zakatnye gariki. Jerusalem: Agasfer, 1998.
Sobranie sochinenii v trekh tomakh. Minsk: MET, 1999.
Sobranie sochinenii v trekh tomakh. Ekaterinburg: U-faktoriia, 1999.
Shtrikhi k portretu. Gariki na kazhdyi den. Ekaterinburg: U-faktoriia, 1999.
Pozhilye zapiski: Pozhilye zapiski, Zakatnye gariki. Ekaterinburg: U-faktoriia, 1999.
Kniga stranstvii. Jerusalem: Agasfer, 2001.
Igor Guberman. Smolensk: Rusich, 2001.
Gariki. Rostov-na donu: Feniks, 2001.

Video Recordings

"Igor Guberman v Moskve." Moscow: Videonet, 1999.
Semen Vinokur, "Igor Guberman s utra do vechera." Jerusalem: Avni Production, 2000.
Back Rubrics (secondary bibliography).

Articles

Zhutovskii, B. "Igor Guberman." *Stolitsa*, 1992, no. 41.
Bossart, A. "Garik iz semeistva Atlantov. *Stolitsa*, 1993, no. 51.
Frolova, I. "Peterburgskie gariki Igoria Gubermana." *Smena*, St. Peterburg (December 26, 1995).
Kovaleva, A. "Ocharovatel'nyi bezdel'nik." *Moskovskii komsomolets* (October 2, 1996).
Okudzhava, B. "Tikhaia ispoved'." *Literaturnaia Gazeta* (March 12, 1997).

Interviews

Fomina. L. "Progulki vokrug granitsy." (beseda s I. Gubermanom). *Moskovskaia pravda* (August 2, 1994).

Ovsova, Marina. "Kur'er kul'tury nezakatnyi Guberman zakatil v Moskvu." *Moskovskii komsomolets* (December 15, 1998).

Shapran, Sergei. "Igor Guberman: 'Tseniu v sebe bezpechnost''." *Belorusskaia Delovaia Gazeta* (December 14, 1998).

Vasenina, Ekaterina. "Igor Guberman: 367 prazdnichnykh dneu v godu. I po krainei mere odin prazdnik—obshchenie s avtorom."
Novaia Gazeta (November 29, 1999).

Chepalov, A. "Nezakatnye 'Gariki' Abrama Khaiama." Trud. Reprinted in *Kaleidoskop* (April 19, 200). Israel.

Biography

V. M. Litvinov, "Igor Guberman." Entry in *Russkie pisateli 20 veka. Biograficheskii slovar'*. Chief editor P. A. Nikolaev. Moscow: Nauchnoe izdatel'tsvto "Bol'shaia Rossiiskaia Entsiklopediia." Izdatel'stvo "Randevu-AM," 2000, pp. 217–218.

Part V

Living Investigations

18

Bilingual Scenes

Sylvia Molloy

Childhood

To simplify matters I sometimes say I'm trilingual, that I was brought up trilingual, although come to think of it, the statement misleads more than it explains. Besides, it's not entirely accurate: I did not learn the three languages simultaneously but in succession, each language occupying a space and taking on an effect of its own. I spoke Spanish (or *castellano,* as it is called in non-Castilian Argentina) first. Then, when I was three and a half, my father started speaking to me in English. Also when I was three and a half my sister was born; instead of throwing dishes out the window, like Goethe when faced with a sibling, I acquired another language, which is another way, I guess, of breaking with safety. French was to come later; it did not coincide with any birth; it was more like a repossession.

Family Romance

Like many English immigrants of her generation, my grandmother, my father's mother, spoke bad Spanish. She had trouble remembering the word for teapot and, much to her son's glee, would ask for a *tetada* and not a *tetera* of tea. It upset her that I didn't know English, that Spanish was my first language. I think it also upset her that my father had married an "Argentine girl." It never occurred to her that my father was himself an "Argentine boy"; she just did not think of him that way. Immigrants and their offspring, regardless of their place of birth, were thought of in terms of language, *were* their language. My mother had lost the French of her childhood; she was monolingual, therefore Argentine. My father spoke English with his mother and sisters, Spanish with his wife and friends. Sometimes people called him *che, inglés.*

My grandmother, my father's mother, died when I was four: I remember visiting her shortly before her death, I remember saying something to her, I don't know in what language. This not knowing what language I used needles me. In fact, I have used the episode on two occasions in fiction: In one version, the child speaks English and makes his grandmother happy before she dies; in the other, the child refuses.

Territory

Each language has its territory, its appropriate time, its rank. The school I went to as a child was divided in two, English in the morning, Spanish in the afternoon. It was therefore a bilingual school, but everybody thought of it as an English institution, *un colegio inglés.* This was due no doubt to the prestige attached to the term, but also to the rules of the school. If a student was caught speaking Spanish in the morning, she was punished. She had to go to the head's office, where she signed a Black Book, which turned out to be a tatty little black notebook, less ominous than it sounded. If you signed three times, however, you were expelled. Other serious offenses that led to signing the black book and to eventual banishment: wearing your socks rolled down, having your hair untied, or cheating on a test. These were serious offenses (as arbitrary as mortal sins in the Catholic church) but to speak Spanish during the English morning period may well have been the worst.

In the afternoon, classes were taught in Spanish. If someone spoke English, no one cared; there was no punishment. Compared to English, Spanish was a lackluster language, at least for those of us who brought it from home. As the mother, in Freud, Spanish was *certissima.* My parents admired this pedagogical system, not just because of the clear-cut division of linguistic time and space but because English was taught in the morning, "when their minds are fresher." They scolded me, scolded us, my sister and me, if we mixed. Our home mimicked the lines drawn by family romance: Spanish with the mother, English with the father. A mixture of both (when nobody heard us) between sisters, a private language of sorts.

I recognized that very same mixture not too long ago, in Buenos Aires, in a shop selling *artesanías.* Two well-dressed women, more or less my age, are fingering some alpaca wool scarves while speaking to each other, "This one will look good on him, *no te parece, pero* it's quite expensive, *che, no quiero gastar tanto, después de todo* I don't know him that well." The switching is effortless: It may have its rules but I, as a speaker, am unaware of them, I can switch *pero no analizar.* I tell myself: these women must have gone to the same school I did, and now that their parents are not around, they mix.

Mix

As I write, another linguistic detour comes to mind. In Argentina people don't say (or didn't use to say: like everything else, bilingualism has its fashions) *bufanda,* scarf, they said *écharpe,* or rather *écharpé,* sounding the final *e*. But the upper classes of course said *écharpe,* in impeccable French, which is the other language of Argentine culture. This is not so much bilingualism as a bilingual *effect,* not the work of switching but the work of citation, so typical of Argentines. Here, a cultural anecdote: José Bianco, admirable Argentine writer and editor of *Sur,* the review founded by Victoria Ocampo, was invited to lecture at Princeton. Distinguished Hispanists asked him what contact, if any, had he had with Américo Castro, the Spanish philosopher who spent years in exile in Buenos Aires before coming to the United States. What did Castro do in Argentina, these Hispanists, many of whom had been Castro's students at Princeton, wanted to know, whom did he converse with, how was he? Bianco: "He was very pleasant, charming, and he spoke like a posh Argentine woman." How could this be, wondered the flustered Hispanists, what on earth did Bianco mean? "Well, for every three words in Spanish he calculatingly dropped two in French, which, I must tell you, he spoke extremely well," Bianco answered quite casually. The conversation ended in general bewilderment. For these Hispanists, so intent on speaking and teaching "pure" Castilian Spanish, it was hard to accept that Castro would dare mix. Why wouldn't he, I wondered, since he championed heterodoxy?

Performance

During childhood birthday parties, my sister and I were often called upon by our cousins on our mother's side, the monolingual ones, to perform our bilingualism. It was both a show and a test: "Digan algo en inglés," they begged. My sister and I remained silent while the plea turned into a challenge: "We dare you to say something in English." Finally, as if plunging into water, one of us said to the other: "These kids are stupid idiots and we can say anything we like because they don't understand," or something to that effect, and our cousins

. Although not quite: When they asked us "¿Qué dieron, what did you say?" we didn't dare tell them. ragment of a novel I have just completed, the title of is *Back Home:*

> They envy you, even if your grandfather was a dirt poor immigrant from Ireland and not a rich Spaniard with silver mines in Peru, they envy you because you're different, because you speak another language, because they're snobs, what can I say. The school I attended was, in principle, an English school, but more and more the students came to it not knowing the language, even children of Anglo-Argentine parents who no longer spoke English at home. Since I did speak it, at least with my father, when they wanted to tease me they pushed me to a corner of the playground and said, Come on, *Inglés,* tells us how you say en inglés la concha de tu madre?

I was never challenged at school to come up with an English translation for my mother's genitalia or, for that matter, my father's. I learned the countless English synonyms for genitalia only much later. Oddly enough, at school, even during the English period, we resorted to Spanish (whispering of course) in order to say *malas palabras,* tell dirty jokes, or refer to unmentionable *partes.*

Punctum

Why do I speak of bilingualism, of my bilingualism, in only one language, and why am I doing it in English? An earlier version of this text was in Spanish: It came more naturally. Another question: How do you translate bilingualism, how do you convert the switching so that the effect of two languages working on each other, against each other, remains? Unavoidably, one must always be bilingual *from* one language, the *heimlich* one (and *heim* can change), the language one settles in first, if only temporarily, the language of fleeting self-recognition. This does not mean the language in which one feels more at ease, or the language one speaks the best, much less the language one has chosen to write. There is (rather, one chooses) a point of support, and from that point one establishes a relation with the other language as absence, or rather as shadow, the object of linguistic desire. Although she has two languages, the bilingual subject always speaks as if she were lacking something, in a permanent state of need. (I think of this last phrase in French: *etat de besoin*. Among others things, the expression describes the state of an addict in need of a fix.)

Loss

To "lose" a language. "A mind is a terrible thing to lose," said Dan Quayle, famously misquoting the motto of the United Negro College Fund. A language is also a terrible thing to lose. There were eleven siblings in my mother's family. The three oldest spoke French as children with their parents, a thick, southern French, I imagine, and then the family became monolingual. Did the parents, my grandparents, continue to speak this French in private when they confided in each other, when they made love? No one can answer my question. It's as if French in that family were in the closet. I think: Had I had children, in what language would I have spoken to them? Which language would I have repressed?

Because French was my mother's language I decided early on to recover it for her sake. I didn't want my father to be bilingual and not my mother. I was quite young when I demanded to learn the language and a teacher was hired, an old friend of one of my mother's aunts, to give my sister and me French lessons. We called her Madame Suzanne. At the beginning she would throw up her arms in despair when, not knowing a word in French, we resolutely Frenchified its Spanish equivalent. *Le café,* we ventured, was stirred with *une cucharite.* In the meantime Madame Suzanne herself, in speaking to our mother, did the same thing in the opposite direction: she would give my mother a recipe for *crème anglaise* and tell her she had to "hacer atención que no se atache," by which she meant she must see that it not stick to the pot. These examples refer (or attach themselves, like the *crème anglaise*) to home, to the spoon, the pot: They create a *heimlich* effect, even if the languages of the bilingual subject are rarely that. The mixing, the comings and goings, the switching, belong to the realm of the uncanny, which is precisely what shakes the foundations of the home.

Limits

To be bilingual is to speak knowing fully that what is being said is always being said in another place, in many other places. This awareness of the inherent strangeness of all communication, this knowing that what is being said is always alien, that speaking always implies insufficiency and, above else, doubleness (there is always an *other* way of saying it), is applicable to any language, but in our need for transparency and contact, we forget it. The explicit bilingualism of the subject wielding more than one language—

through habit, as a provocation, for aesthetic needs; sometimes simultaneously, sometimes sequentially—renders that otherness patent. That is the bilingual subject's privilege; also her *desgracia*, her undoing.

Name

What name does one give the bilingual subject, the newly born for whom one foresees a bilingual life? I have often heard future parents say that they want a name that will work in both languages, with minimal adaptation, without any need for translation. Let us say Tomás/Thomas, or Olivia/Olivia, or Ana/Anna, or Martín/Martin. (No Hermenegildos, please, no Duncans, no Jesuses, no Socorros.) There may be something to the *passepartout* names that may make life easier for the child who navigates between cultures. But, in more general terms, no name works "in both languages"; there is always a need for translation. The same may be said of surnames. Mine is unquestionably Irish to British, Irish, or American ears. But in Argentina, where it is often pronounced with a stress on the first syllable, more than once it has been thought Jewish: If Portnoy, why not Mólloy? And during a trip through Burgundy, years ago, it was considered "un nom du pays": Indeed, there is a little village close to Dijon named Moloy.

Lapsus

In what language does one wake up? When I'm away from home, traveling, and the phone rings, I answer half-asleep, making an effort to do so in the right language, the language spoken there. If I don't, I feel I've made a bad blunder, I've been careless, have been caught off guard. I've allowed something that usually remains unseen to be seen—although I don't quite know what that is. It's as if I had been surprised in a compromising position. One morning, still half-asleep, I started speaking to the woman lying next to me and she seemed not to understand me. She just smiled while I kept repeating my words, exasperated at her failure to understand me. It was like one of those dreams in which you think you're saying something but the words never come out of your mouth. Suddenly I woke up completely and realized that I had been speaking to her in the other language, the language she did not know. I never found out what it was that I really wanted to tell her. And why do I say "really"?

Violence

Jules Supervielle, a Franco-Uruguayan bilingual and a French poet, believed that you could only write in one language: Choosing to become a French poet, he decided to "délibérément ferme[r] à l'espagnol mes portes secrètes, celles qui ouvrent sur la pensée, l'expression et, disons, l'âme." Spanish for him was a remnant, bits and pieces, "borborygmes de langage." *Borborygme*, it will be remembered, is the gurgle caused by flatulence. We're talking here of linguistic burps or farts.

Supervielle's niece, also a writer, tells me that Supervielle had imposed French-only at home and that his wife Pilar, like him a native Uruguayan, found it immensely hard to speak French, "to the point that it was painful to listen to her," says Silvia Baron Supervielle, "she seemed to be doing so much violence to herself, she was another person." The husband's Spanish burps had been replaced by the wife's French ones. What price poetry.

This niece of Supervielle also writes, poetry in particular. She doesn't want to be considered solely a poet. She's a writer, she says. And, moreover, a translator.

Freedoms

In New York City street fairs there are usually several stalls manned by Latin Americans, usually Indians from Andean regions. They sell clothing made of llama or alpaca wool, caps, some pottery, thick linen shirts. A friend tells me that a woman who works in the Peruvian consulate in New York is annoyed by these immigrants, perhaps because they are all too visible, but mainly for linguistic reasons. To be precise, she is irritated by a bilingualism over which, as a representative of the government of her country, she has no control. "These people go directly from Quechua to English," she complains in aggrieved tones.

Escrituras

In terms of writing, how and by what means does the bilingual subject enter language? The Cuban slave Juan Francisco Manzano (of whom it could be said that he worked in two languages, his own hybrid Spanish and the Spanish of his master) learns to write *tracing* the writing of the other. That second language—neoclassical literary Spanish—will become his own for poetry, yet when he writes down his life, at his master's bidding, he goes back to his other Spanish, the messy one. I remember similar exercises in mimesis. When I wrote my first book in French, I tried to imitate the writing of my dissertation adviser, paying close attention to the idioms that peppered his discourse: for example, *qu'à cela ne tienne*. When I wrote my first texts in Spanish, I filtered—the verb is not excessive—everything I wanted to say through my readings of Borges. When I wrote my first book in English, I trained for the exercise like an athlete. Until then, English was a practical language, destined for the everyday life of exile, and also the language of affections, past and present. And it was also the language of memory: the memory of my father. In order to regain ease in written English—ease and authority—I did not follow prestigious examples but practiced a bric-à-brac effect. I would write words on bits of paper, expressions, clauses (usually adversatives) that I liked and wished to use, a little as if I were plagiarizing: *notwithstanding, hitherto, despite, conversely*. It was an adventure in translation.

I have written the key word, *translation*. I will not dwell on its implications, just mark its power for the bilingual subject as a permanent reminder of that "being in between" that marks the bilingual subject's speech, her writing, her tenuous life. And while on the subject of translation, one last anecdote. Many years ago, back in Argentina after many years spent in France, before I attempted to write anything of my own in Spanish, I entered two translation contests together with a friend. One was a translation from French to Spanish (Jean Paulhan), the other from English to Spanish (Virginia Woolf). When we were done (it was a collaborative venture), we had to choose a pseudonym. My friend always claimed that I got depressed when I translated, I was so gloomy, she said, *qué cara de tormenta, che*. For my part, I had just finished reading *Tropic of Cancer* and treasured the scene in the Paris bordello where Miller's friend, the Indian Nanantatee, defecated in the bidet because he had no idea what a bidet was for: It was a culturally alien artifact. My friend and I chose *Gloomy Nonentity* for a pseudonym. We won both prizes. Today, I would certainly not use that adjective to qualify the task of the translator, or the life of the bilingual subject, I would look for something more upbeat. I would, however, keep the noun.

Index